Luke and Acts

EDITED BY

Gerald O'Collins and Gilberto Marconi

Translated by Matthew J. O'Connell

Paulist Press
New York/Mahwah, N.J.

Originally published as *Luca-Atti: Studi in onore di P. Emilio Rasco nel suo 70o compleanno* by Cittadella Editrice, Assisi.

Library of Congress Cataloging-in-Publication Data

Luca-Atti. English.
    Luke and Acts/edited by Gerald O'Collins and Gilberto Marconi; translated by Matthew J. O'Connell.
       p. cm.
    Festschrift published originally in Italian under title "Luca-Atti" to commemorate the 70th birthday of Father Emilio Rasco.
    Includes bibliographical references and index.
    ISBN 0-8091-3360-1 (pbk.)
    1. Bible. N.T. Luke—Criticism, interpretation, etc. 2. Bible. N.T. Acts—Criticism, interpretation, etc. I. O'Collins, Gerald, II. Marconi, Gilberto, 1954– . III. O'Connell, Matthew J.
IV. Title.
BS2589.L827   1993
226.4'06—dc20

92-35226
CIP

Published by Paulist Press
997 Macarthur Boulevard
Mahwah, N.J. 07430

Printed and bound in the United States of America

Contents

In Honor of Emilio Rasco, S.J.

Gerald O'Collins and Gilberto Marconi

Preface

This collection of studies on Luke-Acts addresses itself to topics of contemporary concern. The chapters by Bovon, Conroy, and Prato concern themselves with the question of Luke's use of and background in Jewish scriptures. Caba and Vanni explore the relationship of Luke to the Johannine writings. The contributions by Barbi and Kilgallen bear on the debate over the anti-Jewish sentiments that some find in Luke-Acts. Fusco's paper takes up Lukan eschatology which some scholars have claimed to be sharply at odds with eschatologies found elsewhere in the New Testament. Rigato's chapter relates to current discussions of the question: Has Luke suppressed equal ecclesial roles for women? The piece by Marconi enters the debate over the historical character of Luke's writing. The studies by Betori and O'Collins are relevant to the ongoing discussion over Conzelmann's thesis that Luke uses a threefold division: the time of the Old Testament, the time of Jesus and the time of the church. Farahian's chapter bears on the broad question of Luke's relationship to and presentation of Paul.

Of course, current research and debate leave us with other significant questions: Were Mark and Q really the major sources for Luke's gospel? What was Luke's overall purpose in writing his two works? Without downplaying the importance of these and further questions, we offer this book as a contribution (in collaboration) to present studies on Luke-Acts.

This work also celebrates Emilio Rasco, S.J., on the occasion of his seventieth birthday, December 14, 1991. Since he began teaching at the Gregorian University in 1959, his inspiring scholarship, teaching and writing have encouraged many students and colleagues to deepen their knowledge of the New Testament—in particular their appreciation of Luke-Acts. With gratitude and affection we present this volume in his honor.

We wish to thank the McCarthy Family Foundation for its generous

1

help in covering costs involved in the preparation and publication of this volume.

Gregorian University
Rome
New Year's Day, 1993

Milan,
February 12, 1990

Reverend and dear Father,

Although I am unable to contribute to the Festschrift commemorating the seventieth birthday of Father Emilio Rasco, I do want to express my keen appreciation of the undertaking.

I think it my duty, moreover, to pay public homage to Father Rasco; I regard him as a friend, and I am grateful for the extensive work to which he has given so many years of research and teaching. We toiled, to some extent, in the same field: the Acts of the Apostles, and I have always admired his interpretative skill and the balance he has shown in this area of study.

I hope to profit by his studies in the time to come, and I take the opportunity to assure him of my gratitude and to wish him every blessing in the Lord.

In Christ,
CARDINAL CARLO MARIA MARTINI

Notes on Contributors

Augusto Barbi is Professor of Exegesis and Biblical Theology at the Theological Institute of St. Zeno (Verona).

Giuseppe Betori is Professor of Exegesis of the New Testament at the Theological Institute of Assisi.

François Bovon is Professor of New Testament and of Christian Origins at the University of Geneva. He is a distinguished Lukan scholar.

José Caba, S.J. is Professor of New Testament at the Pontifical Gregorian University (Rome).

Charles Conroy, M.S.C. is Professor of Exegesis of the Old Testament at the Pontifical Gregorian University (Rome).

Edmond Farahian, S.J. is Professor of New Testament Exegesis in the Faculty of Missiology at the Pontifical Gregorian University (Rome).

Vittorio Fusco is Professor of New Testament Exegesis at the Pontifical Theological Faculty of Southern Italy, St. Louis Division in Naples.

John Kilgallen, S.J. is Professor of New Testament at the Pontifical Biblical Institute (Rome). He lectures widely in the United States and abroad.

Gilberto Marconi is Professor of New Testament Exegesis and Biblical Greek at the Pontifical Gregorian University (Rome).

Gerald O'Collins, S.J. is Professor of Fundamental Theology at the Pontifical Gregorian University (Rome).

Gian Luigi Prato is Professor of Old Testament Exegesis at the Pontifical Gregorian University (Rome).

Maria–Luisa Rigato is Professor of Biblical Theology at the Pontifical Gregorian University (Rome).

Ugo Vanni is Professor of New Testament Exegesis at the Pontifical Gregorian University (Rome). He is an eminent scholar on the Book of Revelation.

PART ONE

Ugo Vanni

The Apocalypse and the Gospel of Luke

1. INTRODUCTION: A PROBLEM SOLVED OR A PROBLEM FORGOTTEN?

Present-day critics, with some exceptions, treat the relationship between the Apocalypse and the synoptic gospels with the rapidity and brusqueness of those anxious to dismiss an awkward subject. On the one hand, they take it for granted that the Apocalypse makes use of synoptic material.[1] On the other, they display remarkable hesitancy when it comes to making more precise statements; the inevitable result is vagueness.[2] Is it possible to advance beyond this indeterminateness, which risks locking up the problem in a vicious circle by leaving the Apocalypse in that literary isolation from the rest of the New Testament which E.B. Allo lamented in his day?[3] Efforts at such an advance have not been lacking. In 1953 M.-E. Boismard called attention to points of contact between the Apocalypse and Luke, as well as the Apocalypse and some passages of the fourth gospel.[4] Two works are of special interest: the spacious study by L. Vos[5] and the more narrowly focused contribution of R. Bauckham on the "parousia parables."[6] These three studies have not received proper attention in the commentaries (which usually only list them in the bibliographies), and yet they reached stimulating conclusions that show how important and complicated was the road traveled by the synoptic traditions before they reached the Apocalypse.

Vos, who looks at the matter from the vantage point of the Apocalypse, emphasizes a synoptic tradition by now fixed in regard to the sayings of Jesus. Bauckham complements Vos as he brings out how, in the broad context of the church's parenetic activity, the exercise of a degree of prophetic creativity had led to a "deparableization." If we accept their conclusions, then we must ask, even before studying the development of the traditions, whether it may not be time to explore once again the extent and effectiveness of the literary contacts between the Apocalypse and the synoptics at the level of the text.

9

The study of such contacts is in fact always a necessary point of departure before going on to a thorough investigation of the underlying traditions.

The timeliness of this approach is brought home by the studies listed above, which give preference to certain passages over other possible ones, as well as by the contribution in this area of R.H. Charles, author of a now classical commentary on the Apocalypse.[7]

Charles takes it for granted that the Apocalypse contains passages directly dependent on, or parallel to, other books of the New Testament. He does not hesitate to claim that the author of the Apocalypse "appears to have used Matthew, Luke, 1 and 2 Corinthians, Colossians, Ephesians. . . ."[8] With his characteristic concern to document what he says, Charles then supplies a lengthy list of passages in which he sees a literary contact—dependence or parallelism—with the other books of the New Testament.[9]

The list has for the most part been disregarded. Charles himself takes up each item of the list in the course of his commentary, although he limits himself in each case to pointing out the dependence or parallelism. The development in the literary study of both the gospels and the Apocalypse—a development reflected in the above-mentioned three studies of Boismard, Bauckham, and Vos—makes us more demanding today. The set of similarities must be checked, thoroughly investigated or revised, extended or narrowed from case to case. Furthermore, we are interested today in a more nuanced kind of connection: a literary contact with proto-Paul or those walking in Paul's steps is one thing, a contact with Q is another, and a specific contact with one of the synoptics or 1 Peter still another.

At this point, the course of the present essay becomes clear. An investigation of all the points of contact would take me too far afield. A choice is required: the Lukan character of this Festschrift suggests that I take the gospel of Luke, while Boismard's above-cited study, although, as we shall see, it is focused especially on the demonic, shows that contacts between Luke and the Apocalypse, at least as a working hypothesis, are of particular interest.

I shall therefore first study the points of contact with Luke listed by Charles, weighing them critically and at the same time pointing out any new perspectives that come to light.

Second, I shall indicate some other points of comparison between the two works.

Finally, I shall summarize the analytical observations made in the course of the study and thus be able to pass an at least hypothetical judgment on the relevance, or lack of it, of contacts between Luke and the Apocalypse. This will be my conclusion.

2. LUKE AND THE APOCALYPSE: THE SIMILARITIES LISTED BY R.H. CHARLES

The first similarity we come across in the Book of Revelation links Rv 1:3 with Lk 11:28. Here are the two passages side by side:

Rv 1:3	*Lk 11:28*
makarios ho	autos de eipen, Menoun
anaginōskōn kai hoi	makarioi hoi akouontes ton
akouontes tous logous tēs	logon tou theou kai
prophēteias kai tērountes ta	phulassontes.
en autē gegrammena, ho gar	
kairos eggus.	

Vos' detailed analysis of the similarities between the two texts deserves careful consideration.[10]

Two similarities catch the eye immediately: the literary form of the macarism and the parallel construction of the phrases "to hear the word" and "to keep" it.

But in addition to the similarities which have led many commentators to emphasize the contact,[11] there are considerable differences. First of all, there is a difference in context: in Luke the macarism is a reply to one which a woman utters about the mother of Jesus;[12] in the Apocalypse we are at the beginning of the book and the macarism refers to a liturgical assembly now in progress.[13] In addition, the verb used for "keeping" the word is different: *tērein* in the Apocalypse and *phulassein* in Luke. Finally, Luke speaks of "the word of God" while the Apocalypse speaks of "the words of prophecy" that are expressly said to be written down in this book.

Vos concludes: "John does not methodically *quote* this saying of Jesus. Rather, he *employs* it. And this employment is consistent with John's use of the Old Testament materials in so far as the original context of the passage is totally ignored, and the passage is adapted to John's revelation by the use of both insertions into and alterations of the original saying."[14]

As far, then, as a direct contact with the gospel of Luke at the redactional stage is concerned, Vos does not exclude it but he does regard it as unlikely, given the differences I have pointed out and especially the use of the different verbs, *tērein* and *phulassein,* with reference to the word. The contact would therefore be at the level of tradition and would precede and be independent of the written gospel.

Vos' conclusions are completely acceptable as regards the use of the saying of Jesus by the author of the Apocalypse. But the reasons offered for the unlikelihood of a contact with the written gospel do not seem cogent. In fact, the use of *tērein* and *phulassein* is simply a matter of style, as Charles pointed out long ago: "*phulassein* is a Lucan word: cf. Luke 18[21], Acts 7[53] 16[4] 27[24], whereas our author does not use *phulassein* at all, but uses *tērein* in the same sense."[15]

But there is more: Vos establishes a parallel between the author's use of the saying of Jesus and his use of the Old Testament. The latter was known to the author in written form, to the point that he is familiar with the original Hebrew-Aramaic text as distinct from the LXX.

This fact gives plausibility to the view that the author had contact with the gospel in its written form, just as he did with the texts of the Old Testament.

The Apocalypse displays an obvious literary development. The saying of Jesus now appears not as an isolated episode but is placed at the beginning of the book as a programmatic statement that is to guide the entire reading which follows.

The second similarity Charles mentions is between Rv 3:5, on the one hand, and both Lk 12:8 and Mt 10:32, on the other:

Rv 3:5	*Lk 12:8*	*Mt 10:32*
kai	Legō de	Pas oun hostis
homologēsō to	humin, pas	homologēsei en
onoma autou	hos an homologēsē	emoi emprosthen
enōpion tou	en emoi	tōn anthrōpōn,
patros mou	emprosthen tōn	homologēsō kagō
kai enōpion	anthrōpōn, kai ho	en autō
tōn aggelōn autou.	huios tou	emprosthen tou
	anthrōpou	patros mou tou en
	homologēsei en	[tois] ouranois.
	autō emprosthen	
	tōn aggelōn tou	
	theou.	

Vos assigns great importance to this similarity and discusses it in detail.[16] He observes in particular that while the verbal similarities, though present, are not overwhelming, there is a striking correspondence of thought between the three passages: all speak of Christ who bears witness at a transcendent level to the meritorious behavior of Christians. This correspondence is enough to warrant the conclusion that there is an undeniable connection between the three texts.[17]

But how is the relationship to be represented? A close examination of the three texts shows agreements in terminology: the verb *homologēsō* is common to all three.[18] According to the Apocalypse the confession of Christ is made *enōpion tou patros mou kai enōpion tōn aggelōn autou;* Matthew mentions the Father (*emprosthen tou patros*) but not the angels; in Luke the witness is given to Christ in the presence of the angels (*emprosthen tōn aggelōn*), but no mention is made of the Father. The *enōpion* of the Apocalypse is equivalent in meaning to the *emprosthen* of the two gospels; the variation is merely stylistic.

Given this lack of complete correspondence, any precise identification of the connection remains problematic.

Vos regards it as unlikely, though not impossible, that the author of the Apocalypse combined the two gospel texts. He would have had to know both of the synoptic traditions in order to reproduce the characteristic traits of each. But even this supposition would not explain the use of Matthew's "in heaven" or the change of Luke's "the angels of God" to "his angels."

At this point:

A more plausible solution would be that the saying of Jesus found in Rev. 3:5 preserves the more original form, which both Matthew and Luke employ only in part, in accordance with the general tenor of their gospels. This would mean that the combination of "before my Father" and "before his angels" was already present in the original saying and that Matthew includes only "before my Father," in keeping with his emphasis upon God as Father of Jesus, and Luke employs only "before the angels . . . ," which is consistent with the Judaistic conceptions of the place of the angels in the judgment scene.[19]

But Vos' entire procedure is not persuasive. Q, the source on which both Matthew and Luke draw, existed prior to the redaction of the Apocalypse, which is also later than the redaction both of Matthew and of Luke. It is not likely that Q, passing first through Luke and Matthew, then directly reached the author of the Apocalypse. Any documentation that would suggest this is lacking.

B.M.F. van Iersel had earlier proposed a different solution: The Q tradition was present in Luke, and Matthew modified it. Vos is aware of this alternative possibility, which is decidedly more probable, but he does not investigate it further.[20]

If we adopt van Iersel's suggestion, the relationship between the three texts acquires a different appearance: Luke would have taken over the original saying in Q; Matthew would have modified it at the redactional stage by having the testimony rendered to the Father rather than to the angels (because he was bent on giving primacy to the person of the Father in his gospel).

The author of the Apocalypse, who pays a great deal of attention both to the Father and to the angels, would have taken both formulations and combined them. The fact that he assigns the saying directly to the risen Christ, as well as the liking for variations that is typical of his style, would have led him to omit Matthew's words "who is in heaven" (applied to the Father) and to change Luke's "the angels of God" to "his [the Father's] angels." All this supposes a direct use not only of the synoptic traditions but also of the final text of both Luke and Matthew. The author of the Apocalypse would be using the gospel passages in the same way in which he uses passages from the Old Testament.[21] This interpretation of the passage in the Apocalypse is confirmed by the grammatical substitution of *homologein* with the accusative for the semitism *homologein en* with the dative. The variation points to a later development, as exemplified by 2 Clement, which has *homologēsō auton.*[22]

Given the diversity of contexts and personages, the similarity between the words "Do not weep" which Jesus addresses to the widow of Nain in Lk 12:8 and the words "Do not weep" which one of the elders addresses to John in Rv 5:5 (this is Charles' third correspondence) appears to be accidental and negligible.

On the other hand, a degree of close correspondence is recognizable between Rv 6:10–11 and Lk 18:7–8. The contexts are similar: in both there is question of an intervention of God who has been ardently entreated in prayer, an intervention aimed at restoring for the sake of Christians a balance disturbed by the forces of evil. In Luke the saying is preceded by the parable of the judge who is compelled by a widow's persistence to render her justice at last (Lk 18:1–6). The parable emphasizes the need of constancy and persistence in prayer to God in order to win justice. Christians "cry to him day and night," and God, says Jesus, "will quickly grant justice to them."

Rv 6:10 speaks of the martyrs in heaven who, "with a loud voice," call upon God to act and "avenge our blood." The situation is the same as in Luke, although the Apocalypse stresses the tension between the injustice suffered and the divine intervention that is being requested. The language used is similar: *ekdikeis* in the Apocalypse corresponds to *poiēsē tēn ekdikēsin* in Luke; *ekraxan phōnē megalē* in the Apocalypse corresponds to *boōntōn autō hēmeras kai vuktos* in Luke.

In addition, the assurance given by Jesus that God "will quickly grant justice to them" is explained in the Apocalypse: God responds immediately to the cry of the martyrs, but tells them that they must wait "a little longer," until his plan is completely carried out. The quickness of which Luke speaks (*en tachei*) is interpreted in the Apocalypse as a short time of waiting (*eti mikron chronon*) which the martyrs must accept.

There are some other points of contact that have a certain interest. The Lukan parable describes a "judge" (*ho kritēs*), while in applying the parable the author passes directly to God, who is therefore thought of as a judge who infinitely transcends the level on which human judges act. This passage is made explicit in the Apocalypse: God is invoked as "Lord" (*despotēs*)[23] and as "holy and true"; it is expected that he will act as a judge (*krineis*).

The close similarity of the language (with the variations typical of the Apocalypse) and the equivalence of the two contexts make the contact highly probable. There is an advance, a development: what is said in Luke is explained in detail in the Apocalypse. Furthermore, the fact that the Apocalypse speaks explicitly of a judicial action of God indicates a reference to the parable and supposes that the parable has already been connected with the saying of Jesus. From this it follows that the contact was with the text of Luke at the redactional stage or with an equivalent Lukan tradition already formed. For we are dealing here with a parable and a saying that are peculiar to Luke. This would suggest a special link between Luke and the Apocalypse.

The contact (once more, in Charles' list) between Rv 6:15–16 and Lk 23:30 and 21:36 is a more complicated matter. There is a general similarity between the three contexts, all of which are eschatological. Also typical of both Luke and the Apocalypse are both the citation of Hos 10:8 and the idea of being able to "stand" (*stathēnai*) before Christ as he manifests himself at the end.

But are the general similarity of contexts and the two specific similarities, namely, the citation of Hosea and the use of *stathēnai*, enough to show a literary contact?

We are left uncertain. And the uncertainty increases when we observe that Rv 6:15–17 displays a literary structure which is both flowing and dramatically effective and joins together the two passages of Luke, though these are from different chapters. Then, too, the personages are completely different. In Lk 23:30 Jesus addresses the "daughters of Jerusalem," telling them that the situation described by Hosea will be fulfilled; Lk 21:36 is part of an exhortatory discourse addressed to everyone. In the

Apocalypse, on the other hand, in a unified, well-constructed context (as I noted above), it is the leaders of human society who apply the passage in Hosea to themselves and declare their inability to endure their meeting with God and the Lamb.

All this does not permit us to give a quick answer. The fact, however, that the citation of Hosea and the use of *stathēnai* are typical does suggest a hypothesis: the author of the Apocalypse, familiar with the text of Luke or with the traditions that lie behind Luke but are already fixed, is inspired by it (them) and undertakes his own development of them, combining them in a setting that is materially different, just as he often does when drawing upon the Old Testament. It is to be noted, however, that in the hypothesis of some kind of literary contact, the movement is from Luke to the Apocalypse and not vice versa. The passage in the Apocalypse undoubtedly becomes clearer if we suppose a contact with the two passages in Luke that inspired the author of the Apocalypse.

The similarity of Rv 11:6 and Lk 4:25 is fortuitous. In both passages a reference is made to the drought in the time of Elijah; the reference is clear and explicit in Luke, but is much more allusive in the Apocalypse. Inasmuch as the other references made, in both contexts, to Old Testament events do not correspond, the reference to the drought derives directly, in both Luke and the Apocalypse, from the Old Testament.

In contrast, the contact between Rv 12:9 and Lk 10:18 calls for special attention. Even Boismard, who systematically studies the contacts between the Apocalypse and Luke from the standpoint of the demoniacal,[24] devotes special attention to this similarity and establishes a parallel not only between Lk 10:18 and Rv 12:9[25] but also and above all between Lk 10:18 and Rv 9:1–11.[26]

I shall take for granted the thematic unity given by the demoniacal, to which the passages refer, and I shall examine the two contacts together.

I shall begin with the one which Boismard emphasizes as he sets the similarities side by side:

Rv 9:1–4	*Lk 10:17–19*
1. Kai ho pemptos aggelos esalpisen* kai eidon astera ek tou oranou peptōkota eis tēn gēn, kai edothē autō hē kleis tou phreatos tes abussou.	17. Hypestrepsan de hoi ebdomēkonta [duo] meta charas legontes, Kurie, kai ta daimonia upotassetai hēmin en to onomati sou.
2. kai ēnoixen to phrear tes abussou, kai anebē kapnos ek	18. eipen de autois, Etheōroun ton Satanan hōs

tou phreatos hōs kapnos
kaminou megalēs, kai
eskotōthē ho hēlios kai ho aēr
ek tou kapnou tou phreatos.

astrapēn ek tou ouranou
pesonta.

3. kai ek tou kapnou
exēlthon akrides eis tēn gēn,
kai edothē autais exousia hōs
echousin exousian hoi
skorpioi tēs gēs.

4. kai errethē autais hina mē
adikēsousin ton chorton tēs
gēs oude pan chlōron oude
pan dendron, ei mē tous
anthrōpous hoitines ouk
echousi tēn sphragida tou
theou epi tōn metōpōn.

19. idou dedōka humin tēn
exousian tou patein epanō
opheōn kai skorpiōn, kai epi
pasan tēn dunamin tou
echthrou, kai ouden humas
ou mē adikēsē.

The points of contact which Boismard points out between these two texts are many and detailed. Rv 9:1 and Lk 10:18 show (he says) a very close likeness: the "star fallen from heaven" of Rv is said to be equivalent to "Satan falling from heaven like lightning." Both passages—Rv 9:3 and Lk 10:19—mention "scorpions." Finally, the specific action of the scorpions is indicated by the same verb, *adikein*, in Rv 9:4 and Lk 10:19.

But the two passages (I am still giving Boismard's interpretation) adopt different perspectives. Luke emphasizes

the idea that the disciples of Christ will be protected henceforth against the harmful action of the demons; this implies the end of Satan's power as signified by his fall. The author of the Apocalypse, on the other hand, emphasizes the harmful action which Satan, now fallen to earth, is going to exercise against the wicked.[27]

Despite this difference in perspective, it would be difficult to maintain, says Boismard, that the similarities are accidental. Therefore, "while the rather notable difference in perspective seems to exclude a direct dependence of the Apocalypse on Luke or of Luke on the Apocalypse, the two texts certainly stem from a common tradition, and a tradition had doubtless found *written* form."[28]

It is stimulating to hear so unqualified an assertion. But a critical examination of it leads to further details that are of some interest.

Leaving aside for the moment the dubious parallel between "star" and "lightning," I note a certain inconsistency between the interpretation of *pesonta* in Luke as signifying a defeat and the interpretation of *peptōkota* in the Apocalypse as signifying a negative presence on earth. It is difficult to assign two such different meanings to the same verb in the same setting of a fall from heaven.

While a demonic presence on earth is a fully acceptable meaning for the Apocalypse, the idea of a defeat attached to the fall of Satan from heaven in Luke is not equally so.

The saying of Jesus which Luke reports, and in which the verb *pesonta* occurs, should be taken as a symbolic statement rather than as a vision in the full and proper sense.[29]

In this perspective adequate value must be given to all the elements in the symbolic nucleus: the lightning that flashes from heaven to earth rouses chiefly surprise and fear and suggests danger and harm inflicted on the earth. The image does not of itself convey the idea of a fall in the sense of a defeat. The saying seems to express not the fall of Satan in the mythological sense of a dethronement but rather a threat at the human level where the action of Satan comes like a flash of lightning and manifests itself in harm inflicted on human beings. The power which Jesus gives the disciples over the "scorpions" and all the negative powers, so that nothing can "hurt" them, is to be understood symbolically as meaning an ability to counter the action of Satan when he strikes at human beings. Broadly speaking, then, the "scorpions" are located within the symbolic sphere of the demonic.

The lack of harmony between the two "falls" has now disappeared, since in both Luke and the Apocalypse the "fall" signifies an active, baneful presence of the demon on earth. In Luke this presence is viewed in terms of the disciples' obligation to combat it and their ability to do so. The Apocalypse, on the other hand, develops, in a highly structured form, the effects which the demon has on human beings. These effects, indicated in the figure of the locusts in vv. 7ff, bring a pressure to bear on human beings who are far from God that is comparable to the bite of scorpions.

The similarity between the two passages then becomes even closer, the movement here again being from Luke to the Apocalypse. Satan, who is falling (*pesonta*) from heaven, becomes a "star" that has already fallen (*peptōkota*) to earth. As is clear from a comparison with Rv 12:4, where the dragon sweeps down a third of the stars from heaven and throws them on the earth, the reference is to a result produced, a negative effect on the earth.

The image of the "scorpions," too, is given a new interpretation. There is a shift from a generalized belonging to the world of Satan in Luke to—in the Apocalypse—a precise action of torment, which is limited in time but is beyond human powers to tolerate and is connected with the action of the demonic.

This crescendo of similarities removes the reason for Boismard's reservations as to whether the author of the Apocalypse knew and could have used the text of Luke. His use of it may also be explained as the use of a written tradition that is not identical with the text of Luke but very close to it (a tradition, however, which is not documented). The fact that the passage in question is peculiar to Luke obviates a comparison with the other synoptics in terms of the development of the tradition. But if we suppose a knowledge of the redacted text, the development of the reinterpretation seems clear, without there being need of appealing to other hypotheses.

As I noted above, there is a similarity between Lk 10:17–18 and another passage of the Apocalypse, 12:8–11, which Charles lists but to which Boismard pays no special attention.

I.H. Marshall remarks with regard to Lk 10:18 and especially to the verb *pesonta* as applied to Satan: "*piptō* may be meant as a passive of *ballō* . . . , in which case the picture is of Satan being cast down from heaven."[30] This interpretation establishes a very close connection between the text of Luke and Rv 12:7–9, where the author, using a midrash which he himself perhaps composed, speaks of a struggle in heaven between Michael and his angels, on one side, and the dragon and his angels, on the other. The struggle goes against the dragon who is thrown down from heaven to earth (the passive, *eblēthē*, of *ballō* is used for "thrown down"). The author of the Apocalypse describes this occurrence in an emphatic way that deserves close attention: he repeats *eblēthē* and, in between, describes the many forms which the demonic takes in human history and the resulting names which it has: the dragon is "that ancient serpent, who is called the Devil and Satan, the deceiver of the whole world" (Rv 12:9). I can say, therefore, that subject of *eblēthē* in both cases is Satan. Consequently, the two expressions: "(I watched) Satan fall from heaven like a flash of lightning" and "Satan was thrown down to earth" are to be seen as substantially equivalent. The second interprets the first. It is in keeping with this line of interpretation that we find explicit in the Apocalypse that sense of threat and terror, with all the resulting harm, which lightning causes when it strikes the earth. And in fact the author adds: "Woe to the earth and the sea, for the devil has come down to you with great wrath, because he knows that his time is short!" (Rv 12:12).

All things considered, then, a contact between Luke and the Apocalypse at this point seems highly probable.

The fact that a contact with the same passage of Luke occurs twice in the Apocalypse, in differing contexts, is important, for it calls to mind the way in which the author uses the Old Testament. He often repeats the same passage in different contexts and with differing interpretations.

Another similarity which Charles lists would be between Rv 14:4 and Lk 9:57, both of which have to do with the following of Christ.

Rv 14:4	*Lk 9:57*
houtoi hoi akolouthountes tō arniō hopou an hupagē.	kai poreuomenōn autōn en tē hodō eipen tis pros auton, Akolouthēsō soi hopou ean aperchē.

The points of contact do show a certain closeness. Not only is the same verb, *akolouthein,* used, but there is also the detail (undoubtedly more specific) *hopou an hupagē / hopou ean aperchē.* The incident is found only in Luke, which strengthens the likelihood of a contact. Even though the verb *akolouthein* is often used of the following of Jesus, the added idea of an unconditional readiness occurs only in these passages. The movement would once again be from Luke to the Apocalypse: the desired future in Luke becomes in the Apocalypse a reality constantly being verified, as the present participle *akolouthountes* indicates. Furthermore, in Luke the reference is to the following of Jesus before his resurrection; in the Apocalypse the one being followed is the dead and risen Christ who is actively involved in the struggle against negative forces, as is clear from the fact that Christ is referred to as the Lamb (see Rv 5:6).

According to Charles, another similarity exists between Rv 18:24 and Lk 11:50.

Rv 18:24	*Lk 11:50*
kai en autē haima prophētōn kai hagiōn heurethē kai pantōn tōn esphagmenōn epi tēs gēs.	hina ekzētēthē to haima pantōn tōn prophētōn to ekkechumenon apo katabolēs kosmou apo tēs geneas tautēs.

There is a close similarity in the words *haima* and *prophētōn,* which are common to both passages, and, more broadly, between *pantōn tōn esphagmenōn epi tēs gēs* in the Apocalypse and *to ekkechumenon apo kataholēs kosmou* in Luke. As for Luke, it is to be noted that the substance of the text seems to come from Q (it is also found in Mt 23:35), but the explicit reference to the prophets is characteristic of Luke. The Apocalypse speaks of Babylon as a city of consumers and the representative of an earthly system that is closed in upon its own immanence and opposed to the reign of God and his Christ. The system which Babylon represents is intolerant and seeks to eliminate its rivals by violence, but the blood shed by these rivals remains in it and is "found" on the day of its judgment.

In Luke the perspective is similar but is not developed in detail as in the Apocalypse. By closing itself against him, the generation which Jesus addresses is following in the footsteps of Babylon.

A degree of similarity between the two passages is undeniable, given the similarity of the two contexts and the sharing of some words; this is especially true of Luke as compared to Matthew. The author of the Apocalypse may have gotten an idea from Luke, even though in this instance the model that inspires him is more probably still the Old Testament.[31]

The final similarity listed by Charles—Rv 19:9 and Lk 14:15—calls for particular attention, in view especially of Vos' lengthy treatment of it in the thematic perspective of the spouse and the banquet.[32] Vos studies the entire symbolic picture of marriage, from engagement to wedding feast, that is present in Rv 19:9. Repeating a remark of J. Jeremias, he notes that while the image of a marital relationship between God and his people is everywhere present in the Old Testament, neither there nor elsewhere in Judaism is it applied to the Messiah.[33] It follows (according to Vos) that the only source "for the nuptial depiction in Rev. 19, 6ff. is the sayings of Jesus."[34] Vos makes a detailed study of each element, from its terminology to its contexts. The points of contact with the sayings of Jesus come together in the parable of the wedding guests. The parable comes from Q and has been reported for us, in differing contexts, by Luke and Matthew. Luke (14:15–24) links it to a passage, peculiar to him, that is concerned with precedence among guests at a dinner (Lk 14:7–14). Matthew (22:1–14), on the other hand, links it to the controversy between Jesus and the ruling class: the parable is a reply to the hostile attitude of this class toward Jesus. Vos gives preference to Matthew's redaction and connects it especially with Rv 19:7–9. An outline of the points of contact[35] brings out the connection.

Vos' documentation and analysis seem relevant, though not indisputably conclusive. In fact, the objection can be raised that the Apocalypse transfers directly to the risen Christ many prerogatives of God which are found in the Old Testament.

The image of the marital relationship, which in fact pervades the entire Apocalypse,[36] can be regarded as one of these. Then it has to be asked whether it is indeed so necessary to appeal to the sayings of Jesus as the only possible source. On the other hand, the correspondences between the synoptic material and the Apocalypse are so numerous and so close as to make a contact highly likely.

Now—to return to my main theme—the same argument applies to Luke: close points of contact, equivalent to those which Vos observes in Matthew,[37] can also be found in Luke. Moreover, the immediate context of the parable in Luke seems closer to the text of the Apocalypse.

Rv 19:9	*Lk 14:15-16*
Kai legei moi, Grapson•	15. Akousas de tis tōn
Makarioi hoi eis to deipnon	sunanakeimenōn tauta eipen
tou gamou tou arniou	autō, Makarios hostis
keklēmenoi.	phagetai arton en tē basileia
	tou theou.
kai legei moi, Houtoi hoi	16. ho de eipen autō,
logoi alēthinoi tou theou eisin.	Anthrōpos tis epoiei deipnon
	mega, kai ekalesen pollous.

The macarism form is an undeniable characteristic of both texts. This does not of itself prove a contact, but, as a characteristic literary form, it certainly has some probative value.[38]

The content of the macarism in the two passages is quite similar. In Luke the words express an enthusiasm for participation in the banquet in the kingdom of God, but only in global terms. In the Apocalypse, on the other hand, they take the more specific form of an invitation to the wedding feast of the Lamb, which is an eschatological feast. The kingdom of God is already established (see Rv 11:15). Thus, in the Apocalypse the Lukan idea of sharing a banquet typical of the kingdom of God undergoes a dizzying intensification along the same lines and becomes an invitation to the wedding feast of the Lamb, now that the kingdom of God has been established.

Turning directly to a comparison between Rv 19:9 and the development of the parable, I note first of all a general fact: the "deparableization" which R. Bauckham spotted in the parables of the parousia[39] has occurred here as well.

In the Apocalypse the feast is a real one and in no sense parabolic. In addition, several words directly echo Luke, while others, but less directly, suppose Matthew's redaction. Thus the *deipnon mega* of Luke corresponds to the *deipnon* of the Apocalypse. There are invited guests (*tois keklēmenois:* Lk 14:17) who do not accept, and it is these, the "invited" (*tōn keklēmenōn:* Lk 14:24), who will be excluded from the dinner.

Matthew speaks of a wedding feast (*gamous:* Mt 22:1) which a king celebrates for his own son. Here again, the "invited" (*tous keklēmenous:* Mt 22:3) refuse to come.

The passage in the Apocalypse seems to combine the two redactions: Luke speaks of a *deipnon*, as does the Apocalypse, but the wedding context, with its reference to Christ, is found only in Matthew.

What conclusion can be drawn? We can, I think, agree fully on the importance that Vos assigns to the sayings of Jesus about marriage which apply to him and which by the time of the Apocalypse have already developed into set traditions. The process of deparableization which can be seen in the Apocalypse by comparison with the synoptics and which Bauckham emphasizes seems to be confirmed.

In all probability, however, more must be said. There are no grounds for supposing two partially different traditions of the parable of the wedding feast, both of which would have been present in Q and would then have been taken over by Luke and Matthew respectively. It is easier to assign the variations to the redactional activity of Matthew and Luke. Then, accepting that we find the more pertinent aspects of the two combined in the Apocalypse, it is natural to assume that the author of the Apocalypse knew the redacted text of Matthew and Luke. If this be the case, we have the explanation of how the author of the Apocalypse took over, and incorporated into his own context, the macarism form of Luke, the content of which corresponds to that of the Apocalypse; the movement is always, of course, from the less to the more.

3. OTHER SIMILARITIES

I have thus far been considering the similarities listed by Charles. Numerous though these are, however, they do not make an exhaustive list; other leads could be followed up and discussed, but this would take me too far beyond the limits of this essay. I shall limit myself to pointing out one such similarity and briefly explaining it; I refer to the attention, typical of both Luke and the Apocalypse, that is given to the category of realized salvation.

The term *sōtēria,* used only by Luke in the synoptic gospels, occurs three times (out of four occurrences in all) in the canticle of Zechariah (Lk

1:69, 71, 77). The three occurrences of the term in the Apocalypse are all
in doxologies (Rv 7:10; 12:10; 19:1). In both Luke and the Apocalypse the
idea of *sōtēria* is so deeply felt that it finds lyrical expression in song.

Salvation is taking place now. In Luke this aspect of the matter is
emphasized in the conversion of Zacchaeus, which is interpreted as the
coming of salvation upon his entire household: *sēmeron sōtēria tō oikō
toutō egeneto* (Lk 19:9). Here we have the fourth occurrence of the word
sōtēria in Luke. In Rv 12:10 salvation is again a present reality: *arti egeneto sōtēria* (Rv 12:10). These two passages correspond fairly closely:
sōtēria and *egeneto* are accompanied by two other common synonyms,
sēmeron and *arti*, which bring out the present reality of the salvation.

One final remark. Luke speaks of a knowledge of salvation that is to
come as a gift of God: *tou dounai gnosin sōtērias* (Lk 1:77). In the Apocalypse this knowledge is seen as now present: salvation is known to belong
to God and the Lamb (see Rv 7:10) and to be associated with the power
and ongoing reign of God as well as with the power (*exousia*) that is
specific to and characteristic of Christ (see Rv 12:10). In the area of
sōtēria, then, there is a progression, the movement being again from Luke
to the Apocalypse.

4. CONCLUSIONS

It is now time for me to pinpoint some conclusions.

All the passages listed by Charles have, with two exceptions, raised
problems of great interest when it comes to contacts between the gospel of
Luke and the Apocalypse. By analyzing them in detail and in light of the
three contributions of Vos, Boismard, and Bauckham, I have been able to
show a broad and interconnected series of correspondences. These are not
always very close, but, taking them as a whole, I reach a general conclusion that can hardly be challenged: there has been contact between the
text of Luke and the text of the Apocalypse.

In some instances, closer examination has led me to move from the
text of Luke to an investigation of Matthew as well and has allowed me to
broaden the view: there has also been a direct contact with the text of
Matthew or, more generally, with Q. The contact with Luke, however, has
stood out in special relief; Boismard's insight was accurate. A further
study of contacts between the three synoptics and the Apocalypse would
nonetheless be of interest.[40]

Sticking now to the relationship between Luke and the Apocalypse, I
have noted on each occasion that this involved a crescendo and a forward
movement. This means—at least—that the stage of tradition is different:

more developed, more complete and complex in the Apocalypse by comparison with Luke. This implies a separation in time. At this point, a further problem arises: Should the points of similarity which I have shown be regarded as due to contacts between traditions or to contacts between redacted texts? Vos' work shows the fruitfulness of a study of traditions, and the same can be said of Bauckham's article. But an analysis of some similarities has led several times to a direct contact with the redactional work which the Apocalypse seems to suppose has been already completed.

All of this makes possible a comparison which has already cropped up here and there in various studies and deserves to be emphasized. It is the comparison between the use which the author of the Apocalypse makes of the Old Testament and the use he makes of the gospel of Luke. An impressive parallel emerges: as is well known, the author of the Apocalypse takes over the Old Testament text without citing it and incorporates it into his own, while introducing such variations as a Christian rereading allows him to make. The Old Testament is very often a point of departure, never a point of arrival. Moreover, it is a point of departure in two ways: it serves as an inspiration (a literary model) and it provides details which can be repeated. The same can be said of the text of Luke: at times (as in the case of the demoniacal) it provides an idea which serves as an inspiration; most often, however, the text is taken over in detail, but always with further developments. The date of the Apocalypse—end of the first century or, preferably, the first decades of the second—allows a passage of time sufficient for this kind of development.

In any case—this is a final observation, and one that takes me back to where I started—the problem of a connection between the Apocalypse and Luke and between the Apocalypse and the synoptics generally deserves to be tackled anew and thoroughly investigated. To leave it aside or to settle it with general assertions would be to neglect a further source of light that could play a decisive role in the interpretation of the Apocalypse.

The Role of the Scriptures in the Composition of the Gospel Accounts: The Temptations of Jesus (Lk 4:1–13 par.) and the Multiplication of the Loaves (Lk 9:10–17 par.)*

I

What formative part did the Old Testament, which was the sacred scriptures of the first Christians, play in the development of the gospel stories? In answering this question I shall set aside at the outset two extreme solutions. According to the first, the prophetic texts of the Old Testament played so normative a role that they made inevitable a particular, and necessarily fictitious, formulation of the New Testament narratives. According to the second, the gospel events and the first narratives of them had such a solid historical basis that the Old Testament exerted no influence at all; only later on was the correspondence between promise and fulfillment underscored by scriptural references or citations.

II

In my judgment, the relationship between history and the scriptures is not one-directional; it resembles rather the gropings and subsequent corrections that we see in cybernetics. To take the temptations of Jesus as an example[1]: the event that takes place is individual and unique (Mt 4:1 // Lk 4:1). But the happening on this occasion resembles other, earlier events that have already been described in religious terms; the likeness is seen because a theological consciousness is at work that is alert to the element of continuity and therefore to the fidelity of the one same God. The story of what is specific and unique (Jesus, who is neither Moses nor

Aaron nor Elijah) is thus brought into harmony with the story that preceded it, namely, the presence of the lawgiver on Sinai (Ex 19–20; 24; 32–34). The withdrawal of Jesus into the wilderness is therefore not the first such action; the guidance of the Spirit displays continuity; the devil is not here tempting someone for the first time; and the length of the withdrawal—forty days—matches that of Moses' ordeal in the wilderness (Ex 34:28).

But the interaction does not involve only two poles, namely, the event of Jesus' temptation and the scriptures. It also includes the gospel story—as distinct from the Jesus event which makes its own demands—as well as something too often forgotten: the ongoing reading and actualization of the Old Testament as seen first in Jewish and then in Christian exegesis. In short, we are dealing with a passage that has four sharply defined points of reference: *the historical event* in the life of Jesus; his withdrawal and sojourn in the wilderness; *the biblical echo* of Moses' forty-day stay on the mountain; *the narrative logic* of the gospel stories which show lack (fasting) being followed by desire (hunger); and, finally, *Jewish exegesis*, which, in the form of midrash, a good translation, is the end-result of long-term meditation on the scriptures and which considers the fruit of its reflections to be legitimate commentary, namely, that what is encountered in the wilderness is not only the "biblical" God but also the "intertestamental" devil who seeks to bring about the downfall of believers.[2]

III

Life is made up of countless incidents, and the scriptures of countless stories. How is the selection from these two sources made? Who establishes the correspondences? Christian tradition has kept the memory of an incident from the beginning of Jesus' ministry, because people like beginnings to be sharply defined, and a temptation story in particular, because they admire the tests that certify and empower heroes.[3] This selection of incidents is therefore neither fortuitous nor arbitrary. Neither is the selection of scriptural correspondences: Jesus is the mediator of a new order; was not Moses at the source of the former blessings, namely, the covenant and the law? In order to give expression to what is new, the first Christians turned instinctively to the past. The New Testament story, which is an irreducibile *ephapax*, is altered by being brought into correspondence and connection with the scriptures (resemblance, crescendo, or antithesis). If Jesus is to be understood, he must be like someone already known, in this case Moses, since knowledge increases only through comparison of the object to be known with objects already known and through the discovery of likenesses.[4]

In the final analysis, this is what the typological exegesis of antiquity and the middle ages saw very clearly. But if the correspondences between Adam and Christ or between the high priest and Christ are now part of the Christian inheritance, this is due not to the gospel stories but to the reflections of the first theologians: the apostle Paul and the author of the letter to the Hebrews. As for the evangelists, the point that caught their attention in the inexhaustible store of the Bible is chiefly the comparison with Moses.[5]

IV

The gospels often set a prophetic figure alongside the typical image of Moses as leader and legislator. According to the gospel story Jesus was a prophet—a new Elijah or the prophet like Moses—as well as son of David and royal messiah.[6] The gospel account of the multiplication of the loaves (Mt 14:13–21 // Mk 6:32–44 // Lk 9:10–17 // Jn 6:1–13) makes it possible to check this claim; but this example also reminds us not to forget the points of reference listed earlier, namely, the constraints proper to the literary genre which is that of the miraculous gift[7]; these are: Jewish exegesis, which sometimes interprets the quail from the sea (Nm 11:31) as flying fish and thus explains the presence here of the two fish (Lk 9:13 par.)[8]; the event that is the starting point but is difficult to define; and, finally, the scriptures. But which passage of scripture? The stories of Elijah and Elisha multiplying meal and oil (1 Kgs 17 and 2 Kgs 4). These stories represent, of course, only stages in a tradition of faith according to which God satisfies the hunger of his people, as attested in the proverb cited in the story of Elijah: "The jar of meal will not be emptied and the jug of oil will not fail until the day that the Lord sends rain on the earth." Nevertheless, one of these stories, that of Elisha, did provide the gospel account with its structure and development.

2 Kings 4:42–44	*New Testament*
A man comes to Elisha; there are numerous spectators	The crowds come to Jesus
The man brings bread	People in the crowd have bread
The prophet's servant is present	The disciples of Jesus are present

The prophet orders that the people be fed	Jesus (immediately or after discussion) orders that these people be fed
Reaction of the servant	Reaction of the disciples
New order from the prophet	New order from Jesus
Carrying out of the order (distribution)	Carrying out of the order (distribution)
There is bread left over	There is bread left over

Understood in the context of the scriptures, the New Testament story emphasizes the fact that God continues to feed his people and that he is still faithful; that he makes use of an intermediary, a prophet—in this case, Jesus; that the food, though material, is a manifestation of salvation and even anticipates the blessings of the eschaton; that Christian worship and the ecclesial community are the present locales or settings of this anticipation.[9] The biblical model is thus related to the gospel story as the Lord's supper is to the banquet of the kingdom.[10]

V

Let me return to the story of the temptations, especially as told by Matthew. We read in Mt 4:12–13a that after this test Jesus returns to Galilee, going first to Nazara (Luke 4:16 has the same strange form of the name Nazareth), then to Capernaum. The evangelist's intention is to show Jesus' first preaching as following upon the certifying trial, as Mark has done before him and as Luke does contemporaneously. The two poles of reference, conversion and kingdom (which are in the inverse order here as compared with Mk 1:15), are regarded by Matthew as an adequate summary of this preaching (Mt 4:17). Matthew then continues, as Mark does, with the call of the first disciples (Mt 4:18–22).

However, between the return to Galilee and these two events, Matthew seeks to convince us, almost to force our hand, but in any event to prove a truth to us, to *tell* us something therefore about a *reality*, or, more accurately, to prove the conformity of a prediction to a fact (Mt 4:13b–16). The prediction took the form of a prophetic oracle, *to rhēthen*, which originally lacked substance but has now been filled (*plēroō*). There is here a different relation to the scriptures than at the beginning of the chapter, at the time of the sojourn on the mountain, or later on in the multiplication of the loaves. We have here an instance of a citation (Is 8:23–9:1) that has a tremendous effect.[11] The citation first universalizes, then dramatizes, and finally sets free. It universalizes by describing the encounter between Jesus and Galilee as a manifestation of God to all of his people. It dramatizes by situating all Galileans, like it or not, in darkness. Finally, it sets free by offering the salvation it describes, or, more specifically, by an anticipatory interpretation of the preaching of Jesus (Mt 4:17) as the dawning of a saving light (Mt 4:16). For all Jewish readers, and even all Greek readers, are aware of the connection between light and salvation.[12]

Matthew the evangelist, who can in other respects be so conservative, goes on to be even bolder than he has been in offering this application of the scriptures (4:15–16): He does not hesitate even to intervene in the living reality of history; I mean, of course, the history that he is narrating. He makes Zebulun and Naphtali the rivets that attach history to scripture and scripture to history. Jesus must betake himself not only to Nazara and Capernaum in Galilee but also to the "land of Zebulun, land of Naphtali, on the road by the sea" (Is 8:23, cited in Mt 4:15). If he must, then he will. This explains Mt 4:13b and the movement it describes as intimated by the scripture, which is felt to be achieving its fulfillment (with the help of an entertaining ambiguity: in the Old Testament, the sea to which Isaiah refers is the Mediterranean; in the gospel citation of that passage the sea can only be the Lake of Gennesaret).[13]

VI

If we look now at the scriptural content of the temptations (Lk 4:1–13; Mt 4:1–11), we will note first of all that the superhuman wrestling between the Son of God and the devil is located at the level of human beings and takes the form of a rabbinical dialogue between protagonists who strike blows with verses from the Bible. Alongside the imitation of the scriptures that draws its inspiration from the narrative forms, and biblical prophecy looking for fulfillment, there is here a third usage of the scriptures. The latter are seen here as a norm that applies not just now and then but permanently. The future tense used in the citations is the future not of prophetic promise but of concrete obedience.

Both parties accept the scriptures as law. Jesus recalls the passages that fit the circumstances and shows his adversary how to use them properly. Against the devil's misuse of scripture Jesus appeals to Moses, whereas in the multiplication of the loaves he imitates and completes Elijah and especially Elisha. In the episode of the temptations the scriptures do not provide the form of the story as they do in the passage on Zebulun and Naphtali, but they do serve as an explicitly cited norm for the decisions and actions of Jesus, who is presented as hero of faith and obedience. The tempter's formal fidelity but real infidelity to the scriptures is met by the faithful fidelity of Jesus, a fidelity characterized by trust and dedication. Thanks to the passages he chooses, Jesus outlines a behavior, based on faith, that the people should have demonstrated at the exodus: reliance on the word of God (Dt 8:3), determination to adore God and God alone (Dt 6:13), refusal to put God to the test (Dt 6:16).

This is an obedience that is not so much moral as theological. The Son of God chooses to use neither the miracle-working power which he possesses (he refuses to transform the stones into loaves) nor the political power that is his inheritance (he renounces the kingdoms of this world) nor the immunity bestowed by the Trinity and attested by the princely escort at his disposal (he does without the help of the angels' wings). The story of the temptations is messianic but also ethical and theological and can be read as christological as well as parenetic. It leads us to the scriptures as well as to other areas by reason of new events and experiences. Here on this still unknown terrain of spiritual experience and testing, Jesus, the principal protagonist, who is located, if we may so put it, in his own time and context, refers to scripture as norm of faith and life. This is what the evangelists Luke and Matthew are saying in the story of the temptations.

VII

At the close of this short analysis I may conclude that the evangelists, Luke and Matthew in particular, have a vital relation to the scriptures, a relation which refuses both haughty rejection of them and servile dependence on them. Desirous of respecting the scriptural record of the first fulfillments, the ancient promises, and the constant will of God, the evangelists establish numerous correspondences of various kinds between the sacred scriptures and the saving event which is ultimate and decisive in their eyes as believers, namely, the life, death, and resurrection of Jesus, the messiah and Son of God, whose story they are carefully reporting and whose significance they want to define.

The stories they tell of the temptations of Jesus and of the multiplication of the loaves enable us to uncover at least three uses of scripture: imitation of the biblical story, fulfillment of prophecy, and understanding, in faith, of the scriptural norm.[14]

Methodological Reflections on Recent Studies of the Naaman Pericope (2 Kings 5): Some Background to Luke 4:27

INTRODUCTION

In recent years NT scholars have increasingly noted the influence of the Elijah and Elisha texts of the books of Kings on various NT texts, particularly in Luke and Acts,[1] and the Naaman pericope has been singled out for special attention. It may then be of interest here to examine some studies of 2 Kgs 5 within its OT context. The purpose of the present essay is not to offer a new reading or exposition of 2 Kgs 5 but rather to survey, and comment on, the different approaches and goals of a representative selection of recent studies, with the hope of making a small contribution to the methodological debate that is characteristic of the current situation of OT (as well as NT) studies.

A quick look at two recent commentaries on 2 Kgs, published in prestigious series in Germany and the U.S., can serve both to illustrate the wide diversity of approach to the task of studying this biblical text and to underline the need for methodological reflection. Ernst Würthwein's volume on 2 Kgs in the series Das Alte Testament Deutsch was published in 1984.[2] His treatment of 2 Kgs 5 begins with a translation in which different typefaces are used to indicate the different redactional strata which he discerned in the text. The reader of the commentary is therefore confronted immediately with a processed form of the biblical text, in line with what in fact is the main emphasis of Würthwein's commentary, namely, redaction-criticism and redaction-history. The detailed comments on 2 Kgs 5 are divided into three sections, which correspond to the three redactional strata detected by Würthwein; each section is discussed on its own and its purpose is defined, but no attempt is made to examine the overall effects produced by combining the three stages. Is it too much to say that readers are given the impression that the final form of the text is regarded simply as raw material to be dissected by scholarly analysis into its component strata and is not worth examination for its own sake?

When one passes from Würthwein's volume to the commentary on 2 Kgs in the Anchor Bible series, one finds oneself in a different world, and not only geographically.[3] The authors, the Israeli scholars Mordechai Cogan and Hayim Tadmor, proceed in another way, partly but not totally determined by the editorial norms of the series. First they offer a translation of the text; then a set of notes follows, where verse-by-verse comments are given on philological details, matters of history and geography, and cultural features, with an occasional stylistic observation and reference to parallel texts; finally a more synthetic comment is given, dealing with the dynamics of the narrative and its main themes. Cogan and Tadmor see the chapter as an unstratified literary unity, dating to the period that preceded classical prophecy. Their reading of the chapter, then, focuses on this historical context. What one misses here is not only a discussion with those scholars who propose the existence of redactional strata in the text (and, as will be seen below, Würthwein was by no means the first to do so) but also a more developed examination of the function of 2 Kgs 5 in its present literary context (and not only in its putative ninth century historical context).

Enough has been said to suggest that the two commentaries just mentioned, for all their merits and usefulness (which is beyond question), do not succeed in giving a reasonably comprehensive view of what readers need to deepen their understanding of the biblical text. At this point, one might ask what would be involved in "a reasonably comprehensive view"; the rest of this study will attempt to sketch an answer to this question by surveying a number of monographs and articles that have contributed one or other aspect to this comprehensive view. Put in a very summary way, the thesis proposed here (in agreement with one line of contemporary methodological reflection)[4] is that scholarly study of 2 Kgs 5 should be built on the foundation of an accurate text-critical and philological analysis and should then proceed in two phases, focused first on the final form of the text (as the product of text-critical analysis) and then on the genesis or pre-history of this text. This two-phase model is not intended to be a closed system; it is quite likely that one's study of the pre-history of the text will throw further light on the final form of the text. The following survey of studies on 2 Kgs 5 will be structured according the model just outlined.[5]

I. THE TEXT-CRITICAL FOUNDATION

Up until recently it was usual for scholars to proceed in a rather eclectic, even haphazard, way in making text-critical decisions in the books of Kings. The critical apparatus in the *BHS* exemplifies this approach, and one finds it also in the commentary of Würthwein. The Qumran discoveries, however, have had an impact on the study of the text of Kings too, even though no major manuscript finds have come to light comparable to those of the books of Samuel. A greater awareness of the variety and fluidity of textual witnesses has brought about a move away from automatic option for the Masoretic text-form and a readiness to see that the Old Greek version (in those cases where access to it is possible behind the later Greek recensions) was based on a *Vorlage* that may at times offer a text that is preferable to that of the MT. For the books of Kings in general much valuable work in this line has been done by Julio Trebolle Barrera,[6] and for 2 Kgs 5 in particular one finds an important contribution in the monograph of Herrman-Josef Stipp.[7]

Stipp examines the occurrence of the title "man of God" and the personal name "Elisha" in the MT and in the old versions, notes that the Old Greek used the title less than the MT, and concludes that this represents an older state of the development of the textual tradition. Hence Stipp holds that, on text-critical grounds, one should favor the Greek data in 2 Kgs 5 and treat the occurrences of the title "man of God" in vv. 8.14.15.20 as secondary.[8] As will be seen below, this conclusion (if accepted) will have important implications for the redaction-critical study of the chapter. Stipp stresses the value of the Old Greek text-form in general here and regrets the unfortunate fact that direct witnesses to it do not exist for 2 Kgs 5 (one has to reconstruct the text-form mainly from later Greek recensions). He adds a sobering note: if we had the full text of the Old Greek, there might well be other places in 2 Kgs 5 where we might prefer it to the MT text-form, and consequently the literary-historical analysis of the chapter (which he goes on to offer) might have to be modified in places.[9] In other words, the fact that we do not have all the data we would wish for in order to reconstruct the textual history of the chapter puts a question mark over all our subsequent work, especially in the literary-historical field.

The position of Cogan and Tadmor in text-critical questions is different. They are well aware that the MT may not be the oldest or the best form of the text, but they are more hesitant about proceeding on the basis of retroversions from the Greek (necessarily a hypothetical operation). Consequently they base their commentary on the MT text-form, emending it by the Greek only where the MT seems clearly to be faulty.[10]

In either case, one sees that study of 2 Kgs 5 must face up to the text-critical problems in a more explicit and systematic way than was often the case in the past. Brief references to the *BHS* apparatus as the ultimate authority should be (but regrettably are not) a thing of the past.

II. FINAL-FORM STUDIES

Some scholars have focused their attention exclusively, or at least principally, on the present form of 2 Kgs 5. In some cases these final-form readings are interested above all in the internal semantics of the text; in other cases there is also an interest in pragmatic considerations, that is, to whom did the final form of the text speak originally, in what circumstances and for what purpose. A survey of some of these studies now follows.

A text-immanent reading of 2 Kgs 5 using the full panoply of Greimasian semiotic narratology was presented by Cécile Turiot (in collaboration with a group of readers) in 1979.[11] This study seems to have had little or no influence on subsequent work on the chapter, partly perhaps because of the complex terminology typical of the Greimas method of analysis, partly also because the study was based on a translation of the biblical text and not on the original Hebrew. In fact, however, the latter difficulty is less serious in the present case than might appear at first sight, because the observations made in the article are very largely accessible in a good translation as well as in the Hebrew. Finer details of style, it is true, will escape the reader of a translation, but Greimasian narratology is not greatly interested in these in any case. The article is divided into the two parts that are typical of the method: first the narrative component of the text, and then its discourse component. The former involves an analysis of two narrative programs ("healing and good health," and "recognizing that there is a prophet in Israel"), and discusses their relationship. The second part of the article describes the "composante discursive" on two levels: that of the surface of the text (recurrent motifs and themes, and role-complexes) and that of the deep structure (with much attention given here to the so-called "semiotic square," characteristic of Greimas' semantics).

It is not possible here to explain the semiotic method in further detail; interested readers may wish to consult one or other of the available manuals.[12] The article's contribution seems to me to reside especially in two areas: first, its acute analysis of the intricate interrelationship between the various components of the narrative (especially the narrative function of the Gehazi-episode in vv. 19–27), and, second, its discussion of the surface features of linguistic formulation (pp. 19–24) where it makes several interesting observations and suggests relationships on the paradigmatic axis that are not easily noticed in a sequential type of close reading which privileges the syntagmatic axis. On the other hand, at least for readers who are not committed members of the Greimas school, the concluding section on the deep semantic structure and the semiotic square may well give rise to the feeling that the text of 2 Kgs 5 has become merely an object on which to demonstrate semiotic theories that often appear strained in practice and may even be flawed in theory.[13] In addition, of course, Turiot's article (as is usual for the school which it represents) has nothing at all to say about the author or implied author or narrator (questions of focus, point of view, manipulation of the readers' reactions, and so on). One has to add that it would be more accessible to other scholars if it were "translated" into a form of French less jargon-ridden and less reserved to initiates. In spite of all this, however, students of 2 Kgs 5 would do well not to ignore Turiot's study.[14]

Robert L. Cohn's study, published in 1983,[15] exemplifies another tradition of text-immanent reading, that of Anglo-American "close reading," which was popularized in general literary studies by the New Critical movement of the 1940s and 1950s and which began to be applied to biblical texts from the 1960s on. Cohn's article is a fine example of the potentialities of this type of analysis, written in a style that is far more accessible than that of Turiot's study. Cohn begins with a series of perceptive remarks about the complex plot movement of the chapter with its two apparent endings (vv. 14 and 19) before the definitive ending at v. 27. The reader immediately senses a literary competence here, which one regrets to say is painfully absent at times in studies produced by *some* scholars whose competence appears to be limited to literary-historical analysis. The bulk of Cohn's study is given over to a sequential reading of the Hebrew text, in which he notes narrative features, stylistic devices and thematic aspects. He concludes by characterizing 2 Kgs 5 as "an especially apt example of a biblical narrative in which art and theology are symbiotically related" (p. 184). Cohn refers briefly to the question of the literary genre of the text, opting to see it as "a didactic *legendum*" (p. 183), but apart from this he does not engage in discussions typical of historical-critical study, especially the question of a possible literary stratification within the chapter. Nor does he suggest what the story might have meant to the first readers of its final form. In brief, the article is an excellent example of a final-form reading but it does not engage in explicit dialogue with the full range of scholarly discussion of 2 Kgs 5.

A more recent study was published in Dutch by Klaas A.D. Smelik in

1988, and a German translation with small modifications appeared later in the same year.[16] Smelik is one of the scholars associated with the so-called Amsterdam School,[17] and his study of 2 Kgs 5 is explicitly presented as an example of the "Amsterdam approach." In fact, the type of reading found in Smelik's article is very similar to the close-reading method used by Cohn, as indeed Smelik himself notes; the two scholars do not always coincide in their detailed observations, but that is only to be expected in literary study. Smelik begins by offering what he terms an "idiolectal" translation of the text, that is, a version which tries to convey as far as possible the literary form of the original Hebrew even at the cost of inelegance in the target language (Dutch or German). Then he examines in sequence the six episodes into which he divides the chapter, commenting simultaneously on narrational and linguistic (or stylistic) aspects. The procedure here is practically the same as that of Cohn's article, though Smelik's presentation is somewhat less technical. Finally, the purpose or narrative intention of the whole chapter is examined: Smelik finds that the dominant theme is to teach that "there is no God in all the earth but in Israel" (v. 15) and that Elisha is his prophet. Naaman and Gehazi are confronted with these realities, and their narrative function is to illustrate them in different ways. Smelik holds that the whole chapter comes from one author, who may perhaps have used older traditions. At several points he engages in debate with recent redaction-critical proposals, especially those of E. Würthwein (see below). In this respect, Smelik's study is more comprehensive than Cohn's, but still there is no *detailed* discussion of historical-critical questions.

The foregoing studies of Turiot, Cohn, and Smelik are all predominantly text-immanent, in the sense that they do not devote much (or any) attention to questions about the author and readers of the final form of the text. Two other studies, which can be termed final-form essays to a certain extent anyway, showed greater interest in these questions about the pragmatic dimension of the text of 2 Kgs 5.

The earlier of these was the article of Françoise Smyth-Florentin which appeared in 1970.[18] Though the main part of her study consists of a double sequential reading of the text (first for philological details, then for narrative, stylistic, and thematic aspects) and there are clear signs of early literary-structuralist influence (though without the intimidating terminological apparatus of the Greimas school), there is also a strong historical awareness. Right through the sequential reading one finds remarks about the late (that is, post-exilic) dating of various phrases, and this leads to the conclusion that the present form of the text can best be seen as meant for readers who needed to be warned and defended against the attractions of

Babylonian therapeutic magic. Smyth-Florentin envisages a long period of genesis of the story in oral or literary stages, but her interest lies in the present form of the text and no details are given about its genesis.

Hermann Schult's study (1975) can be mentioned as the second example,[19] even though it is not a final-form approach in the full sense. In fact, he focuses on vv. 1–19a, adding only a short note on vv. 19b–27 which he sees as a dark contrast to what precedes. Vv. 1–19a, however, are studied as they stand now, and there is no analysis of the process of formation of the text. Schult's reading is primarily directed to discerning the purpose of the narrative. His conclusion, based on many textual details, is that the text is best understood as being a "conversion-story" or the "narrative document of a mission-theology"; as such, it is comparable with other late post-exilic texts dealing with non-Israelites who revere Yahweh (e.g., Jon 1:9, 14–16; Est 8:17; Dan 2:47). In general, then, it must be said that Schult's approach is strongly historical, and literary observations tend to be used primarily as evidence for historical conclusions.

To conclude this section on final-form readings, it must of course be added that one will find scattered references to the final form of 2 Kgs 5 in most commentaries on the text (Würthwein's avoidance of this, noted above, is an extreme exception).[20] However it is often unclear in such cases whether the commentator in question intends to speak about the final form of the text as a synchronic whole or about the final redactional phase in the process of formation of the text. These two perspectives need to be kept carefully distinct.[21] A final observation: the authors mentioned in this section do not all come up with the same results or conclusions. But in most cases the differences will be seen to stand in a relation of complementarity, not as contradictories. One author stresses one aspect of the text, privileging perhaps certain linguistic features; another author stresses another aspect, perhaps on the basis of other linguistic features. For the reader, however, this situation does not usually generate a sense of confusion but rather constitutes an enrichment of one's reading. Different literary readings, in other words, can help the reader to appreciate better the wealth of possible sense-effects that the text can generate. This is surely a positive value.

III. THE GENESIS OF THE TEXT OF 2 KGS 5

While final-form study deals with the implied author or narrator (a text-world entity),[22] historical study is interested in the question of the temporal and spatial coordinates of the person or persons responsible for the production of the text. If that question can be clarified, then further circumstances affecting the formation of the text can be investigated, the ultimate aim being to understand the text better as an historical entity. Since we are dealing with a text that comes to us from the distant past, it is obvious that the more historical information we can have about that text, the greater are our chances of understanding it better. The problem is how much historical information is accessible to us in a *sufficiently probable* way to justify further conclusions on the basis of those results. How to determine the degree of probability to be attributed to the results of literary-historical studies of biblical texts is one of the main components in the present-day debate about the practice of the historical-critical method.

1. Literarkritik

The complexity of the methodological problem at issue here can be exemplified by surveying the answers given by scholars to the questions: Was 2 Kgs 5 the work of one or of several authors (redactors, etc.), and when was this work carried out? It may be helpful to divide the answers into several groups.

(a) The chapter is held to be the work of one author, with (at most) a few small glosses added later. This position has been defended by von Rad, Montgomery, De Vries, Rehm, Hobbs (apparently), Stipp, and Cogan-Tadmor.[23] Almost all these scholars situate the author in pre-exilic times; Stipp, however, holds for a post-exilic date (as will be seen in further detail below).

(b) Two strata are distinguished, the Gehazi episode (vv. 19b, or 20, to 27) being seen as a later expansion by another hand. Thus, for instance, van den Born, Fricke, Gray and Seebass[24] (though it is not altogether clear whether Gray held that the expansion took place already during the phase of oral transmission—in which case the first written form of the story would have included the Gehazi episode—or whether the latter verses were literarily secondary). In any case, Gray holds that both strata were pre-exilic, prior in fact to 721 B.C.

(c) More complex proposals:

(i) In 1972 Hans-Christoph Schmitt published an important monograph on the Elisha texts, in which he argued for a decidedly complex history of redaction of the material.[25] 2 Kgs 5, he held, originated essentially in three literary stages: the miracle story of vv. 1–14* which also contains elements of mockery against Aramaean religion, the problem-oriented unit of vv. 15–19a* dealing with the situation of proselytes, and the narrative critique of self-seeking on the part of prophetic individuals and groups in vv. 19b–27. (Smaller additions of various kinds are also distinguished within these sections, but we can prescind from such details here.) The criteria on which Schmitt relied to establish his conclusions were mainly two: different thematic interests and subtle differences in terminology. As to the chronological sequence of the three strata, he held that vv. 1–14 were pre-exilic, vv. 15–19a* belonged to a post-exilic (early fifth century) redactional reworking characterized by its insistence on the title "man of God," and vv. 19b–27 were later still (a precise date is not offered). This complex analysis, proposed with some diffidence by Schmitt himself, was taken over in large measure by Jones and by Würthwein in their recent commentaries.[26]

(ii) Georg Hentschel discussed 2 Kgs 5 in an article published in 1982 and then again in his 1985 commentary.[27] In the former study he seems to hold that there were at least two literary strata in the text: vv. 1–19a and vv. 19b–27. He also notes many tensions within vv. 1–19a, but prefers to explain these (in good measure at least) as due to developments within the phase of oral transmission of the story. He sketches several stages in this oral transmission, and he criticizes Schmitt for not considering this sufficiently and limiting his study essentially to redaction-critical aspects.[28] In the 1985 commentary Hentschel proposes, with small modifications, the same general picture of the formation of 2 Kgs 5. The basis was a short miracle-story that originated in pre-exilic times (the material of vv. 1–3, 10b, 14). A series of pre-exilic additions within the material of vv. 1–19a followed (apparently this still belongs to the phase of oral transmission). Vv. 19b–27 were added later, but it is not clear whether Hentschel situates this in pre-exilic or post-exilic times. Verse 18 is held to be certainly post-exilic, since it focuses on the problems of proselytes.

(d) The recent monograph on the Elisha texts by H.-J. Stipp (1987)[29] calls for special consideration because of its high level of methodological awareness and reflection, which shows the influence of a line of research initiated by Wolfgang Richter in his important methodology book of 1971.[30] As noted above, Stipp devoted much attention to text-critical questions, but our interest here is primarily in his literary-critical analysis. Two criteria guide his work in this area: repetitions and tensions within a text. He systematically lists all the instances of these two phenomena in 2 Kgs 5 and asks whether some or all of them are best explained by the hypothesis of a plurality of authors. His conclusion is that the text is the work of one hand, except for the later addition of the phrase "and two changes of clothing" in vv. 22b and 23b. The principal author (in practice, the sole author) worked in post-exilic times.

Stipp offers a detailed critique of the arguments adduced by H.-C. Schmitt, whom he faults for having first determined the purpose or intention of sections of the text and then on that basis proceeding to eliminate as literarily secondary those parts of the text which do not stand in line with the pre-determined intention.[31] Though it is not altogether clear that Schmitt's procedure is quite as simple as that, Stipp's critique is useful at least as a warning to the more reckless forms of *Tendenzkritik.* Stipp urges that one should first engage in *Literarkritik,* using the criteria of repetitions and tensions, and only then establish the intentions of the various diachronic units discovered by literary criticism.

One has to add, however, that in practice matters may be somewhat more complicated than Stipp's approach would lead one to think. To take the criterion of repetition: if we want to come to a decision whether a particular case of repetition should be termed a "doublet" and thus constitute an argument for the presence of more than one author's work in the text, then it seems necessary that we should have at least a preliminary idea of what sort of text we are dealing with, and this includes at least a vague idea about the intention or purpose of the text. It would seem, as John Barton has stressed,[32] that one cannot get away from a certain measure of circularity in practicing *Literarkritik.* All the more so for the second criterion, that of tensions: depending on the sort of text we are dealing with, tensions may be explained in different ways, in some cases no doubt as indicators of the presence of different hands but in other cases perhaps as revelatory of a complex literary texture created by a skillful author. Furthermore, it seems doubtful whether the criteria of repetition and tensions constitute a sufficient basis for literary-critical decisions in *every* case. Theoretically, at least, it seems possible to imagine a case where a later redactor inserted new material so skillfully into an existing text that no instance of repetition resulted and no obvious syntactical or thematic tension was created by the addition; the added material might express a more developed form of theology, in line with but also going beyond the older theology of the earlier stratum or strata. Of course, Stipp might term such a case an instance of tension (*Spannung*) also, but that would be a very wide sense of the term indeed. In other words, it may not be possible to eliminate ideological criteria altogether from the practice of literary criticism. And this is an area where *Literarkritik* is undoubtedly exposed to the danger of uncontrolled subjective positions, as Stipp has well pointed out.

Returning now to Stipp's own presentation, we can note his criticism of some other aspects of the current practice of literary criticism: the habit of some scholars of taking results gained from the study of one text and extending them without further proof to other texts (Stipp's colorful expression for this is "Literarkritik nach dem Lawinenprinzip")[33]; secondly, the unjustified logical shift which occurs when the secondary nature of a particular passage is first said to be possible and then a couple of pages

later (without further arguments or new evidence) this position is regarded as proven and is used as the basis for further conclusions.[34] Other
scholars are faulted by Stipp for a hypercritical tendency, others for subjective arbitrariness, and others again for making ungrounded (and un-
groundable) statements about alleged subtle differences in formulation
during the phases of oral transmission of a narrative.[35] Prescinding again
from the relevance of these criticisms for the particular scholars named by
Stipp, one can certainly agree that a critical scrutiny of the criteria and
arguments used in *Literarkritik* is a much-needed contribution, especially
in the area of German-language studies.

It can be said at the end of this survey of recent studies devoted to the
problem of the genesis of the text of 2 Kgs 5 that the task of the literary
historian here is not an easy one. When a group of competent scholars,
sharing the same general presuppositions and operating with the same
data, arrive at very different results, one begins to doubt whether it will
ever be possible to produce an account of the genesis of the text that will
win *general* acceptance for the pertinence and perspicuity of its arguments. Some may feel that such pessimism is excessive, but at least it has
to be said that those who think that the elucidation of the process of
formation of a text is the indispensable *basis* for all further exegetical
work do not exactly stand on firm ground in the case of 2 Kgs 5 (and very
many other biblical texts too).

2. Form-Criticism

Another area of research in recent studies of 2 Kgs 5 has to do with
the genre or genres exemplified in the text. Some proposals made in these
studies will now be surveyed.

Reference has already been made to H.-C. Schmitt's form-critical
characterization of the three parts of the text which he decided to treat
separately; however Schmitt did not develop these remarks in a very detailed way, because his main interest was in redaction-criticism. A number of subsequent studies attempted to modify and refine the form-critical
categories used with regard to 2 Kgs 5.

In a monograph on 1 Kgs 22, which also included a discussion of
many other prophetic narratives, Simon J. De Vries (1978)[36] elaborated
a complex set of descriptive form-critical terms applicable to such
narratives. He assigned 2 Kgs 5 to the class "prophetic legend"
(De Vries' general term for prophetic narratives), to the genre "power-
demonstration narrative" in its third sub-genre "prophetic word story." A
power-demonstration narrative was "a marvelous story exemplifying
charismatic power"[37]; this genre, which originated in the schools of disci-

ples of particular prophets, aimed at providing edifying illustrations of prophetic activity. The sub-genre "prophetic word story" is also represented by 2 Kgs 2:23–24 and 8:1–6—texts where the emphasis is less on the prophet's actions (as e.g. in 2 Kgs 4:8–37) than on his efficacious words. One sees that considerations of content and theme tend to predominate in De Vries' form-critical method.

A different approach was suggested briefly by Robert C. Culley in 1980[38] when he studied a group of narratives which all display the action-sequence "wrong/punishment of wrong." Examples include 1 Kgs 13:7–20; 20:33–43; 21; 2 Kgs 1:2–17; 2:23–25; 5:20–27. The action-sequence is common to all these texts, though each differs in the way in which it is filled out in details. Culley refers briefly to 2 Kgs 5:1–19 too; he terms it a "miracle story," where vv. 15–19 have the double function of concluding the miracle story and preparing for the punishment story. One sees that here (at least for vv. 20–27) form-critical considerations are based on a narrative-level structure (as distinct from a syntax-level structure).

Alexander Rofé's important monograph on the prophetical narratives of the Hebrew Bible appeared in English translation in 1988.[39] Our concern here is limited to his form-critical discussion, though Rofé's work includes many other aspects too. However his form-critical remarks are particularly interesting, in that they represent the latest statement by a scholar who had earlier published several important studies precisely in that area.[40] Rofé now distinguishes no less than twelve distinct genres within the corpus of prophetic narratives, the criterion of distinction being the presence of "a recurring plot pattern" (which in practice seems to refer more to theme and purpose rather than to the narrative-level patterns of Culley's study noted above). 2 Kgs 5 is assigned by Rofé to the genre of the "ethical *legenda*"; these are texts where "principle would dominate plot, the miracle would become secondary and the homily primary."[41] In line with other types of *legenda,* the characters are portrayed in a dynamic fashion, but the "ethical *legenda*" go further, in that they present the miraculous happening not simply as an act that benefits one of the characters but rather as aiming to increase belief in God. As Rofé puts it, "The problem was not the miracle but whether the message expressed by it would be heard and understood."[42]

At this point one may well begin to feel that each of the various form-critical proposals just surveyed contains useful and illuminating observations, without however being able to exclude as invalid all the observations made by the other proposals. And this suggests that form-critical study does not fit as easily into the framework of historical-critical study as books on methodology often present the matter; rather it is a task which, ideally at least, is to be carried out on several levels. There is a

text-immanent aspect in the first place. Here one examines the structure
of the literary unit, bearing in mind the possible relevance of at least three
orders of observations: syntactical considerations, which may be struc-
turally significant in many places (but not everywhere); narrational
aspects (plot development, text-semantic oppositions or patterns of correspondence); general thematic considerations. Second, there is a text-
comparative aspect, where the given text is compared with other texts
which seem to resemble it in one or other of the above-mentioned ways
(syntactical features, narrational, and thematic aspects). This type of comparison can sharpen one's awareness of certain aspects of the given text,
by seeing their recurrence in other texts or by noting contrasts in their
regard with other texts. Third, there is a diachronic aspect, where one
attempts to discover the historical development of the genre. That is to
say, form-critical study can also serve to improve one's understanding of
the individual text, as well as to contribute to a textual typology
(synchronically first, and then diachronically).

3. Composition-History

The third, and final, question that can usefully be outlined here concerns the historical relation of 2 Kgs 5 (or its component strata) to its
immediate literary context (namely, the prophetic narratives about Elisha) and then to its wider context in the book of Kings (or in the Deuteronomistic History or even in the large complex of Genesis–2 Kings as
a whole).

Two main types of answer to this question can be distinguished in
recent research. The first, and up to recently at least the more usual,
position holds that 2 Kgs 5 existed as a component part of an Elisha-cycle
of prophetic narratives; this cycle, united with an Elijah-cycle, was inserted practically as it now stands into the Deuteronomistic History by a
deuteronomistic editor or redactor.[43] The Elisha-cycle had its own internal history of composition; opinions differ as to when precisely 2 Kgs 5
took its place in the cycle, but in any event the bulk of the chapter was
pre-deuteronomistic in its written state. At most, parts of vv. 15–19a*
may have been added to the text already inserted in the Deuteronomistic
History.

A very different position is held by a smaller number of scholars, who
think that the Elisha narratives (and related prophetic material) were inserted into their present literary context after the completion of the Deuteronomistic History in the strict sense, sometime in the post-exilic period. Two examples of this second position can now be outlined. H.-C.
Schmitt (1972) concluded from his redaction-critical analysis that the

deuteronomistic edition of Kings contained only one of the Elisha-texts (namely, the account of Jehu's coup in 2 Kgs 9:1–10, 27).[44] Most of the Elisha-narratives, which had their own literary pre-history in several earlier small collections, were inserted into the book of Kings in post-exilic times, probably in the first half of the fifth century; this was effected by a redactor termed by Schmitt "the man-of-God redactor" because he inserted the title "man of God" into many texts. 2 Kgs 5 was one of the texts whose older basis was worked over by this redactor and then inserted with other texts into Kings. At a still later stage, Schmitt held, the "man-of-God" version of the Naaman text was expanded by extensive additions (such as vv. 5b*, 15b–17a*, 19b–27). H.-J. Stipp (1987) agreed with Schmitt that the Elisha-cycle and related texts did not form part of the exilic edition of the Deuteronomistic History. However, as a result of his text-critical work (as noted above), Stipp was unable to accept Schmitt's thesis of a "man-of-God redaction" and he concluded that the Elisha-texts were inserted into Kings by a series of non-deuteronomistic post-exilic redactors.[45]

It is clear that the enormously complex question of the redaction-history of the Deuteronomistic History, on which present-day scholars are widely divided,[46] is involved in the debate between the two positions sketched above. But there are consequences too for one's understanding of the theology of the deuteronomistic school or movement. If one accepts the first, and more common, position (that a more-or-less complete Elisha-cycle was inserted into its present context by a deuteronomistic editor), then one will be entitled to ask whether the theology implicit in 2 Kgs 5 can be taken as having been shared by the deuteronomistic school or at least by part of that school. And if so, one will also have to consider how the theology of 2 Kgs 5 might affect the theological status of other texts in the Deuteronomistic History that seem to be much less open to non-Israelites. On the other hand, if one prefers the second position (either in the form proposed by Schmitt or in that of Stipp), then the theology of 2 Kgs 5 cannot automatically be credited to the deuteronomists and may indeed have to be read as a critique of a more inward-looking deuteronomistic theology.[47] Thus, one's view of the historical development of religious ideas or of theology in Israel will vary depending on one's option in the question of the composition-history of the Elisha-texts in the book of Kings.

To conclude this section on literary-historical studies, we have to ask what is to be made of the fact that different scholars have arrived at widely different conclusions here, especially in the areas of *Literarkritik* and redaction-history. This problem has been illustrated above with regard to 2 Kgs 5, but it holds for many, perhaps most, other OT texts and is one of the main causes for the disorientation of many students interested in these texts. Most questions regarding the literary history of a text call for precise empirical answers. If one asks whether 2 Kgs 5:19b–27 was inserted later into the Naaman text, the answer has to be yes or no, and only one answer can be right. That is to say, different conclusions in questions of literary history are usually mutually exclusive and stand in a relation of contradiction to one another. There are exceptions to this situation (for instance, the question of the traditions or concepts that may have influenced a given text), where different answers may complement one another to some extent at least, but these exceptions do not alter the general picture, which is that in literary-historical study one has to look for the one correct answer to a given question. It has been noted above that the situation in final-form study is different; if one finds different views there about a particular topic, these usually complement one another and thus enrich the reader's understanding of the text. In brief, one should not overlook the different epistemological status of a set of variant conclusions in literary-historical study on the one hand and in final-form study on the other. It is more fruitful and less frustrating for readers to find themselves confronted with different views in the latter area of study. This would seem to constitute a strong practical reason for engaging in final-form study before beginning an investigation of literary-historical questions.

CONCLUSION

In recent years several scholars (R. Rendtorff and E. Talstra, to mention just two)[48] have drawn attention to the importance of seeing the exegetical task as one which involves a plurality of methods and approaches. Above all, it is urgent that scholars do not enclose themselves in little methodological ghettos ("Here we do only literary-historical work," "Here admission is reserved for disciples of Greimas," and so on). The ability to operate on different planes of investigation, using different methods and entering into scholarly dialogue with different neighboring disciplines (e.g. general historical methodology,[49] general literary theory and critical practice) is something that should be regarded as normal for all exegetes nowadays. Certainly, some may prefer to work more on historical questions, others may prefer literary studies (and so on), but one would expect a basic competence in all the main areas to be part of the formation of all exegetes. The foregoing survey of recent work on 2 Kgs 5 has been structured in such a way as to suggest one possible application of these requirements.

If one wishes to do a reasonably comprehensive study of 2 Kgs 5, then the starting point should be a thorough text-critical investigation. Ideally this would provide us with the best possible readings; if, in practice, this ideal cannot be realized in every instance, then at least we are alerted to certain readings that are text-critically dubious, and we are warned that any further conclusion based on those items must carry with it a large question-mark. On the foundation, then, of text-critical (and philological) study, one proceeds to build one's exegetical edifice in two phases initially. First, one studies the final form of the text insofar as it can be established by text-critical work; this first phase will use any method (and all methods) suitable to advance one's understanding of the text. The precise choice will depend in part on the sort of text one is dealing with, in part on the researcher's own preferences. Then one moves on to Phase Two, which stresses historical factors as a means of adding another dimension to one's understanding of the text; this second phase will use both the traditional methods of literary-historical study (*Literarkritik,* genre-history, redaction-history, and composition-history) and the more recent methods taken from the human sciences (sociological and anthropological analysis, perhaps also psychological text-analysis, and so on). The Two-Phase model is not intended to constitute a closed system; it is perfectly possible to return to the final form of the text when one has completed the work of Phase Two, and it may well be that one's observations about the final form can be expanded or made more precise as a result of study of the diachronic dimension.

The practical utility of a more comprehensive and integrated approach, such as the foregoing, needs of course to be exemplified by detailed work on specific texts. This would not only help to refine the theoretical considerations but would also encourage those scholars who still persist in some form of "Methodenmonismus"[50] that it is now time to move on to a more pluralistic and interesting approach to exegesis.

From Lukan Parenesis to Johannine Christology: Luke 9:23–24 and John 12:25–26

INTRODUCTION

In a setting that is both typically and exclusively Johannine (Jn 12:20–33) we find two texts that are widely reported in the synoptic tradition. One of them has to do with the following of Christ (Jn 12:26); this saying is found in synoptic contexts in the threefold tradition (Mt 16:24; Mk 8:34; Lk 9:23) and also in the twofold tradition (Mt 10:38; Lk 14:27). The other text contains the paradoxical statement that life is to be ensured or gained by losing it (Jn 12:25); a similar text appears both in the three synoptics (Mt 16:25; Mk 8:35; Lk 9:24) and again in two of them (Mt 10:39; Lk 17:33). We are dealing here with a typical case in which one and the same logion or saying of Jesus displays its rich content according to the different contexts in which it is found and the different nuances it has.

As can be readily imagined, two texts so lavishly cited in the gospel tradition have been the object of numerous studies from different points of view. I shall mention here only one such study, written thirty years ago.[1] In his article, Father Emilio Rasco focused his attention chiefly on the passage about the grain of wheat that can produce much fruit if it falls into the ground and dies (Jn 12:24); he did, however, attend also to the context (Jn 12:25–26) and to the synoptic parallels. In his comparison of the two traditions, Father Rasco saw in the synoptics an ascetical principle valid for all Christians; he then warned of the danger of applying the same criterion to the verses in John, thereby losing sight of their characteristic christological stamp.[2]

As a contribution to this tribute to Father Rasco I want to follow up on his suggestion. In his article he analyzed chiefly the verse concerning the grain of wheat (Jn 12:24); in these pages I shall study the verses that follow in John (12:25–26). In order to stay within the framework set for the present book I shall compare these two verses with the parallel passages in Luke. My aim will be to uncover in these texts the characteristic traits of Lukan parenesis and Johannine christology.

I shall begin by discussing the texts in Luke (9:23–24); in doing so I shall have to take into account the parallel synoptic passages (Mt 16:24–25; Mk 8:34–35) and the repetition of the verses in the gospel of Matthew (10:38–39) and in Luke himself (14:27; 17:33). I shall then turn to the passage in John, with attention especially to its context. Finally I shall be in a position to evaluate the contrasting theologies of Luke and John in each of the sayings that are being studied. I shall stay always at the redactional level in the discussion both of each text in itself and of its context and its parallels.

A. THE LUKAN SAYING ON THE FOLLOWING OF CHRIST (9:23; 14:27)

This theme is thrown into special relief in the gospel of Luke because of its repetition. The theme is evidently not exclusive to Luke, but he has given it an emphasis of his own by reason of the nuances he brings to it and the context in which he places it. I shall first take each text separately and then compare them.

1. Luke 9:23 (par. Mt 16:24; Mk 8:34)

(a) The *context* in which Luke here records the saying about the following of Christ is common to the three synoptics. Attention to what immediately precedes the text is essential for a correct understanding of what the evangelist is conveying in it. In the threefold tradition the saying is preceded by the confession of Peter, which Matthew (16:13) and Mark (8:27) locate at Caesarea Philippi, but which Luke simply records, not in connection with any particular place but in a climate established by the solitary prayer of Jesus (9:18). Peter's confession itself is given different formulations: the Christ (Mk 8:29), the Christ, the Son of the living God (Mt 16:16), or a formulation that combines the two essential points: the Christ of God (Lk 9:20).

After Jesus has commanded silence on the subject (this too is common to the three synoptics: Mt 16:20; Mk 8:30; Lk 9:21), he begins a teaching in which he tells them of his passion, death, and resurrection on the third day (Mt 16:21; Mk 8:31). While Luke transmits the same message regarding the sufferings of the Son of Man, he does not present it as the beginning of a teaching but rather as something that Jesus says (9:22) to the disciples whom he has just ordered to say nothing about the object of the preceding confession. Only Matthew and Mark tell of Peter's opposition to the announcement of the passion and of Jesus' stern rebuke to him (Mt 16:22–23; Mk 8:32–33). In Luke, the announcement of the passion is succeeded immediately by the saying about following, which I am now considering (9:23).

If I summarize all the nuances proper to Luke in the context for the saying, the saying itself will emerge with greater clarity. The announcement of the sufferings of the Son of man is closely connected with the saying about following; the passion of Jesus is thus brought closer to home for those to whom he is speaking.[3] This teaching does not give the impression of a new beginning, but of something that has been going on since Peter's confession of Jesus as the Christ of God. Both the announcement of the passion and the saying on following derive their importance from what has preceded, not only in the confession of Peter but also in the prayer of Jesus.[4]

(b) The *introduction* to the saying has a nuance peculiar to the Lukan narrative. Both Matthew and Mark use the aorist tense, denoting a particular point in time: *eipen* (Mt 16:24; Mk 8:34). Luke, on the other hand, introduces the saying with a verb in the imperfect tense, *elegen* (Lk 9:23), which expresses continuity and suggests an insistence. The use of this tense in the Lukan account effects a closer link between the announcement of the passion and the saying on following, especially since Luke alone has used the same verb in introducing the announcement of the passion (9:22).

But despite the close connection between the two verses, there is also a strong contrast between them in Luke's redaction. Mark introduces the saying with a simple copulative *kai* (8:34), just as he did with the announcement of the passion (8:31). Matthew uses the particle *tote* (16:24), which he has already used at the beginning of the prediction of the passion (16:21). Luke, on the other hand, sets up a strong contrast by using the adversative *de* (9:23), just as, by means of another *de,* he alone has previously established a contrast between the confession of Peter (9:20) and the command of silence (9:21). The point of the Lukan contrast emerges from the difference between the aorist *eipen,* with its reference to a point in time, which introduced the announcement of the passion (9:22), and the continuative imperfect *elegen* which gives the setting for the saying on following (9:23).[5]

But this contrast extends especially to the addressees of each of the verses. Here Luke exercises his redactional role uninhibitedly. He follows a procedure similar to that which he has used previously in formulating the confession of Peter: "the Christ of God" (9:20), which is a synthesis of what is found in the accounts of Mark: "the Christ" (8:29), and Matthew: "the Christ, the Son of God" (16:16). He does the same now when specifying the addressees of the saying about following. Mark shows Jesus calling to himself the multitude along with his disciples (8:34); Matthew shows Jesus speaking to his disciples (Mt 16:24); Luke, for his part, effects a merger by having Jesus address "all": *pros pantes* (9:23). The purpose of Luke's formulation is clear: what follows acquires a universality.[6] The words about the following of Christ are meant for "all," not just the multitude that surrounds him but also those Christians who will later on form the community.[7]

(c) The *text of the saying* on following has a similar structure in the three synoptics. But while the formulation is completely identical in Matthew and Mark, Luke's has special nuances that set it apart. Here, first, is a synoptic view of the text:

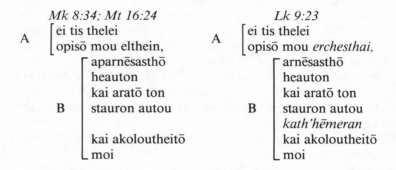

Mk 8:34; Mt 16:24		*Lk 9:23*	
A	ei tis thelei opisō mou elthein,	A	ei tis thelei opisō mou *erchesthai,*
B	aparnēsasthō heauton kai aratō ton stauron autou kai akoloutheitō moi	B	arnēsasthō heauton kai aratō ton stauron autou *kath'hēmeran* kai akoloutheitō moi

In both cases the *structure* consists of a real conditional protasis: "if any wish to come after me" (A), followed by a three-membered apodasis: "let them deny themselves, take up their cross, and follow me" (B).

The text, though clear in its general *meaning,* does give rise to ambiguities. A first stumbling block is the condition with which the saying begins. This clause does not express a mere wish or something left to free choice; it expresses not an uncertainty but an affirmation.[8] The real condition refers to the situation of those who have chosen to come after Jesus, that is, to be his disciples; the call to discipleship takes the form of a call to come after him (see Mt 4:19; Mk 1:17, 20).[9] Thus the real state of being a disciple is set down in the protasis, while the apodasis, with its three parts, explains the content of this "coming after" Jesus. The first member of the apodasis: "let them deny themselves," states the very essence of "coming after" him; the denial of self is a determined "no" to the self,[10] a radical renunciation of the self.[11]

The second member of the apodasis is introduced by an explicative *kai;* this second member explains the preceding statement about the denial of the self.[12] The "denial of self" is explained by "let them take up their cross." Many interpretations have been given of the meaning of this second member of the apodasis.[13] The most plausible explanation seems to be that it is an expressive image derived from the common practice of the time, which was that a condemned criminal carried the instrument of his execution[14]; the image becomes even more effective once Jesus himself has taken up his cross (see Jn 19:17). This vivid image shows that by the following of Jesus is meant the attitude of those who have broken with their former life or have said "no" to the self, to the point even of surrendering their very life.[15]

Unlike the second member of the apodasis, the third, *kai akoloutheitō moi,* does not explain the denial of self. Rather there is a certain discontinuity between this third verb and the two preceding: *akoloutheitō* is a present imperative, while *aratō* and *arnēsasthō* are aorists. By reason of the continuity which the present imperative expresses, it adds a nuance to the two preceding verbs. Unless we are willing to accept a tautology with the protasis, the meaning of *akoloutheitō* cannot be "follow me," for then the protasis would simply be repeated: "if any want to come after me (= follow me), let them follow me."[16] The verb *akoloutheō* can also have the meaning of "accompany someone on the road" (see Mt 4:25; 8:1, 10; Lk 23:27; Jn 6:2).[17] And in fact this "keeping company" with Jesus is a characteristic trait of disciples (see Mk 3:14). Disciples, therefore, who follow after Jesus not only deny themselves and take up their cross, but also accompany him[18]; this last action must be continual, as we are given to understand by the use of the present imperative (*akoloutheitō*).[19]

The special features which the saying has in Luke become clear in a synoptic presentation of the text. One feature has no special importance, namely, the use of the simple verb *arnēsasthō* instead of the compound *aparnēsasthō,* since the two verbs have the same meaning.[20] The other two variants may be due to the evangelist's greater concern for parenesis. One is the use of the present infinitive *erchesthai* instead of the aorist used in the redaction of Matthew and Mark (*elthein*); by using the present tense Luke stresses the element of continuity in a disciple's following of Jesus: "if any want to come after me."[21]

But the most characteristic point in the Lukan redaction is the reference to taking up the cross "daily" (*kath'hēmeran*). Without losing its original reference to the wood of crucifixion, the cross takes on a broader meaning that can apply to daily life; that is, it can refer to the difficulties inherent in the lives of all those to whom, according to the evangelist, Jesus is speaking. Thus understood, it is in harmony with Paul's statement, "I die every day!" (1 Cor 15:31).[22] In its Lukan formulation, then, the saying is not only addressed to all but can be applied continually and in daily life.

2. *Luke 14:27 (par. Mt 10:38)*

The saying under discussion is also found in the tradition common to Matthew and Luke, although in different settings. The new context in which Luke places it, and this second formulation of it, can fill out for us the evangelist's vision.

(a) The *context* of this new version of the saying is important. The evangelist Matthew has it addressed to the disciples, almost at the end of the missionary discourse (10:38). Luke, on the other hand, has Jesus uttering these words on his journey to Jerusalem. While Jesus is at table (14:1), one of his fellow guests says to him: "Blessed is anyone who will eat bread in the kingdom of God!" (v. 15). Jesus answers with the parable about the guests invited to a dinner. He then turns to the large crowd that has been following him (v. 25); at this point the evangelist brings together a series of sayings which are directed to the followers of Jesus and which set down the conditions for sharing in the banquet of the kingdom.[23] Among these conditions is the necessity of carrying one's cross.

(b) The *text* itself has some distinctive traits.[24] A comparison with the parallel in Matthew, and with the formulation of the saying which we have already studied, suggests various thoughts.

	Mt 10:38		*Luke 14:27*
A	kai hos ou lambanei ton stauron autou kai akolouthei opisō mou,	A	*hostis* ou *bastazei* ton stauron *heautou* kai *erchetai* opisō mou,
B	ouk estin mou axios.	B	*ou dunatai einai* mou *mathētēs.*

In structure, the text is once again a combination of a protasis (A), made up in this case of two members joined by the copula *kai,* and an apodasis (B). The saying expresses the theme we have already seen: taking up the cross and following Jesus as the elements constitutive of discipleship. A comparison of Luke's version with Matthew's brings out Luke's special perspective.

Luke begins the first member of the protasis with the pronoun *hostis,* whereas Matthew has *hos;* the greater indefiniteness given by the *tis* calls attention to the universal scope of the pronoun.[25] Luke does not have the simple verb *lambanei,* as Matthew does, but another that is more Lukan and primitive[26]: the expressive verb *bastazei,* which implies carrying with one or upon one; thus Jesus is said to take our infirmities upon himself (Mt 8:17; see Is 53:4) or to carry the cross on his shoulders (Jn 19:17).[27] The cross to be carried is the one intended for each individual,[28] therefore the one peculiar to the disciple; Luke stresses this aspect by using the pronoun *heautou* instead of Matthew's *autou.* But inasmuch as Luke has Jesus utter this statement during his journey to Jerusalem, the word "cross," while meaning the one peculiar to the disciple, cannot but make us think also of the passion of Jesus himself.[29]

The verb *erchetai* has the same meaning as Matthew's *akolouthei* but conveys the impression of being closer to the original.[30] Finally, this taking of the cross and following after Jesus is the very essence of discipleship; Luke alone uses the word *mathētēs* here; in addition, he places it at the very end as being the concept on which everything converges. Moreover, the statement in its Lukan form speaks of an unqualified necessity if one is to be a disciple of Jesus, since without this taking of the cross and following him one cannot be (*ou dunatai einai*) a disciple. There is no question, then, simply of greater or lesser appropriateness or worthiness, such as is expressed in Matthew's weak phrase "is not worthy of me" (*mou axios*); Luke's more concrete formulation underscores an absolute impossibility.[31]

(c) A *comparison* of Luke's two formulations (9:23; 14:27) shows that they have elements in common but also differences which fill out the meaning.

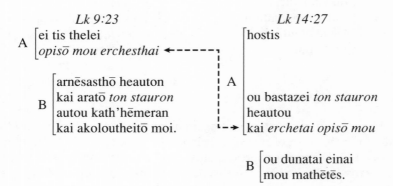

In both cases, the overall structure consists of a conditional (*ei tis*) or equivalently conditional (*hostis*) protasis (A) and an apodasis (B). The theme of both is the attitude of disciples to their own cross (*ton stauron*

autou—heautou) as they journey with it after Jesus (*opisō mou*). Nevertheless there are important differences, which may be observed even in the structure. Lk 9:23 enlarges the apodasis (B); Lk 14:27 makes the protasis lengthier (A). The second text even changes the order of the members, since the theme of the cross, which appears in the apodasis of the first, is found here in the protasis. The very formulations differ: the first text speaks of taking (*aratō*) the cross, while the second speaks of carrying it (*bastazei*).[32]

The greatest difference is to be seen in the positive or negative cast given to the saying. The first text speaks in positive terms in both protasis and apodasis; the second has a negative in both parts, which gives it a more primitive character.[33] The greater age of Lk 14:27 is confirmed by its assertion that it is absolutely impossible to be a disciple of Jesus (*ou dunatai einai mou mathētēs*) unless one carries one's own cross and goes after him.

All these differences tell us that there are two completely different traditions for one and the same saying. Luke reflects the more primitive formulation in the text that belongs to the twofold tradition (14:27). It can be said, however, that in contrast with the formulations found in the other two synoptics, both of Luke's redactions of the same saying are characterized by a more radical demand, a greater universality, and a more personal application when they speak of the necessity of carrying one's own cross after Jesus if one is to be his disciple.

B. THE LUKAN SAYING ON THE LOSS AND GAIN OF ONE'S LIFE (9:24; 17:33)

This second saying is as widespread in the synoptic tradition as the one I have just been studying. I shall stick basically to the two redactions in Luke, while trying to shed light on them by contrasting them with the texts of the other two synoptics.

1. Luke 9:24 (par. Mk 8:35; Mt 16:25)

(a) The *context* in which the saying occurs is the one already discussed in connection with Lk 9:23, since this verse immediately follows. Here too, then, light is derived from the announcement of the passion of Jesus (9:22); also relevant is the introduction in which Jesus urgently addresses all: *elegen de pros pantas* (9:23).

(b) I shall set alongside the Lukan *text* only the foundational text in Mark (8:35), although at various points I shall indicate what is peculiar to Matthew (16:25) as well.

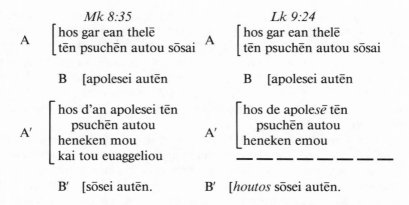

The *structure* in both cases is given by an antithetical parallelism in which "save" (A) and "lose one's life" (B) are paradoxically contrasted with losing it (A') and saving it (B'). The antithesis is brought out, in both texts, by the adversative particle *de*. At the same time, the text is arranged to form a chiasmus:

A   sōsai
   B   apolesei
   B   apolesei(ē)
A   sōsei

Thus through two kinds of loss, which are placed in the center (B − B'), we pass from one to another of two different kinds of salvation (*sōsai–sōsei*), so that the saying opens with the one (A) and closes with the other (A').

Light is shed on the *content* of the text by the causal particle which introduces it (*gar*).[34] The entire saying is geared to explaining the reason why self-denial in the form of a break with one's own self and life, even to the point of surrendering this life, is essential for anyone who wishes to follow Jesus as his disciple. The key word is *psuchē;* reference is made to it twice through the word itself and twice through the pronoun *autēn.* This reality is the subject of a paradox: to save it is to lose it, and to lose it is to save it. *Psuchē* is not, as in the Greek dualist conception of the human person, the soul which informs the body; it signifies rather the very life of the human being, who continually receives the breath of life from God.[35] This life is the limited form in which the concrete existence of each person is passed.[36]

This concrete existence can be "saved," that is, keep itself intact, without suffering the consequences of the "self-denial" or "carrying of the cross" that were explained above. Or this concrete existence can be "lost" by being made the object of a denial of the self, even to the point of its complete elimination in martyrdom. When the life or human existence is "saved" in the manner indicated, then it is "lost," because it did not remain open to an eschatological future, inasmuch as it was closed in upon itself and failed to surrender the self to him from whom it had received its existence. On the other hand, when the existence of the person is "lost" through the complete denial of self and the carrying of the cross, then it is "saved" because of the openness it manifests through the surrender of the self to him from whom its life has come; in the eschatological phase those who surrender their lives are "saved" by finding what they had given away and by their encounter with him for whose sake they had denied themselves. It is in Matthew's redaction that this eschatological salvation is described as a "finding" (*heurēsei*) again of the life that had been lost (Mt 16:25).[37]

In this saying, then, *psuchē* cannot be interpreted as a word with two meanings: temporal life that is saved or lost, thus yielding the loss or salvation, respectively, of eternal life.[38] When the same word *psuchē* is repeated as the object of opposed verbs (*apolesai—sōsei* [*heurēsai*]), the reference in both instances is to the same concrete existence of human beings who, depending on the attitude they take during this earthly sojourn, remain open to a future, after death, of salvation or loss; if they are saved they will be admitted into the life of the future eon; if they are lost, they will be excluded from it.[39] The reason for the future loss is that here on earth they have grown attached to their own life as if death were the ultimate eschatological reality, and have not seen the possibility that God might exclude them in a further stage. On the other hand, the reason for salvation or the future finding of life is found in the renunciation they have made of their existence while trusting in a God who can save it even after death.[40]

In addition—and this is common to the three parallel texts (Mk 8:35; Mt 16:25; Lk 9:24)—the saying gives the immediate reason why the disciples of Jesus lose their human existence in this world in order to be able to save it in the beyond: *heneken emou.* These words make explicit what had earlier been said implicitly in speaking of self-renunciation and the taking up of one's cross in order to be able to follow after Jesus and be his companion (Mk 8:34; Mt 16:24; Lk 9:23).[41] Mark has an additional redactional explanation: *kai tou euaggeliou:* to lose one's life for the sake of the gospel is to lose it for the sake of Jesus himself.[42]

The *special features* in Luke's formulation of the saying are slight ones. He makes a stylistic correction (as does Matthew) which distinguishes his text from Mark's: he replaces the rather strange construction in Mark, namely, an *an* with the indicative (*hos d'an apolesai*), with a more normal one, *an* with the subjunctive (*hos d'an apolesē*). More important is his introduction of the pronoun *houtos* as subject of the future salvation that is won through the loss of one's life here; by using the pronoun Luke puts the emphasis not so much on the loss as on the future salvation.[43] The omission of Mark's redactional addition (*kai tou euaggeliou*) can be explained as emphasizing the christological meaning of the *heneken emou* that motivates the daily following and the daily carrying of the cross, to the point even of losing one's life.[44]

2. Luke 17:33 (par. Mt 10:39)

The paradoxical saying on saving one's life by losing it is given two other formulations in parallel passages of Luke and Matthew. The two texts in question echo a common source (Q), although they are located in different settings and have each their distinctive characteristics.

(a) The *context* in which each evangelist places the saying can help to a deeper understanding of its basic content. Matthew makes it part of the instruction given to the twelve as they set out on their mission; the addressees of the saying are thus the disciples (see Mt 10:1–5), just as they are on the other occasion with which the first evangelist connects the saying (see Mt 16:24). In sending his disciples, Jesus gives them rules that are to govern their activity (Mt 10:5–15); at the same time he warns them of the difficulties they must face (Mt 10:16–36): in the discharge of their mission they will become objects of hatred and persecution. The situations that await them call to mind the conflicts of the last days as described in the eschatological discourse (Mt 10:22; compare 24:9, 13).[45] It is in this context of difficulties in carrying out the apostolic mission that Matthew locates the theme of finding life through losing it.

Luke, on the other hand, connects this other version of the saying with the journey of Jesus to Jerusalem (see Lk 17:11), just as he does the second version of the saying on following Jesus by carrying one's cross (14:27). This second saying on saving one's life by losing it is part of a short eschatological discourse on the day of the Son of Man (17:22–37). The discourse, although introduced by a question from the Pharisees (17:20), is addressed to the disciples (17:22) and warns them of what will happen on the day of the Son of Man. Immediately after this reference to the manifestation and final coming of the Son of Man, Jesus says how necessary it is for the Son of Man to suffer (17:25). This is as it were a secondary clause within the eschatological thematic that is developed in this passage, but it is of some help in once again connecting the saying about the loss of one's life with the suffering of the Son of Man.

On the day of the Son of Man, when he manifests himself like the lightning that flashes from one end of the sky to the other (17:24), everything will be as it was in the days of Noah (17:26–27) and Lot (17:28–29). Since all will happen unexpectedly (see 17:30), the disciples must be detached from their possessions and not try to take them along (17:31–32). More than that, since the day of the Son of Man will come by surprise, they must be detached from their own lives,[46] while knowing, however, that by living in this fashion and losing their lives they will make their lives secure (17:33). Such is the context in which Luke places the saying about the loss and salvation of one's life; the eschatological perspective of the coming of the Son of Man, who has much to suffer from the present generation (17:25), will help the disciples to cultivate the attitude that enables them to lose their lives in order to save them.

(b) The *text* is identical in structure in Matthew and Luke, but has different nuances in each, due in part to the different contexts and in part to the distinctive redactional stamp of each writer.

	Mt 10:39			*Lk 17:33*
A	⌈ ho heurōn ⌊ tēn psuchēn autou		A	⌈ hos *ean zētēsē* | tēn psuchēn autou ⌊ *peripoiēsasthai*
	B [apolesei autēn,			B [apolesei autēn,
A′	⌈ kai ho apolesas | tēn psuchēn autou ⌊ heneken emou,		A′	[kai hos an apolesei
	B′ [heurēsei autēn.			B′ [*zōogonēsei* autēn.

In both texts, just as in the triple tradition, the structure retains the form of antithetical parallelism (A − B − A′ − B′); at the same time, the verbs are arranged in a chiasm which is very clear in Matthew (*heurōn* − apolesei − apolesas − *heurēsei*) but weakened somewhat in Luke because of the change of verbs at beginning and end (*zētēsē . . . peripoiēsasthai* − apolesei − apolesei − *zōogonēsei*).

Matthew has as part of the saying the reason for the loss of one's life (*heneken emou*), as explained earlier in connection with the saying in the triple tradition. By doing so, he makes the saying fit better into its context here, namely, into the discourse for the sending of the disciples, in which they are told in advance that for Jesus' sake they will be brought before governors and kings to bear witness to him (10:17–18). Matthew also keeps the idea of finding one's own life again (*heurēsei*) after losing it; he thus gives an eschatological coloring to the time in which one will recover one's life. The final verb (*heurēsei*) of the text, which is already present in its other formulation in the triple tradition (16:25), determines that the text will begin with the same verb (*heurōn*). In view, then, of the persecutions which the disciples must face, Matthew encourages them to lose their life for Jesus in order to find it again, since those who find it here will lose it hereafter.

Luke's version, on the other hand, omits here the motive for the loss of one's life (the *heneken emou*); the omission is to be explained by the fact that in this context the saying is inspired not by concrete situations of persecution or martyrdom but by the normal situation, namely, the continual coming, by surprise, of the day of the Son of Man. In contrast, the first part of the Lukan version (*hos ean zētēsē . . . peripoiēsasthai*), a part which is exclusively Luke's,[47] may be inspired by the preceding exhortation not to retrieve one's possessions on the last day: "On that day, anyone on the housetop who has belongings in the house must not come down to take them away" (17:31). The tendency to hold on to one's external possessions extends to another, more deeply personal possession: "Those who try to make their life secure will lose it." The combination of verbs: "try to make secure," shows how useless is the effort to preserve one's life.[48] Luke sees a different destiny in store for those who lose their life: they will "keep it alive" (*zōogonēsei autēn*). This final expression, which is peculiar to Luke in the formulation of the present saying,[49] is especially thought-provoking, since the verb *zōogonēsei* implies that the life (*psuchē*) which is lost is transformed, inasmuch as it refers to *zōē*, the life that will take on its full meaning in the Johannine version of the saying (Jn 12:25).[50] The use of the future tense in *zōogonēsei* suggests the certainty with which life will be preserved in the eschatological stage, in contrast to the unsuccessful attempt to preserve it here.[51]

Given the context in which the saying is found in Luke, it becomes, in this version of it, a further exhortation to detachment not only from possessions but from one's very self, in view of the eschatological day of the coming of the Son of Man. The disciple will thus be prepared for this coming of the Son of Man and, by losing his life, will be able to save and transform it.

(c) A *comparison* of Luke's two formulations (9:24; 17:33) shows that a saying can express different perspectives even within the same author and while having the same literary structure. It is the difference in context that determines the nuancing and different applications of the saying.

	Lk 9:24		*Lk 17:33*
A	⎡ hos gar ean *thelē*		⎡ hos ean *zētēsē*
	⎣ tēn psuchēn autou *sosai*	A	tēn psuchēn autou
			⎣ *peripoiēsasthai,*
B	[apolesei autēn	B	[apolesei autēn,
A′	⎡ hos d'an apolesē	A′	[kai hos an apolesei,
	⎢ tēn psuchēn autou		
	⎣ heneken emou,		
B′	[houtos sōsei autēn.	B′	[*zōogonēsei* autēn.

Both texts show the same structure: antithetical parallelism (A − B − A′ − B′). Both arrange the verbs chiastically. The chiasmus is clearer in the first text (9:24), which begins with *sōsai* and ends with *sōsei;* in the middle are *apolesei* and *apolesē.* The second text (17:33) also has *apolesei* (twice) at the center; at the extremes, the opening protasis expresses the vain attempt to preserve one's life: *hos ean zētēsē . . . peripoiēsasthai,* while the final verb expresses the effective preservation, live, of one's existence: *zōogonēsei.* The very structure causes both sayings to give greater emphasis to final salvation. This emerges clearly in the first text (9:24) from the contrast, at the two ends of the sentence, between the salvation sought in the present life (*ean thelē . . . sōsai*), and the certain salvation at the end (*sōsei*), a certainty further emphasized by the preceding pronoun (*houtos sōsei autēn*). The second text (17:33) also emphasizes the theme of salvation: it begins with the unsuccessful attempt in this life (*hos ean zētēsē . . . peripoiēsasthai*) and ends with the assured attainment of life in the beyond (*zōogonēsei autēn*) by those who lose their life here.

Despite this common framework the *differences* between the two texts are evident and important. The first formulation (9:24), set as it is in the light shed by the first prediction of the passion (9:22), gives the ultimate reason (*heneken emou*) why disciples lose their life in order to save it. The second formulation, which is influenced more by its eschatological context (17:22–37) than by the prediction of the sufferings of the Son of Man (17:25), says nothing about this motive. In the one case (9:24), the text is faithful to its source (Mk 8:35) and repeats the same verb for salvation (*sōsai − sōsei*); in the other (17:33), Luke gives the saying a form that is more properly his, by speaking of the attempt to preserve one's life (*hos ean zētēsē . . . peripoiēsasthai*) and then asserting the permanence of the life won (*zōogonēsei autēn*), thus emphasizing the transformation of this life.

Both texts have a strongly hortatory character, either by reason of the way the saying is introduced: *elegen de* (9:23) or by reason of the context, namely the urgency created by the final events (17:22–37). In both texts there is an invitation to the loss or renunciation of what is closest to oneself, namely, one's very life: in the one case, by living this life daily for Jesus and in the light of his example (9:24); in the other, by living in daily expectation of the eschatological events that will accompany the day of the Son of Man (17:33). In both instances, the loss of one's life is connected with a sure promise that this life will be saved and transformed.

C. LUKE'S TWO SAYINGS IN THEIR JOHANNINE FORMULATION (JN 12:25–26)

The repetition of the two sayings which I have been studying is not limited to the numerous formulations of them in the synoptics. A similar tradition has left its mark in the fourth gospel as well. This is not a unique occurrence in the gospel tradition; it is, however, of special interest both by reason of the convergence in the transmission of the same content and by reason of the difference in perspective due to the setting in which the texts, each with its own individual formulation, are located. In turning now to the Johannine texts (12:25–26), I shall look first at the context which the two sayings share, since the one follows immediately on the other; then I shall discuss the characteristic Johannine formulation of each; at the end I shall compare the theologies of Luke and John as seen in the transmission of these texts.

1. The Context in John

The two verses are found in chapter 12, where, at the same time that the activity of Jesus in his public life is ending because his hour is at hand (12:23), a universal perspective is being opened up thanks to the presence of some Greeks (12:20). The Greeks approach two of the disciples, Philip and Andrew, whose very names have a Hellenistic flavor, and tell them of their desire to see Jesus (12:21). The two disciples act as intermediaries between the Greeks and Jesus (12:22). Although the Greeks are not mentioned again, they are still present in the ensuing response of Jesus; they do not disappear like ghosts.[52] Nor can their presence be interpreted simply as a point of departure for the following words of Jesus,[53] for his response is addressed to all the persons previously introduced.[54]

Jesus begins by saying that the hour of his glorification has come (12:23); this hour of the Son of Man coincides in fact with the hour of the Greeks who want to see Jesus (12:21). Further on, Jesus will make this point more explicit when he speaks of drawing *all* to himself when he is lifted up from the earth (12:32). The hour of Jesus' glorification is here described as the falling into the earth of a grain of wheat that dies and produces much fruit (12:24). This is immediately followed by the two verses that are my concern here (vv. 25–26); in this context the verses take on a universality that embraces all.

2. The Saying About the Loss and Salvation of One's Life (Jn 12:25)

The fourth gospel cites the synoptic saying, but in characteristically Johannine phraseology:

A   ho philōn tēn psuchēn autou
B   apolluei autēn,
A'   kai ho misōn tēn psuchēn autou en tō kosmō toutō
B'   eis zōēn aiōnion phulaxei autēn.

The structure, here again, is created by an antithetical parallelism; two contrasted attitudes regarding one's own life (A − A': *ho philōn − ho misōn*) produces effects that are likewise different (B − B': *apolluei − phulaxei*). Within this common structure the variations introduced by John are significant. The two verbs that are used to express the disposition of persons (*ho philōn − ho misōn*) in regard to their own lives reflect the style of the fourth gospel.[55] In keeping with semitic usage, "love" and "hate" do not have a psychological meaning but express a preference and a lesser regard.[56] The preference for life leads to its loss (*apolluei*); this is the term also used in the synoptic tradition (Mt 16:25; Mk 8:35; Lk 9:24). The lower value set on life brings a different result; here John introduces a further variation.

These two attitudes—of preference for one's life or scorn of it—are cultivated "in this world" (*en tō kosmō toutō*). While a spatial meaning (the existing world around us) is not excluded from the typically Johannine term "world" (see Jn 8:23), it certainly has in addition a temporal meaning: the present world as distinct from the future world. Those who scorn their life in the present world will keep (*phulaxei*) it for eternal life. The verb "to keep" (*phulassein*), which sometimes means "to observe" (e.g. the word; see 12:27), here means "to protect" from external forces that can destroy what is being preserved (see 17:12); the contrast with the preceding verb (*apolluei*) demands this meaning here.[57] The existence (*psuchē*) that is lost in this world is contrasted with a life (*zōē*) that is a participation in the life of God and therefore eternal (*aiōnios*); the existence that is scorned in this world is preserved for a subsequent stage in which it shares in a life that is divine and therefore eternal (*eis zōēn aiōnion*).

This saying about the loss and salvation of one's life (12:25) is a restatement of what was said previously about the grain of wheat which produces much fruit after falling into the earth and dying. If this saying about the grain of wheat refers in its very formulation to Jesus who by dying is glorified,[58] then the saying about the loss and salvation of one's life also applies to Jesus who, by losing his life, preserves it for ever. But this second saying (12:25) reaches further. The indefiniteness of the formulation (*ho philōn – misōn*) makes it applicable to all disciples who, like their master, lose their life and so save it for an eternal life. This application to the disciples of Jesus is given another concrete form in the saying that follows immediately.

3. The Saying About the Following of Jesus (Jn 12:26)

This further saying, which is also found in the synoptic tradition, here shows variations that are peculiar to the fourth gospel.

(a) In its very *structure* the saying breaks with the previous molds:

A   ean emoi tis diakonē,
    B   emoi akoloutheitō,
       kai hopou
          a   eimi
             b   egō
    C   ekei
             b'   kai ho diakonos ho emos
         a'   estai

A'   ean tis emoi diakonē
    B'   timēsei auton ho patēr.

The text is characterized by parallelism and correspondence: two conditional statements about those who serve Jesus (A – A': *ean emoi tis diakonē*), each followed by a further statement in the form either of an urgent exhortation (B: *emoi akoloutheitō*) or of a sure promise (B': *timēsai auton ho patēr*). In the first set of corresponding clauses (A – A') the writer plays with the pronouns in a provocative way by ordering them in a chiastic form that links Jesus and his servant: *emoi – tis – tis – emoi*. The nature of this reciprocal relationship is set forth in the central section (C). Here there is a correspondence of adverbs referring to the spheres of

Jesus (*hopou*) and the disciple (*ekei*); the two are then named again—Jesus (b: *egō*) and his servant (b': *kai ho diakonos ho emos*)—as persons who draw near to one another (a − a': *eimi* − *estai*).

(b) The *service* rendered to Jesus (*diakonē*) is not expressly described here[59]; its content emerges from what has just been said about despising one's own life (12:25), while at the same time the idea of "service" brings out what is at issue in hating one's own life. The "service" here consists in giving one's life for Jesus' sake; they serve Jesus who love him to the point of preferring him to their own life. In other words, taking the two verses together as shedding light on each other: they who hate their own life, that is, do not love it more than they love Jesus but rather consider him more important than their own life—these are the ones who serve him.[60] The emphatic place given to the pronoun *emoi* (= Jesus) at the beginning (*ean emoi tis diakonē*), and the inversion of the pronouns in the second part of the verse (*ean tis emoi diakonē*), make clear the christological focus of the service. The universal applicability of the saying is underscored by the repetition of the pronoun *tis,* which, being indeterminate, can refer to anyone who adopts this attitude of service.

(c) The *invitation to follow* is the first categorical directive given to those who would serve Jesus: *emoi akoloutheitō.* The putting first of the pronoun *emoi* continues the highlighting of the christological perspective of the saying. The invitation to follow does not refer here to a literal going after or behind Jesus, as it could at an earlier stage (see Jn 1:37–38), but rather to the assent of faith which accepts what it hears from Jesus, and then applies it to the person's life (see 8:12; 10:27). The verb *akoloutheō* thus has a theological meaning: to follow the directives given in the preaching and teaching of Jesus. The use of the imperative ("must follow") suggests that service is a necessary concomitant of following; the invitation thus acquires the force of an urgent exhortation, a kind of order. The present tense used in the imperative suggests that the following has already begun in the attitude of service; for this reason the exhortation here is not so much to begin as to continue this consistent following.[61]

(d) The *promise* of Jesus is a further stimulus to serve and follow him: "Whoever serves me, the Father will honor (*timēsei*)." The verb *timaō* refers to the honor given to persons in recognition of their condition and traits.[62] In the fourth gospel the recipients of this honor are: the Father, whom Jesus honors (8:49) by acknowledging that he, Jesus, has been sent by him; the Son, whom all are to honor as they honor the Father (5:23), by acknowledging his power to give life and to judge (5:21–23). In the verse I am now considering, it is the servant of Jesus who will be honored by the Father. The use of the future (*timēsei*) makes two points clear: the certainty of this honor that comes from the Father, and the

futurity of the honor. The fact that it is the Father who will confer honor
on the servant of Jesus helps unite the servant even more closely with
Jesus. Jesus has already spoken of the coming of the hour for the Son of
Man to be glorified (12:23); behind the use of the "divine passive" (*dox-
asthē*) stands the Father as the one who glorifies the Son. It is the same
Father who glorifies Jesus and honors the servant of Jesus.

(e) *The goal of the following and glorification* of the servant of Jesus
is at the center of the present saying. After urging his disciples to follow
him, Jesus adds: "And where I am, there will my servant be also."

The *goal of the following* is for the servant of Jesus to be where Jesus
is; there, two different levels converge. The sphere in which Jesus moves
(*hopou*) must become that of the servant (*ekei*). For Jesus this sphere is
already present (*eimi egō*); it is still in the future for the servant (*kai ho
diakonos ho emos estai*). There is not only a juxtaposition of persons,
expressed in the very structure of the text (b − b': *egō − kai ho diakonos ho
emos*), but also a communion of destiny (a − a': *eimi − estai*), since they
share the same goal (*hopou − ekei*). This destiny is already realized for
Jesus; the saying does not tell us what it is that he already possesses, or
what the goal is in which the servant will meet Jesus, but it is possible to
infer this from what has immediately preceded. Jesus has previously spoken of this hour as something already at work; the hour that is meant is the
moment of the glorification of the Son of Man (12:23). This glorification
is comparable to the death of the grain of wheat and the abundant fruit it
produces by dying (12:24); the glory consists in renouncing one's life and
thereby preserving it for eternal life (12:25). This, then, is the very goal to
which the following of Jesus will lead his servant, namely, participation in
the glory of Jesus by sacrificing even one's life in his service and so preferring Jesus to oneself.

The goal of the glorification of the servant of Jesus is also to be where
he is. The place where the glorified Jesus is (*hopou eimi egō*) is where the
Son of Man had previously been (6:62: *hopou ēn to proteron*). He returns
to that place when he returns to his Father (8:21, 22; 13:33; 14:4), but he
does not return there without first passing through the cross and death
(12:24). This future glorification of Jesus is in some manner also already
present in him (*hopou eimi egō*), inasmuch as he lives in an atmosphere of
ineffable union with the one who has sent him (7:34, 36: *hopou eimi egō*).
This present glorification of Jesus will be given to his servant in the future.
The lowliness of the servant of Jesus (*ho diakonos ho emos*) is already
exalted by the one who is being served (*ean emoi diakonē*) and to whom
the servant belongs (*ho diakonos ho emos*). This glorification is already
being accomplished when the servant is able to share the same lot as the

one whom he serves by surrendering his own existence for the master's sake; this is already an honor granted by the Father. But the Father will honor the servant of Jesus most fully when he sees to it that in a future, eternal life, "where I am, there will my servant be also."

D. THE THEOLOGIES OF LUKE AND JOHN COMPARED

Now that I have discussed the Lucan and Johannine formulations of the sayings on the following of Jesus and on the loss and saving of one's life, it is time to conclude with a comparison of the theological orientations of the two evangelists. The two writers have certain elements in common in their transmission of the two sayings, while in other respects each has left his personal impress on the texts.

1. Points in Common

(a) The *very transmission of the two sayings* is something the two evangelists have in common. As a matter of fact, these two sayings are an exceptional instance of multiple attestation. Each of the two sayings comes to us in six formulations: the following of Jesus = Mt 16:24; Mk 8:24; Lk 9:23//Mt 10:38; Lk 14:27//Jn 12:26, and the loss and saving of one's life = Mt 16:25; Mk 8:35; Lk 9:24//Mt 10:39; Lk 17:33//Jn 12:25. If we take multiple attestation as a criterion of historicity,[63] then it will not be rash to judge that, as far as the basic content is concerned, we have in these sayings material that comes from a single original source, namely, Jesus himself, even though this material has been transmitted in various traditions and divergent formulations which make explicit the wealth of meaning contained in the original. The fact of transmission is something which not only Luke and John but all four evangelists have in common.

(b) The *universalist perspective* in the two sayings is a point common to Luke and John in particular. In the *third gospel* the two sayings have a universality that is notably underscored by presenting them together (Lk 9:23–24) and introducing them with words that apply to all that follows: *elegen de pros pantas* (9:23). When the two sayings are repeated, each retains this universalist perspective; see the generalized formulation of the saying about following: *hostis ou bastazei ton stauron heautou* (14:27), and the eschatological context, with its urgency for all, in which the saying on the loss and saving of one's life is placed (17:33).

The *fourth gospel* likewise emphasizes the universal application of the two sayings by means of the context in which it places them. After ironically repeating the Pharisees' assessment of their situation in relation to Jesus: "Look, the world has gone after him!" (12:19), John tells us of the presence of some Greeks who want to see Jesus (12:21). What Jesus says next (12:25–26) holds true for the disciples to whom he is replying (12:23), for the "world [that] has gone after him," and also for the Greeks who want to see him. In fact, this hour of the glorification of Jesus (12:23) is the moment in which he draws *all* to himself (12:32).

(c) The *eschatological perspective* is a further note common to both evangelists. In *Luke* the saying on the loss and saving of one's life (17:33) acquires this perspective because the evangelist places it in an apocalyptic context (17:22–37) and brings up the day of the coming of the Son of Man (17:24, 30) as an incentive to lose one's existence and thereby save it and keep it alive.

John makes the reference to a future life even clearer by contrasting the loss of one's life in this world (12:25: *en tō kosmō toutō*) with the future life for which it is preserved (12:25: *eis zōēn aiōnion phulaxei autēn*). In the saying on the following of Jesus (12:26) the end-result is explained as the future participation of the servant of Jesus (*ekei . . . estai*) in the glory which Jesus already possesses (*hopou eimi egō*).

2. Points Peculiar to Each Evangelist

The special characteristics distinguishing the formulations of the two evangelists are even more prominent. It is these that are of greatest help in bringing out the theological direction taken by each of them.

(a) Luke

(1) The specific *contexts* in which Luke has placed the two different sayings are already peculiar to him. On the one occasion when he connects the two (9:23–24) he follows a tradition common to the three synoptics and places them after the first prediction of the passion (9:22). When he repeats each of them he shows greater originality. With his starting point perhaps in a tradition that he shares with Matthew, he places the saying on carrying one's cross and following Jesus (14:27) among the other points that distinguish the disciple, such as the preference for Jesus over parents, wife, children, and brothers and sisters (14:26) and the renunciation of possessions (14:33). The saying on losing and saving one's life (17:33) is introduced into the short apocalyptic discourse (17:22–37) which is intended to describe the nature of the kingdom of God (17:20–22).

(2) A *christological meaning* is not excluded from Luke's redaction, but it is not the aspect most emphasized. The christological slant of the several Lukan formulations shows distinctive features. Thus in 9:23 going after Jesus (*opisō mou*) consists in taking up one's cross daily and accompanying him (*akoloutheitō moi*); it is this that makes a person *his* disciple (14:27: *einai mou mathētēs*). The losing of one's life in order to save it is done for the sake of Jesus (9:24: *heneken emou*). Both the saying on following (9:23) and the saying on the losing and saving of one's life (9:24) follow upon the first prediction of the passion, thus showing that the disciple will share the master's lot.

(3) The *parenetic and moral* aspect is the one most emphasized in the Lukan redaction. The words that introduce the two combined sayings (9:23–24) point to an ongoing exhortation addressed to all and thus already give us a glimpse of the urgency with which Jesus speaks (9:23: *elegen de pros pantas*). The main content of the saying on following is self-denial (9:23) and the daily (9:23: *kath'hēmeran*) taking up of one's cross (9:23; 14:27); this gives a daily opportunity for putting the exhortation of Jesus into practice. The moral and parenetic power of this Lukan saying emerges more clearly when the saying is compared with the other synoptic redactions of it (Mt 16:24; Mk 8:34). Self-denial and the daily taking up of one's cross are the practical form of losing one's life in order to save it (9:24) and in order to preserve it alive (17:33). The ultimate basis of this parenesis is surely the christological meaning already pointed out.

(b) John

(1) The *parenetic* note is not missing in the Johannine redaction of the two sayings. Their content is part of the reply which Jesus gives to the disciples and to the Greeks who want to see Jesus (12:21). They are an exhortation to follow Jesus (12:26: *emoi akoloutheitō*) and to prefer Jesus to one's own existence so that one may thereby preserve this existence for eternal life (12:25).

(2) The *christological orientation* is primary in the Johannine formulation of the two sayings. This purpose is served by several features with their different emphases.

First of all, the *context* in which the two sayings are placed helps to this christological orientation. The two texts are introduced at the moment when the hour of the glorification of the Son of Man is beginning (12:23); the glorification takes the form of the abundant fruit which the grain of wheat produces by dying (12:24). This statement of Jesus is immediately followed by the two sayings which are here integrated into the discourse as a whole.

The saying *on losing and saving one's life* (Jn 12:25) applies first and foremost to Jesus himself. The christological meaning derives chiefly from the fact that Jesus fulfills in his own person what Luke and the other synoptics had applied to the disciples. John thus extends the meaning of the grain of wheat by referring it to Jesus who by falling to the earth and dying produces abundant fruit. Jesus did not so love his own life as to think he ought to keep it; on the contrary, he preferred to lose it and thereby to preserve it for an eternal life (12:25). He has preserved this eternal life not for himself alone but for many others as well; such is the abundant fruit he obtained by dying like a grain of wheat. The saying on the loss and salvation of one's life is thus valid first of all for Jesus himself, but with those others in view for whom Jesus obtained eternal life. In addition, the saying is fulfilled at the same time in all who hate their own life and thus preserve it for eternal life (*eis zōēn aiōnion*); this new life (*zōē*) is a participation in the very life of Jesus who by dying bears fruit for others.

The saying on *the following of Jesus* (12:26) is the one that most clearly displays a christological orientation: not because it is applicable to Jesus, for in fact it refers directly only to his servants, but because in its formulation and content it looks entirely to Jesus. It contains many words referring to him: the pronoun *emoi* three times (*emoi* diakonē [twice]; *emoi* akoloutheitō); the pronoun *egō,* once; one verb in the first person (*eimi*); a possessive adjective (*ho emos*). As a result, the attitude of the disciple is focused on Jesus, on his service (*emoi diakonē*), and on following him (*emoi akoloutheitō*). The ultimate goal of the servants of Jesus and of their following of him is the honor which the Father bestows on them; but this honor is identified with the complete assimilation of the sphere of the disciple to the sphere of Jesus (*hopou eimi egō ekei kai ho diakonos ho emos estai*). The convergence of the *hopou* of Jesus and the *ekei* of the servant is due to their sharing the same lot: both are grains of wheat that die to themselves but yield a fruit of glory in an eternal life.

The *inverting of the order* of the two sayings is characteristic of John. When Luke combines the two he speaks first of following (9:23), then of losing and saving one's life (9:24). But when John passes them on together, he inverts this order. He speaks first of losing one's life in order to save it (12:25); as a result, the saying applies first and foremost to Jesus, since it continues what has been said about the lot of the grain of wheat (12:24), even though it is, of course, valid also for the disciple. He then reproduces the saying about following, which is applicable only to the servant of Jesus, although it derives its meaning from a constant reference to the one being served.

CONCLUSION

Thus these two sayings, which Luke cites primarily as an exhortation to all who desire to be disciples of Jesus, acquire in John's formulation of them a primarily christological thrust. In the fourth gospel, the saying about losing and saving one's life is applied first of all to Jesus, even if it also applies to all. The other saying, on the following of Jesus, applies only to the servant of Jesus, but is wholly permeated by christological meaning, since the servant of Jesus shares the lot of Jesus in death and glory. Luke gives the message of Jesus a moral and parenetic formulation of universal application; John uses the same message as a fundamental means of shaping a christology, but without lessening the universality.

Vittorio Fusco

Problems of Structure in
Luke's Eschatological Discourse
(Luke 21:7–36)

1. INTRODUCTION

In his several discussions of the eschatological problem in Luke,[1] the scholar we are here honoring has called attention to two points which I regard as quite important. First of all, there is the complexity of the data[2]: among the eschatological texts there are some[3] that disprove Conzelmann's thesis that the expectation of a proximate second coming has been eliminated from Luke.[4] Second, there is need of radically revising the method followed,[5] making it possible to combine a "diachronic" approach with a "synchronic."

It is with this revision in view that I intend to look again at this passage that is so decisive for Lukan eschatology. It has been the object of concentrated study, but the method applied has not always been a correct one; in fact, attention has often been focused on redactional changes and on an effort to explain these one by one in the light of Luke's supposed theological intention, namely, the dissociation of the parousia from any historical event whatsoever. The danger in this approach is of overrating the importance of certain revisions, while failing to consider other possible motives that may have suggested these changes,[6] and neglecting to consider the function which each element acquires in the new context.

The fact is that even monographs on Luke 21[7] offer only brief remarks on the problem of structure.[8] The studies of J. Lambrecht[9] and J. Dupont[10] pay greater attention to this problem, but they reach different conclusions regarding the central issue. Dupont, along with the majority of exegetes, maintains that the clear dissociation of the parousia from the events of contemporary history is the key to a grasp of "the coherence of Luke's text"[11]; he openly acknowledges, however, that this coherence breaks down in v. 32, thus undermining the various attempts to eliminate the expectation of an imminent coming.[12] Lambrecht, along with a minority of exegetes, concludes that in Luke 21 there is nothing that demands the postponement of the parousia to a distant and unspecified future time.[13] This is the conclusion which I, too, regard as better grounded,[14] although I reach it by an analysis that differs from his on certain points.[15]

2. THE OPENING QUESTION (V. 7)

The entire discourse has as its point of departure (v. 7) a question elicited by what Jesus says about the destruction of the temple (vv. 5–6).[16] It is absolutely necessary, therefore, to be clear on the meaning of this question, both in itself and in the light of Jesus' answer. The question contains in fact two queries that are distinct but connected (as is clear from the repetition of the same subject, *tauta*); one concerns the time of these events (v. 7a: *pote oun tauta estai?*[17]); the other, the possible sign of their approach (v. 7b: . . . *kai ti to sēmeion hotan mellē tauta ginesthai?*). The "sign" in question is to be understood in light of the apocalyptic tradition: "that which makes something that is very specific . . . recognisable as such."[18]

The question in Mt 24:3 explicitly extends to the parousia, and Mk 13:4 too may be referring to it by using the verb *synteleisthai* and by adding *panta* to the second *tauta*. Luke, on the other hand, uses the verb *ginesthai*, omits the *panta*, and adds a "therefore" (*oun*) which links the question more closely to the preceding words of Jesus about the fate of the temple (vv. 5–6). All that is left is the plural *tauta*, but this hardly suffices to express a reference to the end not only of the temple but of the world.[19] The most that can be said, then, is that such a reference is not a priori excluded.[20]

The holy city, including the temple, had suffered other destructions in the course of history; its destruction is therefore not necessarily an eschatological event. On the other hand, such a destruction was frequently connected with the final judgment[21]; especially, therefore, in the context of the gospels this prophecy cannot be taken in isolation from all the other preceding prophecies and from the proclamation of the coming of the kingdom (Lk 4:43; 8:1; 9:2, 11, 27; 10:9, 11; 11:2, 20; etc.). Readers will spontaneously ask themselves whether the two events are not to be linked.

The answer is in fact formulated as though that were precisely the question asked.[22] The horizon is already broadened in a decisive way with the "citation" of the false prophets, for the two expressions "I am he!" and "The time is near!" shed light on each other and make it clear that the reference is not to some historical event or other but to the eschatological and messianic *kairos*.[23] Moreover, the refutation (v. 9) of these false prophets does not stay within a framework that is limited to the fate of the Jerusalem temple. It remains within the eschatological framework; the only limitation introduced is the assertion that these things will not happen immediately. And in fact Jesus goes on to foretell a series of events which continue after the destruction of Judaism's holy city (vv. 20–24) and extend to the entire *oikumenē* (v. 26), climaxing in the glorious manifestation of the Son of Man (v. 27). Only at this point does the discourse take up more directly the question of time and signs with which it began (see Section 4, below), and it does so with reference to the event now specified as "your redemption" (v. 28), "the kingdom of God" (v. 31), and "that day" on which they must "stand before the Son of Man" (vv. 34–36). For good reason, then, there is little acceptance today of the hypothesis that the entire discourse is describing the fall of Jerusalem and nothing more,[24] or that any reference to the parousia is by way of digression.[25]

Some argue that in the opening question Luke does not mention the parousia and so makes it clear from the outset that he excludes any connection between the two events[26]; but the argument is not a valid one. The absence of a reference to the parousia in the question does not in fact prevent Jesus from speaking of it in his answer! We may think that an explicit question along this line has been omitted not because it would have been mistaken in principle but because it is unnecessary,[27] or because the redactor does not want to give (and in fact does not give) an equally explicit answer, either positive or negative, or even, more simply, because it is for Jesus and not his questioners to know the future. It is enough that the questioners provide a point of departure, even if only in a confused manner; then it will be up to Jesus to reveal as much as he wishes. It is risky trying to derive the position of Luke more from the question than from the answer!

3. PRELIMINARY PROBLEM: INTRODUCTORY FORMULAS WITH A VERB MEANING "SPEAK" (VV. 10A, 29A)

In many recent studies of this passages the internal division of the discourse has been based on two formulas: *tote elegen autois* (v. 10a) and *kai eipen parabolēn autois* (v. 29a), which (it is claimed) divide the discourse into three parts: an introduction, a central section, and a conclusion.[28] But a quick survey of Luke's use of these formulas shows that such is not their function.

3.1. The Introductory Formula in V. 29a

If we are to maintain that this formula "introduces" the entire con-cluding part of the discourse, then the term *parabolē* must be applicable to the two sayings in vv. 32 and 33, as well as to the final exhortation (vv. 34–36). But in fact neither the sayings nor the exhortation is a *parabolē;* furthermore, the noun *parabolē* is singular in number.[29] The formula therefore introduces only the immediately following passage, that is, the parable of the fig tree (vv. 29b–31). In this respect, the passage manifests the care which Luke takes when introducing parables—a care long since observed to be a characteristic of his[30]—to state explicitly that they are parables. This is especially true of the shorter parables that might other-wise slip by unnoticed (Lk 5:36; 6:39; 8:4; 12:16; 13:6; 14:7; 15:3; 18:1, 9; 19:11; 20:9). The instances in which such an explicit statement is not made are almost all explicable by the fact that the parabolic nature of the passage has already been brought out in some other way (13:18, 20) or is clear from comparison with preceding passages already designated as "parables" (15:8–10; see 15:3–7; 5:37–39; see 5:36) or is clear from the unquestionably parabolic features of longer, narrative parables (7:36–50; 10:25–37; 14:15–24; 15:11–32; 16:1–8; 16:19–31).[31]

We need also note that these formulas can be used at any point in a discourse: at the beginning (8:4; 15:3), or when the subject changes (14:7; 18:1; 18:9; 19:11), or when a parable is meant to explain things said earlier (5:36; 6:39; 12:16; 13:6; 20:9), in which case the formula with a verb of saying evidently serves to connect and not to signify a break; Lk 21:29a belongs to this last group (see Section 4). Its purpose is served in the immediate context; it has no function in relation to the macrostructure of the eschatological discourse.

3.2. The Introductory Formula in V. 10a

The new introduction *Tote elegen autois* (c. 10a), coming as it does so soon after another, *Kai eipen* (v. 8a), which was followed by only a few words (vv. 8b–9), calls for an explanation. Since no such explanation has been found,[32] it has been regarded as a vestige from some other source than Mark[33] (an opinion generally abandoned today) or as a device for distinguishing the various parts of the discourse, and, more specifically:

(a) some see it as a device for preventing any confusion between the events described in vv. 8–9, which are still distant from the end, and those described in vv. 10–11, which (it is said) are to be identified with the signs of the parousia, these signs being anticipated here and repeated later in vv. 25–27 (see Section 5.1);

(b) others see it as a means of distinguishing a more general statement (vv. 8–9) from the subsequent more detailed statement[34]; but, as we
shall see, vv. 8–9 are not reducible to a few generalities (see Section 5.1);

(c) still others see a distinction based on the negative tone of vv. 8–9
and the positive tone of the subsequent verses[35]; the distinction is valid
enough but does not explain the interruption and the repetition of the
verb for "speak."

An examination of the Lukan use of such formulas quickly shows
that they are never used simply to mark the internal divisions of a discourse. In the "sermon on the plain," for example (6:20–49), even though
there is a succession of quite different themes, more so than in Luke 21,
there are, after the introductory formula at the beginning (6:20), no other
such formulas, except those in 5:36 and 6:39, which serve only to introduce the respective parables as such (see Section 3. 1) and which it would
be absurd to take as criteria for distinguishing the several sections of the
discourse. The same situation can be seen in the missionary discourse (Lk
10:1–16) and in other, shorter didactic passages (Lk 8:5–18).

Such introductory formulas are used, however, when they are necessary: to introduce a discourse (Lk 3:7; 13:18; etc.) or a reply (Lk 13:2;
17:20; Acts 4:8; 10:46; 21:13; etc.) or to signal a change of audience (Lk
12:22, 54; 16:1; 17:1, 22). None of these three types is parallel to the one I
am discussing here.[36]

A partial but not unimportant parallel is, however, to be found in the
controversy on the sabbath (Lk 6:1–5). A first formula, *kai apokritheis
pros autous eipen ho Iēsous* (v. 3a), introduces the reply in which Jesus
appeals to the example of David (vv. 3–4). Then a *kai elegen autois,* taken
from Mk 2:27, introduces a further saying: "The Son of Man is lord of the
sabbath" (v. 5). Luke usually prefers to omit this connecting *kai elegen
autois,* which is characteristic of Mark. In this instance, therefore, there
must have been a reason why he did not think it useless. And in fact, if we
note the tenses of the verbs, we see that the verb in the first formula, *eipen,*
is in the aorist tense, which is characteristic of replies (Lk 3:15; 5:34; 8:30;
10:26, 37; 13:23; 16:6, 7; 17:37; 18:27, 41; 19:34; 20:24; 22:10; 24:19); this
is confirmed here by the added *apokritheis pros autous.* In the second
formula, on the other hand, the verb is in the imperfect tense. This difference suggests that the real and proper answer to the adversaries is to be
found only in the casuistic argument based on an incident in the Bible,
while the further saying, which refers explicitly to the authority of the Son
of Man, is directed rather to believers.

Similarly, in Luke 21, the first formula, *ho de eipen* (v. 8a), which
comes after the question (v. 7), has an aorist verb, while the second formula, *Tote elegen autois* (v. 10a), has the verb in the imperfect. A plausi-

ble explanation, then, is that Luke did not think it proper to present the entire discourse as an answer simply to the opening question; he wanted, instead, to stress the point that Jesus did not limit himself to answering a question, but offered much more.[37] And in fact in a good many verses of the discourse the content goes beyond an answer to the opening question: the reference to the parousia, the unnecessary details on the fate of Jerusalem, the parenetic exhortations, and so on.

This explanation also uses to advantage the distinction between a positive and a negative answer: the immediate reply of Jesus makes it clear that the signs are not the ones claimed by the false prophets. Jesus allows, however, that the events in question, though not proximate to the end, must indeed take place (v. 9). Therefore he goes on (v. 10a) to explain these in greater detail and in the correct and more complete context in which they belong (vv. 10b–36). It is not surprising therefore that the wars and insurrections already mentioned (v. 9) should be described anew in different words (v. 10b), with other events added (v. 11). The purpose of introducing a break is not to remove the events of vv. 10–11 from the historical and chronological sequence (see Section 5. 1).

Unlike the *Kai eipen parabolēn autois* of v. 29a, this *Tote elegen autois* (v. 10a) has a function in the overall structure of the discourse, but it is a somewhat limited and general function. It tells us nothing of the discourse's further internal division, which will be derived essentially from the dynamics of the events being foretold.

4. DIVISION OF THE DISCOURSE

Jesus begins to foretell a series of events. The future tense predominates, interrupted here and there by parenetic imperatives; generally speaking, the exposition follows a chronological order, passing gradually from events closer in time to others more distant, down to the final event, the coming of the Son of Man (v. 27).[38]

In the following section (vv. 28–36) a different guiding thread can be recognized, for here no further events are added, but there is a reflection on those already predicted, as can be seen from the frequent use of pronouns: *tauta* (vv. 28, 31), *panta* (v. 32), *tauta panta* (v. 36), *hē hēmera ekeinē* (v. 34).

This new section is to be seen as beginning not after v. 28 but after v. 27. The solemn tone of v. 27 ("Then they will see 'the Son of Man coming in a cloud' with power and great glory") makes it sound very much like a conclusion, after which there is place for a momentary pause. In v. 28, on the other hand, the very fact of saying, after the appearance of the Son of

Man has already been mentioned, "Now when these things begin to take place, stand up and raise your heads, because your redemption *is drawing near*," amounts to "a step backward." At this point, therefore, we have the beginning of a commentary on the events already predicted. This commentary certainly includes vv. 29–31 as well. As I explained earlier, the formula *kai eipen parabolēn autois* (v. 29a) serves to connect, not to separate (Section 3. 1). The very close connection is also shown by the complete structural parallelism between the saying (v. 28), the parable (vv. 29–30), and the explanation of the parable (v. 31).[39]

Protasis	Apodasis
v. 28:	
archomenōn de *toutōn*	anakupsate kai eparate tas
ginesthai	kephalas
	humōn, dioti *eggizei* hē
	apolutrōsis
	humōn.

vv. 29b–30:	
idete tēn sukēn kai panta	
ta dendra	
hotan probalōsin ēdē,	
blepontes	
aph'heautōn	ginōskete hoti *eggus* to
	theros estin

v. 31:	
houtōs kai humeis	
hotan idēte tauta	ginōskete hoti *eggus estin*
ginomena	hē
	basileia tou Theou.

In each case there is first a "protasis" indicating time (*hotan* in vv. 29–30 and 31; a genitive absolute indicating time in v. 28) which describes the occurrence of certain events. In the first case, these are signified by "these things," with the verb *ginomai;* in the second case, by the corresponding moment in the parable, namely, the appearance of the leaves; in the third, which returns to non-parabolic language, they are signified once again by "these things" and the verb *ginomai.* The ascertainment of the events in question by an observer is expressed in the parable by the construction *blepontes aph'heautōn ginōskete hoti,* and in an analogous manner in the explanation: *hotan idēte . . . ginōskete hoti;* in v. 28 this ascertainment is implied.

In each case there is also an "apodasis," which asserts, as a consequence of the observation made, the certainty of a closeness, expressed by *eggizei* or *eggus estin.* That which is close at hand is, first, "your redemption"; second, the corresponding moment in the parable, namely, the coming of summer; third, and explicitly, "the kingdom of God." There can be no doubt that in this context "liberation" and "kingdom of God" refer to the same reality, that is, definitive eschatological salvation, in keeping with the entire biblical tradition, according to which God's reign and definitive human redemption are one and the same.

In saying all this, I do not intend to exclude completely the possibility that v. 28 may *also* have some connection with the preceding verse (25–27) and may serve as a "transition."[40] It has been pointed out that there is an antithesis between the fearful reaction of other human beings (v. 26) and the believers' reaction of relief (v. 28),[41] although the two responses are not formally structured as an antithetical parallelism (the second is an imperative) and are separated from each other by the appearance of the Son of Man (v. 27), which draws attention away from the situation just described. In any case, the important thing is that v. 28 is not disconnected from the parable and reduced to being an appendage of the preceding unit.[42]

This short section (vv. 28–31), then, begins a commentary on the events already foretold ("these things"), in order at last to relate them to the two questions (in v. 7) that were the starting point for the entire discourse. For, in fact, even though the word *sēmeion* is not used, vv. 28–31 are focused on the possibility of passing from observation of one occurrence to the proximity of another; this amounts to saying that the one is a sign of the other.

Next, following a solemn introduction (*Amēn legō humin*), comes a promise, prophetic in tone, of a future fact: "Truly I tell you, this generation will not pass away until all things have taken place" (v. 32). The word *panta,* used as a pronoun, likewise refers to the events already predicted. At the same time, however, both the form and the content of the statement show a transition to the question of "When?" (see v. 7a), a question which the data already provided did not yet make it possible to answer. The coming (*ginomai*) of the events already predicted, a coming that is no longer only partial (v. 28: *archomenōn;* v. 31: *ginomena*) but complete (*panta*), is not to be taken as a condition that must be fulfilled in order to infer some further event; rather it is the object of a special promise. From the viewpoint of form, indeed, the principal statement is cast as a negation: "This generation will not pass away," while the words, "until all things have taken place," are a conditional clause. In reality, however, the entire sentence is a positive statement: Within the time span of the present generation, that is, while the contemporaries of Jesus, or at least some of them, are still alive, all will be accomplished. The two answers, therefore, on the sign (vv. 28–31) and on the time (v. 32), refer in chiastic order to the two questions on the time (v. 7a) and on the sign (v. 7b).

V. 33 ("Heaven and earth will pass away, but my words will not pass away") assert the abiding authority and validity of the promise and of the entire discourse and bring the prophetic part of it to a solemn conclusion.

This is followed in turn by a parenetic conclusion (vv. 34–36). As a matter of fact, from the beginning of the discourse there has been a succession of exhortations dealing with the attitudes to be adopted in face of the various events; now the conclusion of the entire discourse emphasizes the basic attitudes which Christians must cultivate "at all times" as they live in expectation of the Lord: detachment, watchfulness, and prayer.[43]

I may note, from the viewpoint of form, how the structure of the opening question, *Hotan mellē tauta ginesthai* (v. 7b), is repeated in vv. 28–31: *archomenōn de toutōn ginesthai . . . hotan idēte tauta ginomena,* and more clearly still in v. 36 (conclusion of both the parenetic part and the entire discourse), where *tauta panta ta mellonta ginesthai* forms an inclusion with v. 7b. Here *panta* looks back over the entire series of events. Note, too, a certain parallelism with the *panta genētai* at the end of the prophetic section (v. 32).

Outline of the Discourse

Narrative introduction (5–6)
   —opening question: "When?" (7a) and "What sign?" (7b);
   —first immediate reply (*ho de eipen*), of a negative kind, on some
      events still distant from the end (8–9) (see Section 5. 1);
   —more detailed positive explanation (*Tote elegen autois*) (10–36):
   PROPHETIC PART (10–33):
   —series of future events (10–27):
      —disasters and destructive events not immediately prior to the
         end (10–11); these are preceded in turn by persecutions (12–19)
         (see Section 5. 1);
      —the destruction of Jerusalem (20–24a), heralded by its siege
         (20) and followed by "the times of the Gentiles" (24b);
      —cosmic upheavals, followed immediately by the parousia
         (25–27);

—concluding commentary (28–32):
> —on the *sign* (28–31: statement, parable, explanation; see Section 6. 1);
> —on the *time* (32: before the end of the present generation; see Section 6. 2);
—solemn conclusion of the entire prophetic part (33).
PARENETIC PART (34–36).
Narrative conclusion (37–38).

Now that the overall structure has been made clear, I shall look first (Section 5) at the series of events (vv. 8–27) and then (Section 6) at the commentary on them (vv. 28–32).

5. THE SERIES OF EVENTS (VV. 8–27)

5. 1. Problems of Chronological Order

Vv. 8–9 are not restricted to preliminary information of a general kind. V. 9 makes it clear that the reference is to historical incidents that will occur before others. In v. 8 the only thing that is generic is the condemnation of those who pass themselves off as the Christ (*egō eimi*). The second part of the verse, *ho kairos ēggiken,* is false on the lips of such persons only because the claim is premature *at that moment;* the time will come when *eggizein* can be truthfully claimed (vv. 20, 28, 30, 31). Consequently, even though vv. 8–9 are set apart for reasons already given (see Section 3. 2), they already begin the list of events, in chronological order.

On the other hand, the words, "But before all this occurs" (v. 12a), which come at the beginning of the section on persecutions, show that the chronological order of events is being inverted in the order of exposition.[44] It becomes necessary, therefore, to define what is meant by *toutōn pantōn,* that is, to determine *which* events are shifted out of chronological order and *where.* This problem, however, is interlinked with the problem of the interpretation of vv. 10–11. A first interpretation (which I myself prefer) says that the reference is to other historical phenomena that are concomitant with or subsequent to the wars and insurrections already mentioned and that, like the latter, are not to be regarded as signs of an imminent end.[45] Another interpretation, however, claims that the reference is immediately to the signs of the parousia, which are then repeated in vv. 25–27.[46]

This second hypothesis rests on several arguments:
(a) In the apocalyptic literature and, more generally, in the Old Tes-

tament tradition these phenomena are regarded as precursors of the "day of Yahweh."[47]

(b) By adding to Mark 13:8 plagues, dreadful portents, and great signs from heaven Luke accentuates the range of the phenomena and thus makes them more like those listed in vv. 25–27.

(c) While Mark 13:8 used a *gar* to link the phenomena with what preceded, Luke separates them with his *tote elegen autois* (v. 10a).

(d) The phrase "But before all this occurs" (v. 12a) begins a "parenthetical" list of events that must be located at a previous time. If we include in this parenthetical list not only persecutions (vv. 12–19) but also the destruction of Jerusalem (vv. 20–24), then vv. 10–11 have their direct continuation in vv. 25–27.

(e) Luke's omission of Mark's words, *archē ōdinōn tauta* (13:8c), is to be explained by the fact that, in his reinterpretation of them, these events signal not the beginning but the final moment.

It is to be observed that the divergence does not have to do directly with the problem of the expectation of an imminent end, for in the first case there is question of events which are historical (they have probably already taken place) but which are wrongly interpreted as precursors of the parousia; in the second case, the events are historical but will occur only in their proper time in a vague future. In my opinion, however, the arguments are not persuasive.

(a) The traditional view need not be the same as that of the redactor. At the same time, however, a certain continuity with the apocalyptic tradition is preserved even in my hypothesis, since in that tradition the political upheavals and even the appearance of false prophets (vv. 8–9) could be taken as precursors of the end and since Luke, for his part, does not entirely "de-eschatologize" them but says only that they do not *immediately* precede the end (v. 9). On the other hand, the other hypothesis is not very consistent, since in it this traditional eschatological tone is first overlooked completely (vv. 8–9) and then emphasized to such an extent that the events listed become without qualification the signs of an *immediate* parousia (vv. 10–11).

(b) It is natural therefore that there should be some similarity between vv. 10–11 and vv. 25–27. But if the phenomena in question were not unusually threatening they could not have been used by the false prophets. In vv. 10–11 Luke may be increasing the dosage, as it were, in relation to the parallel passage in Mark, in order precisely to make a point: that while these events are frightening, they are not to be interpreted as precursors of the end.[48] However, verbal contacts, in the true and proper sense, are few (*phobētra*, v. 11, and *phobos*, v. 26; *sēmeia* in vv. 11 and 25, although in both places the word may mean simply "prodigies"; see Section 5. 2). Furthermore, there is clearly a distinction between phenomena that occur in particular places, *kata topous* (v. 11), and those described in vv. 25–27 which cause distress to the entire *oikoumenē*. It is one thing to have *sēmeia ap'ouranou* (v. 11), in which the vault of heaven is simply the background against which the phenomena are observable; it is another to have the *sēmeia* of vv. 25–27 which are manifested simultaneously "in the sun, the moon, and the stars" as "the powers of heaven" are "shaken," that is, the cosmic order reels and the primitive chaos seems to be returning.

On the other hand, at least some of the events in vv. 10–11 are the same as those in vv. 8–9, even if the wording is different (v. 9: *polemous kai akatastasias;* v. 10: *egerthēsetai ethnos ep'ethnos kai basileia epi basileian*). This difference is due to a desire to echo a variety of biblical passages (Is 19:2; 2 Chr 15:6). Nothing is said, however, that would allow the hearers to distinguish the conflicts mentioned first, which *are not* signs of an imminent parousia, from those mentioned in the second place, which (according to the hypothesis) must be interpreted as such signs.

The difficulty here is such that some supporters of the hypothesis modify it by having only v. 11 refer to the parousia.[49] But that kind of a division between vv. 10 and 11 is impossible, since the particle *te* closely connects *seismoi . . . kai . . . limoi kai loimoi* (v. 11a) with the political upheavals of v. 10, and then, in its second occurrence, goes on to add *phobētra . . . kai ap'ouranou sēmeia megala* (v. 11b). Furthermore, like wars, the earthquakes and famines already mentioned in Mark and the plagues added by Luke are occurrences which unfortunately are always possible in the course of history and were in fact taking place with special intensity during those very years. The same can be said of *phobētra te kai ap'ouranou sēmeia megala,* which probably refer to such things as comets, meteorites, eclipses, and other occurrences regarded as omens of evil (*Sib.* III, 796–808), as, for example, the birth of malformed animals and so on.[50] It is therefore not possible to argue: events which Luke regards as so important had not yet happened, therefore they are the events signaling the parousia. On the contrary, if the evangelist means occurrences of this kind to be taken as precursors of an immediate parousia, he would be saying that the false prophets were right!

(c) On the function of *Tote elegen autois* (v. 10a), see Section 3. 2.

(d) Since the inversion created by the phrase "But before all this occurs" (v. 12a) means a departure from the guiding thread, which is chronological, the more obvious course would be to make it refer only to what directly follows, namely, the persecutions (vv. 12–19). It must therefore be supposed that as soon as possible, as soon as this theme is finished, the parenthesis closes. The validity of this supposition is confirmed by the sharp break which the temporal-adversative *hotan de* of v. 20 creates in relation not only to what has immediately preceded but to all the events hitherto listed: in the beginning it was an error to say *ēggiken* (vv. 8–9); now, however, *ēggiken hē erēmōsis autēs* (v. 20).

The reason why the evangelist temporarily abandons a chronological order is this: on the one hand, in order to remove the ambiguity found in Mark, where it is not clear whether persecutions come before, during, or after the other things already predicted; on the other, in order not to have to repeat the entire beginning of the discourse, which opened with a warning against false prophets and with a list of the phenomena to which these prophets appealed and among which the persecution of Christians was evidently not included. The simplest thing, therefore, was to speak of the persecution afterward, while pointing out that they would come first.

Furthermore, the persecutions (vv. 12–19) would take place before *all* the other events thus far mentioned; and therefore not only before those of vv. 10–11 but also those of vv. 8–9 (false messiahs, wars and insurrections[51]), whereas the destruction of the city (vv. 20–24), which is the final act of the war, must evidently come after the first skirmishes (vv. 8–9). Consequently, it is impossible to include vv. 12–19 and vv. 20–24 in a single lengthy parenthesis. Those who would identify the events of vv. 10–11 with those of vv. 25–26 must introduce not one but two inversions of the chronological order into Luke's expository order, by locating vv. 12–19 before vv. 8–9 and 10–11, and vv. 20–24 before vv. 10–11 but after vv. 8–9.[52] This necessity increases the complications of the hypothesis to such an extent as to make it extremely unlikely.[53] This difficulty can be ignored only if one reduces vv. 8–9 to "general" preliminaries by overlooking the elements in these verses (elements already pointed out at the beginning of this Section 5. 1) that give them their rightful place in the chronological order.

(e) A much more plausible reason for the omission of Mark's *archē ōdinōn tauta* (Mk 13:8) is that the redactor was no longer able to say that these events marked the *archē,* since persecutions had to come before them (v. 12)![54]

5. 2. General Observations on the First Part (Vv. 8–27)

At this point some partial conclusions may be drawn regarding the opening question (v. 7). Although no explicit reply has thus far been given to it, it is evident at once that the question has not been rejected, by, for example, a reference to the human unknowability of these future events, which are known to God alone (see Mk 13:32; Acts 1:7), and that it has not elicited rebukes or corrections (as in Lk 17:20–21). We must therefore suppose that it has been receiving an answer.[55]

As a matter of fact, the entire discourse sounds like an answer. To the initial interrogative "When?" (*pote*) corresponds a repeated assertive "When" (*hotan*) that is accompanied by directives which are first negative, then positive (vv. 9, 20, 30, 31). The concept of "sign" is also echoed, although not by use of the term *sēmeion* (vv. 20, 28, 30, 31; see Section 6. 1). Only at the beginning does the reply take a negative form (vv. 8–9); the reason, however, is not to reject the question but rather to warn against a mistaken answer; after this point, the tone is predominantly positive. Also worthy of note is the prominence given to the prophetic aspect of the discourse.[56] The discourse receives its initial impulse from an oracle that is completely in the Old Testament style: "The days will come" (v. 6). It then continues with verbs referring throughout to the future. It uses stylistic devices and rhetorical arguments that are characteristic of the language of the prophets (for example, the "Woe" in v. 23), and cites or alludes to the prophets (compare Lk 21:10 with Is 19:2; Lk 21:22 with Hos 9:7 and Jer 5:29; Lk 21:24 with Is 63:18; and so on). It draws toward its end with the solemn statement: "Heaven and earth will pass away, but my words will not pass away" (v. 33), which confirms the orientation of the entire discourse toward the future, while adding certainty about its complete fulfillment. Jesus, then, does not avoid replying; he will in fact reveal more, not less, than he was asked.

Nonetheless, since more than one event is foretold and since explicit references to the opening question are not made in the course of the exposition, it is not easy to say just what the answer is. I can, however, begin by setting aside the events which are not the requested sign; in light of what I have said thus far, these events include everything in vv. 8–19. This leaves vv. 20–24 and 25–27.

In vv. 25–27 the term *sēmeia* is applied to the cosmic upheavals that are followed by the appearance of the Son of Man. But even if we were to leave aside the word "sign" here, the context itself would allow us to describe the events as "signs." The problem is to determine whether they are the sign corresponding to the opening question, that is, to the exclusion of any other of the signs previously listed among historical occurrences. For the moment, let me point out that neither the construction, with its simple *Kai esontai,* nor the word *sēmeia,* used in the plural and without an article, really calls to mind the opening question: *ti to sēmeion hotan mellē tauta ginesthai.* Among other considerations: *sēmeia* here (and in v. 11, if the interpretation already given in Section 5. 1 is justified) could mean simply "prodigies" or "wonders," as it does in so many passages of the New Testament.

In v. 20, on the other hand, even though the word *sēmeion* is not used, the siege of Jerusalem is clearly said to be the event which makes known the imminence of the city's destruction; in fact, therefore, it is a "sign" of this destruction. Since, however, the reference to the *kairoi ethnōn* (v. 24b) shows that this destruction does not coincide with the end of the world, various possibilities are open:

—will another sign be given of the parousia? (those in vv. 25–26?)

—will no sign be given of the parousia?

—will the two events come in such close succession that the one sign holds for both?

For the moment I shall leave these questions unanswered and shall take them up again in the light of vv. 28–31, which provide further elements of a solution.

Meanwhile, up to this point no basis at all has been given for answering the question "When?" I note simply that the distinction between three stages—events still remote from the end (vv. 8–19), events connected with the destruction of Jerusalem (vv. 20–24), and events connected with the parousia (vv. 25–27)—is never presented in terms of distance between the phases[57]: not in the transition from v. 19 to v. 20, nor in that from v. 24 to v. 25, nor even in vv. 8–9, which describe the first events in the entire series, those most remote from the end. The only precision given in vv. 8–9 is: *ouk eutheōs to telos* (v. 9), while the typically apocalyptic terminology (*dei . . . prōton*) suggests that not even these events fall outside the eschatological perspective.

In v. 20a, the temporal and adversative construction with *hotan de* suggests a certain interval: the *eggizein* that had been excluded earlier (v. 8) is now affirmed; the command not to be terrified (v. 9) is replaced by the command to flee in haste (v. 21). But the interval does not imply chronological distance: the siege is evidently in direct historical continuity with the wars that precede.

Nor can I see, between v. 24 and v. 25, the "separation" (German: "scharfer Einschnitt," distinct break) of which Conzelmann speaks[58]; as a matter of fact, the separation is less than the one to be seen in v. 20. Luke suppresses the Markan notation, *alla en ekeinais tais hēmerais meta tēn thlipsin ekeinēn* (Mk 13:24), which is itself vague enough, and replaces it with a simple *kai* (v. 25), which is not a much clearer indication either of proximity or of distance.

The evidence that the end of Jerusalem does not coincide with the end of the world is rather to be inferred from the end of the preceding section with its reference to the *kairoi ethnōn* (v. 24), although the duration of these *kairoi* is not specified. In fact, if we take into account the verb *plēroun* (v. 24) and the traditional theme of "the trampling down of Jerusalem by the Gentiles" (see Zec 12:3 LXX; Dan 8:13; Rv 11:2), which looks upon the profanation of the holy place as a punishment for the sins of the people, we ought to suppose that the *kairoi ethnōn* are of limited duration, being allowed only temporarily by God in his plan of salvation.[59] Even if these mysterious *kairoi* are to be taken as referring to the evangelization of the Gentiles (Acts 1:6–8; Mk 13:10; Rom 11:25), it would be an anachronism to suppose that they must be of long duration. For the geographical horizon of the day was so much narrower than ours that Paul was convinced the gospel had already been preached to the ends of the earth (Rom 10:18; see 15:14–32; 2 Cor 10:16).

All in all, I do not have the impression that the evangelist's primary concern was to postpone the parousia indefinitely; if it were, he could have done it much more clearly. The future events (vv. 8–27) are predicted in such a way as to exclude neither the possibility of a further delay nor the possibility of their imminent occurrence.

6. THE CONCLUDING COMMENTARY (VV. 28–32)

All that has been said shows the importance of the concluding commentary on the sign (vv. 28–31) and on the time (v. 32). Even here, indeed, some obscurity is caused by the use of pronouns which refer to what has already been said but without making the reference precise. On the other hand, there is material here which can shed further light.

6. 1. *Reply Concerning the "Sign." The Meaning of* Tauta

To which events, then, does the pronominal "these things" refer (v. 28: *toutōn;* v. 31: *tauta*) as a sign of the parousia? Since the events of vv. 8–19 have already been excluded by reason of their position (see Section 5), there are only two possibilities: either the tragic occurrences of 70 A.D. (vv. 20–24),[60] or the cosmic upheavals preceding the appearance of the Son of Man[61] (vv. 25–26).[62] In the first hypothesis, there is but a single sign, although it must be added that once the destruction takes place, it can change from a sign foretold by preceding events to an event which in turn foretells subsequent events; it is logical that the destruction, thus viewed, should itself be included in the sign. This first hypothesis is the one usually adopted.[63] In the second hypothesis there would be two distinct signs: one, the siege (v. 20), for the destruction of the city; the other, the cosmic upheavals (vv. 25–26), for the parousia.

The only argument for this second hypothesis is, in the final analysis, an overall interpretation of Lukan eschatology which would dictate that

Luke cannot refer to a sign of the parousia that makes the latter imminent.

Various considerations can be adduced in favor of the first hypothesis, which I adopt.

Some are negative:

(a) There must be at least a short interval between the "sign" asked for and the event itself; for if the sign came into being only at the last moment, so close to the event as to be one with it, in what sense would it be a "sign"? And in fact the clause, "when these things *begin* to take place" (v. 28), suggests some passage of time, some distance between beginning and end. The same can be said for the use of the present participle *ginomena* in v. 31.

On the other hand, there is practically no interval between the cosmic upheavals and the parousia; rather than preceding the parousia, these events accompany it and are part of it. True enough, the text does speak of an expectation which these events rouse in people (v. 26), but this takes only a moment, and is meant to emphasize the terrifying nature of the event (expectation and terror are parallel: *apo phobou kai prosdokias,* v. 26), rather than to point to a succession of moments within the event. The text immediately goes on to say: "And then they will see the Son of Man, etc." (v. 27). It is *while* people are stunned and dumbfounded by the cosmic upheavals and wondering what is happening that the Son of Man appears. But at this point it makes no sense to say simply that he "is near."

(b) If the Lukan Jesus had indicated as the sign only the cosmic upheavals and not any historical signs, he would have revealed nothing new by comparison with the stereotyped Old Testament descriptions of the "day of the Lord" (see Is 13:10; 34:4; Hag 2:6, 21; etc.). But this was certainly not what was intended in the opening question! Such a hypothesis is reducible in substance to the view already refuted, namely, that no reply is given to the opening question (see Section 5. 2).[64]

More positive considerations:

(c) The verbal contact established by "when you see . . . then (you) know . . ." in vv. 31 and 20 confirms the hypothesis that *tauta* refers to all the historical events of vv. 20–24.

(d) This hypothesis explains better why no distinction of two signs is made in the question (v. 7) or in the answer. In the list of events given in the answer the only reference to a sign (though this term is not used) is to the sign for the end of the city (v. 20). The commentary, on the other hand, speaks of signs in reference to the parousia (vv. 28–31). It is difficult to accept that the Jesus of Luke would have limited his reply to the parousia and said nothing regarding the end of the temple, concerning which he has originally been questioned (vv. 5–7); the entire part on the temple cannot be reduced to a "parenthesis." On the other hand, neither would he have given an answer only about the end of the temple, inasmuch as he himself brings up the end of the world. It would also be odd to allow that he replies to both separately, but to one in only a factual and tacit way (v. 20), while saying nothing about it in the commentary which is explicitly devoted to the problem (vv. 28–31). The only explanation can be that the two events have not yet been dissociated but are thought of as following one upon the other, even if there is an undefined delay consisting in "the times of the Gentiles." This explanation is confirmed by the fact that in the reply concerning the "When?" there is again a single question and a single reply.

(e) The words, "Stand up and raise your heads, because your redemption is drawing near" (v. 28), are better explained if understood as directed not in the abstract to those Christians, left unidentified, who will be alive at the moment of the parousia, but concretely to the contemporaries of the evangelist, whom it serves as a forceful exhortation to hope. Such a reference to the experience of the readers provides a better explanation for several points: the use of the second person (Mk 13:27 used the third person); the construction with the imperative rather than with a simple future; the choice of the word "redemption" from among the many that might be used for final salvation; and the image of "raising your heads," which supposes that people have their heads bowed, being overwhelmed by suffering.[65] We should recall that it is said of the persecutions that they will *begin* before the other things (v. 12a), but not if and when they will end (see Section 4).[66]

6. 2. Reply Concerning the "When." The Meaning of Panta (v. 32)

As we saw elsewhere, the expression "this generation" cannot be emptied of its normal chronological meaning.[67] But the other way of excluding imminence, namely, to make *panta* refer only to the historical events in vv. 20–24 but not to the parousia itself,[68] is likewise to be judged unworkable.[69]

It is mistakenly claimed that the omission of *tauta* with *panta* in v. 32 (Mk 13:30 had *tauta panta*) shows the intention of excluding the events most recently mentioned, namely, the parousia (vv. 25–27), and referring only to what preceded, namely, the destruction of the city (vv. 20–24),[70] or, in another intepretation, the intention of not referring specifically to either set of events but only in a comprehensive way to the fulfillment of the divine plan.[71] But how can the parousia be excluded from this fulfillment? It is one thing to say that *panta* without *tauta* may emphasize more the overall picture than events as separate and distinct[72]; it is another to say that it signifies the exclusion of some events. Not only is such an exclusion not demonstrated, but it is even impossible, because it is contrary to the obvious meaning of *panta,* which expresses totality. Therefore, when *panta* is used pronominally as it is here, it implies a reference to the things already said (*tauta* could therefore be omitted as redundant!). I do not see why some of these things should be omitted, least of all those mentioned most recently! If the author wanted to exclude the things last mentioned, he would have had to omit not only *tauta* but *panta* as well. The opposite of "these things" is not "everything," but "those things"! The omission of *tauta* thus proves absolutely nothing. There is no way in which this omission can cancel out the semantic value that is the basis of the word *panta,* and cause the word to express the very opposite, namely, non-totality.

Another hypothesis: *panta* refers not to the events of vv. 20–24 nor to those of vv. 25–27, but to the repeated *tauta* in the immediately preceding verses (vv. 28 and 31), that is, to the signs of the parousia but not to the parousia itself. The word would express totality, not in the abstract but in the concrete, with reference to the things mentioned most recently. This reference is strengthened by the presence of the verb *ginesthai:*

—v. 28a: *archomenōn de toutōn ginesthai*
—v. 31a: *hotan idēte tauta ginomena*
—v. 32b: *heōs an panta genētai*

In addition, there is a chiastic structure:

A: hotan idēte *tauta ginomena* (v. 31a)
    B: ginōskete hoti *eggus estin* hē basileia tou Theou (v. 31b)
                                 (indication of time)
    B': amēn legō humin hoti *ou mē parelthē hē genea hautē*
    (v. 32a)
                                   (indication of time)
A': heōs an *panta genētai* (v. 32b)

In this case, the parousia would no longer be formally included within the time frame given. This does not mean, however, the elimination of an imminent end, for if the signs occur within the time span of a generation, then the event thus signaled must also follow shortly!

In my own opinion, however, it seems more plausible to include in *panta* not only the signs but the event itself, the parousia. I maintain this, first of all, in the light of the broad context provided by the discourse. We may not lose sight of this context, which renders more obvious the reference of *panta* to the entire series of predicted future events, including also and above all the most important of them. In v. 36, which ends the pare-netic section and echoes the end of the prophetic section, we find this same *panta* which looks back and embraces the entire series of occurrences.[73]

The proximate context points in the same direction. The preceding verse contains not only a "protasis" but also an "apodasis": *ginōskete hoti eggus estin hē basileia tou Theou* (v. 31b). It is upon this, the part of the sentence that is closest to v. 32, that the emphasis falls. There is also a chiasmus embracing vv. 31 and 32 (see above), but this should not make us lose sight of the differing functions of the two verses and of the fact that there is a passage from a reply concerning the sign to a reply concerning the time. Strictly speaking, *tauta* in vv. 28–31 already refers to the entire range of predicted events, whereas reference to the sign is made not simply in the *tauta* but in the *tauta ginomena* of v. 31 or the *archomenōn toutōn ginesthai* of v. 28. In order to have a sign it is not necessary that the events which serve as the sign be already completed; it is enough that they have begun. If one wants to say that *panta* in v. 32 picks up this *tauta,* this is acceptable, but with one restriction: it is not possible to carry over into v. 32 the limited reference to the beginning or onset of events. Such a limita-tion was justified when the matter under discussion was the sign; v. 32, however, contains the reply to the question "When?" and this looks at events no longer as in process but as completed.

Finally, it is to be noted that here again we have the same situation as in the problem of the sign: there are not two different questions and two different answers. There is but one question regarding time, and it has to do with the end of the temple (v. 7a). There is likewise but a single answer (v. 32), but at this point, now that the perspective has been broadened to include the end of the world, it can no longer apply only to the end of the temple. Neither, however, can it have to do only with the end of the world, thus leaving unanswered the opening question, which was the only ques-tion explicitly asked. Here again, the only explanation can be that the answer applies to both events.

7. CONCLUSION

I have shown in outline how Luke is consistent in his redaction of the eschatological discourse—once we free ourselves of the presupposition that he locates the parousia in a distant future. There is consistency be-tween, on the one hand, the way in which the future events are foretold (vv. 8–27), these being distinguished but never distanced each from the others (see Section 5. 2), and, on the other, the answers then given more explicitly on the "sign" (vv. 28–31), which is the destruction of Jerusalem (see Section 6. 1), and on the "when" (v. 32), which is expressed in terms of nearness (see Section 6. 2). It is still necessary to see whether this same consistency is to be found in the eschatology of Luke-Acts as a whole,[74] and in those passages in particular that seem to reject any kind of connection between the parousia and specific historical events (Lk 17:20–21; 19:11; Acts 1:6–8). But this problem requires a further study.

" 'Remember' . . . Then They Remembered": Luke 24:6–8

Reflection on the dignity of women in the church is no longer the preserve of those directly concerned or of women and their male collaborators,[1] especially since Vatican II. The Catholic hierarchy also needs to devote serious thought to the subject. Consequently, we may regard as a "sign of the times" John Paul II's *Mulieris dignitatem* (1988), in which he acknowledges the prerogative of women as the "first eyewitnesses of the risen Christ" (no. 16). The document is a meditation offered to the entire church, which gives thanks "for the 'mystery of woman' and for every woman . . . for all the manifestations of the feminine 'genius' which have appeared in the course of history" (no. 31). These are statements and acknowledgments that would have been unthinkable for a pope as recently as a quarter-century ago. Once this meditation and reflection has begun, it is right and desirable that it should continue, until there is no longer "male or female" in the church, but we are "all one in Christ Jesus" (Gal 3:28).

My purpose in these pages is to reflect on Luke 24:6c–8 in the hope of drawing from our common treasure "what is new and what is old" (Mt 13:51).[2]

The Easter traditions that came together in the redactions of the gospels are well known.[3] The verses I am examining here are found exclusively in Luke. They present no problems from the standpoint of textual criticism; the variants are unimportant.[4] The passage is a familiar one, as is its immediate context:

> 24:3　When they [the women] went in [to the tomb], they did not find the body [of the Lord Jesus].

4   While they were perplexed about this, suddenly two men
     in dazzling clothes stood beside them.
5   The women were terrified and bowed their faces to the
     ground, but the men said to them, "Why do you look for
     the living among the dead?
6   He is not here, but has risen. Remember how he told you,
     while he was still in Galilee,
7   that the Son of Man must be handed over to sinners, and
     be crucified, and on the third day rise again."
8   Then they remembered the words,
9   and returning from the tomb, they told all this to the
     eleven and to all the rest. . . .
23   "They [the women] came back and told us that they had
     indeed seen a vision of angels who said that he was alive."

1. " 'REMEMBER HOW HE TOLD YOU'. . . . THEN THEY REMEMBERED. . . ."

The women are urged, even commanded, to call to mind, to keep present, a prophetic message, a revelation of Jesus.

The verb *mimnēskesthai,* "to remember," occurs 255 times in the LXX, where it translates the Hebrew verb *zakar* 175 times (out of 181 occurrences of this verb). In Luke's work (Lk six times; Acts four times) it is always related to God or Jesus:

Lk 1:54: Mary praises the Lord who has helped Israel, being mindful (*mnēsthēnai*) of his mercy.

Lk 1:72: Zechariah prophesied, blessing the Lord God of Israel who has shown mercy to the fathers and been mindful (*mnēsthēnai*) of his holy covenant.

Lk 16:25: In the parable of the rich banqueter and Lazarus the poor man, Abraham urges the rich man to remember (*mnēsthēti*) that he has received good things (*ta agatha*) during his life, while Lazarus has received evil things (*ta kaka*). Received them from whom? According to the biblical mind, from God; see, for example, Job 2:10: "Shall we receive the good (*ha-tôb / ta agatha*) at the hand of God, and not receive the bad (*ha-raᶜ / ta kaka*)?"

Lk 23:42: One of the two criminals crucified with Jesus turns to him and says: "Jesus, remember (*mnēsthēti*) me when you come into your kingdom."

Lk 24:6: The two men-angels said to the women: "Why do you look for the living among the dead? He is not here, but has risen. Remember how he told (*mnēsthēte hōs elalēsen*) you, while he was still in Galilee. . . ."

Lk 24:8: "Then they remembered his words (*emnēsthēsan tōn rhēmatōn autou*)."

Acts 10:31: Cornelius tells Peter that "a man in dazzling clothes" told him his prayer had been heard and his alms had been remembered (*emnēsthēsan*) before God.

Acts 11:16: In Jerusalem Peter reports the entire story of Cornelius and the descent of the Holy Spirit upon the family of this Roman centurion of the Italian cohort; Peter concludes: "And I remembered the word of the Lord, how he said (*emnēsthēn de tou rhēmatos tou Kuriou hōs elegen*): 'John baptized with water, but you will be baptized with the Holy Spirit.' "

This last passage is especially relevant to the present discussion, because it refers to a specific "promise" and its "fulfillment." The promise of Jesus is in fact cited in Acts 1:5: "John baptized with water, but you will be baptized with the Holy Spirit." In the gospel of Luke this promise is placed on the lips of John the Baptist: "I baptize you with water; but one who is more powerful than I is coming. . . . He will baptize you with the Holy Spirit and fire" (Lk 3:16).

Something similar is the case with the one occurrence in Luke of the verb *hupomimnēskein,* which also means "to remember" and is used four times in the LXX, always for the Hebrew *zakar:*

Lk 22:34: "Jesus said, 'I tell you, Peter, the cock will not crow this day, until you have denied three times that you know me.' "

Lk 22:61: "Then Peter remembered the word of the Lord, how he had said to him (*hupemnēsthē . . . tou rhēmatos tou Kuriou hōs eipen*), 'Before the cock crows today, you will deny me three times.' "

We should note that the words of Jesus the Lord which are to be remembered (Lk 22:61; 24:6; Acts 11:16) or which caused the hearts of the disciples at Emmaus to burn within them "while he was talking (*hōs elalei*) to us on the road, while he was opening the scriptures to us" (Lk 24:32), are introduced by a "citational" *hōs*, just as are texts from the Old Testament scriptures: "As it is written in the book of the words of the prophet Isaiah" (Lk 3:4); "As Moses says . . . ," followed by a citation of Exodus (Lk 3:15; 20:37); "As also it is written in the second psalm" (Acts 13:33; Ps 2:7).[5]

2. "HOW HE TOLD YOU, WHILE HE WAS STILL IN GALILEE"

The two men-angels say that during his stay in Galilee Jesus had revealed his suffering and resurrection to the women.

This "you" (*humin*) must not be allowed to pass unnoticed, especially since without it the words of the angels would still have meaning. On the other hand, Luke knows full well that nowhere in his gospel is there a prediction of the death and resurrection of Jesus that is addressed expressly to the women. We must therefore look for correspondences of wording and content to Luke 24:7 among the combined predictions of the passion and the resurrection and try to determine which of these are placed by the redactor in Galilee.

If I am not mistaken, the third gospel has, before the event, six explicit predictions of the passion-resurrection (Lk 9:22; 9:44–45; 13:32–33; 17:25; 18:31–34; 22:15–38) and four allusions to it (5:35; 9:31; 11:30; 14:27); after the event, it has four "remembrances of the prediction's fulfillment" (Lk 24:6–8, 20–21, 26, 45–46). The latter are all uttered in Jerusalem or its environs. The repeated prediction in Lk 22:15–38 is uttered in the upper room in Jerusalem.

Here are some observations that will help decide whether the other predictions, especially the one in Lk 18:31–34, were uttered in Galilee.

(a) The word Judea (which occurs ten times) does not appear between 7:17 and 21:21.

(b) Luke omits the name of the village of Martha and Mary (10:38). Only from John do we learn that the place was Bethany in Judea (Jn 12:1).

(c) Jerusalem is always in the background as the goal of the journey (9:31, 51, 53; 10:30 [parable]; 13:4 [reference to a calamity that occurred there]; 13:22; 17:11; 18:31), as the place to which Jesus draws near (19:11) and to which he continues to go up (19:28). Luke ends the geographical "ascent" of Jesus to Jerusalem by telling us, not that he entered the city, but that he entered the temple (19:45).

Jesus goes up to Jerusalem either from Galilee as a twelve year old (2:42) or from Judea (19:28).

(d) The saying of Jesus: "Jerusalem, Jerusalem, the city that kills the prophets and stones those who are sent to it!" along with the rest of the citation (Lk 13:34–35), is placed by Luke in a Galilean setting (compare Mt 23:37–39): "At that very hour some Pharisees came and said to him, 'Get away from here, for Herod wants to kill you' " (Lk 13:31). According to Luke, Herod had jurisdiction only in Galilee (Lk 3:1; 23:6–7). But Jesus does not leave Galilee. The sabbath meal in the house of a leader of the Pharisees certainly does not take place in Samaria (Lk 14:1–25).

(e) The observation that as Jesus advanced toward Jerusalem "he traveled through Samaria and Galilee" (17:11, *NAB*) is odd from a geographical viewpoint. It may mean that the predictions in 17:25 and 18:31–34 were located by the redactor in Galilee, which is named in second place. On the other hand, at the beginning of his journey to Jerusalem, Jesus enters a village of the Samaritans (9:52); later on, however, as I noted above, he is in Galilee (13:31). Luke's more or less accurate knowledge of the geography of the "land of Israel" (Mt 2:20, 21) is minimal here.

(f) The formal entrance of Jesus into Judea, though the latter is not named, takes place when he enters the city of Jericho (19:1), which he has been approaching (18:35).

(g) "As he approached Jericho" (*en tō eggizein auton eis Ierichō*) is not necessarily connected in time or space with 18:31: "See, we are going up to Jerusalem." We saw something similar in a passage cited above: "As he continued his journey to Jerusalem (*kai egeneto en tō poreuesthai*), he traveled through Samaria and Galilee" (17:11, *NAB*).

A conclusion may be drawn: all these redactional pointers suggest that, except for Lk 22:15–37, the predictions of Jesus' suffering and the allusions to it are located in Galilee.

3. "THE SON OF MAN MUST BE . . ."

Not all the predictions of the passion are followed by predictions of the resurrection, but only some of them, which I shall now look at more closely.

Lk 9:22: The disciples (*hoi mathētai*) are the recipients of the prediction. To the question of Jesus: "But who do you say that I am?" Peter answers: "The Messiah of God" (vv. 18, 20). The prediction follows: "The Son of Man must undergo great suffering (*hoti dei . . . polla pathein*), and be rejected by the elders, chief priests, and scribes, and be killed, and on the third day be raised (*kai apoktanthēnai kai tē tritē hēmera egerthēnai*)."[6]

Lk 13:31–33: To some Pharisees who warn Jesus that Herod wants to kill him (*se apokteinai*), Jesus replies: "Go and tell that fox for me, Listen, I am casting out demons and performing cures today and tomorrow, and on the third (day) I finish my work (*kai tē tritē* [var. + *hēmera*] *teleioumai*). . . . It is impossible for a prophet to be killed outside of Jerusalem."

Lk 18:31–34: The addressees are the twelve: " 'Everything that is written about the Son of Man by the prophets will be accomplished (*telesthēsetai*). For he will be handed over (*paradothēsetai*) to the Gentiles, and he will be mocked and insulted and spat upon. After they have flogged him, they will kill him (*kai mastigōsantes apoktenousin auton*), and on the third day he will rise again (*kai tē hēmera tē tritē anastēsetai*).'[7] But what he said (*to rhēma touto*) was hidden from them."

During the transfiguration, Moses and Elijah allude to the passion, death, and resurrection[8]: "Moses and Elijah [were] talking to him (*sunelaloun autō*). They . . . were speaking of his departure, which he was about to accomplish (*plēroun*) in Jerusalem" (Lk 9:30–31).

Luke's reference to Jonah: "Just as Jonah became a sign to the people of Nineveh, so the Son of Man will be to this generation" (Lk 11:29–32), lacks the explicitness found in Matthew: "Just as Jonah was three days and three nights in the belly of the sea monster, so for three days and three nights the Son of Man will be in the heart of the earth" (Mt 12:40).

The other predictions of the passion, including the final one in Luke 22, are not accompanied by predictions of the resurrection.

Lk 9:44–45: The addressees are the disciples, whom Jesus urges: " 'Let these words sink into your ears: The Son of Man is going to be betrayed into human hands (*mellei paradidosthai eis cheiras anthrōpōn*).' But they did not understand this saying (*to rhēma touto*). . . . And they were afraid to ask him about this saying (*peri tou rhēmatos toutou*)."

Lk 17:25: The addressees are the disciples, to whom Jesus says: "But first he [the Son of Man, vv. 22, 24] must endure much suffering (*polla pathein*) and be rejected by this generation."

Lk 22: Jesus speaks to the disciples/apostles (vv. 11, 14); the verb "suffer" is used again (*pro tou me pathein*) (v. 15); the scriptures must be fulfilled (*dei telesthēnai*) (v. 37); he must be handed over (*paradidonai*) (vv. 21, 22, 48).

Jesus also alludes to his death when he says: "The days will come when the bridegroom will be taken away from" the disciples, who will then fast (Lk 5:35). In like manner, his statement: "Whoever does not carry the cross and follow me cannot be my disciple" (Lk 14:27) is first and foremost an allusion to his death.

An examination of all these passages shows that only two contain explicit predictions by Jesus of both his death and his resurrection: Lk 9:22 and 18:31–34.

In "remembrances of the event" certain words of the predictions are repeated exactly:

Lk 24:7: The men-angels say to them (*pros autas:* the women): " 'Remember how he told you, while he was still (*elalēsen humin eti ōn*) in Galilee, that the Son of Man must be handed over to sinners (*dei paradothēnai eis cheiras anthrōpōn hamartōlōn*), and be crucified, and on the third day rise again (*kai tē tritē hēmera anastēnai*).' Then they remembered his words (*ton rhēmatōn autou*)."

Lk 24:20–21: The two disciples tell Jesus what has happened in Jerusalem: the chief priests and leaders handed Jesus over (*paredōkan*) to be condemned to death, and they crucified him. "It is now the third day (*tritēn tautēn hēmeran agei*) since these things took place."

Lk 24:26: Jesus replies to the two disciples: "Was it not necessary that the Messiah should suffer these things (*edei pathein*) and then enter into his glory?"

Lk 24:45–46: Jesus says to the twelve and the others with them (v. 33c): "These are my words that I spoke to you while I was still with you (*elalēsa pros humas eti ōn sun humin*)—that everything written about me ... must be fulfilled (*dei plērōthē nai*). ... Thus it is written that the Messiah is to suffer (*pathein ton Christon*) and to rise from the dead on the third day (*kai anastēnai ... tē tritē hēmera*)."

4. LITERARY CORRESPONDENCES

Some comments can now be made on the passages listed above.

Luke 24:6c–8 has a number of elements in common with other passages of the same gospel:

remember			
Jesus *said* (*lalein*)	with		24:32, 44
while still (*eti ōn*)	with		24:44
in *Galilee*			
the *Son of Man*	with 9:22, 44; 17:24–25; 18:31		
must (*dei, edei*)	with 9:22; 17:25;		22:37; 24:26, 44
be handed over	with 9:44;	18:32; 22:22	
into the hands of (men)	with 9:44		
(who are) *sinners*			
be crucified		(aorist active 24:20)	
on the third day	with 9:22; 13:32 (partly); 18:32;		24:46
rise (*anistanai*)	with (9:22 as variant);	18:33;	24:46
word (*rhēma*)	with 9:45 (bis)	18:34	

This table already tells us a good deal, because it shows five literary correspondences of Lk 24:6c-8 with Lk 18:31–34 (as well as 24:44–46!), and three (plus one variant) with Lk 9:22, that is, with the two explicit predictions which Jesus made of his death and resurrection before entering Jerusalem. These statistics, along with the small pointers listed earlier (in Section 2), are a further indication that the redactor is locating Lk 18:31–34 "in Galilee."

There are some other points to be made regarding Luke's terminology.

When the word "must" is missing, we find its equivalent, the "fulfillment of the scriptures," using the Greek verb *plēroun* = accomplish, fulfill (Lk 9:31; [22:22]; 24:44: *dei* + *plēr.*) or the Greek verb *telein* = end, bring to term (18:31; 22:37: *dei* + *tel.*).

The "sinners" (Lk 24:7) to whom Jesus had to be handed over are, in brief, the three groups named in 9:22—elders, chief priests, and scribes—together with the "Gentiles" of 18:32, as can also be seen in other passages of Luke, for example, during the trial before Pilate (23:13, 18, 24). The verb "to crucify" (*stauroun*) is used only from Luke 23:13 on.

The verb "to speak," *lalein,* is especially interesting in Luke. More than that, it is a privileged verb, even if not the only one, for self-expression in the sense of revelation or inspiration. Note the two passages in which it occurs along with the verb *mimnēskesthai* (see Section 1, above): God has been mindful of his mercy "as he said/promised to our ancestors, *kathōs elalēsen*" (Lk 1:55); "as he said/promised through the mouth of his holy prophets. . . . He has shown the mercy promised to our ancestors, and has remembered his holy covenant" (Lk 1:70, 72).

Moses and Elijah, who "*were speaking together* [with Jesus] about his departure, which he was about to *accomplish* in Jerusalem," represent the prophets—scriptures (Moses—prophets—psalms, even though Elijah was not a "writing" prophet) who/which revealed him.[9]

The speech of Jesus[10] too is revelation and must be kept in mind (Lk 24:6c).

5. CONCLUSIONS

Luke 24:6c-8 has been composed in such a way that we need only substitute "I told (you)," *elalēs-a,* for "he told (you)," *elalēs-en,* and we will have a discourse of Jesus in the first person. We may regard the two men-angels in dazzling clothes (24:4) as two messengers of the risen Jesus who possess, as it were, his characteristics.[11]

Jesus has always had:

—someone to announce him: the angel Gabriel sent from God to Mary (Lk 1:26–38); the angel of the Lord sent to the shepherds (2:9–12);

—someone to prepare the way for him: John the Baptist (Lk 1:17, 76; 3:4, 16), a prophet (1:76; 7:26; 20:6) "about whom it is written, 'See, I am sending my messenger ahead of you . . .' " (7:27) and who "before his [Jesus'] coming (*pro prosōpou tēs eisodou autou*) had already proclaimed a baptism of repentance to all the people of Israel" (Acts 13:24);

—two prophets, Moses (Acts 3:22) and Elijah (Lk 4:27), who are at his side at the transfiguration (9:30–32).[12]

—At the beginning of his geographical and theological "journey" to Jerusalem, it was Jesus who "sent messengers ahead of him (lit.: before his face), *apesteilen aggelous pro prosōpou autou,*" which seems to mean James and John (Lk 9:52, 54).

—What more solemn moment than the resurrection could there be to justify having two heralds go before him to proclaim that he is living (24:5) and having two other "men in white robes" come after him at the end of his "journey" (Acts 1:10–11)?[13]

The two messengers in Luke 24 bid the women remember the prophecy of death and resurrection which Jesus had uttered to them in Galilee. The literary correspondences remind us of the predictions made to the twelve[14] in particular and to the disciples generally (Lk 18:31–34; 9:22). In Luke's view, then, the women belonged to both groups.

In chapter 8 Luke tells us that Jesus was passing through cities and villages proclaiming and bringing the good news of the kingdom of God, and "the twelve were with him, as well as some women who had been cured" (Lk 8:1–2).[15] Why does Luke not make the same notation in chapter 18? *Before* the resurrection, the women did not count; this was due to the mindset of the time, which is clearly brought out by Matthew at the end of both multiplications of the loaves and fishes: "Those who ate were about five thousand men, besides women and children (*paidiōn*)" (Mt 14:21; 15:38: four thousand men, besides women and children).[16] *After* the resurrection, the women belong with those who count, namely, the men, and form but a single group with them.

The women were devoted followers and disciples; they "had followed him (*hai sunakolouthousai* [present participle] *autō*) from (*apo*) Galilee" (Lk 23:49); "the women followers [in the literal sense] (*katakolouthēsasai* [aorist participle]) who had come along with [him] (*ēsan sunelēluthuiai* [perfect participle]) from (*ek*) Galilee . . ." (Lk 23:55). These women are therefore among those of whom Acts is speaking when it says: "For many days he [Jesus] appeared to those who came up with him (*tois sunabasin autō*) from (*apo*) Galilee to Jerusalem" (Acts 13:31). The women are also, therefore, among those who "were eyewitnesses" (Lk 1:2). They are part of the group described as "the eleven and all the rest," a group further described in the next verse as "the apostles": "some women of our group (*ex hēmōn*[17]) astounded us: (compare Lk 24:9–10 with 24:22). Consequently, they are with the group of "the eleven and their companions" at the moment of the return of the two disciples from Emmaus and therefore at the moment of the solemn return of the risen Lord to the midst of his church: he "stood among them" (Lk 24:33, 36). The same is true of the time when the group is awaiting baptism "with the Holy Spirit" (Acts 1:5, 14).[18] All these facts suggest that the women were also present at the Lukan passover supper (22:14).[19]

In the eyes of believers, the risen Lord, the Kyrios, is the authoritative interpreter of Moses, the prophets, and the psalms (Lk 24:27, 45). He creates a new tradition that has been transmitted to us in the New Testament writings, in which the women,[20] just like the twelve, are the recipients of the revelation regarding the death and resurrection of Jesus the Lord. They must keep this revelation in mind: their witness is henceforth a duty and a right[21]; above all, however, it is one of the many gifts which the risen Lord bestows on women.

"In the last days it will be, God declares, that I will pour out my Spirit upon all flesh . . . even upon my slaves, both men and women . . . and they shall prophesy" (Acts 2:17–18).

Luke 24:47: Jerusalem and the Beginning of the Preaching to the Pagans in the Acts of the Apostles

In his book on the problem of Lukan theology Father Rasco did not fail to criticize the well-known tripartite division of the history of salvation, which, according to Conzelmann, is peculiar to the work of Luke. In addition, while rightly stressing that the time of Jesus and the time of the church are unified under the sign of the fulfillment of the promise, Father Rasco raised questions about the division into "geographical stages" which Conzelmann finds in Luke-Acts; he thus called for a rethinking of the role of Jerusalem in the work of Luke.[1] He certainly did not deny "the importance of Jerusalem in Luke's work or its privileged situation at the end of the gospel and the beginning of Acts," that is, the fact that it is at once a geographical place and a theological place; but he did urge his readers to remember that the city "is not the goal and boundary either of Jesus himself (see Acts 1:10–11; 2:33) or of the evangelizing activity of the apostles."[2]

My purpose in this essay is to contribute to a more precise definition of the role of Jerusalem in Luke's work, and in particular in the first chapters of Acts, in light of the words with which the risen Lord ends his instructions to his disciples in Luke 24. Following the direction taken by Father Rasco, I want to bring out the profound unity which the history of salvation has for Luke, who makes of Jerusalem not the Judaic stage in the time of the church but simply an exemplary period in the story of a proclamation that was open to all peoples from the very outset.

I

Conzelmann's views on this point are well known. The time of the church is divided, he says, into two distinct periods. Acts 15 marks the

transition from the "primitive Church" to " 'today's' Church,"[3] from the
church of the beginnings, which was still tied to the law, to the church of
the Gentiles, which was free of the law. Jerusalem is a connecting link
between the history of Jesus and the history of the church,[4] but it is also
the link that ensures salvation-historical continuity between Israel and the
church. The initial period of the church in Jerusalem, which is construed
as parallel to the initial activity of Jesus in Galilee, is a unique period,
since it is the period of living eyewitnesses; in its relationship to the law it
cannot be made normative for the present, but it is indeed the historical
foundation of the situation of the later church.[5] The description of the life
of the newborn church does not offer a timeless ideal as a model for the
church of the Gentiles.[6]

But is it in fact true that the beginnings of the church in Jerusalem
display a Jewish character? Do the first chapters of Acts really show us a
community that has nothing to say to the church of later times, since its
function was to be a point of transition between close ties to Israel and the
establishment of a universal church? In the instructions which Jesus gives
his disciples in the final lines of Luke's gospel there is a statement that
seems to provide a basis for a negative answer to these questions. Jerusalem is there seen as an essential element in the scriptures which the risen
Lord says have been fulfilled in him. After referring to the recent events of
his suffering and resurrection, Jesus speaks of the message of salvation
being proclaimed to all nations, with Jerusalem as the starting point:

> Then he said to them, "These are my words that I spoke to you
> while I was still with you—that everything written about me in
> the law of Moses, the prophets, and the psalms must be ful-
> filled." Then he opened their minds to understand the scrip-
> tures, and he said to them, "Thus it is written, that the Messiah is
> to suffer and to rise from the dead on the third day, and that
> repentance and forgiveness of sins is to be proclaimed in his
> name to all nations, beginning from Jerusalem. You are wit-
> nesses of these things. And see, I am sending you what my Fa-
> ther promised; so stay here in the city until you have been
> clothed with power from on high" (Lk 24:44–49).

How is the expression *arxamenoi apo Ierousalēm* (v. 47b) to be understood in light of the context and in the perspective of the role played by
Jerusalem in the first part of Acts? A quick survey of the most recent
commentaries on the gospel of Luke shows general agreement: these
words refer to the fact that the Christian mission was to have its begin-

nings in Jerusalem: "The preaching of repentance was to begin in Jerusalem at Pentecost," to quote Schneider.[7] Consequently there is a
widespread conviction that the words of Jesus underscore the geograph-
ico-theological role of the city as the goal of the missionary journeys of
Jesus (Lk 23:5) and as now "the starting point, whence the 'word' will
spread to the ends of the earth."[8]

Difficulties arise, however, when it comes to determining which Old
Testament texts can serve as the scriptural basis for beginning this preaching in Jerusalem. Those who cite such passages as Isaiah 2:2f, Micah 4:1f,
and Zechariah 8:20–23 cannot ignore the fact that these texts speak of a
gathering of the peoples in the holy city and not of a spread of the message
starting from there.[9] As a result, "beginning from Jerusalem" is interpreted as meaning "beginning from the Jews": "The Christian mission
was to commence in Jerusalem and possibly with the Jews themselves"[10];
"Israel retains its birthright."[11]

In the end this kind of interpretation seems to forget that the expression *arxamenoi apo Ierousalēm* has a quite specific referent. The action
that is to begin in the city is not the preaching of the message to Israel nor
even a preaching in general, which would be realized in successive periods
and involve turning first to Israel and then to all the other nations. The
reference is very specifically to preaching *eis panta ta ethnē*. The importance of this precise specification is often missed even in studies devoted
to the final chapter of Luke. Some completely overlook the problems
raised by the phrase "beginning from Jerusalem."[12] Others see in it only a
heralding of Acts 1:8.[13] Still others, while adverting to the idea of "beginning," see the city only as the place "where the proclamation of the gospel
to all parts of the world will have its point of departure,"[14] even though,
because Jerusalem occupies so central a place in the life and vocation of
the Jewish people, they endeavor to identify the scriptural basis for its role
in the spread of the gospel.[15]

A more precise answer can be expected from studies which endeavor
to bring out the meaning of Luke 24:47 in its context and in the framework of Lukan theology.[16] These studies make clear, first of all, the connection between the divine plan, proclaimed beforehand by the prophets
and entrusted to Christ, and the preaching of salvation to the pagans.
Thanks above all to the contribution made by Dupont's studies, the combination of Luke 24:47 with Acts 1:8 and 13:46–47, as seen also in the
light of such texts as Acts 26:23 and 28:28, brings out the full scope of a
plan which Christ himself carries out and which reaches its fulfillment
through his witnesses, precisely in the proclamation to the nations. Isaiah
49:6, which is cited in Acts 13:47, shows how the expression *heōs eschatou*

tēs gēs is understood as referring to the "pagan nations"; at the same time, it serves as an Old Testament reference for Luke 24:47, which takes over the term *ethnē* from it.[17]

The fact remains, however, that while the passage from Second Isaiah speaks indeed of proclaiming salvation to the pagan nations, it makes no mention of the role which Jerusalem plays in this proclamation, whereas the other prophetic texts mentioned above present a centripetal vision of the function of Jerusalem in relation to the pagans that contrasts with the idea of an extension beyond the city, such as lies behind Luke 24:47 and the whole of Lukan theology.

What, then, is the role of Jerusalem in this thrust of the gospel toward the world? It does not seem accurate to say that Luke 24:47–48 expresses the idea of "the mission having Jerusalem as its point of departure."[18] As Burchard has correctly explained,[19] the preposition *apo* is to be understood rather in an inclusive sense: "beginning in Jerusalem." And in fact it is in this city which is the center of the history of salvation that the activity of proclamation begins. Jerusalem is indeed the center and point of departure for the mission to the entire world,[20] and the base from which the mission spreads[21]; above all, however, it is the place in which the message of salvation is proclaimed for the first time by the witnesses of the risen Lord. There is a clear parallelism between "beginning from Jerusalem" in Luke 24:47 and "beginning from Galilee" in Acts 10:37, just as there is a connection with the other passages that mention the beginning of the public ministry of Jesus (see Lk 1:2; 23:5; Acts 1:1, 22). But the parallelism is one in which, as Samain has shown, the *archē* of the mission of the church is subordinated to the *archē* of the mission of Jesus and is an effect of the latter.[22] Just as, after the descent of the Spirit upon him, Jesus proclaims the gospel message for the first time at Nazareth in Galilee, so, after the coming of the Spirit at Pentecost, the same gospel is proclaimed for the first time by the mouth of the apostles. And since the addressees of the preaching in Jerusalem are Jews—both on the day of Pentecost and in the ensuing period, which is described in the first chapters of Acts—it is not surprising that scholars generally should tend to see in the expression "beginning from Jerusalem" a variant of the expression "first to you [= Jews]" in Acts 13:46 (see also Acts 18:6; 28:28).[23]

In this view, then, Luke 24:47b announces that the mission to the pagans is to be preceded by a period in which preaching is directed to the Jews: Jerusalem and the nations represent respectively the point of departure and the point of arrival of the witness[24]; the turn to the pagan world occurs in the discourse of Stephen[25] or with the conversion of Cornelius.[26]

But how is it possible, then, to justify beginning the fulfillment of the promise and duty of proclaiming forgiveness to the pagan nations with a preaching directed to the Jewish world? The answer given first of all is that we are dealing here with a fact: as Wilckens says of this verse, the mission "begins in Jerusalem and *then* turns to the pagans."[27] But an appeal is also made to the priority of the call to Israel, which is confirmed by the words of the risen Lord[28]: these tell in advance of a mission that looks in the first place to the "harvest of Israel," the Israel represented by Jerusalem.[29] In Jervell's view, then, when the missionaries address themselves to Israel they are already beginning their mission to the pagans, since the latter attain salvation only through Israel, to which they are added.[30] But there are also those who see this beginning in Jerusalem as prefiguring the rejection of the gospel by the city of the Jews, the rejection that will cause the missionaries to turn to the Gentiles; thus the message which is not heard by the city that kills the prophets is already, but in a negative way, the first step on the road of evangelization of the pagans.[31] And, finally, some scholars emphasize the ecclesial dimension in the role of Jerusalem: the apostles carry out their task of preaching in the city for the Jews; only inchoatively and indirectly do they fulfill the universal destination of the proclamation; it is for the story and God himself to fulfill the promise, but always in connection with Jerusalem.[32]

II

The uncertainties just described and the unsatisfactoriness of the solutions offered urge a reconsideration of the problem. This is what I shall attempt, but limiting myself to the meaning to be given to the expression *arxamenoi apo Ierousalēm.*[33]

Let me begin by clearing away the questions raised by textual criticism of Luke 24:47. The form *arxamenoi,* attested by א B C* L X 33 1230 1253 cop[sa,bo] arm eth geo,[2] is a solecism, the participle being in the nominative case instead of an oblique case, in keeping with a pleonastic use of the participle itself with the meaning "to start from."[34] The difficulty of the reading explains the several variants found in the textual tradition, all of them inspired by an attempt to get around the absence of any grammatical agreement by shifting to absolute constructions of the participle.[35] The "hanging nominative" is to be kept as being the form that best explains the rise of the others.[36] In any case, the textual variants do not seem to affect the overall meaning of the text as regards the connection established between this beginning in Jerusalem and its object, namely, the preaching of conversion to all the nations. The only significant difference that might exist is between the singular and plural forms of the participle: the plural (*arxamenoi*) may be meant to draw attention to the doers of the actions as well as to the action itself.[37]

There are those, however, who try to get around the textual problem by giving a different reading of the text. They place a full stop after the words *eis panta ta ethnē* and make *arxamenoi apo Ierousalēm* the beginning of the next statement, *humeis martures toutōn* (Lk 24:48).[38] The syntactical difficulty remains, however,[39] nor is the case an isolated one, since there are analogous constructions in Luke 23:5; 24:27; Acts 1:22; 10:37, as Dupont has conveniently reminded us.[40]

In any case, the problem cannot be looked at solely from a linguistic standpoint. In reality, to link the idea of "beginning" in Jerusalem with the duty of bearing witness, of which v. 48 speaks, is to introduce a change of perspective into the words of the risen Lord, a change that would mean a redefinition of the problem I am discussing here.

It is indeed true that, even if the beginning in Jerusalem be taken as referring to the role of witness with which the disciples are invested in v. 48, the *toutōn* which sums up the object of the testimony includes all the promises in vv. 46–47: the passion and resurrection of Christ, and the preaching of conversion to the pagans in his name. It can therefore be said that either directly, in the generally accepted form of the text, or indirectly, when v. 47b is connected with v. 48, the text undeniably retains the connection established between beginning in Jerusalem and preaching conversion for the forgiveness of sins to all the nations. One may not, however, underestimate the substantial diversity between the two formulations. For if *arxamenoi apo Ierousalēm* is connected with *humeis martures toutōn,* the "beginning from Jerusalem" becomes a characteristic of the action of witnessing which the disciples are to carry out in relation to the messianic prophecies fulfilled in Jesus, even if their witness to the third of these prophecies can be completed only by the act of preaching to the pagans. The passage would then become a further confirmation of a point which Dupont has rightly been making for some time now: in his view, there is a unity in the carrying out of the missionary plan, with Paul replacing the apostles in bringing the mission into its definitive stage,[41] or, as Benéitez has expressed it more recently, there is continuity between the carrying out of the mandate by the apostles in relation to Jerusalem and the Jews, and its completion, in the ensuing story, relative to the pagans, after the beginning made by Peter.[42]

No less significant is the fact that to connect v. 47b with v. 48 is to remove the "beginning from Jerusalem" from inclusion in the *houtōs gegraptai* of v. 46. This eliminates the difficult problem of identifying the

Old Testament texts which Luke has in mind when he says that the preaching to the pagans begins from Jerusalem.

But the two results thus obtained by connecting Luke 24:47b with the next verse must not be allowed to mislead us. True enough, the linking of v. 47b and v. 48 would not yield anything inconsistent with Lukan thought; for this reason the hypothesis cannot be rejected in principle, even though it does not resolve the syntactical problems of the text. But good exegesis does not proceed by making the text easier and eliminating the problems which the text raises. As a matter of fact, if the reference to Jerusalem is removed as an element in the fulfillment of the Old Testament prophecies, the result will be to lessen the inherent importance which "beginning in Jerusalem" has in the work of Luke.[43] If the "beginning from Jerusalem" is made a characteristic of the witnessing assigned to the disciples and not of the act of preaching to the pagans, then we confirm a sure aspect of the Lukan theology of mission, but we exclude a priori the possibility of investigating a new perspective, one that is not an alternative to the other but its complement.

It is along the latter lines that I wish to study the scope and meaning of the expression *arxamenoi apo Ierousalēm,* that is, while keeping its enigmatic connection—therefore a connection that is likely to turn up some new content—to *kēruchthēnai epi tō onomati autou metanoian eis aphesin hamartiōn eis panta ta ethnē.*

I must immediately add at this point that I shall not overemphasize the parallelism between Luke 24:47b and Acts 1:8, lest I run the risk of completely identifying the two meanings, wholly to the advantage of the second, the function of which in relation to the Book of Acts is more explicit. I certainly do not want to deny the connection that exists generally between the end of the gospel and the beginning of Acts and in particular between Luke 24:46–48 and Acts 1:8, and therefore the advantage of having the two texts shed light each on the other.[44] I want only to guard against the tendency simply to assimilate the two passages and consequently to conclude that if, as is obviously the case, Acts 1:8 proposes a detailed program for the various stages of witnessing (Jerusalem, Judea, Samaria, and "the ends of the earth"), then Luke 24:47 also informs us about the development of stages of the mission, even if in a more condensed form: Jerusalem and the nations.[45]

It seems to me that in fact the difficulty in understanding the meaning of "beginning from Jerusalem" is due precisely to this unjustified presupposition, namely, that, like Acts 1:8, Luke 24:47 gives information about the course of missionary activity, the difference being that our text speaks of preaching, while Acts 1:8 speaks of witnessing. This presupposition in turn implies another: that Luke is a writer who likes to repeat the same idea in different ways. Such a claim is at least imprudent when one considers the skill with which our author is able to interweave summarizing descriptions and archetypal incidents while carrying the story forward, and adroitly to vary and advance the content while seeming only to repeat the same forms.[46] If, then, the claim is to be made that Luke 24:47 says something about the successive stages in the development of the mission, this must be verified by an analysis of the text and cannot be the point of departure for such an analysis.

To this negative warning I now add a positive reflection on the use of *archein* in Luke-Acts. The first point that becomes clear is that *archein* never expresses an action different from that of the verb with which it is linked. This is evident from the mainly pleonastic use of the phrase "begin to": Luke 3:8; 4:21; 5:21; etc.; Acts 1:1; 2:4; 11:4, 15; etc.[47] But the formula "begin from" (Lk 23:5; 24:27, 47; Acts 1:22; 8:35; 10:37) likewise never separates two actions; rather it serves to emphasize the initial moment of the one action. In Luke 23:5, for example, that which is done in Galilee is nothing else but the same teaching that then extends throughout the whole of Judea; or, again, in Luke 24:27, the action in question is the interpretation of all the scriptures in relation to Jesus, and Moses and the prophets are simply parts of these scriptures. Use of the construction *archein apo* does not distinguish two actions but expresses the extent of one action or, in general, some modality of the action at its beginning. Therefore, in Luke 24:47b, too, that which is said to begin in Jerusalem is the action mentioned in v. 47a, namely, the preaching of conversion to all nations, and not some other preaching, for example, a preaching addressed to Jews.

Samain attempts to turn to his advantage the difficulty represented by the point I have just made, and to assimilate *arxamenoi apo Ierousalēm* to the formula *arxamenos apo . . . heōs* + the genitive that is found in Luke 23:5 and Acts 1:22. In these two passages it is clear that the words which follow *apo* and *heōs* refer to two different phases of one and the same action: its beginning and its end respectively. In Luke 24:47, Samain says, the words *eis panta ta ethnē* refer to the final stage in the journey; this is better expressed in codex D, which reads *hōs epi panta ethnōn,* a variant which might therefore be regarded as in some degree reliable.[48] In this interpretation, Luke is not speaking of the preaching of conversion to the nations but of the preaching of conversion as such; within this he distinguishes an initial phase in Jerusalem and a final phase among all the nations. We now have a solid foundation for the interpretation of Luke 24:47 that sees in this verse a division of the preaching of salvation into two basic periods: preaching to the Jews and preaching to the pagans.

But Samain's hypothesis does not seem tenable. It runs up against the fact that v. 47 does not have the formula *arxamenos apo . . . heōs* + genitive, though this is quite familiar to the author of Acts. How explain, then, that he should fail to use it here, and replace it with a puzzling expression, if his purpose really was to distinguish two phases of preaching, the first directed to Jews, the second to Gentiles? As for the variant in codex D, it seems risky to rely on a type of text, the tendency of which, in Luke-Acts, is precisely to try to clarify by eliminating problems and using "Lukan" stylistic formulas. It is the difficulty of grasping the novelty of the message that seems to impel D to revise the text and assimilate it to one that is more familiar. These observations make it difficult to think that in this passage Luke is trying to say something different from what the text itself says, namely, that the preaching of conversion to the pagans is to have its beginning in Jerusalem.

If the text cannot be interpreted along Samain's lines, then the hypothesis that "beginning from Jerusalem" refers to a period of the preaching of salvation to the Jews is defensible only if the expression *panta ta ethnē* can be understood as meaning "all peoples," including therefore the Jewish people. This is precisely the claim made by Burchard, who derives this interpretation of the plural *ethnē* from the correct observation that the preposition *apo* is inclusive.[49] But this is a hypothesis that has no basis in Lukan usage. For, as a matter of fact, in Luke-Acts, the plural *ethnē* never includes the Jewish people. Admittedly, the singular *ethnos* is sometimes used of the Jewish people, but always in a context that implies a relation to the pagan world: when describing an attitude of someone who belongs to the pagan world (Lk 7:5; Acts 10:22), when addressing the pagan world (Lk 23:2; Acts 24:2, 10, 17) or an audience made up chiefly of pagans (Acts 26:4), when speaking of matters that come under Roman jurisdiction (Acts 28:19). When Luke speaks to pagans or from the pagan point of view, he adapts his language to the situation. *Ethnos* is never thus used of the Jews in other contexts. In the latter, Luke is careful to keep the term *laos* for the Jewish people. Above all, it is never possible to blend in the Jewish people with *panta ta ethnē* of the world. It would be odd indeed if such a blending were to take place in a programmatic text such as Luke 24:47. I must therefore repeat once again: the preaching of conversion cannot be understood as addressed to all, but has as its specific addressee the world that is made up of the pagan nations.

On the other hand, the idea that Luke 24:47 describes two stages in the course of the proclamation, this being addressed first to Jews and then to pagans, implies that Jerusalem and the Jewish world are understood as co-extensive in a way that does not seem characteristic of Luke's work. If "beginning from Jerusalem" were to be taken as meaning "beginning from the Jews," then Luke would have to regard the holy city as a symbol which has the chosen people for its referent. Now Luke certainly does not deny the Jewish connotations of the city, but when the name is used as more than a geographical identification and takes on what Conzelmann calls a "special theological significance,"[50] it ceases to be simply the "city of the Jews" and becomes the center of the saving event. Behind the special emphases given by various scholars, there is general agreement that Jerusalem is the place where salvation is wrought.[51] Jerusalem is thus two-faced: it is a "negative" city inasmuch as in it and from it arises opposition and the murderous rejection first of the prophets and then of Jesus and his followers, but it is also a "positive" city inasmuch as it is the place of appearances of the risen Lord, of the first outpouring of the Holy Spirit, of the first proclamation of salvation, and of the birth of the first believing community.[52]

As a theological entity, Jerusalem, the turning point between the periods of the history of salvation, is the place where the messianic promises are fulfilled through which God reveals his will to save all of humankind. This perspective helps understand why the city is present at the beginning and the end of the gospel; why it is the goal, which cannot be repudiated, of the journey that leads Jesus to death and resurrection; why it is the place where the church takes its first, decisive steps. The name "Jerusalem" has many associations and connections: with the expectation of the fulfillment of prophecies; with the presence of the suffering and risen Christ; with the encounter of the saving word with the human race for which it is meant; with the very roots of the church's existence. There seems, therefore, to be no reason for thinking that in a text such as Luke 24:47 one can separate out a single component, namely, the relationship to Judaism, from this tissue of reciprocal cross-references, due to which it is impossible that when speaking of Jerusalem one may say "Israel" without also saying "Jesus" and "church," and vice versa. The encounter between Israel, Christ, the word, and the church takes place "in" Jerusalem, but Jerusalem is not a symbol of any one of these things taken separately. Consequently, "beginning from Jerusalem" cannot be intended to mean "beginning from (with) the Jews"; it must be taken more broadly as meaning "beginning from the place in which salvation becomes a reality," inasmuch as "the preaching of conversion to all the nations" is an integral part of the divine plan of salvation as revealed in the messianic promises.

This reference to the messianic promises obliges us, however, to face up to a datum that seems to raise problems for the interpretation of Luke 24:47 that is being proposed here. As I mentioned earlier, Dupont has clarified the connection which this passage has, via Acts 1:8, with Acts

13:46–47, 26:22–23, and 28:28.[53] Acts 26:22–23, in particular, seems to be a parallel to Luke 24:47 by reason of the explicit reference to the prophets and Moses as well as of the connection made between the death and resurrection of Christ and his proclamation of "light both to the people and to the nations." This last theme, derived from Isaiah 42:6 and 49:6, is a favorite of Luke; he has already used it in Luke 2:32 in the composition of the canticle of Simeon, in which the preceding verses (30–31) also refer to other passages of Second Isaiah (see Is 40:5; 46:13; 52:10). Clearly, when Luke 2:32 and Acts 26:23 speak of "people" and "nations," they are suggesting that the messianic prophecy fulfilled by Christ is verified in the preaching of salvation to both Jews and pagans. The same idea seems to be implied in Acts 1:8 where in successive stages the witnessing moves from the Jewish world to the pagan nations, the latter being signified here, as we have seen, by the expression "ends of the earth."

The case seems to be different, however, in Acts 13:47, where the proclamation of salvation to the nations, and to them alone, seems to be the object of the Lord's command to missionaries. This is confirmed by the citation there of Isaiah 49:6, in which Luke, like the LXX in cod. A, reads *tetheika se eis phōs ethnōn,* that is, without the *eis diathēkēn genous* which follows the verb and its object in cod. B and especially in the almost parallel text, Isaiah 42:6. From the viewpoint of the present study, it is unimportant whether the omission of *eis diathēkēn genous* in Acts 13:47 is due to the redactional activity of Luke or, as is more likely, is already in the text-form of Isaiah 49:6 which Luke was using, since, whether the author of Acts formulates or simply accepts this form of the text, in any case he uses it to express his own thought. The important thing is rather that a comparison of these passages seems to show the presence in Luke of two different orientations: depending on cases, he chooses between a comprehensive vision of preaching that embraces both the people (of Israel) and the nations (the pagans), and a more restrictive vision which highlights the messianic novelty of a proclamation addressed to the pagans.

It is this second vision that shows in a passage such as Acts 10:43, as well as in the way in which the citation of Amos 9:11–12 is used in Acts 15:16–18 or, again, in the final declaration in Acts 28:28. On the one hand, the newness of the salvation to be proclaimed can be glimpsed in the unified plan that brings together Jews and pagans; the newness here is located in the fact that while the election of the people of Israel is not withdrawn and therefore the risen Lord addresses his word to them through his witnesses, now the pagan nations as such are likewise the direct addressees of a call to conversion for the forgiveness of sins. The same fluctuation can be seen in the call of Paul, which is first described as having for its purpose to bring the name of the Lord "before nations and kings and the children of Israel" (Acts 9:15); at a later point the purpose is rephrased in a command that mentions only the pagan nations: "Go, for I shall send you far off to the nations" (Acts 22:21); finally, the Lord speaks of Paul's "people" and the "nations," to whom he is sent (Acts 26:16–18).[54]

Both conceptions seem to have a place in Lukan theology: the function of the one is to stress the unity of the plan at work in the history of salvation, a plan which, when it includes the pagans, does not forget to confirm the election of Israel; the other conception highlights the point that in the messianic age the limitations accompanying this election are removed and salvation is made available to the world of the pagan nations. The existence side by side of the two perspectives means that Luke 24:47 is not necessarily to be read in the light of the unity of "people" and "nations," but can be read in the perspective of the revelation of God's concern for the pagans that is suggested by the observations thus far made.

III

It does not seem out of place, therefore, to propose the following hypothesis for the meaning of Luke 24:47: first, that an integral part of the series of paschal events is the fulfillment of the third messianic promise, which has to do with opening up to the nations the proclamation of salvation in the form of a call to conversion for the forgiveness of sins in the name of the risen Lord; second, that this proclamation is to begin in Jerusalem, the central location of the salvific events.

I must ask at this point whether and how all this is brought out in the first chapters of Acts, which describe the kerygmatic activity of the apostles in the holy city. For, in fact, a reading of the text shows that the proclamation is addressed to those Jews who live in Jerusalem or for whom this city is the focus of their world. In the description which Acts gives of the first period in the life of the Christian community in Jerusalem there is no trace of a preaching addressed to pagans. Nor should we expect anything different, once we recognize in Luke a writer who is attentive to the historical dimension of the events narrated. This attention shows both in his spirit and in his procedures, which are those of a "historical monograph" typical of Hellenistic historiography, in which, in addition, use is made of the narrative technique of "dramatic episodes." Luke is an historian and, as such, cannot allow himself to distort reality and offer a reconstruction of events that lacks all probability, simply in order to promote a theological vision.[55] It is logical, therefore, that the first chapters of Acts should show us the encounter of the word in Jerusalem with the Jewish world that lives in the city and passes through it. This is in fact what these chapters show us; they could not do otherwise.

But it is no less clear that, even while Luke remains faithful to the historical data, he is not afraid to interpret them, so as to show Christian preaching to be oriented from the outset to the world of the pagan nations. The facts could not be denied, but they could be filled with a symbolism that is no less real than the events. All this is evidently the case, especially in Acts 2:1–13, where the event of Pentecost takes on a universal significance that goes beyond the reality, since the latter involves in fact only persons belonging to the Jewish people. There can obviously be no question here of exhuming interpretations of the text which, contrary to all the evidence, sought to find in the addressees of the miracle of tongues, and therefore of subsequent preaching, a group made up of Jews and pagans.[56] The audience is in fact made up of Jews: Jews presently staying in Jerusalem, but described as coming not only from Judea but from all the centers of the Jewish diaspora in the Near East; Jews of Jewish descent but also converts to the law of Moses and therefore belonging to the people of Israel as proselytes. Kremer emphasizes this point: Luke seems desirous of showing "a universal representation of Jews from throughout the world."[57]

Those, on the other hand, who find the key to the text exclusively in the Jewishness of the audience do not, in my opinion, grasp fully the meaning Luke finds in the events. The theme of the "gathering of Israel" (Lohfink) or, to put it another way, the theme of the "restoration of Israel" (Fusco) is certainly not alien to the traditional and redactional construal of the pericope. It is necessary, however, to ask whether the ultimate meaning of the passage is to be found in the encounter of the apostolic preaching with the Israel of the diaspora,[58] thus placing the event of Pentecost under the "sign of unbroken continuity," insofar as the "restoration" of Israel would be "the presupposition for the evangelization of the pagans."[59] To follow this path means that one must agree with Jervell and assign to Israel a role as mediator of salvation that is added to, and supplements, that of Christ; but this is a position which Luke, though conscious of Israel's role in salvation history, does not seem to support.[60] Fusco himself cannot deny the presence of the universal dimension at the "symbolic" level in Acts 2:1–13, or the "evocation" of a complete universality that includes the pagans.[61] But this element of universality is not a secondary derivation from the principal theme, namely, the "restoration of Israel"; rather it is a constitutive element in the story. The Jewish listeners who come from all the nations form "a link between Jerusalem and the rest of the world,"[62] so that it is possible to say that on Pentecost the apostles are taking "at least the first steps"[63] in their universal mission.

Two points in particular should give assurance that this universalist interpretation of the Pentecostal event is correct. The first is the use of the word *ethnos* to indicate the wide range of origins of the hearers (Acts 2:5). In a context where a geographical terminology might be expected there appears instead this quasi-technical term for the nations in Luke-Acts.[64] The use of the word is not easily explained unless the writer wanted to allude in a positive way to the pagan world of which Jews from the diaspora become in a way the representatives to the apostles.

The second point I want to make here is the advantage Luke takes of the universalism in the passage from Joel (3:1–5 LXX) which Peter cites at the beginning of his discourse on Pentecost (Acts 2:17–21) and again in his final exhortation (2:39) and which in the structure of the chapter is the interpretative key which the author provides for the event described in Acts 2:1–13. If the passage from Joel interprets what has just happened, then the fact that the Jews from all the nations of the world have heard, each in his or her own tongue, the "mighty deeds of God" (Acts 2:11) is an event which has to do not so much with the bringing together of scattered Israel as with the granting of a new prophetic power to every human being (*epi pasan sarka*). The result is a salvation extended not to the members of a particular people but to "everyone who (*pas hos*) calls upon the name of the Lord" (Jl 3:5a = Acts 2:21).

Like the Septuagint version, which in Joel 3:5b replaces the "remnant whom Yahweh is calling" of the Hebrew text[65] with "they that have glad tidings preached to them, whom the Lord has called," Luke seems to be seeking to transcend a nationalistic vision of salvation in which the only concern is the restoration of Israel. And it is perhaps in this text, Joel 3:5b, which locates the saving event *en tō orei Siōn kai en Ierousalēm,* that we have the Old Testament text to which Luke 24:47 is referring when it says that the preaching of salvation to all the nations begins in Jerusalem.[66] The preaching to all the nations is an event that takes place in Jerusalem in fulfillment of the prophecy of Joel, which had foretold a prophetic manifestation that would bring salvation, in the holy city, to those whom the Lord would call. The fact that all this is now fulfilled only in an image, that is, in the fact that the people of scattered Israel act as representative of the nations of the world, is part of the historical dimension proper to the coming of salvation. Following the lead of Joel (LXX), Luke's vision is one that moves from the fortunes of Israel and its restoration to consider the problem of a proclamation of salvation that must reach every human being. It is not the theme of the gathering of scattered Israel that turns the reader's attention secondarily and symbolically to the proclamation of salvation to the pagans; rather the proclamation to the pagans is expressed in language and images that turn the reader's attention in part to that theme.

In Luke's view, therefore, the Pentecost event is a first fulfillment of what had been foretold in Luke 24:47. But the same universalist perspective continues through the early pages of Acts and especially in the discourses that are a characteristic of these chapters. As Bachmann rightly emphasizes,[67] the preaching undertaken by the witnesses of the risen Lord is from the very outset universalist in scope. The fact that the word of salvation is meant for all the nations is not a theme limited to the Pentecost discourse; it is found elsewhere as well. And it is usually accompanied by an appeal to the scriptures, in full accord with Luke 24:47, which makes this theme the third factor in the messianic prophecies.

The element of universality does not emerge solely through the citation of Joel 3:1–5, particularly in Acts 2:17, 21, and then in Acts 2:39, where the expression "those who are far off" reminds the hearers of still another prophetic text, Isaiah 57:19. The same universality reappears in Acts 3:25, which refers to Genesis 12:3, 18:18, 22:18, and 26:4: The witness given by the apostles makes present the time in which God's blessing reaches "all the nations of the earth" through Christ, the "seed" of Abraham.[68] The subsequent discourse of Peter and John before the Sanhedrin closes in a similar way; here again the climactic moment in the proclamation is the statement that salvation is available to all. Here again, too, the words of the witnesses echo the words of Old Testament prophecy as found, once more, in Joel 3:5: the name by which salvation is given is provided so that it may be invoked *en anthrōpois,* without distinction of nations (Acts 4:12).[69] Even at the second appearance, this time of all twelve, before the Sanhedrin, when the kerygma seems directed wholly to Israel, we see reappearing the words *metanoian . . . kai aphesin hamartiōn* (Acts 5:31), that is, the words which described the preaching to the pagans in Luke 24:47; in addition, the gift of the Spirit, which signifies the gift of salvation, is assigned, without limitations of recipient, to *tois peitharchousin* in God (Acts 5:32).[70]

The proclamation of salvation during the early period in Jerusalem culminates in the discourse of Stephen, a well-constructed indictment of "resistance to the Holy Spirit" (Acts 7:51) by the chosen people throughout their history. At the heart of this indictment Luke places a criticism of the temple that is justified by an appeal to Isaiah 66:1–2; in its context in

Third Isaiah, this passage leads into a vision of judgment and salvation for Jerusalem, a vision culminating in the prospect of a gathering of the scattered Israelites that is linked to the coming of the pagans and to "the proclamation of the glory" of God "to the nations" (Is 66:19). Thus, at the conclusion of this first part of Acts, which has seen the newborn church active in Jerusalem, the prospect of universal salvation is an integral part, even if implicit, of the Old Testament background against which the preaching of the apostles is carried on.

Jerusalem thus makes a direct contribution to the evangelization of the pagans through the prospects which it opens up or confirms in this context.[71] It is from the persecuted community in Jerusalem that the missionaries go forth who, like Philip, will make it possible for those on the periphery of the Jewish people to come into contact with the gospel: the inhabitants of Samaria (Acts 8:4–8) and the Ethiopian eunuch, whose religious identity is blurred in the Lukan redaction, leaving him in a vague area between the world of the proselytes and the world of the pagans (Acts 8:26–30). Again, Jerusalem is the point of departure for the journey of Peter, to whom Luke assigns the function of officially opening the mission to the pagans by his evangelization and baptism of Cornelius (Acts 10), just as it is for those who are scattered by the persecution that breaks out after the death of Stephen and who in Antioch preach to pagans as well as Jews (Acts 11:19–21).[72]

But Jerusalem is not only the starting point of the missionary journey to the pagan world; it is also the center of control and confirmation. Thus it is from Jerusalem that Peter and John go out to examine what has happened in Samaria (Acts 8:9–25). It is to Jerusalem that Saul comes after being called on the road to Damascus, in order that his future missionary activity among the pagans may be authenticated by being based in communion with the apostles in Jerusalem (Acts 9:26–30). It is from the church of Jerusalem that Peter receives approval for what has been done at Caesarea in connection with the conversion of Cornelius (Acts 11:1–18). It is from Jerusalem that Barnabas is sent to approve and encourage the formation of the community of Antioch (Acts 11:22–26). Finally, it is in Jerusalem that a resolution is found of the conflict rending the church in regard to the conditions for the entrance of pagans into the faith (Acts 15:1–35). I could go further and show how in the final analysis all the journeys of Paul are seen as originating in Jerusalem. But the many references I have given already take me beyond the first part of Acts to which I wanted to limit my reflections. I have included them here simply to show how "beginning from Jerusalem" is a perspective that not only is at work in the first chapters of Acts but continues throughout the book to control the relationship of the city with the proclamation to the pagans.

IV

I asked what role Jerusalem plays in the first part of the book of Acts as seen from the viewpoint of Luke 24:47. After the considerations I have offered, I think I can say that Luke quite probably does not think of the holy city as representing a period in which the gospel is addressed to the Jewish world and in which a church comes into existence at the heart of Judaism. The unsatisfactory character of interpretations of Luke 24:47 that are intended to justify such a vision led me to reconsider the meaning of the expression "beginning from Jerusalem" in its context. The various stages of the analysis led me to consider the textual form of the Lukan verse, the relation of the verse to Acts 1:8, the use Luke makes of the terms *archein* and *ethnē,* and his comprehensive theological vision of Jerusalem. I went on then to distinguish two perspectives, which are not in competition with one another, relative to the preaching of salvation to the pagans: on the one hand, the placing of pagans at the side of the Jews is a characteristic of the messianic age[73]; on the other, the newness of this age finds expression precisely in the fact that the message of salvation is now addressed to those who were far off. I was able to show, by locating Luke 24:47 in this second perspective, how in the first chapters of Acts Luke could remain faithful to the historical data and yet at the same time show the proclamation to the nations already emerging, and this both in the model used for describing the Pentecostal event and in the universalism that already marks the first Christian kerygma. In addition, the succeeding chapters of the book carefully make clear how the journey of the message to the pagans outside Jerusalem begins from this city and receives its confirmation there.

If Christian preaching in Jerusalem shows itself from the outset to be directed, in form and in content, to the pagan world, it becomes impossible to see in the church of the earliest days an entity which is bound up with the law and therefore cannot serve as a model for the churches that later come into existence in the pagan world.[74] Luke cannot, of course, deny the evidence of a church that comes into being in a Jewish setting and is made up of Jews who accept the witness of the apostles. He is concerned, nonetheless, to show that from its very beginnings this church is already oriented toward that pagan world to which successive phases of history will lead it and to which it is directed by its nature as an entity of the messianic age. It can be said that, seen in this light, Luke's effort is precisely to tone down, within the limits set by respect for historical facts, the "Jewish" aspects of the first community and to present it as an exemplar for the church of every age; this effort shows with special clarity in the various summaries (Acts 2:42–47; 4:32–35; 5:12–16; 5:42; 6:7–8; 8:1b-4) which form the supporting beam of these first chapters and sum up their content.[75] It is an essential element in this identity of every church in every age that it carries to all nations the message which calls human beings to conversion. The church, born as it is of the call which the risen Lord issues through his witnesses, experiences this finality "beginning from Jerusalem," that is, as already at work in the Christian community that comes into being in the city and is at the same time a model for every church.

PART TWO

The Use and Meaning of (*Hoi*) *Ioudaioi* in Acts

The relationship of the church to Israel in Luke and, more particu-larly, Luke's attitude to the Jews have been debated by students of Luke's work[1]; they have come up with quite different answers.[2] In this ongoing discussion more than one exegete has called attention to a point that may be of some interest: Luke, who in the Acts of the Apostles perceptibly increases his use of the term (*hoi*) *Ioudaioi,* gives it (they claim) a negative or adversarial meaning in some instances. The assertion is made, for the most part, in the form of an annotation that is not supported by a thor-ough analysis. A brief look at some authors (the survey is not meant to be exhaustive) will help the reader understand the question.

Gutbrod[3] in his day pointed out that, as in the gospel of John, so in some passages of Acts the *Ioudaioi* are seen as opponents of the preached Christ and of the Christian community, although this hostility is not auto-matically connected with the name "Jews." Conzelmann[4] sees a harden-ing in the Lukan use of the word *Ioudaios,* so that, in addition to its use as a simple ethnic designation, it comes to have a critical and polemical meaning. This semantic shift is visible (he claims) in 14:1, 2, 4 (and con-tinues in 18:5–12, 14–19; 17:1–5, 10–17); from this point on, the "Jews" in the pregnant sense of the term are those who have rejected the gospel and are now presented as stereotypical enemies of the church.

According to George,[5] in 2:5, 11, 14 the word *Ioudaioi* refers simply to Jewish nationality and has no religious overtones,[6] but from 12:3, 11 on it begins to take on a polemical meaning: unbelievers and enemies of Christians.[7] Especially during the stops on the missionary journeys, stops usually destined to end with the expulsion of the evangelizers, the term "Jews" takes on overtones of hostility.[8] Those among them who have rejected the gospel will continue to make up "the Jewish people," a secu-lar people who, having renounced their own mission, have lost their title of people of God.[9]

According to Zehnle,[10] who thinks the word *Ioudaioi* already has a disparaging meaning in 9:23; 12:3, 11, once the Jews of the diaspora join the Jews of Jerusalem in rejecting the preaching of the apostles, the term becomes almost a "technical term" (as in John) to designate the opponents of Paul, who is the agent of salvation.

Lohfink[11] is surprised by the expression *laos tōn Ioudaiōn* in 12:11 and observes that *Ioudaioi* becomes increasingly frequent—and not by chance—after the story of Stephen. Interpreting this fact in the context of Christian literature, where the name often has a somewhat negative tone and marks a distancing from the church of Judaism, Lohfink concludes that in Acts too it is a name for the Israel that has not believed and has turned into "Judaism."

Hauser has drawn up a detailed table of the use of *Ioudaios-Ioudaioi* in Luke's second volume[12] and points out that, starting with 9:23, in a good twenty-six cases (*hoi*) *Ioudaioi* has a negative meaning and becomes a label for enemies of the gospel and of Christian preachers.[13]

Gaston[14] gives a list of passages in which the Jews are shown as enemies of Paul, and observes that even though the individual texts may suggest the Jews of a particular place, the overall impression given is that *Ioudaioi* refers to Jews generally. In his opinion, the truth is that Luke sees a degree of success being achieved among the Jews at the various stops on Paul's mission; it is no less true, however, that Luke continually shows the Jews in violent opposition to Paul. Moreover, this second aspect seems to have the final word for this author.

On the basis of a series of passages in the Pauline section of Acts, Slingerland[15] stresses the point that Luke not only deliberately uses the term *Ioudaioi,* but also presents their dealings with Paul in a strongly pejorative light. The description of their behavior, which is marked by jealousy, rioting, and intrigue, fits in with an anti-Jewish *topos* that is also to be found in other literature of the time. This presentation of the Jews is born not of a desire for historical accuracy but of a tendency to show opposition to Paul as coming almost exclusively from Jews. We are therefore in the presence of an anti-Jewish reconstruction of history.

Finally, in his voluminous study of Luke's work,[16] Sanders brings out once again the change that occurs beginning with the martyrdom of Stephen. From 9:22 on, the word *Ioudaioi* is often used with an adversarial meaning. Sanders emphasizes especially those expressions that suggest all Jews are opposed to the evangelizers (see 12:11; 18:2; 25:4); he concludes that the "Jews" are presented as enemies of Christianity.

All the views that I have cited are a stimulus to seek a better understanding of the meaning of (*hoi*) *Ioudaioi* in Acts by means of a more detailed analysis of its use. I shall begin with an annotated classification of the occurrences of the word and proceed then to a study of the context in cases in which the word may have negative overtones. The conclusions reached in this essay may give us some little insight into Luke's way of looking at the Jews.

1. CLASSIFICATION OF THE OCCURRENCES OF *(HOI) IOUDAIOI*

Statistics already suffice for a first impression: *Ioudaioi* occurs seventy-nine times in Acts as compared with five times in the gospel of Luke (Mark five times; Matthew six times) and as compared with seventy-one times in John where the term is generally recognized as important. The impression is softened to some extent by the realization that the very content of the story in Acts probably demands the use of the word. In sixty-eight cases in Acts the plural, with or without the article, can be regarded as inclusive. The use or omission of the article does not seem significant for purposes of this study.[17]

A classification based on one important criterion will help to an initial understanding of the use of *(hoi) Ioudaioi*. In my opinion, such a criterion is provided by the interaction (or lack of it) between Jews (explicitly named) and evangelizers. A classification based on this norm provides, first of all, a picture of the relationship between evangelizers and Jews, although the picture is not altogether complete since the passages used are limited to those in which the word *Ioudaioi* occurs. Secondly, the classification makes it possible to distinguish clearly between the instances in which *Ioudaioi* surely has a neutral meaning and those in which negative overtones may be surmised.

A. Passages in Which There Is No Interaction

A series of passages containing the word *(hoi) Ioudaioi* have contexts which display no interaction between Jews and evangelizers.

2:5, 10, 14: Those present at Pentecost are described as "Jews" living in Jerusalem or coming from every nation (v. 5). In the list of peoples the reference to "Jews" (v. 10) is a religious identification. At the beginning of his discourse, Peter addresses his hearers as "Jews" by nationality (v. 14).

10:39: Peter refers to "the region of the Jews" (including Galilee) as the locale of Jesus' public activity.

10:22; 22:12: In a comparable way, Cornelius and Ananias are described as persons with a good reputation among the "Jews."

16:20: Paul and Silas are described as "Jews" and accused of disturbing the city of Philippi and advocating customs not lawful for Roman citizens.

18:2b: Claudius orders that all "Jews" be driven from Rome.

18:14ab: Gallio turns to the Jews and addresses them as such.

19:13: The adjective "Jewish" is used in describing some exorcists who invoke the name of Jesus.

19:33: The "Jews" push Alexander forward, that he may speak to the excited crowd.

25:8: Paul says he has committed no offense against the law of the "Jews."

26:3: Agrippa is addressed as one who is familiar with the customs and controversies of the "Jews."

26:4: All the "Jews" know Paul's way of life.

In all these passages the word (*hoi*) *Ioudaioi* clearly signifies that the persons belong to a race or to the religion of that race. It has, therefore, an ethnic and religious meaning.

B. Passages in Which There Is an Interaction

"Interaction" between Jews and evangelizers is understood here in a very broad sense. It thus allows of further distinctions based on significant collocations, on actions done or suffered by the evangelizers, and on interactions reported in direct discourse.

1. The Phrase *sunagōgē tōn Ioudaiōn*

This phrase occurs four times in Acts and is used in connection with the first step taken by evangelists at the stops on their missionary journeys (elsewhere the same indication is given by the simple word *sunagōgē:* see 9:20; 13:14; 17:17; 18:4, 19; 19:8). This first meeting with Jews in the synagogue occurs at almost every stop made by the missionaries; in view of the *prōton* in 13:46, the meeting must not be taken as merely a pragmatic way of beginning the activity of evangelization but as a manifestation of respect for the priority which the history of salvation assigns to the Jews as recipients of the message of salvation. As regards the meaning of the word *Ioudaioi* in this phrase, it is fairly clear that it serves as an ethnic but also a religious designation, since the synagogue is the place where the scriptures are read (see 13:15; 15:21).

2. The Phrase *Ioudaioi kai Hellēnes*

This phrase occurs five times (14:1b; 18:4; 19:10, 17; 20:21), to which I shall add 11:(19)20.

11:(19)20: Among those scattered by the persecution of Stephen are some men of Cyprus and Cyrene who speak (*laleō*) not only to Jews but also to Greeks.

14:1b: In the synagogue of Iconium Paul and Barnabas speak (*laleō*) so effectively that a large number of "Jews and Greeks" believe (*pisteuō*).

18:4: At Corinth Paul argues (*dialegomai*) every sabbath in the synagogue and tries to convince (*peithō*) "Jews and Greeks."

19:10: Paul argues (*dialegomai*) in the lecture-hall of Tyrannus, so that all the residents of Asia, "Jews and Greeks," hear the word of the Lord (*akouō ton logon tou kuriou*).

19:17: The incident of the sons of Sceva becomes known to all the residents of Ephesus, "both Jews and Greeks"; everyone is awestruck and praises (*megalunomai*) the name of the Lord Jesus.

20:21: Paul tells the elders of Ephesus that he has testified (*diamarturoumai*) to "both Jews and Greeks" about conversion to God and faith in the Lord Jesus.

These passages seems to resemble each other in a consistent way. The context is always the spread and success of God's word. Taken in conjunction with *Hellēnes,* the word *Ioudaioi* is clearly being used as an ethnic designation. The phrase *Ioudaioi kai Hellēnes* is meant to show the universality both of the preaching of the gospel and of its acceptance in varying degrees.

3. Paul's Activity in Relation to the "Jews"

Six passages explicitly name (*hoi*) *Ioudaioi* as the persons to whom Paul's activity is directed.

9:22: Saul becomes increasingly powerful and confounds (*sugchunō*) the "Jews" living in Damascus by demonstrating with a series of arguments (*sumbibazō*) that Jesus is the Christ.

17:17: In the synagogue of Athens Paul argues (*dialegomai*) with the "Jews" and with those who believe in God.

18:5: At Corinth Paul devotes himself to the word, testifying (*diamarturoumai*) to the "Jews" that Jesus is the messiah.

18:19: In the synagogue at Ephesus Paul argues (*dialegomai*) with the "Jews."

18:28: At Ephesus Paul refutes (*diakatelegchomai*) the "Jews" in public, showing (*epideiknumi*) from the scriptures that Jesus is the messiah.

28:17: At Rome Paul calls together the leaders of the "Jews" in order to assert his innocence.

If we except 28:17, which is a special case, this series of passages shows Paul's activity in relation to the "Jews" to be in the form of discourse that is chiefly argumentative and refutational. He develops his thought by using scripture, which is explicitly mentioned in 18:28 and is presupposed in the demonstration of Jesus' messiahship. In this setting the term (*hoi*) *Ioudaioi* has religious associations, for with "Jews" it is possible to argue on the basis of scripture. It is possible that in the passages which emphasize the aspect of refutation (9:22; 18:28) the word "Jews" has a negative meaning, since in these passages the "Jews" emerge as those who resist the force of Paul's arguments.

4. The Activity of the "Jews" in Relation to the Preachers of the Gospel

The reaction of the *Ioudaioi* to the preachers (and especially to Paul) is shown in many passages. It will be helpful to distinguish various kinds of reaction.

(a) Response to Preaching

Two passages need to be considered here. One shows a positive response, the other a negative.

13:43: After the address in the synagogue at Antioch in Pisidia many (*polloi*) "Jews" and proselyte believers in God follow Paul and Barnabas.
13:45: On the following sabbath (again in Antioch in Pisidia) the "Jews" see the crowds and are filled with jealousy; they contradict (*antilegō*) what Paul says and blaspheme.

These two responses come during the same missionary stop: the positive response is partial, the negative seems to be total. I shall leave to a later analysis this seeming inconsistency. For the moment it is enough to point out that the word *Ioudaioi* in 13:43 is clearly an ethnic and religious description, while in 13:45 it may have a negative meaning.

(b) Violence during the Missionaries' Stops

There are quite a few passages, which, taken together, yield a highly negative picture of the "Jews."

9:23: At Damascus the "Jews" plot (*sumbouleuomai*) to kill (*anaireō*) Saul.

13:50: At Antioch in Pisidia the "Jews" incite (*parotrunō*) the devout women of high rank and the leading persons of the city; they stir up persecution (*epegeirō diōgmon*) against Paul and Barnabas and drive (*ekballō*) them from the region.

14:2: At Iconium the "Jews" who have rejected the preaching (*apeithēsantes*) stir up (*epegeirō*) the minds of the Gentiles and rouse them to anger (*kakoō*) against the Christians.

14:4: The crowds in the city are divided; some side with the "Jews," others with the apostles.

14:5: The Gentiles, the "Jews," and their rulers decide to mistreat (*hubrizō*) and stone (*lithoboleō*) Paul and Barnabas.

14:19: At Lystra the "Jews" of Antioch and Iconium, after winning over (*peithō*) the crowds and stoning (*lithazō*) Paul, drag (*surō*) him out of the city, thinking him dead.

17:5: At Thessalonica the jealous (*zēloō*) "Jews" take with them (*prolambanō*) some ruffians from the marketplace and form a mob (*ochlopoieō*); they set the city in an uproar (*thorubeō*) and go to the house of Jason, with the intention of bringing Paul and Silas before the assembled people (see the accusation in v. 6 of turning the world upside down, and in v. 7 of violating the decrees of Caesar by saying that there is another king named Jesus).

17:13: The "Jews" of Thessalonica come to Beroea in order to stir up (*saleuō*) and incite (*tarassō*) the crowds.

18:12: At Corinth, when Gallio is proconsul, the "Jews" unanimously (*homothumadon*) rise up (*katephistamai*) against Paul and bring him before the tribunal (see the accusation in v. 13 of persuading people to worship God in ways contrary to the law).

20:3: Reference is made to a plot (*epiboulē*) of the "Jews."

This list shows that at practically every stop of Paul on his missionary journey, except for Cyprus, Philippi, and Athens (for Ephesus see further on), the final *topos* is the violent activity of the "Jews." This activity ranges from plotting (even the death of the missionaries) to systematically stirring up the crowds or particular groups of Gentiles, to dragging the missionaries before tribunals with false charges, to persecuting, stoning, and driving them from cities. It may be, as Slingerland has suggested,[18] that in describing some of these behaviors Luke has made use of a commonplace of secular anti-Jewish criticism of the time. In any case, we must bear in mind that all of this violent activity is directed against Christian preachers and Paul in particular.

With regard to the use of (*hoi*) *Ioudaioi*, it must be noted that only once is a particular group of these mentioned, namely, *hoi de apeithēsantes Ioudaioi* in 14:2. In the other passages the reference is to the body of "Jews," either with the addition of their city of origin (see 14:9; 17:3: *apo*) or without this addition (13:50; 14:4, 5; 17:5; 18:2; 20:3). In 18:2 the presence of *homothumadon* further accentuates the unanimity of the "Jews." It is probable that in the passages in which the "Jews" are mentioned in an inclusive way as authors of the persecution against the preachers, the term has a negative or adversarial meaning. This possibility will be checked in a second phase of my analysis.

(c) Violence and Accusations in the Section of Acts in Which Paul Is Placed on Trial

In two of these passages the term *Ioudaioi* is used to identify and describe a particular group: "the chief priests and the leaders of the Jews" (25:2) and "the chief priests and the elders of the Jews" (25:15). This group is named as Paul's accusers and plotters against him (25:2) and as desiring to have the apostle condemned without a trial (25:15). It is clear that in these passages the term *Ioudaioi* is simply an ethnic designation.

In five other passages the *Ioudaioi* are more or less directly the leading figures in the action.

21:27: The Jews from Asia, who had seen Paul in the temple, stir up (*sugcheō*) the whole crowd and lay hands (*epiballō tas cheiras*) on him (see v. 28 for the charge: he is teaching everyone everywhere against the people, the law, and the temple, and is defiling the temple by bringing pagans into it).

22:30: The tribune wants to know why Paul is being accused (*katēgoreō*) by the "Jews."

23:12: Joining in a conspiracy (*sustrophē*), the "Jews" bind themselves by oath not to eat or drink until they have killed Paul.

24:9: The "Jews" join together (*sunepitithēmai*) and assert (*phaskō*) that the charges brought by Tertullus are true.

25:7: The "Jews" who have come down from Jerusalem surround Festus and bring many serious charges against Paul but are unable to prove them.

In these passages the "Jews" are described as those who accuse Paul (22:30; 24:9; 25:7; see also 21:27–28) falsely (25:7 and 24:9, if *phaskō* has the connotation of falsehood). Furthermore, they are the ones who attack Paul along with the mob (21:27) and seek his death at any cost (23:12).

Ioudaioi is used in these passages as a comprehensive designation, without any breakup into more limited groups, except for place of origin (21:27; 25:7). Given the context of violent opposition to Paul, the term *Ioudaioi* may have a negative meaning.

(d) Action Indirectly Caused by the "Jews"

There are three important passages which say that rulers, desiring to satisfy the "Jews," take steps against the preachers of the gospel.

12:3: Herod, seeing that the killing of James has pleased (*areston estin*) the "Jews," arrests Peter as well.

24:27: Desiring to do a favor (*charita katatithēmai*) for the "Jews," Festus leaves Paul in prison.

25:9: Wishing to do a favor (*charin katatithēmai*) for the "Jews," Felix suggests that Paul go to Jerusalem, even though he, Felix, is aware of a plot against Paul.

In these passages the "Jews" are pictured as opponents of the Christian community and the preachers of the gospel and as able to influence rulers indirectly, so as to harm Peter and Paul. Once again, in these passages the term *Ioudaioi* is used as a comprehensive description and, given the context, can be thought to have a negative connotation.

For the sake of completeness I shall mention in this context 16:3, where Paul is persuaded by the presence of the Jews to have Timothy circumcised. In this context "Jews" is clearly an ethnic and religious designation.

5. Interaction Between "Jews" and Evangelizers in Direct Discourse

Under this heading I place passages of varying content, which have in common that (*hoi*) *Ioudaioi* are mentioned in direct discourse. The use of direct discourse seems to make these passages function as interpretations of the events narrated. It is worth our while to grasp this rereading of the events and to see the viewpoint from which it is made.

12:11: Peter interprets his miraculous deliverance from prison as the work of the Lord who rescues him from what "the Jewish people" were expecting.

20:19: In his discourse at Miletus Paul looks back over his experiences in Asia and sees them as marked by plots (*epiboulai*) of the "Jews."

21:11: At the beginning of the section on Paul's trials, the prophet Agabus anticipates what is to come and points to the "Jews" as responsible for the arrest of Paul and his being handed over to the Gentiles for judgment.

23:20: The son of Paul's sister reveals the plot of the "Jews" which has already been narrated in 23:14b-15.

21:20, 21: After telling Paul how many thousands of believers there are among the "Jews" of Jerusalem, the Christians of that city warn him that these converts have been given to understand Paul's missionary activity as an attempt to induce all the "Jews" living among the Gentiles to abandon Moses.

24:5: When Tertullus accuses Paul before Felix, he describes the apostle's ministry as a stirring up of rebellion among all the "Jews" of the world.

23:27: In a letter to Felix, Claudius Lysias, the tribune, decribes first the attack on Paul in the temple and the attempt of the "Jews" to murder him and then his own rescue of Paul.

25:24: At his solemn presentation of Paul to Agrippa and all the citizens, Festus tells of how "the whole Jewish community" has asked for the apostle's death, whereas he, Festus, has found Paul to be innocent.

24:19: In the presence of Felix, Paul attributes the attack on him in the temple to "some Jews from Asia" and asserts that the attack has no justification in his behavior.

26:21: In his final defense, Paul reveals that the real reason for the attack on him in the temple is the mission of universal salvation which he has undertaken in obedience to the command of the risen Lord.

25:10: Referring to the accusations against him, Paul tells Festus that he has done no wrong to the "Jews."

26:2, 7: In his final defense before Agrippa, Paul says he considers himself fortunate to defend himself before such a judge against all the accusations of the "Jews" (v. 2), but he goes on to say that what the "Jews" are really attacking is his hope, which is shared by the twelve tribes of Israel and fulfilled in the resurrection (v. 7).

28:19: Paul tells the local leaders of the "Jews" of Rome that he has been forced to appeal to Caesar by the opposition of the "Jews"; the Romans wanted to let him go free.

I have not cited these passages in their proper order because I wanted to set some of them side by side in order to bring out important similarities. When it is the "Jews" who speak, the emphasis is on the falsity of accusations based on a distorted interpretation of Paul's missionary activity (21:21; 24:5). When the Roman authorities speak, the emphasis is on the positive steps they have taken in the face of the violence and murderous intentions of the "Jews." Finally, when Paul speaks, he shows the lack of justification for the attack on him in the temple (24:19) and the accusations made against him (25:20) and brings out the real motive for the actions of the Jews (26:7, 21).

This rereading or interpretation of the events yields a negative picture of the actions of the Jews toward the preachers of the gospel. The Jews were expecting Peter's death as the result of their persecution of him in Jerusalem. During Paul's missionary activity they plotted against him. In Jerusalem they attacked him without any specific reason and would have killed him if the Roman authorities had not intervened. They asked these authorities to put Paul to death and resisted the proofs of innocence which he offered. Their accusations against him are proven false. The real reason for their attacks and their real object of their accusations is his preaching and its universal scope, despite the fact that this is precisely the content of Israel's hope and of the messianic prophecies found in the scriptures (see the connection between 26:7 and 26:23).

As for the use of *(hoi) Ioudaioi,* it must be observed that except for the partitive in 24:19 (but see 21:27) the term is always used without restriction. Especially deserving of attention are expressions which seem to insist that all of the "Jews" are opponents of the gospel: *laos tōn Ioudaiōn* (12:11) and *hapan to plēthos tōn Ioudaiōn* (25:24).

(Hoi) Ioudaioi does not have a single homogeneous meaning in these passages. The ethnic and religious sense seems rather clear in passages which refer to believers among the Jews who also continue to maintain the Jewish religious spirit (21:20), or in which the Jews are the objects of Paul's (misinterpreted) mission (21:21; 24:5), or, again, in which the apostle says he has done no wrong to the Jews (25:10). In the other passages, where the Jews as a body engage in violence and accusations, we may surmise that the term "Jews" has an adversarial meaning, although this must now be further examined.

2. NEGATIVE CONNOTATION OF THE TERM (HOI) IOUDAIOI

The classification I have presented has made it possible not only to set forth the interaction between the preachers of the gospel and the *Ioudaioi* but also to show when the term *(hoi) Ioudaioi* has an ethnic and religious meaning and when, on the contrary, a negative connotation may be assumed. I shall now proceed to a further analysis of these latter passages by placing them in their context. I shall divide the analysis according to sections of the narrative. The criterion I shall apply is a simple one but also, in my opinion, capable of bringing out a possible negative connotation of (*hoi*) *Ioudaioi*. The criterion is this: if even when the author is aware that preaching addressed to the Jews is to some extent successful, he nonetheless uses (*hoi*) *Ioudaioi* without restriction, or other expressions even more indicative of a totality, to describe the opponents of the gospel and its preachers, then the term certainly does not have a neutral ethnico-religious meaning but refers to those members of Israel who have closed their minds to the preaching of the gospel.

A. The Persecution in Jerusalem (12:1–23)

(*Hoi*) *Ioudaioi* are mentioned twice in the context of the persecution unleashed by Herod Agrippa in Jerusalem against some members of the Christian community. They are first named as those who are pleased by the killing of James, and to please whom Peter too is imprisoned (v. 3). Later they are mentioned as those who were looking forward to legal action against Peter and to his condemnation (v. 11).

This depiction of the *Ioudaioi* as enemies of the Christian community has long since been noted by exegetes as a new factor, a sign of a change in the mood of the Jewish people and of a growing rift between Christians and unbelieving Jews.[19] And in fact throughout his story of earlier events in Jerusalem Luke had not failed to emphasize, almost in a kind of refrain, the large number of conversions among the Jews (see 2:41, 47; 4:4; 5:14; 6:1, 7) and had highlighted the favorable attitude of the people to believers in Christ (see *laos* in 2:47; 4:21; 5:13, 26). Only in the episode involving Stephen did the people (*laos*) change its attitude and take part in arresting him and bringing him before the sanhedrin (see 6:12). Now, when the narrative shifts back to Jerusalem and the Herodian persecution, the reference to the *Ioudaioi* (v. 3) as being pleased by violence against Christians becomes significant. The term can no longer mean simply those who are of Jewish origin, since a large number of Jews in Jerusalem have become believers and are now in part the object of persecution; the term can only mean those of the Jews who have rejected the offer of salvation and are now hostile to the Christian community.

Also revealing is the statement that Herod (v. 4) intended to bring Peter before the people (*laos*) for public trial after Passover. We may think that a negative attitude to the apostle is here being attributed to the "people." This impression is confirmed when Peter interprets (v. 11) his own miraculous flight from prison as a deliverance by the Lord from the hands of Herod and from the expectations of *tou laou tōn Ioudaiōn*. The earlier references to *Ioudaioi* (v. 3) and *laos* (v. 4) have sufficiently prepared the way for this final pregnant phrase, which is unmatched elsewhere in the book of Acts.

The presence of the expression *laos tōn Ioudaiōn,* though surprising when taken by itself, no longer astonishes readers who have followed the story of events in Jerusalem. Luke has carefully avoided using such terms as *ochlos* or *plēthos* for the crowds in Jerusalem (except in 2:6, where those present are Jews from the diaspora), preferring the more meaningful word *laos;* he has also shown the "people" to be the addressees of the preached gospel and as favorably inclined to the Christian community. Now, however, after the negative attitude which the people have adopted in the Stephen episode and in the Herodian persecution, he does not hesitate to describe them as *laos tōn Ioudaiōn.*[20] The people have become hostile unbelievers: the addition *ton Ioudaion* seems to underscore the attitude of opposition which the people have adopted toward the gospel and the church. It remains to show how the negative connotations of the term *Ioudaioi* attach in a significant way to the unbelieving people of Jerusalem, once the city has ceased to be the scene of evangelizing activity and Peter, the primary witness, is about to abandon it.

B. The Stops on Paul's Missionary Journeys

Among these I include Paul's first preaching at Damascus (9:19b–25), since this episode seems to show a structure similar to that described for the stops he later makes on his lengthy missionary journeys. It is perhaps not possible to prove apodictically the negative connotation of *Ioudaioi* in this first setting. It can, however, be presupposed in v. 22, provided Paul's continuing refutation is behind the resistance of his Jewish audience to him and their rejection of him, and it can be glimpsed in v. 23, provided the "Jews," with their plot to kill Paul, are regarded as contrasted with the group of disciples who help Paul to escape. *Ioudaioi* would then signify those who reject Paul's preaching and react violently to him, in clear contrast now to the Christian community that has come into existence.

A more precise judgment on the possible negative connotation of the term *Ioudaioi* can be made in connection with certain stages on Paul's missionary journeys, for in narrating these Luke seems to follow, although with variations, a standardized "model" or pattern: entrance into a city, preaching in the synagogue, initial positive response, opposition of the "Jews" (and turning of the preachers to the pagans), stirring up of the crowds by the "Jews," and departure from that city.[21] This model, with its sequence of initial positive response and subsequent violent rejection by the "Jews," may be taken as a way of bringing out the negative meaning of the term *Ioudaioi.*

At Antioch in Pisidia (13:14–52), the entrance into the synagogue and Paul's sermon there (vv. 14–41) are followed by initial success (v. 43):

many of the Jews and devout proselytes follow Paul and Barnabas, who converse with them and try to persuade them to abide in the grace of God. The language used is not explicitly the language of faith (for a different language see 17:34). The verb *akolouthe̅o,* here as in 12:8, 9, and 21:36, means simply "to go after" and not "to follow" in the fuller sense. The verb *peitho̅* emphasizes the effort, including an intellectual effort, which the preachers make to win over their hearers.[22] *Prosmenein te̅ chariti tou Theou* means to persevere (see 11:23) in the grace given through the gospel.[23] While not saying in so many words that this group became believers, is Luke referring in this last phrase (*prosmenein . . .*) to a grace already received,[24] to an initial faith[25] in which these individuals are to remain constant, so that these Jews and proselytes are to be regarded as the nucleus of a new community?[26] If Luke's words are to be read in this way,[27] then the presence in v. 45 of the term *Ioudaioi,* without any accompanying restriction, takes on a definite meaning. *Ioudaioi* can no longer be a neutral ethnic and religious designation, but instead refers simply to that part of the Jewish people that has not been touched by the grace of the gospel and now, jealous (see 5:17) of the success of a mission that reaches out to everyone, opposes Paul's preaching and blasphemes the name of Jesus (see 26:11) in which salvation is offered to all.

The same negative meaning must be assigned to the word *Ioudaioi* in v. 50. After the announcement that the gospel will now be preached to the pagans (vv. 46–47) and the statement that the pagans joyously accept it (vv. 48–49), we are told that the "Jews," hardened in their opposition, incite an uprising among influential groups and drive the preachers of the gospel from the city. The reason for this violent action is not explicitly stated; we may suppose, however, that the wide success of the message, as indicated in v. 49, is the motive.

The pattern is repeated during the stop in Iconium (14:1–6): entrance into the synagogue and initial positive result (v. 1). This result is described as the acceptance of the faith (*pisteusai*) by a large number of Jews and Greeks. The result is, therefore, a new community of disciples who come, in part, from Judaism. In v. 2 the poisoning of the minds of the Gentiles against the Christians is said to be the work of the *apeithe̅santes Ioudaioi.* This is the only instance in which the word *Ioudaioi* is accompanied by a limiting qualifier. The Jews in question here are those who have hardened their hearts and "have not obeyed" the call to faith (see 19:9). After a further period of preaching (v. 3), the city remains divided; the unbelieving and hostile Jews act as a catalyst for part of the population, while another part sides with the apostles-missionaries (v. 4). At this point, however, the faction made up of unbelieving Jews is called simply *hoi Ioudaioi.* The negative connotation of the term *Ioudaioi* could not be clearer.[28] The same pejorative meaning also attaches therefore to the term in v. 5, according to which the Jews, together with their rulers and the Gentiles who have joined them, attempt to do violence to the missionaries and stone them.

The stay at Lystra (14:8–20) does not follow the model I have indicated, because the story focuses on the encounter of the missionaries with the pagan world. But when mention is made in v. 19 of the *Ioudaioi* of Antioch and Iconium as the ones who stir up the crowd to stone Paul, we may think of the embittered Jews whom we have already seen in those cities.

The pattern met earlier is found again at Thessalonica (17:1–9): entrance into the city and the synagogue (vv. 1–2a), preaching to the Jews with suitable arguments (vv. 2b-3), and report of some success (v. 4). The passage tells us that in addition to a great many devout Greeks and not a few women of rank, *tines* among the Jews *epeisthēsan kai prosklērōthēsan* Paul and Silas. The success among the Jews is real, even if much less extensive than among the pagans. The language is not that typically used of access to the faith, but it describes an equivalent occurrence. The passive of *peithō* shows that there has been a positive response to the arguments (see the active form of *peithō* in 13:43; 18:4; 19:8; 28:23, and the passive in 28:24, where it is contrasted with *apisteō*) which Paul has used in his preaching. The passive of *prosklēroō* implies the divine action that entrusts the new converts to Paul and Silas as their disciples.[29] Since some of the Jews have become part of the new Christian community, the word *Ioudaioi* in v. 5 refers to the majority who have not welcomed the preaching; these, envious of the missionaries' great success among the pagans and deprived now of the support of the influential women who have become believers, stir up a tumult in the city and bring accusations against the preachers (vv. 5–8a).

The same narrative scheme is repeated at Beroea (17:10–15). However, the Jews of this city are described as well disposed, and many of them believe, along with not a few Greek women and men of high rank (v. 12). The trouble is caused by the *Ioudaioi* of Thessalonica (v. 13), a term which, as we saw above, refers to the unbelieving Jewish faction of that city. Here again the word has an adversarial meaning.

During the stay in Corinth (18:1–17) the pattern recurs but not in as simple a form. Luke first says that Paul argues (*dielegeto*) weekly (*kata pan sabbaton*) in the synagogue, as he attempts to persuade (*epeithen*) Jews and Greeks (v. 4). He says nothing of any result. In a second phase, after the arrival of Silas and Timothy, the apostle devotes himself entirely to preaching (*suneicheto tō logō*) and exercises his role, in relation to the Jews, of witness (*diamarturomenos*) to the messiahship of Jesus (v. 5). The vocabulary seems to emphasize the elements of proclamation and witness in Paul's activity, elements that turn this into a call to decision. The response is negative and seemingly unanimous. Luke notes no exceptions when he says that the Jews oppose Paul or the message preached (in favor of the latter interpretation see 13:45) and blaspheme against the name of Jesus which has been proclaimed (v. 6a). After making the prophetic and symbolic gesture of shaking the dust from his clothes, proclaiming his innocence, and announcing his intention to turn to the pagans (v. 6b), Paul continues his activity at the home of Titus Justus (v. 7). Only at this point are we told of the success of the mission: along with many Corinthians, Crispus, head of the synagogue, and all his family become believers. The positive result among the Jews is thus minimal and quite limited in comparison with a rejection of the gospel that in v. 6 seemed to be universal. In my opinion, this explains the *homothumadon* with which the *Ioudaioi,* in the time of Gallio, attack Paul and bring him before the tribunal (v. 12), where they accuse him of persuading the people to worship God in a way contrary to the law (v. 13). The adverb *homothumadon* had been used legitimately in 7:57 to express the unanimity with which the mass of embittered Jews (6:12) rushed on Stephen in a rage and dragged him out to be stoned. Now, in Corinth, the vast majority of Jews who oppose the gospel are unanimous in doing violence to Paul and accusing him. The fact that Crispus and his family are named as exceptions shows, I think, that *Ioudaioi* in v. 12 has taken on a pejorative connotation.

I have briefly analyzed some of the stops on the missionary journeys that display in a more typical manner the presence of the *Ioudaioi.* The analysis leads me to think that in 20:3, with its general reference to an *epiboulē hupo tōn Ioudaiōn,* Luke is again thinking of a group of Jews who have closed their minds to the gospel. The same negative connotation is probably to be seen also in 20:19, in the discourse at Miletus, in which Paul speaks of the *epiboulai tōn Ioudaiōn* which he had experienced at Ephesus but of which no mention was made in the report on his stay there.

C. *The Section on the Trials of Paul*

Let me recall the criterion I have been using: if the term *Ioudaioi* is used without limiting modifier and if reference has already been made in the context to the acceptance of the gospel by part of the Jewish population, then the term has the negative meaning already described. Application of this criterion makes the analysis of the many passages in this section of Acts an easy matter.

I wish to call attention first of all to the mention of the "Jews from Asia" (21:27; 24:19), who lead the attack on Paul in the temple. As the commentators point out,[30] these are in all likelihood Jews from Ephesus, since they recognize a fellow townsman, Trophimus (21:29; see 20:4). In his account of the stay in Ephesus (19:8–10), Luke does not explicitly mention the *Ioudaioi* but he does tell of Paul's repeated preaching in the synagogue (v. 8), which breaks off when some members of that synagogue stubbornly resist and do not obey the gospel but rather speak evil of the "way" (v. 9a). At this point Paul departs from the synagogue and causes the departure of his disciples as well, that is, of those Jews who have become Christians; he goes off to argue daily for two years in the lecture hall of Tyrannus (vv. 9b-10). Thus a faction of unbelieving Jews is formed; the predominant pattern followed in the accounts of the stops on the missionary journeys would lead us to expect this faction to create uproars and to plot against Paul. Luke does not tell of such activity at this point but he does refer to it in 20:19, where he expressly attributes it to the *Ioudaioi*. Given this background, it is legitimate to infer that "Jews from Asia" in 21:27 and 24:19 refers to this fringe group of stubborn Jews whom Luke, applying a *topos* already used in 14:19 and 17:13, shows working, in a city not their own, to cause difficulties for Paul. In these two passages, then, the term *Ioudaioi* must be regarded as having a clearly negative meaning.

Except for these mentions of Jews from Asia, all the passages in this section that show the *Ioudaioi* as accusers and opponents of Paul are to be taken, it seems, as referring to Jews of Jerusalem. Now, as I pointed out earlier, Luke has already depicted Jerusalem as a place of evangelization and has emphasized the noteworthy success which the preaching of the gospel had among the Jews there. As though recalling this positive situation that had existed in the past, James and the elders remind Paul, right at the beginning of this section, of the thousands of believers among the Jews (21:20).[31] On the other hand, I have also pointed out that after the episode of Stephen Luke sees the *Ioudaioi* in Jerusalem as opponents of the Christian community (12:3) and refers to the formation in that city of a *laos tōn Ioudaiōn* made up of Jews who have rejected the gospel (12:11).

Given this background, we will be right in thinking that when, in this section on the various trials of Paul, Luke uses the term *Ioudaioi* for the inhabitants of Jerusalem, he means the party, now established in that city, of Jews who are set against the gospel and who become false accusers of Paul and plotters against his life (see 21:11; 22:30; 23:12, 20, 27; 24:9, 47; 25:7, 9, 24; 26:2, 7; 28:19). Among these passages 25:24 in particular makes a strong impression: in a solemn setting which conveys the atmosphere of a trial,[32] Festus states that all of these unbelieving Jews (*hapan to plēthos tōn Ioudaiōn*) are seeking the death of Paul.

3. CONCLUDING OBSERVATIONS

The occasion for this detailed study of the term (*hoi*) *Ioudaioi* in Acts was a series of summary annotations by various exegetes and the realization that the term occurs with great frequency in Luke's second book. The analysis has proved to be of some interest. In these concluding observations I want to remain within the limits of the question I raised for myself and not stray over into the broader area of the relationship between the church and Israel or the question of the salvation of the Jews. Despite this limitation, the results obtained may give an important glimpse into how Luke viewed the Jews, and raise questions about the relationship between his church and Judaism.

A. My tentative classification of the uses of (*hoi*) *Ioudaioi* has made it possible to enumerate a series—not exhaustive indeed but clearly pointing the way—of interactions between preachers of the gospel and Jews. I have been able to bring out the priority given to the Jews in missionary preaching through use of their synagogues, as well as the kind of preaching addressed to them: a preaching that has as its main content the messiahship of Jesus and as its primary method argument and refutation based on the scriptures. The extent of the rational and dialectical effort to persuade that is made in the course of this activity is impressive. Successes among the Jews are noted; they are numerous and are brought out, as far as my analysis is concerned, especially in the phrase *Ioudaioi kai Hellēnes.*

Even more impressive, however, are the negative reactions, first in the form of blasphemous opposition to the gospel and then in the form of uprisings, violence, and underhanded accusations. This violence and these accusations, which are murderous in intent, seem to reach their climax during the period of Paul's several trials. Despite its limits, the picture is a very sad and tragic one: those to whom the gospel was first addressed and indeed offered with passionate zeal have in part become the most implacable enemies of the message and its preachers.

B. With regard more particularly to the term (*hoi*) *Ioudaioi:* I noted in my classification that Luke uses it in its ethnic and religious meaning in passages in which there is no interaction between evangelizers and Jews or in which the action is that of the evangelizers in relation to the Jews or in which the phrase "Jews and Greeks" is used. Only when Paul's action is that of refutation may the word have a pejorative meaning, but there is no way of proving this. On the other hand, the impression that the word has a specific adversarial connotation in passages which describe the reaction of the Jews to the preachers of the gospel has been confirmed by a further, more detailed analysis. Luke often uses *(hoi) Ioudaioi* to mean those Jews who have openly rejected the gospel, have moved others to distance themselves from the Christian community, and have become the most violent opponents of this community and especially of its preachers.

C. It is worth noting the process by which Luke shows the Jews in question becoming *(hoi) Ioudaioi* in the adversarial sense. He seems to make regular use of a pattern or model: preaching of the gospel, greater or lesser success among the Jews, and emergence of the *Ioudaioi* as a faction in violent opposition to believers and especially to preachers of the gospel. The model is applied to the period in Jerusalem, for which the narrative is quite detailed, and then, more schematically, to the more typically Jewish stops on Paul's missionary journeys. Luke seems to want to show by use of this model the ongoing rupture among Jews in relation to the gospel. When Jews accept the gospel they become simply "believers among the Jews" (21:20) and join the Christian community. When they reject the gospel, they become *Ioudaioi* in the adversarial sense. The community of disciples is forced to distance itself from these Jews and their synagogues. It is from this group that a more continuous threat to the community and its missionary activity seems to come.

D. Some further points need to be made. Once we take into account the repeated use of the model that can be glimpsed at work, it becomes impossible to follow some of the authors cited at the beginning of this essay in laying excessive emphasis on the Stephen episode as a dividing point at which the *Ioudaioi,* in the negative or adversarial sense of the term, begin to appear. The martyrdom of Stephen does indeed play a decisive role in the emergence at Jerusalem of a "people of the Jews," but the process by which the group of unbelieving *Ioudaioi* was formed will have to be repeated in the cities of the diaspora and become finally a constant factor in the spread of the gospel. For the same reason, we cannot think of Paul as the sole target of the *Ioudaioi* understood as adversaries. He, along with his communities, undoubtedly is and continues to be the principal figure whom the unbelieving Jews violently oppose. But Peter, too (and James), with the Jersualem community, are objects of persecution by these Jews. The opposition of the Jews is thus viewed as constant and present from the outset.

E. After these conclusions and comments, the questions begin. I shall simply raise them here without trying to answer them, since the answer requires broader foundations than those laid by my inquiry.

Luke rereads those events in the process of evangelization that now lie behind him. Is his presentation of them dictated by his desire to be faithful to the facts and the way they unfolded, or is it (as is likely) the result of an interpretative "tendency"? Is this tendency determined by traces of anti-Jewish polemic or simply by a desire to explain the tragic division that occurred in an Israel faced with the gospel? Does the repeated observation of a distancing of the Christian community from Jews hardened in unbelief reflect a situation in which there has been a now complete break between Luke's community and Judaism? May such a break explain the now prevailing focus on the evangelization of the pagans? Are the violent opposition and underhanded accusations against the preachers of the gospel a memory from the past, or do they still hamper the missionary endeavors of the Lukan churches?

These are interesting questions, but not easily answered. My limited aim has been to show how the use and meaning of a term can yield insights into Lukan theology and the situation of the church as known to Luke.

John J. Kilgallen

Persecution in the Acts of the Apostles

I. THE WHEN, WHERE, AND FREQUENCY OF THE PERSECUTIONS

To determine the when, where, and frequency of the persecutions against Christians, as reported by the Acts of the Apostles, it is useful to consider Acts according to four divisions.

First, there is Luke's story of what occurred in Palestine from the time of Jesus' teaching his disciples for forty days till the death of Herod Agrippa of Galilee. In this period the reader learns of (1) active persecution against Peter and John by the sanhedrin, including imprisonment and whipping, (2) the trumped-up trial and terrible death of Stephen, (3) the persecution and scattering of the Hellenist Jewish Christians of Jerusalem and Paul's bitter part in it all, (4) an attempt on the life of Paul, now witness to Jesus, in Damascus, and (5) the death of James and the imprisonment and lurking death of Peter.

Second, there is the narrative of chapters 13 and 14, where divinely missioned Paul visits a southeastern section of Asia Minor. It can be argued whether the opposition (13:8) of Bar-Jesus, i.e. Elymas, should be classified as persecution. And though the controversy between Paul and the jealous Jews of Antioch in Pisidia might be called a theological difference (13:45), the antipathy these Jews stirred up among influential women and leading men of Antioch expressed itself as a persecution of Paul and Barnabas (13:50–51). Leaving Antioch, Paul and Barnabas not only met with contentiousness, but were threatened also with stoning, from both Jew and Gentile in Iconium (14:5). Having fled (14:6) from Iconium to Lystra, Paul and Barnabas eventually met up with disgruntled Jews from Antioch and Iconium, who, as expressed in a few words, stoned Paul to the point of leaving him, they thought, dead (14:19–20). All this experience led Paul and Barnabas to formulate the cry of the oppressed: "It is our destiny to enter the kingdom of God by many trials" (14:22).[1]

143

Third, with the bitter debate and happy outcome of chapter 15 in place, Paul—and now with him go Silas and Timothy—travels through parts of Asia Minor, through Macedonia and through Greece. A first trouble for Paul and his companions in this travel section of Acts is reported to have occurred in Philippi. Here these Christian witnesses are flogged, then jailed. The cause of this jailing was actually the driving out of a demon from a young lady who was proving financially lucrative to the lady's masters. All this might not add up to persecution of Paul and his companions. Yet the trumped-up accusations which played their part in Paul's jailing are accusations one associates with persecution: agitators, disturbing the peace, advocating customs (Jewish) which are forbidden "to us Romans" (16:20–21). From Philippi the witnesses went to Thessalonica, where eventually they met resentful Jews and their henchmen, who tried to start a riot and bring Paul to trial there (17:5). The accusations we have heard before: disturbing the peace elsewhere, disregarding the laws of Rome, and claiming their own king (17:6–7). Paul escaped from Thessalonica by night (17:10), to reach Beroea, only to meet up eventually with Jews from Thessalonica who stirred up Beroean crowds to a degree that Paul was hurried by his friends out of town to Athens, under escort (17:13–14). One might argue whether or not Paul's appearance before Gallio of Corinth was a persecution, but the accusation against Paul and the violent beating of Sosthenes forewarn of a persecution (18:12–17). And what happened in the theater of Artemis in Ephesus has every mark of being, not just a demonstration or a riot, but the beginning of a persecution (19:29–34, 40). Certainly there were all the marks of persecution in the plot hatched against Paul who intended to travel directly by ship from Greece to Syria, but changed his entire route to avoid those lying in wait for him (20:3). Finally, certain words of the Pauline address to the Ephesean elders raise the specter of imminent persecution: ". . . how I served the Lord in humility through the sorrows and trials that came my way from the plottings of certain Jews. . . . But now I am on my way to Jerusalem . . . not knowing what will happen to me there—except that the Holy Spirit has been warning me from city to city that chains and hardship await me. I put no value on my life . . . none of you will ever see my face again . . . (20:19–25).

Fourth and finally, Luke's Acts ceases to follow a missionary journey narrative model of witnessing, in favor of a witness to Jesus to be drawn out of the final grim years of Paul's life, a life in prisons.[2] These years are preceded and foreshadowed by painful leave-takings in Miletus and Tyre, a fearsome prophecy of doom in Caesarea, and Paul's equally gritty words there, "I am ready, not only for imprisonment, but for death" (21:13).

From chapter 22 to the end of the story, Paul is in chains, at times due to niggardliness, but overall classifiable as persecution.

Such then is the soaking of Acts in this theme of persecution. Few chapters escape all participation in this motif: 1–3; 10; 15.[3] It is not the main theme of Acts certainly, but its omnipresence suggests an importance which might be understood through investigation of certain questions. It is in search of the answers to these questions that this essay now turns.

II. WHO ARE THE PERSECUTORS AND WHY DO THEY PERSECUTE?

To answer this question, let us look at our four divisions again—first at the Palestinian experience of the Christians.

Peter and John

The first three chapters yield nothing on the subject of opposition and persecution, and designedly so, for they promote solely the positive witness to Jesus.[4] It is the fourth chapter which introduces repression, in response to the preaching of Peter (and John) in the temple area of Jerusalem (chapter 3). Here the captors and accusers of Peter and John are *hoi hiereis, ho stratēgos tou hierou kai hoi Saddoukaioi* (4:1). This group swiftly yields to the highest authority, *hoi archontes, hoi presbuteroi, hoi grammateis, Hannas ho archiereus, Kaiaphas, Ioannēs Alexandros* and as many as there were available *ek genous archieratikou* (4:5–6). Why do these people oppose and oppress the Christian witnesses?

Some of the first group mentioned by Luke (4:1) are those who are involved simply in the more immediate work of arresting. Priests are those who function in liturgical services in the temple and thus are present to events taking place in the temple and on the temple platform.[5] The *stratēgos tou hierou* captains the guard responsible for order in the entire temple area; most likely, he is an *archiereus*.[6] In the case of Peter and John, no doubt we are expected to understand that this *stratēgos* utilized priests at hand to arrest the Christians. The Sadducees involve themselves in this arrest gladly, for, though not an arresting body, they are particularly inimical to people who preach the resurrection of even one person from the dead (cf. 4:2: *diaponoumenoi* most properly modifies just *Saddoukaioi*).

It is not altogether clear why the *stratēgos tou hierou* arrested Peter and John. Perhaps the Sadducees pressured him to do this[7]; it is possible that he himself, if he was an *archiereus,* was sympathetic to the Sadducees' anger at Peter and John, for *archiereis* were very often Sadducean in theology.[8]

The motivation, then, which brought about the arrest of Peter and John is their teaching about resurrection from the dead. The Sadducees had already shown their opposition to this teaching when they confronted Jesus over this question (Lk 20:27–40). It is very important to note Luke's phrasing as to what Peter and John were announcing in the temple area: *tēn anastasin ek nekrōn* in Jesus (4:2). This means that the resurrection of Jesus from the dead justifies belief that all will rise from the dead; as Acts elsewhere notes, Jesus is *archēgos tes zōēs* (3:15; 5:31).[9]

That the sanhedrin, together with Caiaphas, John and Alexander and all of the high priestly class, took over the case of Peter and John suggests a partially different motivation from that which drove the Sadducees to arrest the preachers. Though many members of the sanhedrin were Sadducean in outlook and thus opposed preaching about resurrection from the dead, the more aggravating point was the preaching that he is alive whom the sanhedrin just a short time ago had eliminated. At least they thought they had gotten rid of Jesus; now he is preached as alive, at the right hand of the Father, key to salvation and source of that wisdom which represents most surely the wisdom of God regarding how life is to be lived. They had thoroughly eradicated the master from Galilee; it is intolerable that he be urged again on Jews, that the sanhedrin be now preached as having acted unjustly in its elimination of Jesus.[10]

The motive, then, for persecution of the Christian witnesses is twofold: certain quarters insist that witness to the resurrection of Jesus, foundation of belief in resurrection of all from the dead, be brought to a swift end, indeed punished; the highest authority will not have its judgment appraised and argued to be unjust—such a public contentiousness should be punished.

Not much later than this first incident is a second arrest, this time instigated by *ho archiereus kai pantes ho sun autō, hē ousa hairesis tōn Saddoukaiōn* (5:17). Those Christians were jailed by the high priest (also usually Sadducean in belief) and the Sadducees gather the sanhedrin, and the entire *gerousia tōn huiōn Israēl* (5:21) for another trial.[11] The outcome of this confrontation was a flogging, accepted with joy for the sake of the name (5:40–41). Because of the explicit mention of the Sadducees, one again affirms that the basic cause of punitive action is the preaching that Jesus is risen, and the accusation that the Jewish authority was unjust in insisting upon Jesus' elimination.

Stephen

Despite the description of witnesses against Stephen as "false," the accusations against him probably were a fair assessment, at least from the point of view of his enemies, of Stephen's preaching: preaching which nullified certain elements of the Mosaic law, and which argued against the present conception of the Jewish temple—a preaching which thus took issue with Israel's manner of understanding God himself.[12] All of this criticism was held together by a belief that Jesus himself held these opinions, and, worse, that he would come again (and thus is risen from the dead) to destroy the temple and rework the Mosaic traditions (6:11–14).

These accusations were enough to put Stephen on trial for his life. What actually led to Stephen's being stoned to death was his public affirmation before his already angered jurors that at this moment he sees "the heavens opened and the Son of Man at the right hand of God" (7:56). The narrator of the story, Luke, had identified Jesus as the one Stephen saw at God's right hand; it is this identification of Jesus as Son of Man in glory at God's right hand which leads to expulsion from the city and to death by stoning.[13] The sanhedrin responds here, as earlier with Peter and John and other apostles, with great anger and violence to the insistent profession that Jesus is innocent, indeed is glorified and the Son of Man; it is the resurrection of Jesus from death to life that brings about repression, persecution, flogging, imprisonment and violent death. It is those who oppose this claim, then, that are the culprits, so far, of Acts: those who thought they had rid Israel of Jesus, and those who cannot brook any claim that resurrection from the dead is the truth.[14]

Hellenistic Jewish Christians

The death of Stephen unleashed a persecution of Christians (8:1) who thought and spoke like him. This persecution apparently was instigated by the sanhedrin; at least, as Luke presents the matter, it flowed right out of the murder of Stephen. It is in the midst of this terrible death and subsequent persecution that the figure of Paul is introduced to the reader. He becomes one of the most forceful persecutors on behalf of the sanhedrin. Paul is no Sadducee, but rather a Pharisee of the strictest kind. Why would he get involved in all this? Not that he opposed the idea of resurrection from the dead, as did the Sadducees. Rather, he opposed the figure of Jesus, because Jesus, and then his disciples, taught a law of Yahwism which in a number of points contradicted the Mosaic traditions to which Pharisees were totally devoted. But Paul must also have been angered at the preaching that Jesus was glorified by God, for the Christians could hardly have undertaken to continue to make public Jesus' way of living if they had not been convinced of his resurrection from the dead and his glorification at God's right hand. Thus, to the Sadducean and sanhedrin fault-finding is to be added the accusations of Paul against the Christian "way." But no matter how sanhedrin, Sadducees and this Pharisee can be said to differ in their motivations for persecuting Christians, it is becoming increasingly clear that the root of trouble is the figure of Jesus. Whatever the particular reason, it is he who must be eliminated—his followers, yes, but Jesus is the ultimate target. In this the Christian experience is simply a replay of the master's.

Later (11:19), Christians fleeing the persecution after Stephen's murder reach even Antioch on the Orontes. From the preaching in which these Christians engaged, as well as from the earlier, convulsive experience of Paul on his way to Damascus, one continues to get the impression that at the core of the matter is Jesus, particularly because he is risen. It is this Jesus, not God or the Holy Spirit, who turns Paul's life completely around. It is this Jesus whom the Christians preach in Phoenica, Cyprus, and Antioch (11:19–20). All religious discussion seems reduced to the figure of Jesus; on him, and necessarily on him risen, is everything now focused.

James and Peter

Herod Agrippa, whose fullest rule lasted from 41 to 44 A.D., beheaded James (brother of John) and intended to do the same to Peter, whom he imprisoned. It is not clear on what grounds he acted this way; Luke only says that Herod had decided to mistreat *tinas tōn apo tēs ekklēsias.* Involved in this matter, however, are the "Jews"; twice (12:3, 11) Luke notes that the deaths of these men would be very satisfactory to the Jews.

Just who these Jews are is not said[15]; it seems, however, to be inconceivable that every Jew in Israel was concerned with Peter and James. It is more likely that, by chapter 12, "Jews" has become a word by which Luke sums up the viewpoints which the Christians contradicted. Only in chapter 9 (vv. 22 and 23) does the term *Ioudaioi* begin to appear as an inimical word to designate those opposed to the preaching of Jesus as messiah[16] (most clearly seen by virtue of his resurrection). *Ioudaioi,* in its critical sense, is picked up again only in chapter 12. Perhaps what it is meant to suggest is that certain groups or strata of Jews were becoming impatient with the continuous and insistent preaching of Jesus as messiah. Not only had they reacted violently to drive out of Jerusalem the widely critical Hellenist Christian Jews, but now they are taking umbrage at the Palestinian Christian Jews for their continuous public claim that

Jesus alone is the messiah, that only in him is God's salvation to be found. Joined to this explanation of Herod Agrippa's extreme (and apparently sudden, unexpected) action is the very light possibility that Herod Agrippa himself[17] became fed up with preaching in his kingdom about Jesus for whose death his predecessor and relative, Herod Antipas, to some degree had some responsibility.[18]

Opposition to James and Peter, then, seems based on the claim that Jesus is risen, on the claim that his peculiar, untraditional doctrine is God's will—and perhaps implies criticism of a past Herod for his role in Jesus' unjust death.

Such, then, has been the experience of the church in Palestine that its members have been persecuted for a number of reasons, all of which center around the fact that Jesus, thought to have been eliminated in a thorough way for his differences with traditional Judaism and claims made about his identity, is now preached as alive, with every intention of continuing his way of living and his claim to leadership.

Is what has been found to be the case in Palestinian repression the cause of similar persecution in Paul's missionary life throughout Asia Minor, Macedonia and Greece?

The First Missionary Journey

Chapter 13, with its stops in Cyprus and Antioch of Pisidia, reports disagreement, even vigorous opposition, but it is only at the last three verses of this chapter that opposition turns to persecution. In Antioch Paul had made some headway with diaspora Jews in his witness to Jesus; as a result, *polloi tōn Ioudaiōn* followed Paul, primarily because of his heartening message that "the risen Jesus is the one through whom they are now to receive the blessings assured to David: justification from sins and from all that the law of Moses could not free them from" (13:33–39).

Perhaps his other words (13:43) to these Jews followed the lines of the Hellenistic Jewish Christians of Stephen's kind. Whatever, not much later, *hoi Ioudaioi,* from whom the *polloi tōn Ioudaiōn* had come, instigate a persecution against Paul and Barnabas and succeed in having them thrown out of Antioch. One can only depend on context for a clearer understanding of who these enemies are. Previous mention of *Ioudaioi* suggests that these Jews are those who have decided that Jesus is not what Paul and Barnabas preach, that to follow Jesus is to abandon God and his revealed ways, that the decision, which Paul notes, to put Jesus to death in Jerusalem was a just decision and not overturned by God's raising Jesus to life, that Jesus is a false messiah. Perhaps, however, another, equally powerful motive comes to the fore, here and elsewhere: certain Jews are antagonistic at the perceived deception worked on their brethren and want to eliminate what they see as divisive, unjust to their community as the people of God.[19]

Iconium follows the pattern of Antioch. Synagogue discussions as to the definition of the messiah and as to the qualifications of Jesus to fit that definition produced believers and enemies. Once again familiar terms appear to signal converts, *Ioudaiōn te kai Hellēnōn polu plēthos,* and angry opponents, *hoi Ioudaioi.* But this time, for the first time, Luke joins to *hoi Ioudaioi* the significant description *apeithēsantes.* It is relative to the data of Paul's arguments that *Ioudaioi* are found to be believing or disbelieving. The disbelieving remain faithful to the traditional religion and thus are titled *hoi Ioudaioi.* Their title, then, indicates, not their ancestry nor their nation and culture, but their religious preference: to disbelieve in Jesus and to remain with traditional Yahwism. What is said about Jesus represents such a development of Judaism that a disbeliever often felt obliged to respond by forceful rejection of what to him was a pernicious and tempting lie.

The mission of Paul and Barnabas in Lystra met with the same reaction as in Antioch, for *apo Antiocheias kai Ikoniou Ioudaioi* (without the article *hoi*) so invaded Lystra that the upshot confrontation with the Christian witnesses resulted in Paul's being left for dead. To understand these *Ioudaioi,* the reader is asked to return to the speech of Paul in Antioch, whence these Jews came; forceful opposition to a central element of the theme of that speech makes clear the nature of opposition to Paul.[20]

The first missionary journey of Paul indicates that *hoi Ioudaioi* are the source of persecution to the Christian preachers. The Pauline discourse in Antioch is the nearest clearest source by which to understand why Jews persecuted Paul. This speech does not differ in its proclamation from earlier speeches given in Palestine. It seems then that, if the preaching remains the same, opponents to it will become easily defined and predictable. While those who put Jesus to death (even a person of minimum involvement as was Antipas) pass from the scene, as Luke's story passes from Palestine—and thus some of their personal reasons for persecution pass away—opposition is totally from that group that remains the perennial disbeliever, that group that remains faithful to the traditional Yahwism and violently opposes any intrusion of falsehood into it.

The Second and Third Missionary Journeys

In this period a new source of persecution is reported. In Philippi Paul is jailed for having caused a young girl to lose the evil spirit which had empowered her to predict fortunes and thus for having deprived her owners of much money (16:16–24). The opposition from these few owners, Gentiles as far as one can discern, becomes persecution as they complain that Paul and his companions disturb the peace and, being Jewish, urge Philippians to embrace religious practices opposed to Roman law. Such claims led to crowd attack and punishments from city magistrates.

Preaching in Thessalonica (17:2–3), however, brought *hoi Ioudaioi* into opposition with Paul; these *Ioudaioi* resented[21] the conversion of *tines ex Ioudaiōn* and instigated a virulent attack against the Christian preachers, in the form of mob riot. At the source of this opposition, then, is conversion from Yahwism, which conversion must again be understood as centered on the Christian claims made about Jesus.

Reaction to preaching in Beroea follows the same pattern: it is *hoi apo tēs Thessalonikēs Ioudaioi* who promote a commotion once they learn of the preaching of what Luke calls "God's word" (17:13) at Paul's next stop. This "word of God" is the message that Jesus is the messiah Lord, upon whose name, God says, one is to call for salvation and whose way of life one is to follow to final redemption. It is enemies of Jesus who oppose his witnesses.

Amidst a relatively quiet, lengthy preaching period in Corinth, Paul is challenged at one moment by *hoi Ioudaioi homothumadon* (18:12). Their claim against Paul is that he is influencing people to reverence (*sebasthai*) God in ways which are against the law. No doubt, this charge is formulated to appeal to a Roman magistrate; underneath it is the real reason for the opposition of *hoi Ioudaioi:* opposition to Jesus' way of worshiping Yahweh. This is hinted at in the reply of Gallio to their charge; he is not going to be bothered about a case that has to do with Jewish terminology and titles and laws. The real struggle, then, is over the impact Jesus has on the traditions of Israelite religion; advocates of the latter, who turn into persecutors, is the meaning of *hoi Ioudaioi*. Indeed, though it does not deal with a persecution, the story of Apollos (18:24–28) contains a reference to *tois Ioudaiois* (v. 28) who are distinguished by their refusal to accept Apollos' arguments from the Jewish scriptures that Jesus is the messiah.[22]

Ephesus, too, produced Christian persecutors, but these came from the ranks of the pagans, and were motivated by a perceived loss of revenue should Christianity replace the cult of Artemis.

Persecution, then, followed Paul through almost all the major cities he visited on his second and third missionary journeys. Persecutors in this period, however, are mostly *hoi Ioudaioi,* but also pagans. *Hoi Ioudaioi* continue to be identified most particularly by their opposition to Jesus, the messiah, who preached a way of life at times different from Jewish teaching of his time.

Paul Imprisoned

With the inception of chapter 21, the reader is brought back to Jerusalem. Old faces, or at least old factions, reappear.[23] Paul is caught in presumed violation of a temple rule, and for this his death is sought. But this situation is magnified by an enlargement of the familiar accusations against him: he is spreading his teaching everywhere against the people of Israel, against Jewish law, against the Jerusalem temple (21:28). Such charges brought about a riot, it is said, and Paul was on the verge of losing his life on account of them. Paul's first explanation (of many) for his years of Christian activity is met with cries, "Kill him; rid the earth of him!" Here Paul's personal persecution is the result of Jews who will not accept his claims to divine mandate; also involved in their opposition, though it is hard to say to what degree, is rejection of Paul's implicit affirmation that Jesus is Lord, who can appear even in the temple.[24]

Paul is saved so as to be judged more equitably and with equanimity by the national sanhedrin. Whatever the charge first raised against Paul, violator of the temple law or general abuse of the Jewish religion in the diaspora, Paul focuses sanhedrin attention on one issue: he is charged because he professes belief in the resurrection of the dead (23:6). Admittedly this is a ruse to pit Sadducee against Pharisee who, too, believes in resurrection, but it leaves unaddressed that more crucial belief, which Pharisees would have opposed: Jesus is messiah, as the resurrection shows, and Lord, as the sitting at the right hand of God shows, and thus his way should be the way Jews should now walk to God.

This hearing, like the previous hearing, ended without decision— except that, in preparation for trial before the governor Felix, Lysias reports from his pagan ignorance of what is disputed between Jews and Christians that Paul "was accused regarding matters dealing with their own (Jewish) law" (23:29).

Before this note to Felix, but after the hearing before the sanhedrin, *hoi Ioudaioi* enter the story again; actually, as the story unfolds, they number a bit over forty, a salutary consideration in trying to estimate just who is meant in Acts by *hoi Ioudaioi*. It is their goal to kill Paul as he is moved from jail back to the sanhedrin for further questioning.[25] The plot is frustrated, but it should be noted that the sanhedrin, while not called *hoi Ioudaioi,* played along with the plotters.

Neither the hearing before the Roman chiliarch nor the hearing before the sanhedrin produced a decision about Paul; he is now presented to the governor, Felix, in Caesarea. To this trial come the high priest, president of the sanhedrin, and some of the elders who make up part of the sanhedrin. These for the moment are Paul's accusers. The charges presented against Paul are dressed so as to trouble a Roman: Paul is a troublemaker, stirring Jews everywhere to sedition (presumably because he encourages them to believe that Jesus is a royal messiah), a leader of the Nazorean gang (24:6). These charges, Luke says, were supported by *hoi Ioudaioi,* now a term meaning, it is to be presumed, those few Jews present in Felix's courtroom; Acts 26:24 will, however, suggest a broadening of the term.

It is important to note again that Paul made resurrection from the dead the only issue of this trial. Not only did this remove the entire situation far from the qualifications of Felix, but it brings back the reader's attention to the core difficulty between Christians and the vast majority of their persecutors.

Unfortunately, Felix would not rule in Paul's favor; rather, he kept him confined, in hopes of being bribed to release Paul and at the same time trusting that imprisonment would prove to be something satisfactory to *hoi Ioudaioi,* evidently now the Sanhedrin, and the Sadducees who influenced it.

With the replacement of Felix by Festus, the case of Paul is reopened. Against him are now listed *hoi archiereis kai hoi prōtoi tōn Ioudaiōn* (25:2). Some (25:7) of these opponents came to Caesarea to attend Paul's trial before Festus. From Paul's general statement to Festus, that he "committed no crime against Jewish law, Jerusalem temple or Roman emperor" (25:8), one gathers what the accusations consisted of; they are repetitious. Rephrased later by Festus, "they differed with him over matters of their own religion and about a Jesus who had died, but who Paul claimed to be alive" (25:19).

Festus finally arranged for a hearing of Paul before such dignitaries as Herod Agrippa I and prominent men of Caesarea. Introducing Paul to the assembly, Festus says that *hapan to plēthos tōn Ioudaiōn enetuchon moi,* in Jerusalem and in Caesarea, to seek Paul's death (25:24). This phrase of Festus, first of all, appears best to be translated as "the whole Jewish people appealed to me."[26] Obviously this could have happened only in the sense that the sanhedrin, particularly the high priest, had sought the death of Paul (which Luke has indicated) and in so doing had represented the entire community of Ioudaioi in Jerusalem and in Caesarea (which representation Luke has only made clear here late in his book). Perhaps, in the light of Festus' remark, one must reconsider all references to the sanhedrin as references to those who represent the entire Jewish people. In this sense, precisions about certain Jews may at times be appropriate, but do not deny what has now come to light, that all Jews in some sense could be said to be against Paul. Since, however, this is the only time in Acts that "all Jews" are involved in a legal action, one is perhaps better counseled to consider Festus' remark to Agrippa an exaggeration of some proportion.[27] In any event, one must not lose sight of the basic definition of *Ioudaios,* whether here or elsewhere: one who refuses with force the teaching that Jesus is risen, is messiah, and is the one whose teaching is to be followed for salvation.

In his forceful speech before Agrippa I, Paul refers to enemies who have brought him to this present grievous situation. Twice he refers to himself as accused *hupo Ioudaiōn* (26:2, 7).[28] The latter reference defines, as far as Paul is concerned, the most precise source of grievance: the hope of fulfillment of the promise made to the fathers and prayed for even now by the twelve tribes, i.e., evidently, resurrection from the dead (cf. v. 8). The surpassing cause of persecution in Christian eyes, then, is the belief in resurrection; Jesus, risen, inescapably stands at the center of this fundamental opposition.

Paul (v. 3), in his own attempt to render Agrippa friendly to his cause, describes Agrippa as one who is knowledgeable in the customs and disputes *kata Ioudaious.* Paul intends by this not only to flatter Agrippa, but also to indicate from the start the line of his self-defense: Paul intends to split Judaism itself in such a way that at least Pharisees will appear on his side, and that therefore not all Judaism can be said to oppose him. Thus, whereas in the same speech *kata Ioudaious* (v. 3) embraces the widest number of Jews, *hupo Ioudaiōn* (vv. 2, 7), who represent his accusers, are limited to those who reject the resurrection from the dead and, particularly, Jesus' resurrection. Looking backward, the reader can identify this latter group as comprising at least the high priest, the elders, the chief priests, and the Sadducees; notably absent from this list are groups such as the Pharisees and scribes.

Further on in his speech, Paul notes that he was apprehended in the temple; this is the beginning of his woes which today have brought him to stand before Agrippa. It was, Paul says, *Ioudaioi* who captured him in the temple. Clearly (here as in vv. 2, 7), *Ioudaioi* is a term used to describe only a small number of those who apparently qualify to be described by that term. *Ioudaioi,* then, is a denomination which, even in this limited speech of Paul, has only one meaning; in Paul's speech before Agrippa, *Ioudaioi* are persecutors because they oppose preaching that Jesus is risen, that anyone can rise from the dead.

In one other place Acts speaks of persecutors. When Paul explains his presence in Rome to those described as *tous ontas tōn Ioudaiōn prōtous*

(28:17), he notes that he asked to be judged by Caesar because, when he might have been released by Roman authority for lack of evidence against him, *Ioudaioi* opposed this release. The more precise identification of *Ioudaioi* here appears from a rereading of the earlier pages which recount how both Sanhedrin officials and bands seeking to waylay and kill Paul stood in the way of Paul's freedom. These people are those opposed either to belief in the resurrection of the dead or to the claim that Jesus is messiah, the only teacher to be followed in service of God.

In summary, it seems best to say that the vast majority of instances of persecution come from those who can be called Jews because they remain faithful to the traditional Yahwism and violently oppose any challenge to it, whether it be in teaching the way of the Lord or in identification of Jesus as messiah or in affirmation of resurrection from the dead or simply in the conversion of Jews to Christianity.

III. THE EFFECTS OF THE PERSECUTIONS

1. One effect of the persecutions in Acts is, ironically, the spread of the Christian witness; what was intended as a snuffing out of Christianity caused Christianity to be planted elsewhere. There are a number of examples in Acts where it seems that the particular, and often sole, cause of the movement of Christian witnesses to new territory was forceful expulsion from old territory. The witness to Jesus that took place in Phoenicia, Cyprus and Antioch on the Orontes occurred because of the persecution in Jerusalem against Stephen and his class of Jewish Christians (11:19). Preaching in Iconium occurred, it seems, because Antioch in Pisidia drove out Paul and Barnabas (13:50–51). And threat of abuse and stoning drove Paul and Barnabas from Iconium to Lystra (14:5–6), where, after an unorthodox reception, the Christian witnesses were driven (Paul almost dead) to Derbe (14:19–21).

In Philippi, Paul was asked out of town by the magistrates (16:39). The Thessalonians were particularly offensive and caused Paul and Silas to move, under cover of night, to Beroea (17:5, 10); then they chased after these preachers and in Beroea stirred things up to the point that Paul was sent off immediately by the brothers (17:14). Perhaps, finally, Paul's leaving Ephesus (20:1) when he did was the result of the turmoil created by the silversmiths against the new way; certainly Paul's adjustment of his travel mode from Greece to Syria was caused by a plot against him in Greece (20:3).

Whatever missionary plan Paul had, after his meeting with James and the other Christians in Jerusalem, the attacks against him ended that plan, bringing him rather to witness in Rome.

2. Another effect of the persecutions can be said to be the various expressions of piety which result in Acts because of them. At the very core is the courage shown in the face of suffering and in resuming activity which will probably result in further suffering. Added to this are the expressions of joy which resulted from seeing persecution as an opportunity to show and bring honor to the name of Christ. The way in which Stephen's death is presented is meant to teach forgiveness of enemies and trust in God—no mean virtues *in extremis.* One might even suggest with strong probability that the wisdom expressed by Christian witnesses under duress came to be and was sharpened precisely by their anxious situations, and, still further, that the unity Luke eulogizes in the first communities is owed not only to sincere *metanoia* and baptism in the same Lord, but also to common support against enemies.

Noteworthy is the prayer which resulted (4:23–31) from the earliest persecutions. It is characterized by its ability to relate suffering for the name of Jesus to Old Testament sacred literature, by its ability to find in this suffering a divine plan and by its request to God for still further ability *meta parrēsias pasēs lalein ton logon sou.* Persecution sharpened the realization of what it meant to have called on the name of the Lord.

One might even go so far as to note that the prudence of Gamaliel was exercised amidst the conundrum of whether or not to continue persecution against the Christians.

A thesis which is difficult to prove, yet attractive for all that, says that the conversion of Paul was somehow owed to the persecution which he impressed upon Christians. It is "Jesus whom you are persecuting" who is the constant in the changing circumstances which make up the three accounts of Paul's conversion. Such an identification has power over Paul and suggests thereby that it was his experience in dealing in mortal fashion with faithful, devoted Christians that psychologically prepared Paul to question, at the right divine moment, his entire orientation toward Christianity and Jesus.

Acts occasionally reports even righteous indignation (13:51), manifested in "shaking dust from their feet," as a sign of protest and in accord with Jesus' own recommendation (cf. Lk 9:5). Apart from such a gesture and words which explain it, one must marvel that at no time did any Christian witness retaliate or take revenge for sufferings endured. In fact, the expression of Paul near the end of his first missionary experience in today's southeast Turkey seems meant to be extended throughout Acts: *dia pollōn thlipseōn dei hēmas eiselthein eis tēn basileian tou Theou* (14:22).

As Paul progresses through the Mediterranean basin, one is further impressed with two facts which proceed from persecutions, as Luke presents them. First, there is the perplexity of Roman officials and others which results in either indifference (e.g. Gallio at 18:14–15) or a willingness to judge Christians favorably (e.g. Festus at 25:25, Agrippa II at 26:32). Without the persecutions, Luke might not have been able to bring such important material forward in favor of Christianity. Second, there is the clear folly and bad will of those virulently opposed to Christianity. It is the persecutions, inspired by jealousy, forged by connivance and executed with brutality, when unable to stand up against truth, which help most to underline the wrongness of its enemies and the opposite goodness of Christianity; these types of violence usually have such an effect.

3. Finally, one can call an effect of the persecutions what appears to be a conscious effort on Luke's part to correlate the last years of Paul with the last months of Jesus.[29]

Already in the prayer of the community at the return of Peter and John from prison, the Christians of Jerusalem had revealed a consciousness that the apostles' sufferings were reminiscent of the suffering by which "the Gentiles conspired" and "the kings and princes were aligned and gathered" against the Lord and his anointed (4:25–28). The use of *dei* in the observation that "by many trials we must enter the kingdom of God" (14:22) reminds one of the *dei* which forms an essential part of the passion/resurrection predictions of Jesus about himself (9:22, 44; 24:7, 26, 44, 46).

Furthermore, words which are recognized as terms which recall the sufferings of Jesus—*paradidōmi, paschein*—occur on occasion as descriptive terminology of persecutions. Acts 8:3 speaks of Paul as one who *paredidou* Jewish Christians to jail; Paul later on describes this same persecution of Jewish Christians by the same term, *paradidous eis phulakas* (22:4). In 21:11 the prophet Agabus notes about Paul that the Jews in Jerusalem *paradōsousin* Paul *eis cheiras ethnōn*. Indeed, at one point they *paredidoun* Paul *hekatontarchō* (27:1); finally, in Rome Paul describes himself: *desmos ek Hierousolumōn paredōthen eis tas cheiras tōn Rōmaiōn* (28:17). As for the word *paschein*, used to describe the passion of Jesus, Luke quotes Jesus as telling Ananias that Jesus himself will indicate to the repentant Paul *hosa dei auton hyper tou onomatos mou pathein* (9:16).

Most importantly, however, as indicated at the beginning of this section, the last chapters of Acts seem to be written so as to remind the reader how much Paul has become like Jesus.

At Acts 19:21 Paul says (to whom?), "Once I have been there (i.e. Jerusalem), I must visit Rome, as well." This intention may seem innocent of deeper meaning, just the hopes of an eager missionary. But, from the viewpoint of a master storyteller, this is the first of a number of foreshadowings (marked by the very significant usage of the word we have noted earlier, *dei*) of the trials of Paul which eventually brought him to Rome. One might point out a number of parallels to this from the story of Jesus; perhaps, to parallel the timing of a reference to the suffering of Jesus, one might best recall the early prophecy of Simeon which long foreshadowed the time when Jesus would be "a sign opposed" resulting in even the "piercing of Mary by a sword."

At Acts 20:22–25 Paul indicates to the Ephesian *presbuteroi* his sure conviction, all the more ominous for its lack of clear detail, that, though not knowing precisely what will happen to him in Jerusalem, it will include hardship and chains. Such will be this experience that Paul can in the same breath talk about readiness to give up life itself, about not ever seeing his friends again. There is much in all this to make one recall, first, the forecasts by Jesus of his own death (Lk 9:22, 44) and, second, the many dark suggestions in Jesus' last words at his Passover meal (Lk 22:14–38), particularly his opening, tone-setting remark, "With great desire have I wanted to eat this Passover meal with you before I suffer; I assure you, I will not eat it again until its meaning is completed in the kingdom of God" (Lk 22:15–16).

To underline the profound sadness of Paul's discourse in Miletus, Luke records the unrestrained weeping and embraces and kisses, all resulting from the deeply distressing realization that "they would never see his face again" (20:38). This poignant Lucan phrasing of a detail reminds one of the apostles' experience, not revealed as an experience of sorrow, but one of confusion and consternation, whether as to the "why" of Jesus' suffering (Lk 9:45) or as to the identity of a betrayer among them (Lk 22:23) or to the possibility of infidelity (Lk 22:33).

The Spirit is then reported to have revealed to disciples in Tyre an undefined but deadly threat to Paul in Jerusalem; Paul was undeterred by such an authoritative revelation (21:5). The reader recalls Jesus' own resolution: "As the time drew near for his being taken up to heaven, Jesus set his face (determinedly set out) for the journey to Jerusalem" (9:51). One might even see in the Pharisees' warning that Herod was out to kill Jesus (Lk 13:32) something of a parallel to the disciples' warning that something drastic would happen to Paul in Jerusalem.

Once again, this time at Caesarea Maritima, a scene unfolds which augurs ill for Paul in Jerusalem. First, there is another prophecy from the Holy Spirit, done in gesture, then interpreted: Paul, for a moment bound hand and foot in a prophetic action, hears, "In this fashion will the one bound be handed over to the Gentiles" (21:10–11). This symbolic act is followed by great urgings to stay away from Jerusalem (21:12). All this elicits from Paul a statement that, even in the face of weeping and pleading, "I am ready, for the name of Jesus, for imprisonment, even death, in Jerusalem" (21:13). The conclusion to this story is consciously written to reveal, in its pathos, the only true response to the martyr's inner knowledge: "The Lord's will be done" (21:14). The repetition of the forecast of suffering becomes as important as the forecast itself. Luke is very aware of this factor, whether in his gospel or in Acts. Not only did Luke early in the gospel vignette of Simeon suggest Jesus' suffering, but such times as when God identifies Jesus as his *agapētos* (Lk 3:22), thereby suggesting Jesus as the suffering servant of Isaiah (Is 42:1; 49:3), and when Luke programmatically indicates death as the only cessation of anger at Jesus' claims (Lk 4:21, 28–29), and when Luke notes that Jesus speaks with Moses and Elijah about his *exodos* to be fulfilled in Jerusalem (Lk 9:31), and when Jesus responds to the threat of Herod Antipas (Lk 13:31) with his fateful words, "For all that, I must (again *dei*) continue onward today, tomorrow, and its tomorrow, because no prophet is permitted to die elsewhere than in Jerusalem" (Lk 13:33)—throughout the gospel there is a buildup, continual warning and pressure derived from it, that is similar to what Luke does in Acts by the (admittedly less pervasive) repetition of the theme of forthcoming suffering for Paul.

Once one enters Jerusalem with Paul, one sees the precise contours the forebodings of previous chapters take. There is at least one trial in the formal sense (24:1–22), this, as in the case of Luke's story of Jesus, before Roman officialdom. There are a number of hearings, stretching from 22:1 to 28:22, all of which, in one way or another, argue forcefully the innocence of Paul; this is matched by the parallel insistence in the gospel story that no one, Roman or Jew, can find anything really wrong about Jesus. To this point belongs the particular parallellism between the gospel and Acts as regards the charges leveled against Jesus and Paul. In Jesus' case, it was "subversion of our nation, opposition to payment of taxes to Caesar, claim to be king" (Lk 23:2) and, more generally, "stirring up the people with his teaching" (Lk 23:5). In Paul's case (with due allowance made between Jesus and Paul) it was "spreading teaching everywhere against God, temple, Israel" (Acts 21:28), "making trouble, stirring up sedition, a ringleader of the Nazoreans, who desecrates the temple" (Acts 24:5–6), "regarding issues of their own religion and regarding a certain Jesus, put to death, but claimed by Paul to be alive" (Acts 25:19)—this latter formulation of the charge recalls that accusation made in Thessalonica, "Christians pay no attention to the decrees of Caesar and claim that Jesus is king" (17:7).

In the above ways, and others, too (e.g. imprisonment, rough handling), Paul's "way" is completed in a manner which is very reminiscent of Jesus' "way" to ascension—intentionally so, it appears.

CONCLUSION

Persecution surely permeates the Acts of the Apostles story. Not that it is omnipresent, which argues that it is not a fiction. Moreover, persecution is not presented as the main point the reader is to reflect upon; witness is. Given the nature of the writing, "from faith to faith," persecution at times serves to bring out courage and wisdom on the part of Christians, foolishness and evil on the part of the persecutors. Not least at all is the likeness one comes to see between the pattern of Christ's life and the pattern of witness to Christ. One can even consider that fidelity under persecution becomes its own peculiar witness to Jesus. In this way, a subordinate reality of Acts takes a more central place, as it contributes to the great theme of Acts, "You will be my witnesses . . ." (1:8). And in its turn persecution can be seen to flesh out what Luke meant to give to Theophilus, when he assured him that, from reading Luke's presentation of the Christian experience, Theophilus would "grasp the solidity (*asphaleian*) of what he had already been taught" (Lk 1:4). The "truth" blossoms forth from those seeds gone to decay in the earth for what they believed, what they said and did under pressure of persecutions.

Gerald O'Collins

Luke on the Closing of the Easter Appearances

Apropos of Jesus' post-resurrection appearances, some continue to hold that these "appearances" were simply the first example (chronologically) of ecstatic, pneumatic and/or revelatory encounters with the risen Jesus which early believers experienced and which later believers also could and can experience. However, the data from Paul, John and other New Testament witnesses does not support this thesis. What the New Testament indicates is that the appearances of the risen Lord were limited to certain individuals and groups and that, even at the beginning of Christianity, others beyond those individuals and groups did not and indeed could not share in that experience.

This article limits itself to the evidence from the gospel of Luke and Acts. What does Luke say in his two-part work about the duration of the post-resurrection experiences?

In the Lukan scheme the Easter appearances come to an end, and this closure is closely connected with three things: the risen Jesus' ascension (Lk 24:50–51; Acts 1:9–11),[1] the role of the (twelve) apostles as eye-witnesses to him (Lk 1:2; 6:12–16; Acts 1:3, 9–11, 21–22),[2] and the transition from the period of Jesus (which begins with the Holy Spirit descending upon him when he is baptized by John—Lk 3:21–22; 4:1, 14, 18) to the time of the church (which begins when Jesus is taken away into heaven out of sight of the apostles and they are baptized with the Holy Spirit—Acts 1:5, 9.[3] Let us see these points in a little more detail.

In Luke's two-part account of the origins of Christianity the work of Jesus begins with his baptism (Lk 3:21–22; Acts 1:22; 10:37–38). It ends with his ascension when a new stage in salvation history opens the period of the church that will bring the witnesses of Christ right to the ends of the earth (Lk 24:47–48; Acts 1:8) and will close when he comes again at the *parousia* (Acts 1:11).[4] The aorist tense of *ōphthē* in 1 Cor 15:5, 6, 7, 8, suggests that the Easter appearances were over and done with—a point made quite explicit by Paul's "last of all" in 1 Cor 15:8. This notion (that the appearances of the risen Jesus had come to a close) probably helped in the making of Acts 1:1–11.[5] The period when the risen Jesus had let himself be seen (Acts 1:3) ended with the ascension (Acts 1:9–11), an episode which stresses the role of the apostles as eyewitnesses right to the finish:

> And when he had said this, as they were *looking on,* he was lifted up and a cloud took him out of *their sight.* And while they were *gazing* into heaven as he went, behold, two men stood by them in white robes and said, "Men of Galilee, why do you stand *looking* into heaven? This Jesus, who was taken up from you into heaven, will come in the same way, as you *saw* him go into heaven."[6]

Thus Jesus' activity was followed by eyewitnesses from the beginning of his ministry (Lk 1:2; 3:23), through the crucifixion (Lk 23:49), and on to the time of post-resurrection appearances (Lk 24; Acts 1:1–11) that terminated with the ascension. These disciples not only report on the ministry and death of Jesus, but also witness to the resurrection and testify that the risen one was and is personally identical with the earthly Jesus (see also Acts 10:39–42; 13:31). From among these disciples the witnesses par excellence are "the twelve" whom Luke practically identifies with "the apostles." The account of the choice of Judas' successor (Acts 1:15–26) summarizes the Lukan view on the conditions and function of the apostolic office. Peter says: "One of the men who accompanied us during all the time that the Lord Jesus went in and out among us, beginning from the baptism of John until the day when he was taken up from us—one of these men must become with us a witness to his resurrection" (Acts 1:21–22). After prayer Matthias was chosen by lot to become one of the twelve and through the Spirit (Lk 24:49; Acts 1:8) to be empowered (with the others) in his function as apostolic witness.[7]

Thus with the ascension and the coming of the Holy Spirit the period of the church begins, a period that opens with Peter and the college of twelve apostles bearing witness to Jesus and their experience of him which has ended with his being taken up into heaven. For the twelve apostles the post-Easter appearances have definitively come to a close. That being their situation, *a fortiori* is it so for others. Henceforth, instead of seeing him, the new "disciples" (Acts 6:1, 7; 9:1, 10, etc) or "Christians" (Acts 11:26) "turn to" Jesus (Acts 9:35; 11:21), receive the forgiveness of sin through his name (Acts 2:38; 3:26; 4:31; 10:43), "believe in" him (Acts 9:42; 10:43; 11:17; 14:23; 16:31), have "faith" in him (Acts 26:18), are "baptized in his name" (Acts 2:38; 8:16; 10:48; 19:5) and are "saved" through his name (Acts 4:12) or through his grace (Acts 15:11). In these and other ways Acts presents the (old and new) disciples' experience of and relationship to Jesus in the post-ascension situation. He does not, however, "appear" to them nor do they "see" him. Let us look at three exceptions (Paul, Ananias and Stephen) and the possible case of Paul's companions on the Damascus road.

Along with Barnabas, Paul is twice called an "apostle" (Acts 14:4, 14). Like Stephen (Acts 22:20) Paul is called a "witness" (Acts 22:15; 26:16). Like the twelve apostles, Paul is to witness to what he has "seen" and "heard" during his Damascus road experience (Acts 22:14–15; see Acts 9:27) and later during a trance in the Jerusalem temple (Acts 22:17–21). Nevertheless, in the Lukan scheme the real witnesses to Jesus and his resurrection are the twelve apostles (Acts 4:33) and their leader, Peter (Acts 2:32; 3:15; 5:32; 10:39–41). Hence in one of his major addresses (in Pisidian Antioch) Paul speaks not of himself but of those others (who are, above all, the twelve) as *the* witnesses to the risen Jesus: "For many days he [Jesus] appeared to those who came up with him from Galilee to Jerusalem, who are now his witnesses to the people" (Acts 13:31). Thus even if Luke twice calls Paul an apostle and witness, it is only by way of "analogy" to the qualifications and function of the twelve apostles.

Where then does that leave the Damascus road encounter which Luke emphasizes by including it three times (Acts 9:1–19; 22:5–16; 26:12–18)? In the encounter "a light from heaven flashes" around Paul (Acts 9:3; see 22:6 and 26:13) who falls to the ground and hears a voice which identifies itself as that of Jesus (Acts 9:4–5; 22:7–8; 26:34–35). It is not in the actual narration of the encounter but only afterward that the text says that "Jesus appeared to" Paul (Acts 9:17) or that Paul "had seen the Lord" (Acts 9:27; see Acts 22:14–15). In the third version of the encounter it is Jesus himself who adds that language of appearing and seeing:

> Rise and stand upon your feet; for I have *appeared* to you for
> this purpose, to appoint you to serve and bear witness to the
> things in which you have *seen* me and to those in which I will
> *appear* to you (Acts 16:16).

The promise about those things "in which I will appear to you" refers to other (subordinate) encounters with the heavenly Jesus, three of which are narrated by Acts. First, after returning to Jerusalem Paul goes to pray in the temple, a place of central importance in the Lukan picture of salvation history, and later reports: "I fell into a trance and saw him [Jesus] saying to me, 'Make haste and get quickly out of Jerusalem' " (Acts 22:17–21). What Paul hears is much more significant than what he sees, as the heavenly Jesus sends him as apostle to the Gentiles. Hearing like-wise takes precedence over seeing in a second episode which, though chro-nologically later, turns up earlier in the text of Acts. In Corinth Paul is encouraged to teach bravely and prolong his stay after the Lord Jesus *spoke* to him "one night in a vision" (Acts 18:9–10).

The same emphasis on what Paul hears holds true on the third occa-sion: "The following night the Lord [Jesus] stood by him and said, 'Take courage, for as you have testified about me at Jerusalem, so you must bear witness also at Rome' " (Acts 23:11). Thus the three episodes that fulfill the promise "I will appear to you," even if they use the language of "see-ing" and "vision," concentrate rather on what Paul hears Jesus "saying" and "speaking" to him about the apostle's mission to the Gentiles and about the difficulties to be overcome on that mission. These messages from the heavenly Jesus, given during prayer in the Jerusalem temple or at night, are somewhat akin to what Paul himself reports in 2 Cor 12:7–9. On some occasion (after an "abundance of relevations") Paul suffered from "a thorn in the flesh," prayed three times and received from the Lord a message of comfort—the only word from the risen and heavenly Jesus cited by Paul in his letters.[8]

To sum up: in the Lukan scheme the risen Jesus' only clear appear-ance to Paul is the Damascus road encounter. Even there, when narrating the encounter, Luke does not state straightforwardly that Jesus appeared to Paul (as in 1 Cor 15:8) or that Paul saw Jesus (as in 1 Cor 9:1). This detail is added subsequently by Ananias (Acts 9:17; 22:14–15), Paul (Acts 9:27) or Jesus himself (Acts 25:26).

In Luke's first and second version of the Damascus road encounter the disciple Ananias plays a significant role. In the second account he communicates what "the God of our fathers" has called Paul to experi-ence and become (Acts 22:14). It is only in the first version that Ananias experiences the Lord (Jesus) "in a vision" (Acts 9:10–19). Even there the emphasis is all on what Ananias hears (and says) and not on what he sees. The opening verse of the pericope indicates that clearly: "The Lord *said* to him in a vision" (Acts 9:10).[9] Only by way of analogy could one describe Ananias' experience as a christophany or appearance of the risen Christ. It is an auditory (rather than a visual) communication of a message about what Ananias must do immediately and what Paul is to become subsequently.

We can deal rapidly with the third case, that of "the men who were traveling with" Paul on the Damascus road. In Luke's first account they hear the voice (of Jesus) but see no one (Acts 9:7). In the second account they see the "great light from heaven" but do not hear the voice speaking to Paul (Acts 22:6, 9). In the third account the apostle's companions are not said to see the light or hear the voice. In this account, however, the light from heaven shines around them and they too fall to the ground.[10] Nevertheless, none of the three accounts reports that the risen Jesus "appeared" to those others or that they "saw" him. Their case provides no exception to the Lukan scheme of no christophanies after the ascension.

Finally, there is the experience of Stephen minutes before his death by martyrdom: "He, full of the Holy Spirit, gazed into heaven and saw the glory of God, and Jesus standing at the right hand of God; and he said, 'Behold, I see the heavens opened, and the Son of Man standing at the right hand of God' " (Acts 7:55–56). Heaven which had taken the risen Jesus out of sight (Acts 1:10–11) is here opened, and the doomed Stephen gazes into the place where he or his "spirit" is about to go (Acts 7:59). Jesus is said (twice) to be "standing at the right hand of God," presumably waiting to receive the martyr.[11] The point of the scene is neither to establish the fact of Jesus' resurrection nor to turn Stephen into an Easter witness who can function as an apostle. Rather Luke wishes to explain why Stephen's face shone like that of an angel (Acts 6:15 is intelligible because Stephen reflected the glory of God), to link this first Christian martyrdom with the death of Jesus (Acts 7:56, 59, 60 are to be associated, respectively, with Luke 22:69; 23:46; 23:34a) and to connect the killing of Stephen with a leading protagonist in the subsequent chapters of Acts, Saul/Paul (Acts 7:58; 8:1). In short, Stephen's vision is not on a par either with the appearances of Jesus to his original disciples (up to the time of the ascension) or with Paul's Damascus road encounter. The doomed martyr's vision does not really breach the pattern of no post-ascension christophanies.

The solitary real exception to this Lukan pattern is the special case of Paul, whose encounter with the risen Jesus turned him into *the* apostle to the Gentiles (Acts 9:15; 13:46–47; 22:21). Obviously, Luke does not present Paul and his Damascus road experience as a model for what new Christian disciples experienced or could experience. Further, as we have noted, Luke even plays down the parallel between the post-resurrection appearances to the original disciples and Paul's experience on the Damascus road by not stating clearly, when narrating the actual encounter, that "Jesus appeared to Paul" or that "Saul/Paul saw Jesus."

In Acts one episode brings out forcefully the Lukan scheme of no post-ascension christophanies—the baptism of the Ethiopian official on the road to Gaza (Acts 8:26–40). A number of scholars have noted and analyzed the similarities between this story from Acts and the account of the meeting with the risen Jesus on the road to Emmaus (Lk 24:13–35).[12] The common elements include, for example, the theme of persons on a journey (a natural symbol for a search), the meeting with a mysterious

stranger, new insights into scripture, the sacramental theme (breaking of
the bread at Emmaus and baptism for the Ethiopian), the disappearance
of the companions (Jesus himself in Luke and Philip in Acts) and the
joyful continuing of the journey (on the part of the Ethiopian in Acts and
the two disciples in Luke's gospel). In a striking way the two stories parallel each other. Nevertheless, in the Emmaus story the heavenly protagonist is the risen Jesus himself; in the second story "the angel of the Lord"
(Acts 8:26) sends Philip to the Gaza road and "the Spirit" (Acts 8:29)
instructs him to initiate the dialogue that brings the Ethiopian to Christian faith. Jesus appears on the Emmaus road but not on the Gaza road.
The story of the Ethiopian official does not tamper with the Lukan pattern of the christophanies ending with the ascension.

To conclude: Luke is, of course, not the only New Testament witness
to be heard on the question of the duration of the risen Christ's appearances. At all events his evidence is clear: the Easter appearances closed
with the ascension. Neither the visions of Stephen and Ananias nor the
experience of Paul's companions on the Damascus road modifies this
pattern of no christophanies after the ascension. The only (partial) exception is the "appearance" to Paul himself. Even here what Paul hears is
more important than what he sees.

In this way the Lukan data converges with the data from Paul, John
and others to indicate the unique role of those who witnessed to their
experience of Jesus that ended with the post-resurrection christophanies.
Later disciples cannot simply repeat that experience, but are called to
believe in dependence on the testimony of the original disciples.

Gilberto Marconi

History as a Hermeneutical Interpretation of the Difference Between Acts 3:1–10 and 4:8–12

"Methods have their day; poetry abides" (A.M. Ripellino)

INTRODUCTION

Ten years of close acquaintance with Father Emilio Rasco have made me increasingly convinced of the excellence of his research, which is both faithful to historical tradition and open to the demands of hermeneutics. It is by focusing on these two elements—history and hermeneutics—that I shall try to honor the man whose teaching has guided and inspired my own research.

The abundant scholarly literature on the historiographical role of the Acts of the Apostles[1] may well make any further reflection on the subject superfluous and its results quite foreseeable. One possible way of avoiding this pitfall is suggested by some types of written text that require first of all a procedure of a hermeneutical kind. Like any literary document that narrates a history, the Acts of the Apostles does not set before us pure historical fact but rather the latest in a series of interpretations which the facts have undergone before reaching us in the form we now have them.

My purpose, then, is to show the impossibility of distinguishing the historical account of events from their interpretation. Starting from this pre-understanding, which has been abundantly confirmed by historical and philosophical inquiry,[2] I set forth a series of interpretations of the same event in order to ascertain, not the characteristic methods of its redactor but rather a hermeneutical development that includes even the so-called "story of the event." My conclusion is that nothing falls outside the purview of interpretation. In other words: the analysis I offer starts from the presupposition that an objective historiography is impossible and that interpretation alone can yield a satisfactory understanding of history.

The passages I analyze tell of an experience of Peter and John (3:1–10). The leader of the pair interprets the event immediately afterward to the astonished people (3:12ff) and the next day to an assembly gathered to pass judgment on him and his comrade (4:8–12).

CONTEXT

The text in its entirety is mounted as it were between two summaries (2:42–48 and 4:32–33) whose atemporal and generalizing statement of an ideal[3] stands in contrast to the historical and temporal details of the narrative passage (3:1: "at three o'clock in the afternoon"; 3:2, 10: "at the gate of the temple called the Beautiful Gate"; 3:11: "Solomon's Portico"; 4:3: "until the next day, for it was already evening"; 4:5: "the next day"; etc.). It also has its place in the broader context of the entire work inasmuch as it marks the beginning of the testimony, comprising actions and interpretative words, which the risen Lord called for (1:8) at the moment of separation between divinity and visible world when he withdrew himself from the sight of the community (1:9).[4] In keeping with this command, it is in Jerusalem and indeed in the place which best represents the city, namely, the temple, the center of Jewish life and religion,[5] that the proclamation of Jesus' true identity begins. No better place could have been found for making this testimony immediately known throughout the city.

Our section (3:1–4:31) contains a number of literary genres which suggest subdivisions. The opening narrative passage (3:1–10) is a miracle story,[6] and it is followed by a discourse (3:13–26). Next comes an account of persecution, which in its turn comprises a narrative passage (4:1–4: imprisonment) and an account of a trial (4:5–22). The whole section ends with a prayer offered by the gathered community (see v. 23: "their friends"; v. 24: "they raised their voices together"). Each pericope, though set apart internally by the style proper to its literary genre and by a degree of verbal repetition that promotes inclusive forms, is also closely connected to the preceding pericope both by some use of the same words[7] and by the logical succession of actions; this last is also underscored by the initial *de*s which never have their usual adversative meaning.[8]

The pericopes, divided in this way, yield two narrative passages, the first concerning a deliverance (miracle of healing: 3:1–10) and the second an imprisonment (4:1–4). Each of these is followed by a passage of discourse (3:13–26; 4:5–22); the second of these, though more of a dialogue, leaves ample room for a discourse of Peter (4:8–12).[9] While the event that is of greatest interest, or from which at least everything else follows, is the cure of the cripple as told in the opening passage, the other interpretations are included in the successive discourses. Both of these begin with a reference to the preceding miracle, which can give the impression of being simply a means to an end. This impression is perhaps better founded in the first discourse because of its length; in the second, on the other hand, the reference to the miracle takes up half of Peter's discourse. In any case, I shall analyze both discourses, even if 4:8–12 deserves greater space because it manifests a certain structural similarity to the first interpretation given of the narrated event (3:1–10).

It is difficult to derive from the context and the division of pericopes considerations that are decisive for an understanding of the texts. On the other hand, unless we want to distort Luke's intention, it cannot be mere chance that a certain unity emerges: both the first interpretation of the event and the interpretations that follow are contained in the same section and have Peter as principal subject. This unity is further supported by the logical continuity between the pericopes: everything starts with the miracle that is followed by an explanation. This in turn leads to an imprisonment that necessitates a trial. Once the two disciples are acquitted, the community gathers and prays. We are thus able to observe how from the beginning the primitive church experiences predominantly the "external" aspect or at least how the two things with which my analysis in concerned must be thought of as combined at this stage of the church's life.

ARCHITECTURE OF ACTS 3:12, 16

Despite numerous challenges to it, the overall pattern which Wilckens finds in the missionary discourses of Acts[10] is still to some extent valid. In the present context I am interested only in the possibility of generalizing the first of the six elements making up the pattern,[11] namely, the exordium, which links the discourse to the situation in which it is pronounced. In 1962, Dupont criticized Wilckens' position and opted for a closer connection between each discourse and the narrative framework in which it is placed.[12] He returned to the subject in 1973 and seemed to nuance his earlier dialectical position, at least as regards the exordium which he describes as "suitable to the occasion," and as having "for its purpose to ensure the connection between the Christian message and the situation in which the discourse is placed."[13] In the following year, Wilckens gave his response on the general theme.[14] Looking beyond the debate between these two great scholars (a subject that would take me far beyond the restricted scope of my concern here), it seems that the exegetes have

generally assigned little importance to the exordium, regarding it most of
the time as having no value in itself and serving only to recall events by
way of the wonder they aroused or the false interpretations that called for
a satisfactory explanation. I shall look for a possible solution solely
through analysis of the texts, since there is no other way for me to proceed.

In our present passage the exordium is located, from a structural
point of view, in the first part of a discourse that can be divided into two
phases, each beginning with an exclamation (v. 12: *andres Israēlitai;* v.
17: *adelphoi*). Vv. 11–16[15] seem to be organized concentrically. The
verses forming the outer circle (vv. 11–12, 16) are tied together to form an
inclusion by repetition of the pronoun referring to the person healed (this
pronoun does not recur during or after the passage) and by the repeated
reference to all those around:

> v. 11: *pas ho laos*   *autou*
> v. 12: *andres Israēlitai*   *auton*
> v. 16: *pantōn humōn*   *toutōn, hon . . . autō*

The second circle (vv. 13a, 15b) is characterized by the presence of
God, whose action has Jesus as its object:

> v. 13a: *ho Theos Abraam . . . ho Theos . . . edoxasen ton paida*
>   *autou Iēsoun*
> v. 15b: *hon (Iēsoun) ho Theos ēgeiren ek nekrōn*

At the center, the repeated second person plural pronoun is the subject of five coordinate negative actions which again have Jesus as their
object:

> v. 13b: *humeis men paredōkate kai ērnēsasthe*
> v. 14:   *humeis de ērnēsasthe kai ētēsasthe*
> v. 15b: *apekteinate*[16]

Of the three parts only the outermost refers directly to the miraculous
event; the other two tell of opposed behaviors relative to Jesus, cause of
the cure, and not directly to the crippled man.

This structure makes it possible to connect v. 12 with v. 16 and
therefore to consider the exordium as having two levels as it were: the first
is closer to and as it were repeats the action that was the starting point, and
serves as a kind of link; the second is a core containing the christological
explanation and has a greater theological importance.

The other exordia are rather different in character. In 2:15 Peter refutes an erroneous judgment passed on the disciples; he makes only one reference to the "fact" which is the starting point of his discourse, and in doing so he changes the terminology (v. 13: *gleukous memestōmenoi;* v. 15: *methuousin*). In 4:9 the subject of the one-clause exordium is the "event" of the our passage; here again the vocabulary changes (this case will be analyzed separately). In 5:29 an exordium is replaced by the reason for the disobedience to authority. The discourse in 10:34–43 is too different from the others to allow of a comparison, even one limited to the exordium, which is completely missing.

It is my opinion, therefore, that there is no question of an exordium conceived purely and simply as a formal link, at least in the two Petrine discourses which I am examining more closely. On the other hand, both start with an interpretation of the event, and this is followed by an explanation of the causes; consequently the interpretation, in the true and proper sense, of the event is to be sought in the exordium.

ANALYSIS OF ACTS 3:12, 16

Peter's first reference to the miracle comes immediately after it and is addressed to all the people (v. 11: *pas ho laos;* v. 12: *pros ton laon*) who have run to the Portico of Solomon and are amazed as what has happened (v. 10: *eplēsthēsan thambous kai ekstaseōs;* v. 11: *ekthamboi*). His question, which focuses on this amazement, looks to the ultimate cause of the extraordinary happening: *ti thaumazete epi toutō . . . hōs*[17] *idia dunamei ē eusebeia pepoiēkosin tou peripatein auton* (= v. 12: "why do you wonder at this . . . as though by our own power or piety we had made him walk?"). It is to this opening question that I wish to direct attention, and especially to the person for whom the miracle was worked and to the miraculous action.

The crippled man is mentioned simply by means of a pronoun that refers back to the preceding incident and shows that the discourse is a logical continuation of the event and is inseparable from it. In fact, throughout chapter 3, after the *anēr chōlos* of v. 2, every reference to the cripple is in the form of a pronoun.[18]

A second question, which is more closely related to my purpose, has to do with the interpretation of the miracle, which is explained as consisting in the cripple's recovery of his motor function. The verb *peripatein*, which is a characteristic element in the stories of healing in the gospels and Acts,[19] signifies here the simple action of walking in direct contrast to the immobility previously forced upon the man: in addition to the description of his condition in the adjective *chōlos*, his passivity is emphasized by the two verbs in the imperfect tense: *ebastazeto* and *hon etithoun* (v. 2: "was being carried" and "whom they would lay"). After Peter orders him to walk (v. 6: *peripatei*), the chief activity of the cured man is described by that very same verb.[20] This activity, the result of the miracle, is used to describe the miracle itself in Peter's discourse. It seems, in fact, that an interpretation in the true and proper sense is omitted in favor a repeated objective description of the facts. Thus, even as regards the interpretation of the event, there is complete continuity with the event itself; we are led therefore to think that this first reference back to the event is eminently instrumental. In reality, however, inasmuch as only in this first reference does Peter use the very language of the original story to refute an "erroneous" interpretation, we may suppose that the closer we are to the reality, the greater the number of interpretations, or the more "mimetic" the language, the greater the possibility of interpretative readings.[21]

In this same discourse, a further explicit reference to the event broadens the hermeneutical understanding of it. The reference is in v. 16, the rather unique organization of which begins with a formula that brings together, in oblique and dependent cases, the subjects of the next two clauses; the latter are vaguely chiastic in form, with the testimony (T), the verb (V), and the subject (S) following in inverse order:

epi tē pistei tou onomatos autou
touton, hon theōreite kai oidate (T), *estereōsen* (V) *ton onoma* (S)
            autou
kai hē pistis (S) *hē di'autou edōken* (V) *autō . . . apenanti pantōn*
            humōn (T)

The twofold repetition of the two subjects follows a certain logic: it represents the solution to the dilemma introduced in Peter's question in v. 12. It was not the power or piety of the apostles that caused the man to walk but faith in God and the name of Jesus. V. 16 also has in common with this preceding reference (i.e. v. 12) the pronominal reference to the unfortunate man and the logical continuity with the event itself. In fact the result of the miracle is interpreted by means of the same verb used in speaking of the person whose ankles were restored (v. 7): *stereoō* seems to signify physical healing,[22] the description of which is continued and expanded in the second part of the interpretation: *edōken autō tēn holoklērian tautēn.* Here we have the first really new element, not only because the word *holoklēria* occurs only here in the New Testament[23] but also because this compound noun extends the concept of healing to the entire person[24] and may be translated as "wholeness."[25] Back in v. 7, immediately after the miracle, Luke had mentioned the parts of the body that had been afflicted and were now healed, namely, the feet and ankles. But in v. 16 we have a broadening of perspective, even though the semantic field remains exclusively physical.

Another relatively new element in v. 16, at least by comparison with v. 12, is the testimony of those being addressed. In vv. 9–10 it was said that "all the people saw him . . . and recognized him" (*eiden . . . auton . . . epeginōskon de auton*). In v. 16 the verb *horaō* is used again, but *epignōskein* is replaced by *theōrein*. Although the semantic level is not altered, there has been a change: the verb "recognize" (v. 10), which is more logical, given the physical change in the man, and which has for its object the person as such of the cripple, is replaced by the more general "know," which is concerned not with the identity of the person but with the testimony it required to the person and to direct knowledge of him.

The new nuance seems to be further accentuated by the direct discourse. In vv. 9–10 the two verbs were simply parts of the narrative; in v. 16, in direct discourse, the same words acquire a dimension of witnessing which they did not have before. In vv. 9–10 the focus was on recognizing that the man who leaps about and praises God is the same who had formerly been a cripple and used to beg alms in front of the temple. In v. 16 the onlookers are called upon to bear witness to the miraculous event. That seems to be the point of the formula *apenanti pantōn humōn* ("in the presence of all of you"), which is completely new.[26] The testimony of those who have seen becomes a guarantee of authenticity and as such a motive of credibility.[27] The final part of v. 16 that is to be mentioned points in the same direction: *epi tē pistei tou onomatos autou*.[28] The "name" of Jesus is repeated from v. 6, while "faith" is a word that occurs for the first time since the beginning of chapter 3. The whole phrase corresponds to the rhetorical question with which Peter begins his address to the people as he tries to explain to them the mistake they are making (*hōs idia dunamei ē eusebeia*). In parallel fashion, the activity of the man for whom the miracle was worked is given a fuller interpretative formulation: "walking" is understood as "being strong" and having "perfect health."

At the end of the analysis of this first passage, we have the definite sense that in v. 16 the hermeneutical movement is beginning to take visible form as compared with the more repetitive v. 12. Continuity with the initial account of the miraculous event is still to the fore, but new factors make their appearance along with changes in others. We are moving through hermeneutical levels toward a new understanding that will be further developed at the beginning of the next discourse, in which Peter, while harking back to the same event, will be obliged to account for his actions to legitimate judges.

ACTS 3:1–10 AND 4:5–12

The exordium, then, interprets the incident that has led to the discourse; Acts 4:8–12, for its part, takes as its point of departure the same event that lies behind the preceding discourse. The time has come now to compare the "account" of the miraculous event and the passage in which it receives its fuller interpretation.

The beginning of the pericope 4:5–12 not only recalls in a general way the narrative pattern at the beginning of 3:1–10: the chronological setting, the active agents, their action in a particular place. There is also the description of the other person, whose weakness is shown by the condition in which he exists, by the place where he is found, and by the action of which he is the passive object.

3:1: at the ninth hour[29]	4:5: the next day[30]
3:1: Peter and John	4:5b–6: the rulers, the elders, the scribes, the[31] high priests Annas, Caiphas, John, Alexander, and all who were of the high-priestly family
3:1: they were going up to the temple	4:5a: they assembled[32] in[33] Jerusalem
3:1: for prayer	4:5a: (for the trial)
3:2: was carried in and laid	4:7a: made the prisoners stand
3:2: at the gate of the temple called the Beautiful Gate	4:7a: in their midst
3:2: a man lame from birth	4:7a: Peter and John who had been arrested and imprisoned (see 4:3)[34]

The parallel, while deficient as far as the vocabulary is concerned, is legitimate at other levels, beginning with style and function.

To begin with, the chronological indication, while referring to different times, is given in both cases by *epi* with the accusative (3:1: *epi tēn hōran;* 4:5: *epi tēn aurion*).

The actions of the subjects are expressed in verbs of movement. *Anabainō,* which has, among others, a technical cultic meaning,[35] already conveys the purpose of the disciples' "going up." The verb *sun-achthenai,* "come together," which is used for the action of the high priests, is less expressive, but the context leaves no doubt about the judicial intentions of the gathering, intentions that would, of course, be clothed with all the charisms of legality. The distance between the high priests who meet in Jerusalem to prepare a trial, and the two apostles who go to the temple to pray, is fully felt and, in fact, is perhaps even underscored the more by a certain similarity between the two groups because of the authority each has. Peter[36] is the acknowledged chief spokesman for the new community, and in the present instance acts as both miracle-worker and preacher.[37] The sanhedrin for its part was both the highest regional tribunal and the supreme religious authority.[38]

The venues of the activity of the two groups may be said to be practically identical. There is a very close connection between the temple (which had not yet been completed at the time of the events being narrated) and Jerusalem: the temple is the highest embodiment of the holiness that attached to the entire city. Temple and city were regarded as the property of all Israel; that is why the residents of Jerusalem had an obligation to give foreign pilgrims free lodging at the time of the great feasts.[39] If, then, the priests come to Jerusalem, the connection of city and temple becomes one of semi-identity. This idea is supported by the super-fluous[40] mention of Jerusalem as the place for the gathering of the sanhedrin.[41]

Contrasted with these activities and movements are the persons who are the objects of the actions and whose weakness is shown by their situation (the cripple has been a cripple since birth; the two disciples were in prison the evening before), by the place they occupy (the cripple sits at the entrance gate to the inner courtyard of the temple, the one at which cripples begged alms; the apostles are "in the midst" of the judicial assembly which sits in a semicircle around them, that is, they are in the position of persons under accusation), and by the actions of others, of which they are the passive objects (3:2: *ebastazeto, hon etithoun;* 4:7: *stēsantes autous*).

The parallel makes it easy to see a kind of reversal of functions among the persons in this passive role: the cripple with his lack of physical freedom is replaced by Peter and John who the day before had restored that freedom to him; it is as if as a result of liberating him they themselves must now suffer his weakness. One pointer to this kind of relationship may be the fact that after the liberation of the disciples (4:24) as after the cure of the cripple (3:9; 4:21) praise is given to God.

But while the captivity of the apostles remains a fact, we are confronted here with a literary fiction in which, it seems, the author wants to challenge the apparent real situation by a further shift of actantial roles. For at this point the question asked by one in need is placed in the mouth not only of the cripple but also of the rulers of the people and the high priests. This could ordinarily be explained by the two different functions of such a question: in the cripple's case it is connected with a need, while in the case of the judges it becomes a manifestation of power. But in fact, even for the judges, because of their role, the question is a necessity, not only because only by means of it do they manifest their authority, but also and above all because it is indispensable for the proper carrying out of a preliminary investigation; in other words, it is a necessary part of their functioning. Therefore, even though the initial situations of the cripple and the judges are quite different in their presuppositions, both of these parties express through their questions their need of a response. Is this because the judges are to be set beside the cripple as men who are truly needy? This is perhaps what the text is suggesting by its parallel use of the imperfect of two verbs for "ask": *ērōta* in 3:3 and *epunthanonto* in 4:7.[42]

THE FIRST AND THE FINAL INTERPRETATIONS

I have now reached the point that chiefly interests me: a comparison between the initial Lukan interpretation, which is given through the "story of the event," and the final one, which is placed on the lips of Peter as he stands before the sanhedrin. In both passages, after an opening observation placing the apostle in a religious and sacral context which is quite different in the two situations but also has aspects in common, an interpretation is given of the person for whom the miracle was performed; it is here that the nuances of Lukan hermeneutics emerge more clearly than elsewhere. In 3:1 says that Peter and John were going up to the temple (*anebainon eis to hieron*); 4:8 says that Peter was filled with the Holy Spirit (*plēstheis pneumatos hagiou*). Peter and the temple are both holy, but the presuppositions of this holiness are quite different in the two cases. In the one, attendance in the old temple at the hours of prayer made possible, for good or for ill, a contact with authority and tradition. In the other, there is the new reality which does not require their attendance: the Spirit of the new temple to which they need not go up because it is not something external or connected with particular schedules: rather they carry it within them and are even filled with it.

The fact that *plēstheis pneumatos hagiou* is a formula introducing discourses takes away nothing of its semantic significance.

The beneficiary of the miraculous event in 3:1–10 is *tis anēr chōlos;* thus the central personage of the story seems to be a quite particular individual. Despite the variety of senses which *anēr* has[43] and the high number of its occurrences in Acts,[44] it seems in this passage to have the specific sense of "man" as defined by sex, that is, a "male." The adjectival phrase accompanying the noun, *chōlos ek koilias mētros autou,* describes his helplessness in a specific way: he is a cripple, lame from birth; he does not walk at all, so that they must carry him daily to the temple where he displays his full helplessness by asking for alms.

In 4:9 the man is called *anthrōpos asthenēs:* no longer that particular individual, but a person, a human being; the intention is perhaps to underscore the human situation of sickness.[45] The same outlook is indicated by the negative adjective *asthenēs* (*a* privative + *sthenos*), the first meaning of which is "weak"; when the weakness referred to is physical, the meaning may also be "sick."[46] The interpretation of the cripple that is given in this second passage (4:9) is much broader in its negative implications and represents to some extent a universalizing by comparison with the much more specific interpretation in 3:2. It is no accident that in Luke's other two references to the cripple (4:14, 22) he uses the more generic *anthrōpos,* a word that makes its first appearance in Acts in this very passage (4:9).[47]

In the first story (3:3) the question asked is a petition for alms and looks therefore to a personal, material need of the petitioner. In the last story (4:7) the question is: By what power or by what name[48] was the miracle done? The question seems to be connected, therefore, with an inquisition by an authority that is both societal and religious. V. 7 picks up two explicit and basic words from what Peter says in chapter 3 (3:12: *dunamis;* 3:16 *onoma*) and combines them in a single question of the judges. This "name" had already been introduced in the story of the miracle (3:6) and will return again in 4:11, thus showing itself to be the central constituent of the entire section.

Peter's answers are geared to the needs of the petitioner or questioner. In the first story, it disappoints, to some extent, the expectations of the cripple, but what is given goes far beyond these expectations, for the man had been a cripple even in hope. In like manner, the reply to the sanhedrin is more than satisfactory, for it explains with a wealth of detail the history of the person in whose name the miracle was done. The name of Jesus becomes a narrated history in which the present hearers have played a part,[49] but the story also presently involves these same persons not only through remembrance of the events but also through the interpretation given of their role as a result of the question asked.

In direct dependence on the difference between the interpretations of the man for whom the miracle was done and the formulation of the petition or question, there are also readings given of the object, namely, the cure, which is given different names and takes on different nuances. In 3:6–10 a varied vocabulary is used to describe the result of the apostle's miraculous intervention, with active movement being the unifying thread (v. 7: *egeirō, stereoō;* v. 8: *exallomai, istamai, eiserchomai;* but especially *peripatein,* "walk," which occurs four times in vv. 6, 8, 8, 9). The same result is described by Peter in his address to the people, first with the same verb (i.e. *peripatein,* 3:12) and then with *holoklēria* (3:16). Before the sanhedrin, however, an entirely new vocabulary is used: first, *euergesia;* then the verb *sōzein,* the root of which is used three times (v. 9: *sesōtai;* v. 12: *sōtēria;* v. 12: *sōthēnai*). It might be said that the vocabulary of salvation replaces the vocabulary of walking, while remaining in the sphere of history.

Euergesia is a compound of *ergon* and signifies, in a general way, a good action. In the few New Testament uses of the root, the purpose seems to be to call the reader's attention to the divine origin of the benefit rather than to its material content.[50] By comparison with the more concrete and specific *holoklēria, euergesia* neglects the specifically physiological aspect of illness and lays greater emphasis on the high quality of the effect and, in the final analysis, on the one who alone is capable of intervening in this effective manner. As a result, the way is prepared for the verb *sōzein,* which belongs in the semantic field of healing stories,[51] as does the *peripatein* of the previous interpretation (3:12), but at the same time continues the developing hermeneutic of the historical event.

Since the two verbs are used separately in two passages that differ in situation and audience, each is able to offer its own contribution to the movement of universalization[52] and generalization within Peter's interpretation. Even if we remain within the sphere of the physical, it is obvious that the word "save" has a broader scope than "walk"; *peripatein,* "walk," in contrast, was connected with the cripple's situation of immobility. The fact that the sanhedrin, like the cripple, ask a question, as well as the presence of the final clause, "there is no other . . . by which we must be saved" (4:12), probably shows that the meaning of *sōzō,* too, is defined by the contrast, in this case, with the real helplessness of the sanhedrin's religious outlook. Therefore, not only does Peter's reading before the sanhedrin not detract in any way from the historicity of the event; rather it relates the event directly to his listeners.

Let me sum up the course of Peter's interpretation of the object: we have seen a rather varied vocabulary, most of it at home in the literary genre of healing stories, but, more importantly, oriented so as to move, in a manner not entirely harmonious, from the particular to the universal. *Peripatein, holoklēria, euergesia,* and *sōzein* are the terms marking a hermeneutical process that is determined by the historical situations in which the story of the healing is repeated. This vocabulary changes from one referring specifically to the physiology of an individual to lexical forms which generalize and in which the physical aspect is passed over in complete silence; at the same time, there is a shift from the material historicity of the first two terms to a more religious description of the event. This double movement reaches its climax at the end of the passage when the verb *sōzō* and its corresponding noun, *sōtēria,* are repeated (4:12), but now with a quite different semantic density, and one that is clearly theological. The formal echo of v. 9 is evident, but the previous reference to the beneficiary of the miracle is now replaced by a first person plural pronoun: we are all the recipients of salvation. But this is no longer the subject with which I am dealing.

THE HISTORICAL CAUSES
OF THE SEMANTIC DEVELOPMENT

Having reached the end of my journey, I must ask what the historical causes are of this semantic development. The text indicates several of these: there has been a change in the historical situation of the two apostles, in the time, the addressees, the place. . . .

In his first discourse Peter speaks as a free man to people who have witnessed the miracle and been amazed by it. As a result, the vocabulary he uses refers primarily to the physical restoration of the cripple, which is there for all to see. But there is more. In giving his interpretation Peter clearly intends to oppose another, one presumably being given by the bystanders; this can be gathered from the apostle's words (3:12). As in the preceding discourse on Pentecost (2:15), so here Peter gives an interpretation which is meant to correct another; consequently it cannot be based on the more readily perceptible facts, those more properly of the physical order. In parallel, there is also an awareness of the plurality of interpretations which are dictated by hermeneutical necessity and therefore by the choice made.

When the leader of the apostles girds himself for his second discourse, he has already spent a night in prison along with John; therefore on the day following the miraculous event he speaks as one being investigated and before a tribunal that asks him to account for what has taken place. The examining agency is the supreme political and religious institution of Palestine, and this agency is probably concerned more with the social and religious occurrence than with the cure as such.[53] It is evidently concerned also about the new religious movement that is in its first days; therefore, when the sanhedrin sets the two apostles free, it has a reason for ordering them to do no further teaching in the name of Jesus (4:18). The more generic vocabulary with its religious overtones is well suited to meet the demands of the investigating agency, which has little interest in the cripple who has been healed.[54] This does not mean that the story lacks historical status or that the second interpretation is less historical than the preceding. It is simply that Peter now interprets the event from a different standpoint. As a matter of fact, no one challenges the factuality of the story of Peter before the sanhedrin. This proves that Luke's conception of history always presupposes an initial theory that determines each interpretation.

Throughout this essay my concern has been to demonstrate that Peter's interpretation is historical. But the same is true of Luke's narrative: each story he tells, including the story of the miracle at the Beautiful Gate of the temple, is first and foremost an interpretation and presupposes a theory in the background which determines the reading of the story. Consequently, we must speak not of a "story of the event" (3:1–10) and successive interpretations of it (3:12, 16; 4:9), but rather of a series of interpretations that are historical and historicized. There is no history that is not first of all an interpretation, and no interpretation that is not historicized.

CONCLUSION

It is not easy to wind up an analysis that aims solely at identifying procedures. This can be shown by a comparison. Studies of the missionary discourses in Acts have usually taken as their point of departure the "objective" historical datum; having either accepted[55] or denied[56] this datum, scholars move on to the question of "what" Luke has added and why. The course I have taken provides for an alternative journey. I have set aside the problem of the historicity of the discourse as such and have tried to establish the broadest possible relationship that exists between history and interpretation, using as my example Peter's discourse in its relation to the story of the event that led to the discourse. Since we are dealing in every instance with a story, I thought it appropriate to read, within a single section, four interpretations of the same occurrence. Even the first, which is usually called "story of the miracle," is an interpretation, certainly more detailed but not more historical than the interpretations that follow. Each of these is in some respects different from the others, but at the same time there is continuity between them all: external factors, and especially the *intentio auditoris,* determine the differences among them and thus the truth itself.

All this demands a new relationship to the word, which takes on an undeniable relativizing priority with respect to actions, including miracles, and to the readings made of the actions.

Idolatry Compelled to Search for Its Gods: A Peculiar Agreement Between Textual Tradition and Exegesis (Amos 5:25–27 and Acts 7:42–43)

In his speech to the sanhedrin (Acts 7:2–53) Stephen summarizes the fortunes of the most famous persons in the religious history of ancient Israel, from Abraham to Solomon, while dwelling especially on Abraham (vv. 2–8) and Moses (vv. 20–44). Concerning Moses he recalls numerous biographical details which enhance the greatness of the man's person and work (his birth, his killing of the Egyptian oppressor, his flight to the land of Midian, his call: see Exodus 2:1–3:10), and then goes on to speak of the episode of the golden calf (vv. 40–41). This act of idolatry is immediately linked to a punishment, which consists in worship of the heavenly bodies (v. 42a). This assertion is confirmed (vv. 42b–43) by the citation of a passage from the prophet Amos (5:25–27) in which mention is made of a "tent of Moloch"; this seems, finally, to offer Stephen an opportunity to speak of another tent, the one in the wilderness, which was brought into the land of Israel as an anticipation or pre-figuration of the temple (vv. 44–50). This last subject provides Stephen with the conclusion of his speech, in which he says that the dwelling of the Most High cannot be enclosed within the material building erected by Solomon; here again, Stephen bases what he says on a citation from the Old Testament (Is 66:1–2).

The reader of such a succinct review of the history of Israel cannot but be surprised by the unexpected shift to the theme of the tent and the temple, a shift that seems motivated solely by a passage from Amos, although in the prophet the passage refers to something quite different. Furthermore, only one part of the passage cited from Amos could refer to an astral cult practiced by the ancient Israelites. In the Septuagint (LXX) translation, which the author of Acts is using, mention is made in fact of two divinities which do not seem to possess astral traits (v. 43 = Am 5:26). The remaining part of the cited passage refers to sacrifices in the wilderness (v. 42 = Am 5:25) and to an exile in Babylon which may be intended to emphasize and conclude the theme of punishment (v. 43 = Am 5:27, but with a considerable change from the LXX: the Damascus of Amos becomes Babylon!).

In conclusion, there is something jarring about this hypothetical demonstration of an astral cult among the ancient Israelites. This jarring note can already be heard in the very way in which the proof is documented in Acts, which places it in the mouth of Stephen. Then, if we look more closely at the passage from Amos, we are surprised to find that this presents analogous problems in relation to its context, and even greater difficulties as regards its content. For not only do the two divinities in the LXX translation appear to be different from those in the Masoretic text (MT), but the latter themselves may have been "invented" by a textual tradition that sought to clarify a kind of idolatry that was already more or less clear in the original words.

It seems, then, that in this case we are in the presence of an unusual instance of interpretation, one that gives concrete form in the text to what the text says in a general way about an idolatrous cult, and that does so by manipulating the philological possibilities of the language, or languages, of the text and seeking out, from scratch, unknown divinities which it then attempts to situate within an existing pantheon. But modern exegesis seems to follow a comparable path, because on the one hand it wishes to see in the words of the text (especially the text of Amos) proper names of non-Israelite divinities, while on the other it tries to use its philological resources to reduce these same words to simple common nouns which would describe a real, even if unorthodox, Israelite religion. In other words, if it be a fact that idolatry creates its own gods, we find the same thing happening at the level of (ancient) textual tradition and (modern) exegesis, both of which create and annihilate divinities according to a pre-understanding of the text as referring to idolatry.

I would like to illustrate this claim by discussing in this particular light some problems connected with the analysis of Acts 7:42–43 and Amos 5:25–27 (especially v. 26). I shall not take into account, therefore, all the exegetical questions raised by the two passages, but shall focus only on the relationship between each passage and its respective context, to the extent required in order to understand the supposed divine names and their fortunes in the texts. However, in making the comparison I cannot but attend also to the citation of Amos 5:25–27 in the Damascus Document (= CD; see VII, 14–15); this will serve only to give more precise definition to the broader subject.

Acts 7:42b–43[1] cites Amos 5:25–27 LXX[2] with some variants: in v. 42b there are in fact no important changes,[3] whereas for v. 43 it may be noted that in the phrase *tou theou humōn* the *humōn,* which causes no difficulty in LXX, is omitted by some textual witnesses to Acts (among them Codex Vaticanus and Codex Beza[4]), and in the phrase *tous tupous autōn* the demonstrative pronoun, though sufficiently attested for LXX, is omitted by all the witnesses to Acts, while the phrase *epoiēsate heautois* is unanimously given as *epoiēsate proskunein autois* in Acts. Above all, however, the name of the second divinity, *Raiphan* in the LXX of Amos 5:26 (with variants *Remphan* and *Raphan*) is transmitted in Acts 7:43 in a great variety of forms: *Raiphan / Raphan / Rephan / Rephphan / Repha / Rephpha / Rempha / Remphan / Rempham* (= Latin *Rempham*) / *Rompha / Romphan.* A comparison of these forms shows the shift *ai / a / e / o* in the first vowel and the addition of *m* only after *e* and *o* (with one instance of assimilation for the first of these: *Rephpha / Rephphan,* which is little attested).

This textual situation is faithfully reflected in the critical editions of Acts, which accept *Raiphan* (Nestle-Aland, 26th ed.), *Rephan* (Nestle), and *Romphan* (Tischendorf); this last form, which differs most from the forms in the LXX, is accepted precisely because it is regarded as a *lectio difficilior* and therefore more likely to have been brought into uniformity with the witnesses to the supposed original.[5]

Finally, as I mentioned earlier, *epekeina Damaskou* in Amos 5:27 LXX becomes *epekeina* (var. *epi ta mērē*) *Babulōnos* in Acts 7:43. If we prescind from the divine name and from this last-mentioned geographical substitution, the variant *heautois / proskunein autois* lays perhaps even greater emphasis, for the author of the citation in Acts, on the idolatrous significance of the actions described in v. 43.[6] Another point to be mentioned in the comparison of the two passages is a syntactic one: in Ziegler's and Rahlfs' editions of Amos the question asked is limited to v. 25, while in Tischendorf's and Merk's editions of Acts the whole of Amos 5:25–26 is understood as a question. Nestle-Aland (26th ed.) retains the punctuation of the two critical editions of the LXX; this is also the punctuation followed by the translations of almost all the commentators.[7] It is clear that if both verses (25–26) of Amos are taken as a question, then the accusation of idolatry in Acts 7:43 could be read as expressing a doubt or as a rhetorical question, in which case the citation of the passage becomes even less intelligible in this context.

But even if the passage of Amos, as cited in Acts, is read as a question

(Am 5:25 = Acts 7:42), followed by a statement (Am 5:26–27 = Acts 7:43), further problems arise with regard to the two meanings which the tent takes on and therefore the two meanings given to the word *tupos*. For in 7:43, in keeping with the text of Amos, *tupos* means "image," "statue" (of the divinity), while in 7:46 it is a "model" of the tent erected by Moses in the wilderness.[8]

First of all, it may also be noted that with the introduction of the passage from Amos Stephen is led to speak of a twofold punishment. The first consists in the fact that the Israelites gave themselves up to the worship of the "host of heaven"; this is understood as an automatic consequence of their idolatry, or, more accurately: idolatry itself is already a punishment. We see here the application of a principle of compensatory retribution, according to which the very thing by which the people were led astray becomes the instrument of punishment. This principle, which is already implicit in earlier Old Testament traditions, is later on categorically asserted and illustrated above all in the book of Wisdom (see especially Wis 11:16; 12:23, and, with a diversified application, 11:5). The verb *estrepsen* (v. 42) may emphasize even further this kind of intrinsic retribution if it be taken as reflexive in meaning: God "withdrew himself" (from them).

The second punishment consists of exile and comes about through a positive intervention of God who "deports" (*metoikiō*) the Israelites to Babylon (v. 43); in the perspective of the author of Acts the Babylonian exile was the climactic historical punishment as compared with the more precise deportation "beyond Damascus" in Amos 5:27 LXX. The text of Amos allows only for this second punishment; if what is said in 5:26 is understood as referring to the future, then the passage can at most be already foreshadowing the exile or be somehow connected with it.[9] In Acts 7:43, however, the text of Amos 5:26 does not simply render v. 42a more explicit: by citing the LXX version of Amos 5:26, in which reference is made to two divinities, the author of Acts turns these divinities into examples of the astral cult in which the first punishment consists. By comparison with v. 42b (= Am 5:25), which contains a question (expressed in the negative) about sacrifices offered by Israel in the wilderness, v. 43 seems to have scant importance, unless we look for a fuller explanation of it from its context in Stephen's speech.

As a matter of fact, the relation between Amos 5:25 and Amos 5:26 is rather complex in itself, especially in the MT, but here in Acts it takes on a different shape. Exegetes who have tackled the problem seem at times to approach it with the sole concern of keeping Stephen, or the speech attributed to him, from contradicting other Old Testament statements according to which the Israelites were already offering sacrifices while in the wilderness. Therefore either v. 42b denies these sacrifices,[10] or else it is a rhetorical question ("Did you not . . . ?") and calls for a positive, even if conditioned answer: sacrifices were offered in the wilderness, but they were not the ideal, or else they were provisional or tainted with idolatry, or else they were simply outright idolatrous. Up to this point, the explanations offered do not fall outside the range of possible interpretations of the text of Amos considered in itself.[11]

Other exegetes, however, contrast Amos, for whom the time in the wilderness is an ideal period in the life of ancient Israel, and Stephen, who makes the wilderness a place solely of idolatrous worship.[12] Or else they are even more explicit and interpret Amos' words as calling for a negative answer (Israel did not offer sacrifices in the wilderness), whereas Stephen gives a different interpretation (Israel did offer sacrifices in the wilderness, but to idols).[13]

A more plausible solution, however, is the one proposed a while back by M. Simon and revived by H. Conzelmann in his commentary on Acts: Acts reflects the rise of the radical opposition to the temple and its cult which can be seen in some currents of Judaism and primitive Christianity and which views the sacrificial worship of Israel as negative and idolatrous from the very beginning.[14] Although this explanation manages to link vv. 42 and 43 by means of a hermeneutic that is not tied solely to the text of Amos or to the Old Testament, and although it has a basis almost only in later documents (Simon appeals in fact chiefly to Justin and the Pseudo-Clementines), yet it does shift the focus of the problem to the theme of the temple, which represents the climax of Stephen's speech (Acts 7:44–50).

In this broader setting it becomes necessary to determine who or what is really responsible for the negative vision of the temple: Stephen himself? A passage attributed to him? A redactor who has introduced material for this purpose? E. Haenchen[15] maintains that vv. 39–44 were introduced for polemical purposes into a neutral speech on Moses, but what is said in these verses could not have persuaded the court, since use is made of a passage from the LXX which differs from the Hebrew. According to T. Holtz,[16] however, Stephen's speech is already marked by a negative vision of the cult, as shown in the reference to astral idolatry (v. 42a); Luke would simply have added documentation by citing Amos (vv. 42b–43), but would have failed to realize that the text to which he made his addition already regarded worship of the heavenly bodies as a punishment. A. Weiser[17] makes Holtz's hypothesis his own but is even more specific: the original speech contained only a description of history that came from Jewish circles faithful to the temple (vv. 2–34, 36, 38, 44–47); later on, a group of Hellenistic Christians (close to Stephen) turned the speech into a sermon of conversion that was addressed to Jews, by adding

vv. 39–42a (thus introducing a deuteronomistic conception into the text: Israel rejects the saving deeds of God); finally, Luke introduced into this material scriptural citations (vv. 42b–43 and 48b–50) and a criticism of the temple in v. 48a (he had a basis for doing so in 6:11, 13–14 and 7:55–56). R. Pesch, for his part,[18] maintains that the citation of Amos, thus inserted into an earlier speech, pre-dates Luke.

Without going into this question, which has to do with the literary composition of Stephen's speech, I would simply like to call attention to the way in which the passage from Amos, whatever its meaning in its context in LXX and MT, is here adduced as proof of an idolatrous cult which is *astral* in character: even though the Old Testmant contains numerous references which place such a cult in a negative light (see Dt 4:19; 17:3; Jer 7:18; 8:2; 19:13; Zep 1:5; 2 Chr 33:3–5), the important thing to note here is that the content of the passage from Amos is read and interpreted as proof of this kind of idolatry. The two divine names in v. 43 (= Am 5:26) are adapted to this purpose as proper names and independently of their true character; it is more important that hearers and readers think of two divinities as such rather than that these be identified. It is significant, moreover, that the commentaries and monographs on Acts 7 do not have much to say about the characteristics of these two gods and are satisfied to rehash, at most, the discussion of the subject that is usually found in commentaries on Amos; the matter is thus reduced almost to a matter of idle curiosity or of erudition that is quite secondary in relation to the essential exegesis of the passage in Acts.[19] It is no less significant that both of these divine names have acquired a place in language dictionaries of the New Testament and in "Bible dictionaries," where they occur, evidently, in their Greek form; as a result, we are given only a summary of the few points of information connected with the original passage in Amos, and it is from the latter that the identity of these divinities is deduced.[20] At this level, Moloch and Raiphan (with their variants) are divinities not further defined; their probative efficacy seems to reside solely in the ill-omened powers evoked by their names. Given the astral nature of the idolatry they exemplify, their usual connection with the planet Saturn, which, it is thought, can be deduced from the text of Amos, seems not to create any problem.

As regards a direct study of the text of Amos 5:25–27, it is appropriate to begin by presenting some textual data from MT and the ancient translations, but I shall limit the comparison to v. 26, which is more closely related to my subject. I shall therefore give 5:26 as found in the MT, the LXX, Targum Jonathan (= TJ), the Peshiṭta (= S), and the Vulgate (= V).

MT   *ūn^eśā'tem 'ēt sikkūt malk^ekem | w^e'ēt kiyyūn ṣalmēkem*
               kōkab 'ĕlōhēkem 'ăšer 'ăśîtem lākem

LXX   *kai anelabete tēn skēnēn tou Moloch | kai ton astron tou*
               theou humōn Raiphan,
               tous tupous autōn hous epoiēsate heautois

TJ   *wntltwn yt sykwt ptkrykwn | wyt kywn ṭ'wtkwn*
               kwkb ṣlmykwn d'bdtwn lkwn[21]

S   *'l' šqltwn mšknh dmlkwm | wkwn ṣlmkwn*
               kwkb' d'bdtwn lkwn 'lh'[22]

V   *et portastis tabernaculum Moloch vestro, et imaginem*
               idolorum vestrorum,
               sidus dei vestri, quae fecistis vobis

A first comparative study of these five texts suggests the following remarks:

(1) MT makes the plural *ṣalmēkem* ("your images") refer to both of the preceding objects, *sikkūt malk^ekem* and *kiyyūn,* and raises the problem of *kōkab 'ĕlōhēkem* ("the star of your god"), which is singular and can refer to only one of the preceding objects, but seems to be poorly located after the plural *ṣalmēkem.* In the LXX the two difficulties are eliminated by moving *kōkab 'ĕlōhēkem* forward and having it refer explicitly to the second object alone; the latter is thus defined as an astral reality.

The other translations stop at times halfway. TJ describes the second object (*kywn*) as "your idol," but by continuing with "star your images" it seems to offer an unharmonized text, if the two words be understood as in apposition to what has preceded, without any connection between them.[23] V tries to make the *kiyyūn ṣalmēkem* of MT intelligible by translating it as *imaginem idolorum vestrorum,* thus combining the two terms in a single genitive and creating a phrase that should be synonymous with the following phrase, *sidus dei vestri;* however, the plural *quae fecistis vobis* seems not to refer to the second object alone, but to both. S harmonizes the second part of the verse: by taking *ṣalmēkem* as a singular and shifting *'ĕlōhîm* to the end it obtains the sequence: "and *kwn/k'wn* your image, the star which you formed for yourselves (as) a god"; it thus makes specific the astral character of the second object, but in a different way than the LXX.

One should note also that in the Greek version of Theodotion the syntactic sequence of the second part of the verse reflects the MT; however, by translating *amaurōsin eidōlōn humōn astron tou theou humōn* it intends to make *eidōlōn humōn* a specification of the second object only.

Finally, the Arabic version follows the LXX exactly (and therefore speaks of two divinities, Mûlûḥ and Râfân).

(2) The names of the two objects vary widely. *sikkūt malkᵉkem* of the MT becomes *tēn skēnēn tou Moloch* in the LXX, which thus interprets the first term as a common noun and the second as the name of a divinity. V does the same (*tabernaculum Moloch vestro*), although the adjective *vestro* here retains the suffix of *malkᵉkem*, which seems to have been lost in the LXX. Symmachus renders the MT as *tēn skēnēn tou basileōs humōn*, thus using two common nouns; Theodotion does the same in his *tēn horasin tou basileōs humōn*, but the *suskiasmous Molchom* of Aquila is close to the LXX. Also like the LXX and Aquila is S with its *mšknh dmlkwm* ("tent of Milcom"). TJ, on the other hand, does not resolve the difficulty: *skwt/sykwt ptkrykwn/ptkwmrkwn/ptkmrykwn* means only: "*s.* of your idols."

The second object, *kiyyūn* in the MT, is *Raiphan* in the LXX (with variants *Remphan/Raphan*) and *chion* in Aquila and Symmachus, to which can be joined the *kywn* of TJ and the *kwn/k'wn* of S. Only Theodotion (*amaurōsis*) and V (*imaginem*) turn it into a common noun.[24] Later on I shall come back to the possible meanings of these terms.

For a more complete overview we need also to keep in mind the citation of Amos 5:26–27 in CD VII, 14–15, which gives it in the following form:

whglyty 't skwt mlkkm w't kywn ṣlmykm m'hly dmśq[25]

The subject of the sentence here is no longer "you," as in the MT of Amos 5:26, but God, and the two objects are connected with the verb in v. 27 (*whglyty* = "I shall take into exile"). The objects seem to be simplified by the elimination of the words *kōkab 'ĕlōhēkem 'ăšer 'ăśītem lākem* of the MT, but it must be noted that in the exegesis of the passage, which follows immediately in CD, *skwt* is repeated in the form *swkt* (VII, 15, at the end); the second object is given in two forms, *wkynyy hṣlmym* and *wkywn hṣlmym,* the first of which seems to be a mistake and should be deleted; finally, *kwkb* reappears, after seemingly having been omitted from the citation. Apparently the text of Amos is simply abbreviated here, and the conclusion cannot be drawn that the author had the text in a different form from that of the MT; this is true despite the reading *m'hly* ("from the tents") in place of the *mhl'h* ("beyond") of Amos 5:27.[26] CD's interpretation at the exegetical stage is another matter, but it is significant that there is no reference here to divinities or divine names. To this point, too, I shall have to return further on.

It is difficult to assign Amos 5:25–27 a precise place within vv. 21–27, a pericope in which the prophet criticizes an unacceptable kind of worship.[27] Exegetes often assign these verses a secondary role, but have divergent, though not mutually exclusive, reasons for doing so.

As far as the literary genre of the pericope is concerned, it is to be regarded as a composition made up of diverse elements: in substance, it is a prophetic discourse in which an introductory formula (vv. 21–22) expressing a (negative) view of the temple cult (*Kultbescheid;* according to W. Rudolph the tone is one of irony) is followed by a warning of a sapiential kind (vv. 23–24) and a threat of punishment (exile in the direction of Damascus, v. 27).[28] Vv. 25–25 would then link the cultic ideal set forth by Amos with the situation in the wilderness, although this connection still does not settle the problems within these two verses and, on the other hand, the threat of punishment proves rather violent (in fact, v. 27 is sometimes considered to have been introduced by a redactor[29]). Still on the literary side, O. Loretz has recently suggested that vv. 25–27 be regarded as post-exilic, because of their incompatibility with the context as well as because of their content; the author reaches this conclusion by applying "colometric analysis" to Amos 5:21–27.[30]

These results in the literary order are often explained at the level of religious history by assigning vv. 25–26 to the deuteronomist milieu and at times also by insisting that if v. 26 speaks of two non-Israelite divinities, there was no trace of them in Israel before 722 B.C. when they would have been introduced by the Assyrians (see 2 Kgs 17:24–41); in addition, it is claimed that Amos did not speak elsewhere of foreign divinities.[31] This argument is not convincing, partly because it is based on the supposition that the Assyrians forcibly imposed their own gods or their own religion on conquered peoples, partly because historians and archeologists today commonly accept that in the time of Amos there were foreign influences at work in ancient Israel, especially in the northern kingdom.[32]

Considered in themselves, vv. 25–26 present further difficulties, especially as regards the relation of the first verse to the second. According to some interpreters, the question asked includes v. 26; thus the entire passage may be taken as a rhetorical question.[33] But this still leaves open the question of the temporal relation between the two verses: the reference to the sacrifices in the wilderness (in the past) could in fact include also the idolatrous objects in v. 26, which would thus likewise be part of a cult in the wilderness; in this case, the question being asked in v. 25 could without difficulty be extended to include v. 26.[34] Or else v. 26 is not part of the question and refers to the present or the future; in the second case, the idolatrous cult would be in some way connected with the threat of exile.[35] When v. 25 alone is taken as a question, the exegetes often explain its connection with v. 26 by arguments based on an *a priori* conception of the religious history of ancient Israel. They say that v. 25 requires a negative answer, because the wilderness was the ideal time during which no sacrifices were offered. This claim would even contradict those Pentateuchal literary traditions (E, P) which see Israel's cultic institutions as having their origin precisely in the wilderness and at Sinai; on the other hand, it would be consistent with statements made by the prophets (see Jer 7:22f).[36] But if this exegetical explanation of v. 25 be valid, then v. 26, if understood as likewise referring to the past and the wilderness, would create an even greater difficulty; it is understandable, therefore, that proponents of this religious conception of the wilderness should simply eliminate v. 26.[37]

In order, therefore, to continue connecting v. 25 with v. 26, it must be accepted that the question is rhetorical and that it refers to an inadequate or unclean cult practiced in the wilderness.[38] The question can certainly be limited to v. 25; then the two idolatrous objects in v. 26 can be located chronologically in the wilderness, that is, in a distant past, but also in the present or the future. If these objects are divinities, resolution of the chronological question requires determining who they are concretely and when the Israelites began to revere them. In fact, therefore, the entire exegetical question seems conditioned by the presupposition that the idolatry in Amos 5:26 is connected with divinities which are specific, even if difficult to identify. It is for this reason, too, that v. 26 is at times regarded as one of the most complicated texts in the book of Amos.[39]

The exegetical perspective changes completely, however, if the two objects are given a different interpretation: they may be simple objects—a position taken not out of an unwillingness to allow other divinities alongside YHWH, but solely because of the fact that worship of Yahweh in ancient Israel could find expression in forms different and distant from the official one that finally prevailed. V. 26 would then be criticizing a Yahwist cult that was unorthodox or diverging from the ideal; at a later time, however, this heterodox form of worship would have been interpreted as a form of idolatry (this is already the case in the ancient translations) and would have been provided with concrete divinities, to some extent astral in character, the original text having supplied the idea that set this hermeneutical process in motion.

Most of the commentaries and some of the monographs see in the two words *sikkūt* and *kiyyūn* of the MT the names of two Babylonian divinities. The vocalization in the MT would be attributable to a "dysphemism" (opposite of euphemism) in which the vowels of *šiqqûṣ* ("abomination") or *gillûl* ("idol," but this word is used almost always in the plural in the MT; for the singular see Sir 30:18[40]) are used for the two words. The first term, when read as *sakkût*, is sometimes likened to *sukkôt-bᵉnôt,* one of the Assyrian divinities introduced into Samaria according to 2 Kings 17:30, and is interpreted as a Hebrew form of the Babylonian divinity *Sag/Sak-kud,* who is identified with the god of war, Ninurta (or Nin-ib, according to the old reading), and to whom some would also assimilate the astral divinity, Saturn.[41] The second name, read as *kêwân,* should (it is claimed) go back to an Akkadian adjective applied to Saturn and intended to emphasize the stability or steadiness of this god (*kayyamānu/ kayyawānu*).[42] If these identifications are valid, then we should read Amos 5:26 as containing the names of two gods who share an astral character, or two names for a single god (Saturn).

The first to propose this interpretation of the names was K. Schrader, who based it on a few scattered Akkadian texts used for the purpose,[43] but it received further backing and was spread abroad above all when H. Zimmern, in 1901, published an Akkadian text in the series of so-called *Šurpu* supplications, in which, according to Zimmern's reading, one and the same line (*Šurpu* II, 179) mentions the two divinities *ilSak-kut* and *ilKaiamānu* (which Zimmern translates as Sakkut and Kewan).[44] The same reading was confirmed in a later publication of the same text by E. Reiner: this editor transcribes the second name with the logogram *dSAG.UŠ,* which, she claims, corresponds to the reading *Kajamānu.*[45]

Recently, however, R. Borger has noted that the reading is erroneous, and Zimmern himself may have been aware of it, although he did not let this be known; Borger's new collation of the copies of the text shows that the name of the second divinity (actually the third in the line, since a *dTI.BAL* is mentioned at the beginning of the line) is to be read not as *dSAG.UŠ* but simply as *dUŠ,* which corresponds therefore not to *kayyamānu* but to *dNita,* another equivalent of the god Ninurta.[46] It is, therefore, no longer possible to appeal to this Akkadian text as a basis for assigning the same astral character to the two supposed divinities of Amos 5:26 and making them the equivalents of the god Saturn. True enough, the mistake pointed out by Borger applies only to the second divinity in Amos 5:26, but the correction can be extended to the first as well, so that the reading *sakkut* and the connection with the god *Sag/Sak-ud* also become quite questionable.[47] It must be said in addition that the god Ninurta does not have astral characteristics, despite the scattered evidence adduced in favor of this claim,[48] and a connection with Babylonian divinities is difficult to establish even for the first part of the name *sukkôt-benôt* in 2 Kings 17:30.[49] It is clear, in any case, that another direction must be taken in the effort to identify *kêwân* (if one wants to so read the name of the second divinity).[50]

Alongside this first line of exegesis there has developed another which reduces the two words in Amos 5:26 to common nouns and either keeps the Hebrew consonantal text unchanged or introduces only a few changes. E. Sellin in his day was already claiming that the words could be read as *sukkat* ("tent") and *kēn* ("pedestal").[51] In like manner, M. Bič translated them as "hut" and "statue (?)," and had in mind a ceremony in which the king was carried in procession on a festival of Yahweh that was marked by Baalist elements.[52] V. Maag keeps the consonantal text even for the second word and vocalizes it as *kiyyôn* ("pedestal"), while for the first he too accepts *sukkat* ("hut").[53] A. Weiser does not explain the second term, but for the first he proposes *massekôt* ("cast images").[54] S. Gevirtz has suggested an analogous correction, but for a gratuitous reason: on the basis of a hypothetical equivalence between nominal forms in *qittûl* and *mqtl* he changes *sikkût* to *mskt* and *kiyyûn* to *mākôn,* but simply, in the final analysis, in order to be able to assimilate the first to the Phoenician *mskt,* "little temple," which appears in an inscription at Karatepe.[55]

There have also, of course, been eccentric hypotheses to explain this verse—for example, that of H.H. Hirschberg, who takes Arabic as his starting point and would see in Amos 5:26 two symbols of fertility: in *skwt* a pole, that is, a phallus, and in *kywn* the clitoris/vagina.[56] On the other hand, É. Lipiński[57] offers a rather persuasive explanation of the first word: he links *skwt* to the Ugaritic *sknt,* "image," the shift taking the form *sakkantu > sakkat;* for the second vowel it would not be impossible to apply here the change *a > o* of Ugaritic and Phoenician, or if this vowel is considered long, it is possible further to get *ō > ū.* In support of his hypothesis Lipiński also cites Akkadian *šukuttu,* which in the Erra poem can signify the "statue" of Marduk. At the oral suggestion of M. Dietrich, K. Koch proposes both of these linkages, but independently of Lipiński and without knowledge of the latter's article.[58]

Faced with this alternative solution, those who have dealt more recently with the problem of Amos 5:26 have shown themselves to be at a loss; sometimes, however, they use the new hypotheses, but only in order to prove other points.[59]

If the common noun hypothesis, which does not of itself require any change in the consonantal text, is accepted, it is still necessary to see how the second part of the verse is to be read. Very often exegetes see it as containing glosses, especially in the words *ṣalmêkem* and *kôkab,* chiefly because of the shift from plural to singular and the connection of the two words with the following *'ĕlōhēkem,* which in turn can be understood as meaning either "your god" or "your gods." The text is therefore shortened, both by those who read it as containing divine names and by those who prefer to see common nouns. If, however, we accept this second interpretation, against which there are no difficulties, and if we prescind from the Masoretic vocalization, which is late and subsequent to the ancient translations (therefore *skwt,* "hut," and *kywn,* "pedestal"[60]), then Amos 5:26 speaks of two cultic objects which may refer to one and the same god but which remain distinct as "images," and the last part of the verse becomes explanatory. Here, then, is a possible translation of the verse:

> And you have carried the hut of your king and the pedestal, your images. The god you have made for yourselves is a star.[61]

The text thus speaks of objects connected with a divinity who may, of course, be the god YHWH; these objects are built and "carried" by the Israelites. The last part of the verse then seems to identify this god with a star or at least assigns him astral characteristics. It is, however, difficult to decide further whether this explanation is original or from a later time[62]; if from a later time, it is possible to speak of a gloss, but a gloss which is already ancient and, in any case, earlier than the LXX, which continues precisely this kind of interpretation.

We are now in a position to follow the probable evolution of the text and the origin of the divine names that have been introduced into it. In the second half of the verse the Greek translator (= LXX) found a text in which *kwkb 'lhkm* had already been moved ahead of *kywn,* or else he himself made this transposition, and he took the expression as a construct genitive, so that the second word became an explanation of the first; at the same time, however, the second person plural suffix in *ṣalmêkem* was changed into the third person plural, and, in addition, the word was made to refer to the two preceding objects (*tous tupous autōn; autōn,* however, is missing in part of the tradition, as it is also in Acts 7:43). The substantive *kywn* became instead *Raiphan* (variants: *Remphan/Raphan*).[63]

In the syriac version, the Peshiṭta, *kywn* is rendered as *kwn* (= *kêwân*), a word which in this form or in the graphic forms *kywn* and *k'wn*[64] is connected with a god, known also in Persian, Arabic (= Kaiwān), and Mandean (= Kiwan), where it always signifies Saturn.[65] It is commonly agreed that *Raiphan* is a corruption of *Kaiphan* (whence the other Greek variants are readily explained). The Greek construction ("and the star of your god *Kaiphan*) is therefore justified insofar as it acknowledges the astral character of *Kaiphan.* The Syriac translation, "and Kewan your image (or: your idol), a star which you made for yourselves (as a) god," keeps the construction of the Hebrew, but reads *ṣalmêkem* as a singular; on the other hand, in the second part of the verse, the Syriac is still close to the Hebrew noun sentence inasmuch as it retains a predicative relation between "star" and "god."

In Targum Jonathan the word *kywn* is simply transcribed, but it is described as "your idol," at least in the textual tradition that translates *'ĕlōhêkem* as *ṭ'wtkwn* and locates it immediately after the name *kywn*.[66] The next part of the verse can still be read as a noun sentence: "the images you have made for yourselves are a star."

Finally, it should be noted that in the Greek translation of Theodotion (⟨*kai tēn*⟩ *amaurōsin eidōlōn* ⟨*humōn*⟩ *astron tou theou humōn*) the Hebrew construction is kept, but *kwkb* is interpreted as being in the construct state, while *kywn* is translated as *amaurōsis* ("darkening," "dulling"), a negative description of the "your idols" that follows (Aquila and Symmachus translate as *chion,* showing that they take the word to be a proper name, but they do not identify it).[67]

The Latin *imaginem idolorum vestrorum,* whatever its origin, eliminates every reference to a divinity. It is possible, therefore, to see in the second part of the verse an interpretative approach that makes *kwkb* ("star") the starting point for an accentuation of the astral character of the word *kywn,* to the point of turning it into the god Saturn.

In the first half of the verse the Greek of the LXX has the expression *tēn skēnēn tou Moloch* ("the tent of Moloch"), and the Syriac has *mškn dmlkwm* ("the tent of Milcom"). Neither translation, therefore, takes the first word to be a divine name (or, rather, they understand the Hebrew *skwt* as *sukkat,* "tent"), but they have introduced another god into the text. In the case of Moloch we perhaps have an anomaly. The issue is not whether the Hebrew word to which "Moloch" is usually referred is understood in the Old Testament as a divine name or as the name of a sacrifice: the Hebrew word is in fact *mlk* (vocalized as *mōlek* by the Masoretes) or *mlkm* (vocalized as *milkōm,* the god Milcom of the Ammonites, or as *malkām,* "their king"), but the form *mlkkm* of Amos 5:26 is never found. According to the traditional interpretation, *mōlek* is a kind of sacrifice, but the LXX turned it into a person by translating it as *archōn* (in Lv 18:21; 20:2, 3, 4, 5) and as *Moloch* (see 2 Kings 23:10); this last became the basis for Masoretic vocalization *mōlek,* which recalls that of *bōšet,* "shame." *Moloch* would thus be an invention of the LXX.

Today, however, scholars hold that the *mlk* of the Hebrew text can, in itself, be the name of a god known to ancient Israel and to other eastern peoples.[68] Furthermore, the relation of the Greek text to the Hebrew is seen in a more nuanced way. It is pointed out that in some cases in which the Hebrew has the form *mlk,* the Greek translation has *Moloch,* but also a proper noun ending in *-m* (for example, in 2 Kgs 23:10 *Moloch/ Melchom*). The conclusion drawn is that this tradition, represented by the "Old Greek" translation, knows a Hebrew text in which the name in question is *mlkm* (= Milcom), while a more recent tradition, represented by Proto-Theodotion and "the *kaige* recension," reflects a (protomaso-retic) Hebrew text with the form *mlk,* from which *Moloch* is derived. If this hypothesis is sound, it follows that an older Hebrew text spoke of the god Milcom, while *Moloch* would be a more recent invention, which then entered into the present Masoretic text.[69]

The *Moloch* of Amos 5:26 LXX would, then, have its place in this more recent tradition, but in fact it does not seem that the word is a direct translation of the Hebrew *mlkkm.* Aquila's *suskiasmous Molchom* would seem to go back to an older tradition, but here again without any direct basis in the Hebrew.[70] Theodotion's *tēn horasin tou basileōs humōn* like-wise interprets the first word as a common noun,[71] but it does not turn the second into the name of a divinity. As I pointed out, the Syriac has Mil-com, while the Latin, following the LXX, has here *tabernaculum Moloch vestro* and therefore supposes a suffix which, however, is joined to an already "divinized" noun. None of these translations understands the Hebrew *skwt* as the name of a god; the name of a god, where it appears as the identification, is the result of interpretation and, in addition, is not founded on the *mlkkm* of the original text. Finally, Targum Jonathan keeps the transcription *sykwt/skwt,* but understands *mlkkm* to mean "your idols,"[72] and thus in its own manner judges idolatrous the word governing it. Consequently, the *Moloch* of the LXX seems due to the translator's intention of expressing by means of this divine name an even more marked idolatry, though not of an astral kind.[73] But perhaps it is not without some justification that in the LXX the astral idolatry should be concentrated entirely in the second part of v. 26.

The state of the Hebrew text and the interpretive approach thus far observed receive some confirmation from the citation and interpretation of Amos 5:26–27 in CD VII, 14–15. As I pointed out earlier, the citation does not include the last part of v. 26 (the part corresponding to *kôkab 'ĕlōhêkem 'ăšer 'ăśîtem lākem*), but in the exegesis that follows the cita-tion attention is in fact paid to the word *kôkab.* This is a sign, first of all, that the Hebrew text used by CD may still have made clear the secondary character of this word, as well as its noun function, since CD picks up the word in isolation, without the *'lhkm* that follows it in the Hebrew. CD, therefore, does not know a text in which, as in the LXX, the "star" has become the object of the verb "carry" and is even identified with its second object. In the CD exegesis of the passage from Amos the *skwt mlkkm* of the citation (VII, 14) is repeated and interpreted as a genitival expression and is applied to the books of the Torah: *spry htrh hm swkt hmlk* ("the books of the Torah are the tent of the king": VII, 15–16). This assimilation is confirmed by a citation from Amos 9:11, which is intended to explain the meaning of the tent ("and I will raise up the fallen tent of

David") and to make possible the identification of the king with the assembly itself.

Secondly, the *kywn ṣlmykm* of Amos, cited first in VII, 15, is repeated[74] and applied to the prophetic books: *wkywn hṣlmym hm spry hnby'ym* ("and the *kywn* of the images are the books of the prophets": VII, 17). Finally, the statement is made: *hkwkb hw' dwrš htrh* ("the star is the interpreter of the Torah"); the text continues by saying , "he comes to Damascus, as it is written: 'a star comes from Jacob and a scepter rises out of Israel' " (CD VII, 18–20, citing Nm 24:17). In this final application, which combines the texts of Amos and Numbers, scholars see stated the doctrine of the two messiahs: the messiah of Aaron and the messiah of Israel,[75] but my concern here is rather to point out that no negative or idolatrous meaning is given to the "star," and the same holds for the two words *skwt* and *kywn*. Furthermore, it would be very strange if such an exegesis were practiced on a text in which the names of two gods were to be read: it is most unlikely that the community would have dared to change so radically two concrete expressions of idolatry and make them refer to itself. We do not know how the author of CD read *skwt* and *kywn* in Amos 5:26; he certainly did not pronounce them in accordance with the reading followed by modern exegesis, and therefore it would be a mistake to translate the two words as "Sakkut" and "Kewan" in the citation of Amos in CD VII, 14–15; at most, one might retain the masoretic vocalization of the words as *sikkût* and *kiyyûn*.[76] But this vocalization is doubtful for the period of history to which CD belongs; it may in fact owe its existence to a later stage in the interpretive process I have been trying to retrace, when the Masoretes, precisely in order to maintain it, would have understood as "abomination" (perhaps thinking of *šiqqûṣ*, as is usually maintained) two words by now "divinized" and become symbols of idolatry.

It was thought that by "inventing" various divinities a concrete face might be given to idolatry of an astral kind, with the text of Amos 5:26 certainly providing a cue and some material. This idolatry in turn became synonymous with radical aberration and apostasy; one attestation, among others, of this view is the citation of Amos 5:25–27 in Acts 7:42–43. Just as the ancient text tradition developed its own interpretation of Amos 5:26, a development that was conditioned by a negative vision of idolatry and that transformed cultic objects into divinities in the true and proper sense, so too later exegesis, including that of our own time, has taken the same presuppositions as its starting point and has often tried to track down illusory divine beings that not only have never existed *in mente Dei* (as those rightly say who talk of "idolatry") but have never had any kind of solid existence *in mente textus*.

Paul's Vision at Troas (Acts 16:9–10)

The Acts of the Apostles tell us that while at Troas Paul had a vision, a dream, in the night (Acts 16:9–10). This event, which determined his subsequent life and apostolate, is reported briefly in two verses which also tell us that after the vision Paul did not go to Asia, as in all likelihood he would have, but instead took the road to Europe.[1] As everyone knows, the result was that Christian communities would flourish in Europe down through the years, but would arise in Asia only centuries later and would, at least apparently, be much less successful down to our own time.[2]

If we think even briefly about it, the new direction taken at this point in the church's missionary expansion seems quite mysterious. The impression can be gotten that the future of the church was jeopardized because of chance circumstances or, for practical purposes, of credence given to a dream. How are we to understand the incident? And what significance is to be attached to all this when it comes to interpreting the will of God? The passage which I shall be studying can prove especially helpful because in it we see an event in an individual's history playing an important role in collective history. What I would like to accomplish in this essay[3] is to bring out anew the real importance of the passage. My aim is to show, on the basis of available studies, the place of the dream among the literary devices which the author of Acts uses in making the will of God clear to his personages and his readers.

As for bibliography: the studies devoted to Acts 16:9–10 are few,[4] while the commentaries on Acts, for their part, do not give the dream the attention it deserves.[5] A survey of these works shows that for the great majority of authors the dream signifies that the mission is not simply the fruit of human activity (whether of Paul or of anyone else) but is directly dependent on the will of God. Some years back, C.M. Martini wrote on this point in his commentary: "But Luke wants to give the reader the impression that this journeying through Asia Minor has for its sole ultimate goal to open the way to Greece."[6]

But it is not enough to recognize the direct dependence of the mission on God. To stop there would be to risk not bringing out the balance between divine will and human freedom.[7] Moreover, while it is important that this theological truth be evidenced and affirmed, it seems to me even more important that we see "how" this will of God is manifested and made known, first of all to the personages involved and then to the reader. But scholars generally have thus far not been interested in this aspect. Only two, as we shall see, have pointed us in the right direction.

My review of the exegetes shows a variety of alternative approaches.

Some exegetes do not see any problem about how to know God's will. Others focus on the person of the Macedonian. Some devote themselves to tracing the actual route followed by Paul and his fellow workers; others notice and study the "we"; still others discover Hellenistic religious influences; finally, there are those attentive to whatever has to do with the Spirit. I shall describe these positions; when I think it opportune, I shall add my own observations.

THERE IS NO PROBLEM

A good many commentators fail to see anything problematic about the manifestation of God's will.[8] For practical purposes they repeat what the text says: after encountering various difficulties, Paul makes his way to Macedonia to begin the evangelization of that region.[9] The fact that Paul meets with obstacles leads some to look for explanations and plausible arguments, as, for example, that Paul had some difficulty with his eyes (they have in mind Galatians 4:13–15).[10]

IDENTIFICATION OF THE MACEDONIAN

Other scholars devote themselves instead to speculation about the person of the Macedonian.[11] Who was he? How did Paul recognize him? More extreme hypotheses identify him with Luke, who supposedly appears to Paul in the dream.[12] It may be supposed that the Macedonian was identified by a particular dress and, of course, by a particular accent as well. I think it more likely that he was just any Macedonian. There is no basis for thinking that Paul was faced with the angel of the local church, as some have claimed.[13] Still less is there any question of Luke himself and his first meeting with Paul. This is pure fantasy. The text does not offer any basis for such a possibility. It is no less necessary to set aside all the speculations of a psychological kind that appear every so often.[14] The text provides no basis for such constructions. On the other hand, I think it important to observe that the author of Acts has a certain interest in this event. The Macedonian origin of the author might explain his emphasis on the story of the incident.[15]

THE JOURNEY

Other authors turn immediately to the concrete itinerary of Paul and his companions and try to determine its several stages.[16] It may be observed that these stages are not easily identified. The reason is perhaps that, in my opinion, the text itself gives no information.

THE "WE"

At times the interest of the commentators shifts to the "we" that appears for the first time in v. 10; their preoccupation with the author's journal keeps them from perceiving other aspects.[17] But the first "we" that we see in 16:10 should not turn our thoughts in that direction. In fact, if we suppose that the reference is to Luke, the companion of Paul, we find ourselves in disagreement with early tradition, according to which Luke was from Antioch and not Macedonia.[18] This is a difficulty that is often overlooked.[19]

We have to be very cautious and not use the "we" in the so-called "we-sections" of Acts as the basis for hasty conclusions about Luke's relation to Paul.[20]

If we try to locate the Troas vision within Paul's life as we see this emerging in the Pauline letters, we must recognize that there is no point at which to locate the vision. How are we to explain this silence in the letters when we reflect that the remainder of the story in Acts 16–28 depends on this vision?

Was Paul simply forgetful? Or, more probably, was the omission due to the difference between the Paul of the letters and the Paul of Acts, a difference that scholars have increasingly emphasized? In Acts we have a Paul who already lives "in the odor of sanctity." In speaking of his life, which was now over, certain aspects are exaggerated and extolled, as will happen later on in the "classical" type of hagiography.[21]

If, on the other hand, we approach the real person on the basis on what Paul says about himself in his letters, we see that while he experienced charisms and spiritual gifts (see 1 Cor 12–14) and mentions "visions and revelations" (2 Cor 12:1) and spiritual favors (Gal 2:20) received during his life, he never speaks of the vision he supposedly had at Troas according to Acts 16:9–10. Furthermore he does not rely on more or less paranormal phenomena or make apostolic decisions under the influence of inspiration from dreams. He regards his life as essentially a spiritual struggle in which the outcome is never attributed to factors such as Acts describes. Finally, he is never hesitant in his apostolic activity nor does he feel the need of strength from sources outside himself.[22] Moreover, he never looks for signs (on the contrary: see 1 Cor 1:22!).

Silence in the letters about the quite different side of Paul that we find in Acts is not due to Paul's reserve about himself or his restraint in speaking about his accomplishments. No, what is said in Acts should in all likelihood be attributed to another hand, that of the author of the book of Acts, who thereby shows that he was not a close acquaintance of the apostle to the Gentiles.

HELLENISTIC INFLUENCES

Still other authors, adopting a variety of approaches, study the phenomenon in question from a different angle. They view the dream as a Hellenistic literary device for solemnizing key moments in the life of great individuals by means of revelations given in dreams.[23] Alexander the Great had a dream which was a turning point in his career: something similar happened to Paul.[24] Such a model and influence are plausible. But even if this provenance were demonstrated (the author, after all, comes from a Hellenistic milieu), the use of such cultural models when speaking of the true God, and their consequent introduction into Acts, remains an open question, for there can be no question of a *fatum* or blind determinism.

THE SPIRIT

Finally, there are those who focus on the role of the Spirit in this passage and on the unusual expression "Spirit of the Lord"; they emphasize the Spirit and its role in Acts generally. However, as they proceed in their interpretation they abstract from the immediate context.[25] When they look more concretely at the obstacle placed by the Spirit they do not say that it has its origin in the Spirit.[26]

But there is something more to be said. There are two contributions that fall outside this analysis and move in an entirely different direction. With regard to the manifestation of God's will two authors have pointed out factors that enable us to go further. At the same time, however, their contribution is restricted to brief remarks.

The first is an observation of E. Haulotte in a short commentary on the book of Acts. According to this French exegete, Paul wants to go southward, after the stay in Lystra, and therefore to follow the road to Ephesus, but an obstacle prevents him. "*Oddly enough,* the account," says Haulotte, "attributes the incident to the Holy Spirit." Therefore Paul tries to go northward into Bithynia, that is, toward the Black Sea, "but *the same* obstacle reappears, described now as the Spirit of Jesus."[27] Haulotte's study unfortunately stops here, being satisfied to note the opposition but without seeing what precisely is at issue. He makes his point, then continues on.

The other contribution comes in a phrase of M. Dibelius, which, despite its brevity, is perhaps the most relevant observation I have come across. He notes "the threefold divine intervention" that accounts for this new shift in the direction of the mission,[28] but he does not explain further.

THE GENERAL CONTEXT OF THE VISION AT TROAS

The vision at Troas comes after the treatment of the council of Jerusalem,[29] in the second half of the book of Acts. More specifically, the text comes in the midst of various incidents in which the miraculous is not lacking.[30] We should not be surprised that at the dawn of Christianity's expansion throughout the world there were many signs and wonders (see Acts 2:17–19), perhaps more than in other, later periods.

These elements of the extraordinary should not make us forget that the events narrated in Acts took place in real history, and therefore between the years 30 and 60 A.D. During this time the church spread according to the program briefly summarized in 1:8. After the first Pentecost, preaching was initially addressed to the Jews, then to the Samaritans and Hellenists, and finally to the pagans, so that it reached the ends of the earth. The activity described in Acts is chiefly that of Peter and Paul; they are the two principal personages around whom, for practical purposes, the entire account revolves.[31] Both men receive abundant spiritual favors. It is in this broad framework that the Troas vision has its place; only in this setting does it reveal its meaning.

THE TEXT

Everything becomes complicated when the reader turns to the passage. The immediate context of the dream calls for careful reflection. While the vision sequence itself is easily delimited, we are forced to push back the beginning of the pericope to 16:6, for 16:5 contains a kind of concluding "summary" of the stage in the journey that has just been completed. At the other end, the pericope stops at 16:10, for this last verse speaks of the departure for Macedonia in accordance with the instruction received in the dream. This is confirmed in 16:11, where the opening words, "having set sail from Troas," show that what follows is part of this new stage.[32]

Textual criticism of our two verses, like that of the book of Acts as a whole, has left us with two versions, a long and a shorter, which are regarded as two editions of the same work, one before and one after the death of Paul.[33]

In the verses that concern us here the long version has simply explained the short text with the help of minor amplifications.[34]

The content is the same in both versions and can be easily summarized: Paul is experiencing a short period of great indecision, not knowing where to go; he finds his answer in a nocturnal vision or dream, in which a Macedonian asks him (in direct discourse) to come to his aid. As a result, Paul and his companions set out immediately to carry out this new assignment. The verses thus describes two steps: the Macedonian's appeal for help, and the conviction of Paul that he must now travel to Europe to preach the gospel.[35]

The entire pericope (16:6–10) thus makes known, before the "opening" given in the dream, the presence of two "closures" which are often passed over in silence: in 16:6 the Holy Spirit prevents them from proclaiming the word in Asia; in 16:7 the Spirit of Jesus (an expression that occurs only here) does not allow them to go into Bithynia. Twice, then, the Spirit bars the way to missionary activity before opening a new path for the witnesses.

These various parts of the passage show first of all that there are two opposed "poles" in the text. On the one hand, there is the "no" of the Holy Spirit; on the other, the "yes" given by the dream, and therefore the importance of the last two verses (vv. 9–10). The passage thus also leads us to suppose that there were two attempts at missionary action, each of which might well have had good results but which were rejected. The human persons involved are not simply robots under the control of the Spirit. But, once again, what does all this mean?

A strictly methodical answer to this question requires that we allow ourselves to be guided, first of all, by the vocabulary of the passage. Every passage is as it were a piece of material, the threads of which are the words making it up.

The first point to be noted is the large number of names of places or cities in this pericope. This is not surprising since the passage tells of movements which circumstances allow or prevent. On the other hand, it is clear that all this is not simply geographical information, still less a guidebook for tourists.

Vv. 6–10 have, in fact, a quite different purpose. The way in which they are formulated and their use of pronouns show us on what we ought to focus our attention. Vv. 6–8 are in the plural ("they went," etc.) and describe what happens to the group of missionaries. Vv. 9–10a speak only of Paul's experience, and v. 10b describes the results of this experience for the entire group, using the plural pronoun but shifting to the first person. This final "we" ("us") underscores the unity that, according to Luke, exists between the missionary group and their head, Paul. His experience determines the course of the entire group. Before this transforming event took place, there was nothing that was normative for all. Without their head the group was unable to act. With him, all take up once again the way of the Lord's service. We find a similar phenomenon in the Old Testament: God acts through great individuals—patriarchs, kings, prophets, and so on—in leading his people.[36]

Within this framework another important fact emerges: in vv. 9–10a the story shifts from the stagnation of aimless wandering to a properly directed movement. There is no more circling around, no more danger of turning back. Confident progress is again possible.

In addition, the word *horama*, "dream" or "vision," occurs twice in these same verses.[37] This is a heavy concentration of a word that is rather rarely found: of its twelve occurrences in the New Testament, eleven are in Acts[38]; of these, eight are in the first part (chs. 1–12) of the book (7:31; 9:10, 12; 10:3, 17, 19; 11:5; 12:9) and three in the second part (chs. 13–28), two of them in the present passage and the last in 18:9.[39]

In Acts 7:30–31 (in Stephen's discourse) the reference is to a vision not of the protomartyr but of Moses at the time of his call and mission.[40] In a burning bush Moses sees an angel who orders him to take a different road and become leader of his people that he may bring them out of Egypt and into the promised land. Here the rereading of a past event is called a "vision."

Acts 9:10–12 tell of two appearances, one to Ananias and one to Saul-Paul, while Acts 10:3–8, 10:9–16, and 11:5 explain the two appearances to Peter and Cornelius. In both cases the visions-appearances serve to explain the origin of attitudes which otherwise would have been not only completely unpredictable but even impossible.

In Acts 12:9, in the story of Peter's miraculous deliverance from prison, the leader of the apostles for a moment confuses vision and reality. His deliverance is to be seen as a prolongation of those interventions in salvation history in which God snatches his people from the grip of their persecutors.[41] As a result of the divine action, Peter can continue on his way.

In Acts 18:9, Paul receives in a vision encouragement for continuing his apostolic activity in Corinth. Here the chosen witness is urged to remain, and in fact he stays a year and a half in Corinth (18:11).

Finally, in Acts 16:9–10 we are told of the dream at Troas in which Paul is called to go into Macedonia and evangelize that region.

The distribution of the word *horama* is quite striking. Not only does it seem to be the characteristic word of the entire book of Acts; in addition, it is easy to see that only great individuals have dreams or visions: Moses, Peter, Paul. This association suggests that the recipients are equals and have a like dignity; and in fact the recipients of dreams or visions are the principal personages in the history of salvation. In any event, the vision of dream they have received proves in each case to be determining for the remainder of their lives—it affects reality; the dream or vision is not restricted to the realm of the oneiric. The case of Peter, in 12:9, is very significant in this perspective. It is worth noting also that the change brought about affects not only these important individuals but also the entire people, the church!

What we see happening here should not surprise. In fact, it has already been brought up and explained by the author of Luke–Acts at the beginning of the second volume of his work, in his use of the words *horasis* and *enuption*. These two words appear together in the citation from Joel (3:1–5) by Peter in his sermon on Pentecost (Acts 2:17). The passage cited links dreams and visions with the new irruption of the Spirit: "In the last days it will be, God declares, that I will pour out my Spirit upon all flesh, and your sons and daughters shall prophesy, and your young men shall see *visions* and your old men shall dream *dreams.*" This passage not only sets the tone for Peter's sermon; it remains present in the author's mind in the later chapters as a key for reading successive events, especially those having to do with the conversion of the pagans.[42]

"The last days" have now begun, and the time of the church is part of this final period.[43] We are living in a new age. The period begun by the descent of the Holy Spirit will be marked by direct communication between God and human beings. Dreams are a means of such communication. This is especially true of the dream in 16:9–10 and of all the other dreams listed above in which the word *horama* is used. In all these cases, and unlike the dreams in the citation from Joel, the dreams or visions have a well defined content that is connected with mission or apostolate, and they make known the will of God.

But dreams cannot be considered the only means of such direct communication; it tends rather to be combined with other words to form a kind of net adapted to the purpose. At times *horama* is joined to *aggelos,* "messenger" or "angel," or to *phōnē,* "voice." More than once it occurs in association with *pneuma,* "spirit," or *Iēsous,* "Jesus." More rarely, it occurs near *cheir,* "hand," which may refer to the hand of God or the hand of human beings.[44] These literary devices are used to describe communication between God and human beings. Reduced to their essentials, these mediations all focus on Jesus or the Holy Spirit (see chapter 18).[45] In this setting more particularized and "sensible" forms of communication multiply: dreams or visions, words, hand, and so on.

Since Jesus Christ is no longer sensibly present after his resurrection and ascension, his disciples are compelled, in their effort to remain faithful to him, to act and proceed without now being able to refer directly to him or to his spoken word. They are therefore obliged to seek and find solutions to the difficulties they encounter in new situations, just as all Christians must who live in the period between the resurrection of Jesus and his second coming.

Since God's will is not already determined before events and *a fortiori* is not known before these events take place, it is of interest to see how choices are made.

Decisive interventions from on high direct the actions of the principal personages, but not independently of their will. They have been looking for solutions; they have tried various avenues; they have experienced doubt and indecision.

A careful reading of the text has made it possible to discover the traces of all this. In the present passage, the evidence is the holes and voids still to be found in the text. To fill them up, as it were, recourse has been had to literary devices.

"An angel," or "the Spirit," or "a vision" or "dream," or "a hand," or "a voice" has, in different passages, taken the concrete place of Jesus Christ and helped the human personages to go forward in fidelity to him.

In the vision at Troas, as Haulotte has correctly observed, the two poles are the Holy Spirit or the Spirit of Jesus, on the one hand, and the dream or vision, on the other. But it would be too hasty a conclusion to say that the Spirit is the obstacle or acts as an obstacle. He may simply be the first cause, which the author invokes because he does not know the second.[46]

It is much more relevant to observe that both the Spirit and the dream have the same importance in the argument and therefore the dream, too, takes on a "spiritual" character. It is the means by which the word of God is communicated.

In addition, we can gain a deeper understanding of the passage if we compare it, on the one hand, with the account of Paul's vocation (Acts 9;

22; 26) and, on the other, with the vision of Peter in Acts 10:11, a vision which occurs three times over.

In chapter 9 Ananias and Paul have a vision, each of the other; the way is thus prepared for a fruitful meeting of the two men. In Acts 22:10, after hearing the voice, Paul asks what he is to do; an unobtrusive allusion to the role of Ananias in Damascus enables him to overcome any indecision. (There is a close parallelism here with Acts 16:9–10. The Macedonian of the dream plays the same role that Ananias played at the time of Paul's conversion; to say this does not mean that one must identify the Macedonian of the dream with Luke—a fanciful view which I rejected earlier.) An obstacle has been overcome. Ananias receives Paul into the church. The human personage blends into the heavenly and serves as the latter's embodiment.

In chapter 10 we have the same situation but with Peter instead of Paul. As Peter prays on the roof he has a vision which makes it possible for him to accept Cornelius and his household into the church and thus to cross the mental boundaries to which he had been accustomed. Here again, the words *horama, aggelos, pneuma,* etc., relate all to the world of God, but the human factor exists and is acknowledged; in fact, Peter emphasizes it by insisting with his hearers that he is only a mortal (in 10:26 his hearers are tempted to treat him as a heavenly being).

In Acts 12 the story of Herod's death displays the same tendency but in the contrary direction. There is no question of any spirit of revenge! But the tyrant's death does display the opposite of what should characterize the agents of the Christian mission. The word *horama* does not occur, but is replaced by a "voice" and an "angel of the Lord." Herod delivers an address and receives an ovation: "The voice of God, and not of a mortal!" (12:22). On the spot, the angel of the Lord strikes him and he dies eaten by worms (12:23). The human being who has gone beyond what is permitted to him is immediately cut down to size.

Peter's attitude is directly opposed to that of Herod. Further on (14:15), Paul too will say that he is only a mortal. Even human beings who accomplish great things are little before God.

From all this it can be concluded that the heroes of the story are fully human and in real communication with God. By the power of Jesus Christ they succeed in doing great things and in writing the history of salvation: a history that is not prefabricated. Obstacles and hesitations mean that the involvement of freedom weighs upon the decisions taken. Even in the way he tells the story the author does not gloss over the gaps in his information or the real difficulties which the first disciples faced. All the literary devices which I have pointed out, especially dreams or visions, serve to give us a glimpse of the interplay of numerous influences and to preserve a sufficient area of obscurity that lets us sense the *sunergeia* between God and human beings. The narrator is skillful enough that, without ever saying exactly the same thing twice over, he lets us see how their action of God elicits that of human beings in a true symbiosis. It is perhaps this subtle way of writing that explains this author's great fascination for all his readers down the centuries. Each of the passages I have recalled is a little masterpiece of verbal skill; this is true in a special way of the vision at Troas.

Abbreviations

AB	Anchor Bible
AfO	*Archiv für Orientforschung*
AHW	W. von Soden, *Akkadisches Handwörterbuch*
AnBib	Analecta Biblica
AnGr	Analecta Gregoriana
ANRW	*Aufstieg und Niedergang der römischen Welt*
AOAT	Alter Orient und Altes Testament
ASOR DS	American Schools of Oriental Research Dissertation Series
AssSeign	*Assemblées du Seigneur*
ATD	Das Alte Testament Deutsch
ATS	Arbeiten zu Text und Sprache im AT
BASOR	*Bulletin of the American Schools of Oriental Research*
BBB	Bonner biblische Beiträge
BETL	Bibliotheca Ephemeridum Theologicarum Lovaniensium
BEvT	Beiträge zur evangelischen Theologie
BHS	*Biblia hebraica stuttgartensia*
BHT	Beiträge zur historischen Theologie
Bib	*Biblica*
BK	Bibel und Kirche
BKAT	Biblischer Kommentar: Altes Testament
BL	*Book List*
BWANT	Beiträge zur Wissenschaft vom Alten und Neuen Testament
BZ	*Biblische Zeitschrift*
BZAT	Beihefte zur Zeitschrift für die alttestamentliche Wissenschaft
BZNW	Beihefte zur Zeitschrift für die neutestamentliche Wissenschaft

CAD	*The Assyrian Dictionary of the Oriental Institute of the University of Chicago*
CAT	Commentaire de l'Ancien Testament
CBQ	*Catholic Biblical Quarterly*
CSS	Cursus scripturae sacrae
ConNT	*Coniectanea neotestamentica*
DBAT	*Drielheimer Blätter zum AT*
EdF	*Erträge der Forschung*
EHS.T	Europäische Hochschul schriften. Theologie
EKKNT	Evangelisch-katholischer Kommentar zum Neuen Testament
ErbAuf	*Erbe und Auftrag*
EtB	Etudes bibliques
ETL	*Ephemerides Theologicae Lovanienses*
EvT	*Evangelische Theologie*
ExpTim	*Expository Times*
FRLANT	Forschungen zur Religion und Literatur des Alten und Neuen Testaments
FzB	Forschung zur Bibel
Greg	*Gregorianum*
GTT	*Gereformeerd theologisch Tijdschrift*
HALAT	W. Baumgartner et al., *Hebräisches und aramäisches Lexikon zum Alten Testament*
HAT	Handbuch zum Alten Testament
HNT	Handbuch zum Neuen Testament
HTKNT	Herders theologischer Kommentar zum Neuen Testament
HTS	Harvard Theological Studies
ICC	International Critical Commentary
IDB	*Interpreter's Dictionary of the Bible*
Int	*Interpretation*
JAAR	*Journal of the American Academy of Religion*
JBL	*Journal of Biblical Literature*
JSOT	*Journal for the Study of the Old Testament*

KAT	Kommentar zum Alten Testament
KEKNT	Kritisch-exegetischer Kommentar über das NT
KNT	Kommentar zum Neuen Testament
LD	Lectio divina
LUÅ	Lunds universitets årsskrift
MeyerK	H. A. W. Meyer, Kritisch-exegetischer Kommentar über das Neue Testament
MiscCom	*Miscelaneas Comillas*
NCeB	New Century Bible
NICNT	New International Commentary on the New Testament
NIGTC	New International Greek Testament Commentary
NT	*Novum Testamentum*
NTD	Das Neue Testament Deutsch
NRT	*Nouvelle revue théologique*
NTS	*New Testament Studies*
OBO	Orbis biblicus et orientalis
OkTKNT	Ökumenischer Theologischer Kommentar zum NT
OTL	Old Testament Library
RB	*Revue biblique*
RCatalT	*Revista Catalana de Teologia*
RivB	*Rivista Biblica*
RNT	Regensburger Neues Testament
RSR	*Recherches de science religieuse*
RTP	*Revue de théologie et de philosophie*
SANT	Studien zum Alten und Neuen Testament
SB	Sources bibliques
SBS	Stuttgarter Bibelstudien
SBT	Studies in Biblical Theology
SEÅ	*Svensk exegetisk årsbok*
SemBib	*Sémiotique et Bible*
SNTSMS	Society for New Testament Studies Monograph Series
ST	*Studia theologica*
STANT	Studien zum Alten und Neuen Testament
STö	Sammlung Töpelmann
StudOr	Studia orientalia

TDNT	*Theological Dictionary of the New Testament*
TGUOS	*Transactions of the Glasgow University Oriental Society*
ThHK	Theologischer Hand Kommentar zum NT
TLZ	*Theologische Literaturzeitung*
TPINTComm	Trinity Press International Commentaries
TQ	*Theologische Quartalschrift*
TRE	*Theologische Realenzykolopädie*
TRu	*Theologische Rundschau*
TU	Texte und Untersuchungen
TWAT	G.J. Botterweck and H. Ringgren (eds.), *Theologisches Wörterbuch zum Alten Testament*
TZ	*Theologische Zeitschrift*
UF	*Ugarit-Forschungen*
UTB	Unitas TaschenBücher
VD	*Verbum Domini*
VT	*Vetus Testamentum*
VTS	Vetus Testamentum, Supplements
WMANT	Wissenschaftliche Monographien zum Alten und Neuen Testament
WUNT	Wissenschaftliche Untersuchungen zum Neuen Testament
ZAW	*Zeitschrift für die alttestamentliche Wissenschaft*
ZBK	Zürcher Bibel Kommentare
ZNW	*Zeitschrift für die neutestamentliche Wissenschaft*
ZTK	*Zeitschrift für Theologie und Kirche*

Notes

THE APOCALYPSE AND THE GOSPEL OF LUKE (VANNI)

1. H.B. Swete wrote as follows: "If we accept the later date of the Apocalypse, it may be assumed that the Churches of Asia were already in possession of some of the earlier books of the New Testament. Certain of the Pauline Epistles, and if not one or more of our present Gospels, some collection or collections of the sayings of the Lord were probably in their hands, and familiar to our author" (*Commentary on Revelation* [3rd ed., London, 1911; reprinted: Grand Rapids, 1977], clvi). J. Sweet takes an equivalent position: "It can be questioned how far he has moved beyond the spirit of the Old Testament (see p. 48), but there are echoes of most of the New Testament, especially the gospels and Pauline epistles" (*Revelation* [London, 1979], 40). U.B. Müller simply points out the presence and importance of Q traditions (*Die Offenbarung des Johannes* [Würzburg, 1984], 51).

2. P. Prigent sums up with clarity what is today a current impression: "As regards the relation of the Apocalypse to the other New Testament writings (except for the Johannine literature, which needs to be studied separately), not even here are any very specific conclusions to be had. Various resemblances suggests various literary relationships, but it is never possible to conclude to a dependence of the Apocalypse on a gospel or vice versa. Either the dependence is mediate, or it may be supposed that the Apocalypse and the parallel passage both go back to a common tradition" (*L'Apocalisse di S. Giovanni,* trans. P. Brugnoli [Rome, 1985] 735–36). J. Sweet has his own explanation of this lack of certainty; referring to the author of the Apocalypse, he says: "His practice of alluding rather than quoting makes for uncertainty in detecting references to New Testament books" (*Revelation,* 40).

3. E. B. Allo, *L'Apocalypse* (Paris, 1934[4]), cxii: "The critics have until now looked upon the Apocalypse as a book apart in the New Testament."

4. M.-E. Boismard, "Rapprochements littéraires entre l'Evangile de

Luc et l'Apocalypse," in *Synoptische Studien (Festschrift A. Wiken-hauser)* (Munich, 1953) 53–63.

5. L.A. Vos, *The Synoptic Traditions in the Apocalypse* (Kampen, 1965).

6. R. Bauckham, "Synoptic Parousia Parables and the Apocalypse," *NTS* 23 (1976–77) 162–76.

7. See R.H. Charles, *Revelation* I–II (Edinburgh, 1921).

8. Charles I, LXXXIII.

9. Charles I, LXXXIV–LXXXVI.

10. See Vos 54–60.

11. Vos 55, note 4, cites Charles, Swete, Lohmeyer, Bousset.

12. Of interest is the documentation supplied by Vos (54, note 10) and his criticism of Bultmann who judged the saying and its setting to be unauthentic.

13. See U. Vanni, *L'apocalisse: ermeneutica, esegesi, teologia* (Bologna, 1988) 106–08; Vos 57, note 11.

14. Vos 59.

15. Charles I, LXXXIV, note 7.

16. Vos 85–94.

17. Vos 89: "It is evident from the similarities in both thought and wording that there is a very certain relationship between this saying as it is found in the Apocalypse, in Matthew and in Luke. However, it is also evident from the variations in wording that neither passage is directly dependent upon the other as they are presently found in their Greek form."

18. There is, however, a grammatical difference. In the Apocalypse *homologeō* is used with the accusative; in Luke and Matthew it is used with *en* and the dative. The two synoptics show an aramaism, while the Apocalypse has the regular Greek construction (see Bauer-Aland, s.v.).

19. Vos 89–90.

20. See Vos 191, note 157, where van Iersel is cited.

21. Vos himself suggests this possibility: "It has been noted, however, that John does take similar liberties and makes similar alterations in his use of Old Testament materials" (91, note 158).

22. 2 Clem 3, 2, cited by Bauer-Aland (s.v.) and Vos (89, note 144).

23. It is to be observed of the New Testament linguistic field that only Luke and the author of the Apocalypse use the title *despotēs* of God: Lk 2:29; Acts 4:24; Rv 6:10.

24. This concentration is made clear at the very beginning of Boismard's essay. He writes: "The person of Satan occupies a very important place in the Johannine writings" (53).

25. See Boismard 56. But Boismard does not regard this contact as either the only one or the most important: he refers to it only in parentheses and along with others: Rv 20:1–3; 20:4–6. The main contact which Boismard emphasizes is between Lk 10:18 and Rv 9:1–11.

26. See Boismard 56–58.

27. *Ibid.* 57–58.

28. *Ibid.* 58.

29. This point is made by I.H. Marshall, *The Gospel of Luke* (Exeter, 1978), 428, who provides ample documentation.

30. *Ibid.*

31. Vos (163) holds that there is a close dependence between the texts of Luke and Matthew, on the one hand, and that of the Apocalypse, on the other. J.P. Ruiz, however, maintains that a dependence of the Apocalypse on these synoptic passages "is far from certain"; see his *Ezechiel in the Apocalypse: The Transformation of Prophetic Language in Revelation 16, 17–19, 10* (Frankfurt/M., 1989) 477. The question may be asked: Can Matthew and Luke be put on the same level in relation to the Apocalypse, if the more detailed similarities to the Apocalypse are found only in Luke?

32. Vos 163–74: "The Bridegroom and the Marriage Feast."

33. Vos 165: "The important element for our study, the identification of the Messiah with the bridegroom, is completely lacking in rabbinical Judaism as it was in the Old Testament."

34. Vos 166.

35. Vos 174: "We can list the following:

Rev. 19:7–9	*Matt. 22:1–14*
—The marriage of the Lamb is come	—marriage feast made for the son by the king
—the wife (bride) is properly attired	—a guest is not properly attired
—blessings on those bidden	—many are bidden; the object of the bidding is prominent
—marriage supper	—marriage feast.

John was evidently well acquainted with this parable of Jesus."

36. See Donal A. MacIlraith, *The Reciprocal Love between Christ and the Church in the Apocalypse* (Rome, 1986).

37. See note 27.

38. Swete unhesitatingly accepted a direct literary contact: "The words are a Christian interpretation of the remark which called forth the parable

of the Great Supper" (*Apocalypse* 246). Vos (172) disagrees: the macarism form is of no special importance, while the fact that its content corresponds to the parables of Matthew (22:1–13; 25:1–13) is indeed important. In particular, Vos says, there is a contact between the *keklēmenoi* of Rv 19:9 and the statement in Mt 22:14: *polloi gar eisin klētoi, oligoi de elektoi.*

39. See Bauckham (note 6).

40. A point worth investigating would be, for example, the relation among the three synoptics in regard to the *Weckformel* ("awakening formula"): "Let anyone who has ears (*ōta*) to hear with listen," which is found in a more elegant form in the Apocalypse, where the singular "ear" replaces the plural "ears": "Let anyone who has an ear (*ous*) to hear with listen." See Vos 71–75.

THE ROLE OF THE SCRIPTURES IN THE COMPOSITION OF THE GOSPEL ACCOUNTS (BOVON)

* I am happy to offer these pages in homage to Father Emilio Rasco, S.J., whose friendly welcome has always touched me, both at Rome and at the various meetings of the Society for New Testament Studies. Common theological interests and, in particular, a similar focus on Luke the evangelist helped give rise to this friendship, as did also Dom Jacques Dupont, whom I take this occasion to thank.

1. On the temptations of Jesus and the vast bibliography to which they have given rise see U. Luz, *Das Evangelium nach Matthäus (Mt 1–7)* (EKKNT I/1, 2nd ed.; Neukirchen-Vluyn and Zürich, 1989) 158–67; ET: *Matthew 1–7,* trans. W.C. Linss (Edinburgh, 1989); F. Bovon, *Das Evangelium nach Lukas (Lk 1, 1–9, 50)* (EKKNT III/1; Neukirchen-Vluyn and Zurich, 1989) 191–204.

2. See J. Steinmann, *Saint Jean Baptiste et la spiritualité du désert* (Maîtres spirituels; Paris, 1955) 155–57; ET: *Saint John the Baptist and the Desert Tradition,* trans. M. Boyes (Men of Wisdom 5; New York, 1958).

3. For a semiotic analysis of the temptation stories and their commentaries see L. Panier, *Récit et commentaires de la tentation de Jésus au désert. Approche sémiotique du discours interprétatif* (Paris, 1984).

4. See B.E. Gärtner, "The Pauline and Johannine Idea of 'To Know God' against the Hellenistic Background: The Greek Philosophical Principle 'Like by Like' in Paul and John," *NTS* 14 (1968) 209–31.

5. For a bibliography on Moses in the New Testament and especially in the work of Luke, see F. Bovon, "La figure de Moïse dans l'oeuvre de

Luc," in R. Martin-Achard (ed.), *La figure de Moïse. Ecritures et relectures* (Publications de la Faculté de Théologie de l'Université de Genève 1; Geneva, 1978) 47–65; reprinted in F. Bovon, *L'oeuvre de Luc. Etudes d'exégèse et de théologie* (LD 130; Paris, 1989) 73–96.

6. See F. Gils, *Jésus prophète d'après les Evangiles synoptiques* (Orientalia et Biblica Lovaniensia 2; Louvain, 1957).

7. See G. Theissen, *Urchristliche Wundergeschichten. Ein Beitrag zur formgeschichtlichen Erforschung der synoptischen Evangelien* (Studien zum Neuen Testament 8; Gütersloh, 1974) 111–14; ET: *Miracle Stories in the Early Christian Tradition* (Edinburgh, 1983).

8. See J.-M. van Cangh, *La multiplication des pains et l'eucharistie* (LD 86; Paris, 1975) 105–09.

9. For a bibliography on the multiplication of the loaves see F. Bovon, *Das Evangelium nach Lukas* (note 1) 465–66.

10. On imitation of the Old Testament see T.L. Brodie, "Towards Unravelling Luke's Use of the Old Testament: Luke 7. 11–17 as an *imitatio* of 1 Kings 17. 17–24," *NTS* 32 (1986) 247–67; J. H. Charlesworth, "The Pseudepigrapha as Biblical Exegesis," in C.A. Evans and W.F. Stinespring (eds.), *Early Jewish and Christian Exegesis: Studies in Memory of W. H. Brownlee* (Homages Series 10; Atlanta, 1987) 139–52.

11. On the concept of citation see F. Bovon, " 'Schon hat der Heilige Geist durch den Propheten Jesaja zu euren Vätern gesprochen' (Apg 28, 25)," *ZNW* 75 (1984) 226–32; reprinted, in French, in F. Bovon, *L'oeuvre de Luc* (note 5) 145–53.

12. See H. Conzelmann, "phōs," *TDNT* 9:310–58.

13. On the episode of Zebulun and Naphtali see U. Luz, *Das Evangelium nach Matthäus* (note 1) 169–74.

14. On the part played by the Old Testament in the work of Luke see F. Bovon, *Luc le théologien. Vingt-cinq ans de recherches (1950–1975)* (Le monde de la Bible; 2nd ed.; Geneva, 1989) 85–117; J. Jervell, "Die Mitte der Schrift. Zum lukanischen Verständnis des Alten Testaments," in U. Luz and H. Weder (eds.), *Die Mitte des Neuen Testaments. Einheit und Vielfalt neutestamentlicher Theologie. Festschrift E. Schweizer* (Göttingen, 1983) 79–96; J.T. Sanders, "The Prophetic Use of the Scriptures in Luke-Acts," in *Early Jewish and Christian Exegesis* (note 10) 191–98.

METHODOLOGICAL REFLECTIONS ON RECENT STUDIES OF THE NAAMAN PERICOPE (2:KINGS 5) (CONROY)

1. See, for example, T.L. Brodie, *Luke the Literary Interpreter. Luke-Acts as a Systematic Rewriting and Updating of the Elijah-Elisha Narra-*

tives in 1 and 2 Kings (Rome, 1987: = dissertation 1981); idem, "Jesus as the New Elisha: Cracking the Code," *ExpTim* 93 (1981–82) 39–42; idem, "Towards Unraveling the Rhetorical Imitation of Sources in Acts: 2 Kings 5 as One Component of Acts 8, 9–40," *Bib* 67 (1986) 41–67.

2. E. Würthwein, *Die Bücher der Könige. 1. Kön. 17—2. Kön. 25* (ATD 11, 2; Göttingen, 1984).

3. M. Cogan – H. Tadmor, *II Kings* (AB 11; Garden City, 1988).

4. See, for instance, W. Egger, *Methodenlehre zum Neuen Testament.* Einführung in linguistische und historisch-kritische Methoden (Freiburg–Basel–Wien 1987); W. Stenger, *Biblische Methodenlehre* (Düsseldorf, 1987).

5. For related considerations see also C. Conroy, "Methodological Reflections on some recent studies of the 'Confessions' of Jeremiah," *Proceedings of the Irish Biblical Association* 12 (1989) 7–25; idem, "Reflections on the Exegetical Task Apropos of Recent Studies on 2 Kg 22–23," *Pentateuchal and Deuteronomistic Studies.* Papers read at the XIIIth IOSOT Congress, Leuven, 1989 (eds. C. Brekelmans and J. Lust) (BETL 94; Leuven, 1990) 255-68.

6. See, among other studies of his, J. Trebolle Barrera, *Jehú y Joás.* Texto y composición literaria de 2 Reyes 9–11 (Valencia, 1984); idem, "Historia y crítica del texto del Libro de los Reyes," *II Simposio Bíblico Español (Córdoba 1985)* (ed. V. Collado Bertomeu y V. Vilar Hueso) (Valencia–Córdoba, 1987) 143–58; idem, *Centena in libros Samuelis et Regum.* Variantes textuales y composición literaria en los libros de Samuel y Reyes (Textos y Estudios "Cardenal Cisneros," 47; Madrid, 1989). For a discussion of 2 Kgs 5:18 see 168–70 of the last-mentioned work.

7. H.-J. Stipp, *Elischa—Propheten—Gottesmänner.* Die Kompositionsgeschichte des Elischazyklus und verwandter Texte, rekonstruiert auf der Basis von Text- und Literarkritik zu 1 Kön 20.22 und 2 Kön 2–7 (ATS 24; St. Ottilien, 1987).

8. Stipp, *Elischa* 6–46, 301, 478.

9. Stipp, *Elischa* 486.

10. Cogan – Tadmor, *II Kings* (see n. 3 above) 9–10.

11. C. Turiot, "La guérison de Naaman. Analyse du texte de 2 Rois 5, versets 1 à 27," *Sémiotique et Bible* 16 (1979) 8–32.

12. See, for instance, *Analyse sémiotique des textes,* par le Groupe d'Entrevernes (eds. J.-C. Giroud et L. Panier) (Lyon, 1979). On a more systematic level, see A.-J. Greimas – J. Courtés, *Sémiotique. Dictionnaire raisonné de la théorie du langage* (Paris, 1979); ET: *Semiotics and Language. An Analytical Dictionary* (trans. L. Crist, D. Patte, et al.) (Bloomington, 1982).

13. See D. Greenwood, *Structuralism and the Biblical Text* (Berlin–New York–Amsterdam 1985) 34–36, 72.

14. For another example of semiotic narrative analysis of 2 Kgs 5 (limited to vv. 1–19a), together with suggestions for homiletic application of this type of reading, see F. Siegert, "Narrative Analyse als Hilfe zur Predigtvorbereitung—ein Beispiel," *Linguistica Biblica* 32 (1974) 77–90.

15. R.L. Cohn, "Form and Perspective in 2 Kings v," *VT* 33 (1983) 171–84.

16. K.A.D. Smelik, "De Betekenis van 2 Koningen 5. Een 'Amsterdamse' benadering," *GTT* 88 (1988) 98–115; idem, "Das Kapitel 2. Könige 5 als literarische Einheit," *DBAT* 25 (Dec. 1988) 29–47.

17. The periodical associated with this group is entitled *Amsterdamse cahiers voor exegese en Bijbelse theologie* (1980ff). For further description and discussion see R. Oost, *Omstreden Bijbeluitleg*. Aspecten en achtergronden van de hermeneutische discussie rondom de exegese van het Oude Testament in Nederland. Een bijdrage tot gesprek (Kampen, 1986); see the notice by J. Barr in *BL* 1988, 114.

18. F. Smyth-Florentin, "Histoire de la guérison et de la conversion de Naaman, II Rois 5, 1–19," *Foi Vive* 69, 3 [Cahiers Bibliques 9] (1970) 29–43.

19. H. Schult, "Naemans Übertritt zum Yahwismus (2 Könige 5, 1–19a) und die biblischen Bekehrungsgeschichten," *DBAT* 9 (Sept. 1975) 2–20.

20. A particularly useful commentary in this regard is that of T.R. Hobbs, *2 Kings* (Word Biblical Commentary 13; Waco, 1985) 55–69.

21. A failure to take note of this distinction seems to be found in H.-J. Hermisson, "Einheit und Komplexität Deuterojesajas. Probleme der Redaktionsgeschichte von Jes 40–55," *The Book of Isaiah. Le Livre d'Isaïe. Les oracles et leurs relectures. Unité et complexité de l'ouvrage* (éd. J. Vermeylen) (BETL 81; Leuven, 1989) 287–312, esp. 287–90.

22. These concepts are discussed in most contemporary treatments of literary theory. See, for instance, S. Rimmon-Kenan, *Narrative Fiction. Contemporary Poetics* (London–New York, 1983) 86–105; G. Genette, *Nouveau discours du récit* (Paris, 1983) 93–107.

23. See G. von Rad, "Naaman. Eine kritische Nacherzählung," *Gottes Wirken in Israel* (Hrsg. O.H. Steck) (Neukirchen-Vluyn, 1974) 53–64; J.A. Montgomery – H.S. Gehman, *A Critical and Exegetical Commentary on the Books of Kings* (ICC; Edinburgh, 1951) 373–81; S.J. De Vries, *Prophet against Prophet*. The Role of the Micaiah Narrative (1 Kings 22) in the Development of Early Prophetic Tradition (Grand Rapids, 1978) 120–21; M. Rehm, *Das zweite Buch der Könige. Ein Kommentar* (Würzburg, 1982) 61; T.R. Hobbs, *2 Kings* (cf. n. 20 above); H.-J. Stipp,

Elischa (cf. n. 7 above) 312–19; Cogan-Tadmor, *II Kings* (cf. n. 3 above) 68.

24. A. van den Born, *Koningen* (De Boeken van het Oude Testament IV/2; Roermond–Maaseik, 1958) 145–49; K.D. Fricke, *Das zweite Buch von den Königen* (Stuttgart, 1972) 68, 74; J. Gray, *I & II Kings.* A Commentary (London, ³1977) 470–71, 508–10; H. Seebass, "Elisa," *TRE* 9 (1982) 506–09, esp. 507. For a variant of this position see M. Sekine, "Literatur-soziologische Betrachtungen zu den Elisaerzählungen," *Annual of the Japanese Biblical Institute* 1 (1975) 39–62, esp. 52–53; Sekine held that the earliest stratum consisted of vv. 1–14, 17–19a, while the later part (which presupposed classical prophecy) included vv. 15–16, 19b–27.

25. H.-C. Schmitt, *Elisa: Traditionsgeschichtliche Untersuchungen zur vorklassischen nordisraelitischen Prophetie* (Gütersloh, 1972). On 2 Kgs 5 see esp. 78–80, 211–15.

26. See Schmitt, *Elisa* 80 n. 44; G.H. Jones, *1 and 2 Kings.* Volume II: 1 Kings 17:1–2 Kings 25:30 (New Century Bible; Grand Rapids–London, 1984) 412–21; Würthwein, *Könige* II (see n. 2 above) 296–303.

27. G. Hentschel, "Die Heilung Naamans durch das Wort des Gottesmannes (2 Kön 5)," *Künder des Wortes.* Beiträge zur Theologie der Propheten (FS. J. Schreiner; [Hrsg. L. Ruppert, P. Weimar, E. Zenger] Würzburg, 1982) 11–21; idem, *2. Könige* (Neue Echter Bibel; Würzburg, 1985).

28. One has to add, however, that Hentschel's account of various stages in the oral development of the Naaman story is highly speculative; it is not easy to see how such considerations are amenable to inter-subjective scholarly control. This is not to deny that the story may have had a period of oral transmission; what is questionable is whether scholars today have the capacity to get to know anything in detail about it.

29. Stipp, *Elischa* (see n. 7 above).

30. W. Richter, *Exegese als Literaturwissenschaft.* Entwurf einer alt-testamentlichen Literaturtheorie und Methodologie (Göttingen, 1971). This work has also had decisive influence on the widely-used manual of G. Fohrer – H.W. Hoffman – F. Huber – L. Markert – G. Wanke, *Exegese des Alten Testaments.* Einführung in die Methodik (UTB 267; Heidelberg, ⁵1989).

31. Stipp, *Elischa* 316–17.

32. J. Barton, *Reading the Old Testament.* Method in Biblical Study (London, 1984) 16–18, 65–67.

33. Stipp, *Elischa* 61 n. 38.

34. Stipp, *Elischa* 116 n. 134.

35. For these three points see respectively Stipp, *Elischa* 193 n. 109, 261; 214; 317–318.

36. De Vries, *Prophet against Prophet* (see n. 23 above).

37. De Vries, *Prophet against Prophet* 53.

38. R.C. Culley, "Punishment Stories in the Legends of the Prophets," *Orientation by Disorientation*. Presented in Honor of William A. Beardslee (ed. R.A. Spencer) (Pittsburgh Theological Monograph Series 35; Pittsburgh, 1980) 167–81.

39. A. Rofé, *The Prophetical Stories*. The Narratives about the Prophets in the Hebrew Bible. Their Literary Types and History (Jerusalem, 1988); the original Hebrew edition was first published in 1982 and revised in 1986. On 2 Kgs 5 see esp. 126–31 of the 1988 edition.

40. See, for instance, A. Rofé, "The Classification of the Prophetical Stories," *JBL* 89 (1970) 427–40; idem, "Classes in the prophetical stories: Didactic legends and parables," *Studies on Prophecy*. A Collection of Twelve Papers (VTS 26; Leiden, 1974) 143–64.

41. Rofé, *Stories* 126. See also pp. 8–9 for his remarks on the twelve genres in general.

42. Rofé, *Stories* 129.

43. Thus, for instance, M. Noth, *Überlieferungsgeschichtliche Studien*. Die sammelnden und bearbeitenden Geschichtswerke im Alten Testament (Tübingen, ²1957) 78–79, 83; J. Gray, *I & II Kings* (see n. 24 above) 28–30, 465–71; M. Rehm, *Könige* II (see n. 23 above) 24–27, 260; G. Hentschel, *1. Könige* (Neue Echter Bibel; Würzburg, 1984) 11–14.

44. Schmitt, *Elisa* (see n. 25 above) 138. The other pre-exilic Elisha traditions continued to be transmitted in separate collections, according to Schmitt. See the synthesis of his literary-critical results on pp. 137–38. Würthwein, *Könige* II (see n. 2 above) 366–68 follows, with some modifications, the conclusions of Schmitt. G.H. Jones, *1 and 2 Kings*. Volume I: 1 Kings 1–16:34 (New Century Bible; Grand Rapids–London, 1984) 68–73 acknowledges the importance of Schmitt's work, agrees that the existence of a pre-deuteronomic cycle of Elisha-traditions is questionable, but hesitates to accept all the late datings proposed by Schmitt.

45. For a synthesis of Stipp's conclusions about the composition-history of the Elisha texts see his *Elischa* (as n. 7 above) 463–80.

46. See, for instance, H. Weippert, "Das deuteronomistische Geschichtswerk. Sein Ziel und Ende in der neueren Forschung," *TRu* 50 (1985) 213–49; M.A. O'Brien, *The Deuteronomistic History Hypothesis: A Reassessment* (OBO 92; Freiburg–Göttingen 1989).

47. On this theological problem in general see W. Groß, "YHWH und die Religion der Nicht-Israeliten," *TQ* 169 (1989) 34–44; on 2 Kgs 5 see esp. 42–44.

48. R. Rendtorff, "Jesaja 6 im Rahmen der Komposition des Jesaja-

buches," *The Book of Isaiah* (see n. 21 above) 73–82; E. Talstra, "Clio en de 'agenda van de toekomst'. Het Oude Testament van verhaalkunstenaars, gelovigen en historici," *GTT* 89 (1989) 212–25 (for some remarks on 2 Kgs 5 see 221–25). See also the overview by L. Alonso Schökel, "Trends: plurality of methods, priority of issues," *Congress Volume Jerusalem 1986* (ed. J.A. Emerton) (VTS 40; Leiden, 1988) 285–92.

49. It is surprising, and worrying, to notice how little dialogue with general historiographical theory and method one finds in most biblical studies in the historical-critical mode. For a recent exception to this comment see R. Liwak, *Der Prophet und die Geschichte. Eine literarhistorische Untersuchung zum Jeremiabuch* (BWANT 121; Stuttgart, 1987).

50. The term comes from R. Rendtorff, "Jesaja 6" (see n. 48 above) 74.

FROM LUKAN PARENESIS TO JOHANNINE CHRISTOLOGY (CABA)

1. E. Rasco, "Christus granum frumenti. Jo 12, 24," *VD* 37 (1959) 12–25, 65–77.

2. *Ibid.* 13: "Since the parallel verse in the Synoptics does not refer to the work of Christ but rather enunciates what I might call an ascetical principle for all Christians, there is danger of interpreting the verses in John in pretty much the same way, so that the christological meaning of the entire pericope is lost.'

3. W. Grundmann, *Das Evangelium nach Lukas* (ThHK 3; Berlin, 1964) 190; H. Schürmann, *Il vangelo di Luca* (Commentario Teologico de Nuovo Testamento 3/1; Brescia, 1983) 1:843–44.

4. Schürmann (note 3) 1:830.

5. According to Lagrange, the use of the imperfect weakens the reference to a particular historical moment; see his *Evangile selon Saint Luc* (7th ed.; Paris, 1948) 268; but the redactional element is thereby accentuated.

6. J. Schmid, *L'evangelo secondo Luca* (Brescia, 1961) 218.

7. Schürmann, *Luca* (note 3) 1:844.

8. P. Bonnard, *L'évangile selon Saint Matthieu* (Neuchâtel, 1963) 249; the statement applies to the text of Matthew but also to the other synoptics.

9. A. Schulz, *Nachfolgen und Nachahmen. Studien über das Verhältnis der neutestamentlichen Jüngerschaft zur urchristlichen Vorbildethik* (SANT 6; Munich, 1962) 83: "The expression '*ei tis thelei opisō mou*

elthein (= *akolouthein mou*),' reflects the rabbinic term הַלַּךְ אַתְרָי; it is an image that signifies the intention of becoming a *mathētēs* of Jesus."

10. Schürmann, *Luca* (note 3) 1:846. The Greek verb *aparneisthai* can be explained in light of the Lukan Aramaism *misein tēn psuchēn heautou* (Lk 14:26); see A. Fridrichsen, "Sich Selbst Verleugnen," *ConNT* 2 (1936) 1–8, especially 3; Schulz, *Nachfolgen und Nachahmen* (note 9) 99; Schürmann, *Luca* (note 3) 1:846, note 87.

11. H. Schlier, "arneomai," *TDNT* 1:469–71; H. Riesenfeld, "The Meaning of the Verb *arneisthai*," *ConNT* 11 (In honorem A. Fridrichsen; Lund–Copenhagen, 1947) 207–19, esp. 218.

12. Bonnard, *Matthieu* (note 8) 249; F. Blass, A. Debrunner, and R.W. Funk, *A Greek Grammar of the New Testament* (8th ed.; Chicago, 1972) no. 442 (9).

13. For a summary of the main opinions see J. Schneider, "stauros," *TDNT* 7:574–79. Especially interesting has been the suggestion that at the historical level of Jesus himself the expression should be viewed as an allusion to the text of Ez 9:4–6, which speaks of the *Tau* carried on the forehead as a sign of protection by the Lord and of belonging to him; after the crucifixion of Jesus the *Tau* has been seen as the historical cross of Jesus. Thus E. Dinkler, "Jesu Wort vom Keuztragen," *Neutestamentliche Studien für R. Bultmann* (BZNW 21; Berlin, 1954) 110–29, especially 124–29; R. Pesch, *Il Vangelo di Marco* (Commentario teologico del Nuovo Testamento 2/2; Brescia, 1982) 101. According to J. Schneider, taken as a whole, this idea of being marked with a seal does not fit in with the views of Jesus (see "stauros," *TDNT* 7:578–79); see F.M. Uricchio and G.M. Stano, *Vangelo secondo Marco* (Rome, 1966) 400.

14. Uricchio-Stano, 399–400; Schürmann, *Luca* (note 3) 1:846.

15. Schneider, "stauros" (note 13) 989; W. Grundmann, *Das Evangelium nach Markus* (ThHK 2; 3rd ed.; Berlin, 1965) 175.

16. Lagrange seeks to exclude this repetition of the idea in *opisō mou eltherin* but it persists in his explanation of the meaning: "One who wishes to come after Jesus must understand clearly that this means to follow him" (*Luc* [note 5], 168). The identity of meaning in the two expressions is shown by Schulz, *Nachfolgen und Nachahmen* (note 9) 83.

17. F. Zorell, *Lexicon Graecum Novi Testamenti* (Paris, 1931) 53: "I follow or accompany someone as he goes; I am someone's companion on a journey" (see Mt 4:25; 8:1).

18. J. Schmid, *L'evangelo secondo Marco* (Brescia, 1961) 223.

19. V. Taylor, *The Gospel According to St. Mark* (London, 1963) 381; S. González Silva, "El seguimiento de Cristo en los logia *akolouthein*," *Claretianum* 14 (1974) 124.

20. Luke himself uses them interchangeably (see 12:9a, 9b); see

González Silva, "El seguimiento" (note 19); Riesenfeld, "The Meaning of the Verb *arneisthai*" (note 11) 208.

21. Lagrange, *Luc* (note 5) 268: "It is not a question of following Jesus in a given situation but of walking always in his steps."

22. D.E. Miller, "Lc 9, 18–24," *Int* 37 (1983) 66; Schürmann, *Luca* (note 3) 1:847.

23. J. Ernst, *Il vangelo secondo Luca* II (Brescia, 1985) 631.

24. This verse of Luke (14:27) is omitted in some codices (R, Γ) and ancient translations. The omission is easily explained by the phenomenon of homeoteleuton, since v. 26 and v. 27 end in the same way. See J.A. Fitzmyer, *The Gospel according to Luke* X-XXIV (AB 28a; Garden City, 1985) 1065.

25. M. Zerwick, *Graecitas Biblica* (4th ed.; Rome, 1960) no. 215. ET of an earlier edition: *Biblical Greek,* trans. J. Smith (Rome, 1963).

26. E. Dinkler, "Jesu Wort vom Kreuztragen" (note 13) 111.

27. Zorell, *Lexicon Graecum* (note 17) 220: "I carry on my shoulders, I take upon myself."

28. Schmid, *Luca* (note 6) 317.

29. Ernst, *Luca* (note 23) 2:632.

30. *Ibid.* 630, note 4.

31. *Ibid.*

32. Although it is difficult to determine which is the earlier formulation, the verb *bastazei* contains a clearer allusion to the person of Jesus (see Jn 19:17) behind whom one walks. See Schulz, *Nachfolgen und Nachahmen* (note 10) 84, note 63.

33. Ernst, *Luca* (note 23) 2:632.

34. Grundmann, *Markus* (note 15) 175–76; Pesch, *Marco* (note 13) 2:103.

35. X. Léon-Dufour, *Life and Death in the New Testament: The Teachings of Jesus and Paul,* trans. T. Prendergast (San Francisco, 1986) 33; idem, "Luc 17, 33," *RSR* 69 (1981) 102.

36. G. Dautzenberg, *Sein Leben bewahren. Psuchē in den Herrenworten der Evangelien* (SANT 14; Munich, 1966) 58; Schürmann, *Luca* (note 3) 1:850.

37. Bonnard, *Matthieu* (note 8) 251.

38. Thus Taylor, *Mark* (note 19) 382; Schmid, *Marco* (note 18) 223–24; Uricchio-Stano, *Marco* (note 13) 400.

39. Dautzenberg, *Sein Leben bewahren* (note 36) 58–60; Schürmann, *Luca* (note 3) 1:850; Léon-Dufour, *Life and Death* (note 35) 33–34.

40. Pesch, *Marco* (note 13) 2:103.

41. Dautzenberg, *Sein Leben bewahren* (note 36) 61; Schürmann, *Luca* (note 3) 1:851.

42. W. Marxsen, *Der Evangelist Markus. Studien zur Redaktionsge-schichte des Evangeliums* (2nd ed.; Göttingen, 1959) 85; Dautzenberg, *Sein Leben bewahren* (note 36) 63.

43. *Ibid.;* Schürmann, *Luca* (note 3) 1:850.

44. *Ibid.* 1:851.

45. Léon-Dufour, *Life and Death* (note 35) 37–38.

46. Léon-Dufour, "Luc 17, 33" (note 35) 109.

47. The verb *peripoieomai* occurs only here in the gospels; the meaning is "to preserve," or, in the middle voice, "to preserve something of one's own." It occurs twice more in the New Testament with the meaning "to obtain" (Acts 20:28; 1 Tm 3:13); see Zorell, *Lexicon NT* (note 17) 1042. The verb *zēteō* signifies not only the desire for something but also the effort to obtain it, as, for example, the kingdom of God (Lk 12:31); see Léon-Dufour, "Luc 17, 33" (note 35) 102; Dautzenberg, *Sein Leben bewahren* (note 36) 63.

48. Dautzenberg 63.

49. *Zōogoneō* in the sense of "to keep alive" likewise occurs only here in the gospels; it also occurs in Acts 7:19; 1 Tm 6:13.

50. Léon-Dufour, "Luc 17, 33" (note 35) 103.

51. Dautzenberg, *Sein Leben bewahren* (note 36) 63.

52. This is the view of Schwartz, Renan, Wellhausen, and Spitta, who are cited in J.M. Lagrange, *Evangile selon Saint Jean* (8th ed.; Paris, 1947) 328.

53. R. Schnackenburg, *The Gospel according to John* 2, trans. C. Hastings *et al.* (New York, 1960) 384–86.

54. B.F. Westcott, *The Gospel according to St. John* (London, 1958) 189; R.E. Brown, *The Gospel according to John* I-XII (AB 29; Garden City, 1966) 466–67; G. Ferraro, *L'"ora" di Cristo nel Quarto Vangelo* (Rome, 1974) 180; F.J. Moloney, *The Johannine Son of Man* (2nd ed.; Rome, 1978) 176.

55. The two verbs taken separately are typical of John: *phileō:* Mt five times, Mk once, two times, Lk Jn thirteen times; *miseō:* Mt five times, Mk once, Lk seven times, Jn twelve times. So too is the combination of the two verbs to express two contrasting attitudes—love, hate—on the part of the world (Jn 15:18–19).

56. O. Michel, "miseō," *TDNT* 4:690–93; Brown, *John* (note 54) 464.

57. Westcott, *John* (note 54) 243.

58. Rasco, "Christus granum frumenti" (note 1) 76.

59. The verb *diakoneō* appears only one other time in the fourth gospel, to describe the service given to Jesus by Martha at the dinner in Bethany (12:2).

60. R.C.H. Lenski, *The Interpretation of St. John's Gospel* (Columbus,

1942) 866; C.K. Barrett, *The Gospel according to St. John* (2nd ed.; London, 1978) 424.

61. Lenski, *John* 866.

62. Zorell, *Lexicon NT* (note 17) 1320; W. Bauer, *A Greek-English Lexicon of the New Testament,* ed. and trans. W.F. Arndt and F.W. Gingrich (4th ed.; Chicago, 1957) 824–25.

63. J. Caba, *De los evangelios al Jesús histórico* (BAC 316; 2nd ed.; Madrid, 1980) 439–40; R. Latourelle, *Finding Jesus through the Gospels: History and Hermeneutics,* trans. A. Owen (Staten Island, 1979) 221–23.

PROBLEMS OF STRUCTURE IN LUKE'S ESCHATOLOGICAL DISCOURSE (FUSCO)

1. See F. Bovon, *Luc le théologien. Vingt-cinq ans de recherches (1950–1975)* (Neuchâtel–Paris, 1978); M. Rese, "Das Lukas-Evangelium. Ein Forschungsbericht," *ANRW* II.25.3 (1985) 2258–328; V. Radl, *Das Lukas-Evangelium* (EdF 261; Darmstadt, 1988).

2. E. Rasco, "H. Conzelmann y la *Historia salutis.* A proposito de *Die Mitte der Zeit* y *Die Apostelgeschichte,*" *Greg* 46 (1965) 286–319, at 309–16.

3. E. Rasco, *La teología de Lucas. Origen, desarrollo, orientaciones* (AnGr 201; Rome, 1976) 167.

4. H. Conzelmann, *Die Mitte der Zeit. Studien zur Theologie des Lukas* (BHT 18; Tübingen, 1954; 5th ed., 1964); ET: *The Theology of Luke,* trans. G. Buswell, from 2nd German ed. (New York, 1960). [I shall cite the ET, unless the fifth German edition, which the author is using, has introduced some change.—Trans.]

5. E. Rasco, "H. Conzelmann" (note 2) 301–05, 318; *La teología de Lucas* (note 3) 98–114.

6. See some examples below in Sections 2 (Mk 13:4//Lk 21:7), 3 (Lk 21:10a, 29a), 5.1 (Mk 13:8c//Lk 21:11), and 6.2 (Mk 13:30//Lk 21:32).

7. J. Zmijewski, *Die Eschatologiereden des Lukas-Evangeliums. Eine traditions- und redaktionsgeschichtliche Untersuchung zu Lk 21, 5–36 und Lk 17, 20–37* (BBB 40; Bonn, 1972); R. Geiger, *Die lukanische Endzeitreden. Studien zur Eschatologie des Lukas-Evangeliums* (EHS.T 23/16; Frankfurt M.–Bern, 1976); F. Keck, *Die offentliche Abschiedsrede Jesu in Lk 20, 45–21, 36. Eine redaktions- und motivgeschichtliche Untersuchung* (FzB 25; Stuttgart, 1976).

8. Zmijewski, *Echatologiereden* (note 7) 53–59 (some factors giving unity to the text); 69–72 (division into eight short parts); further remarks in Keck (*Abschiedsrede* [note 7] 29–35) who rejects the method that de-

rives the structure of Luke 21 from Mark 13 (*ibid.* 31–32); but he too falls back on this explanation when he derives the division (*Gliederung*) of Luke from a comparison with Mark (*ibid.* 186).

9. J. Lambrecht, "Redactio sermonis eschatologici," *VD* 43 (1965) 278–87; idem, "Reading and Rereading Lk 18, 31–22, 6," in *A cause de l'évangile. Festschrift J. Dupont* (LD 123; Paris, 1985) 585–612.

10. J. Dupont, *Le tre apocalissi sinottiche* (Bologna, 1967); see also his *Distruzione del tempio e fine del mondo. Studi sul discorso di Marco 13* (Rome, 1979); *Le discours eschatologique* (Ad usum privatum; (Rome: Pontifical Biblical Institute, 1971) 43–77; "Il cristiano durante il tempo dell'attesa (Lc 21, 5–19)," in *33a domenica "per annum"* (La parola per l'assemblea festiva; Brescia, 1970) 127–40.

11. Dupont, *Distruzione* (note 10) 67.

12. *Ibid.* 201; Dupont, *Le tre apocalissi* (note 10) 144.

13. See e.g. R. Maddox, *The Purpose of Luke-Acts* (FRLANT 126; Gottingen, 1982) 122: "Nothing in our examination of Luke 21, 5–36 has emerged to support the "delay"-theory."—Other authors are cited in my own studies that are listed in the next footnote.

14. See V. Fusco, "Lc 21, 32 alla luce dell'espressione 'questa generazione,'" *Asprenas* 31 (1984) 397–424; idem, "Chiesa e Regno nella prospettiva lucana," in G. Lorizio and V. Scippa (eds.), *Ecclesiae sacramentum. Studi in onore di A. Marranzini* (Naples, 1986) 113–35; idem, "Progetto storiografico e progetto teologico nell'opera lucana," in *La storiografia nella Bibbia* (Atti della XXVIII settimana biblica; Bologna, 1986) 123–52.

15. See below, Section 3 and note 28; Section 4 and note 43; Section 5.2 and note 53.

16. Keck, *Abschiedsrede* (note 7), has the discourse begin in 20:45 with the redactor's introduction: "In the hearing of all the people, he said to the disciples . . ."; but in Luke's mind, once Jesus has entered Jerusalem, everything is a follow-up, dealing with various themes, on his teaching in the temple (see 19:47–48; 20:1, 6, 9, 19, 26, 45; 21:37–38). It is not clear why his eschatological teaching should be especially connected only with 20:45–21:5.

17. One proceeds arbitrarily when one eliminates the chronological element on the grounds that for Luke the question is only whether or not there will be a parousia; thus J. Ernst, *Das Evangelium nach Lukas* (RNT; Regensburg, 1977) 569.

18. K.H. Rengstorf, "sēmeion," *TDNT* 7:232.

19. Thus I.H. Marshall, *The Gospel of Luke* (NICNT 3; Grand Rapids, 1978) 761.

20. See note 26.

21. P. Volz, *Die Eschatologie der jüdischen Gemeinde im neutesta-mentlichen Zeit, nach den Quellen der rabbinischen, apokalyptischen und apokryphen Literatur* (2nd ed.; Tübingen, 1934; Hildesheim, 1966) 148–52.

22. Consequently I cannot accept G.B. Caird's view in his *The Gospel of St. Luke* (Pelican New Testament Commentary; London, 1963) 230: "Matthew has removed the inconsistency by making the question fit the answer, Luke by making the answer fit the question."

23. J. Wellhausen, *Das Evangelium Lucae* (Berlin, 1904) 117.

24. Including vv. 25–27 where a purely literary use is supposedly made of the lively details of the Old Testament judgment theophanies: A. Feuillet, "Le discours de Jésus sur la ruine du Temple d'après Marc XIII et Luc XXI, 5–36," *RB* 55 (1948) 481–502; 56 (1949) 61–92; F. Spadafora, *Gesù e la fine de Gerusalemme* (Rovigo, 1950); A. Salas, *Discurso escatológico prelucano. Estudio de Lc 21, 20–36* (Biblioteca de *La Ciudad de Dios,* I/16; El Escorial, 1967); idem, "Los signos cósmicos de Lc 21, 25–28 a la luz del concepto bíblico 'día de Yahvé,'" *La Ciudad de Dios* 180 (1967) 43–85; idem, "'Vuestra liberación està cerca.' Dimension liberacionista del acto redentor," *ibid.* 189 (1976) 3–22; O. da Spinetoli, *Luca. Il van-gelo dei poveri* (Assisi, 1982) 636–56.

25. Thus F. Godet, *Commentaire sur l'évangile de Saint Luc* (2nd ed.; Paris–Neuchâtel, 1872) II, 338; M.-J. Lagrange, *Evangile selon Saint Luc* (EtB; Paris, 1921) 532–33; H. Lattanzi, "Eschatologici sermonis Domini logica interpretatio (Mt 24, 1–16; Mc 13, 1–37; Lc 21, 5–36)," *Divinitas* 11 (1967) 71–92.

26. Thus, for example, W. Marxsen, *Der Evangelist Markus. Studien zur Redaktionsgeschichte des Evangeliums* (FRLANT 67, NF 49; 2nd ed.; Göttingen, 1959) 130; ET: *Mark the Evangelist,* trans. J. Boyce *et al.* (Nashville, 1969); W. Grundmann, *Das Evangelium nach Lukas* (ThHK 3; 6th ed.; Berlin, 1971) 379; E. Grässer, *Das Problem der Parusie-verzögerung in den synoptischen Evangelien und in der Apostelgeschichte* (BZNW 22; Berlin, 1957) 155–56.

27. See A. Loisy, *Les évangiles synoptiques* (Geffonds, 1907–8) II, 399.

28. Zmijewski, *Eschatologiereden* (note 7) 104, 121–22, 265; Geiger, *Endzeitreden* (note 7) 170, 229; Keck, *Abschiedsrede* (note 7) 29–30, 108–15, 189, 263–65, 322; Lambrecht, "Reading . . ." (note 9) 603; C.H. Giblin, *The Destruction of Jerusalem according to Luke's Gospel: A Historical-Typological Moral* (AnBib 107; Rome, 1985) 78–86.—Dupont is more cautious and has had second thoughts, at least about v. 29a; *Discours* (note 10) 72–73; *Distruzione* (note 10) 64, note 83, and 67, note 88; *Le tre apocalissi* (note 10), 110, 136, 141.

29. See note 31.

30. H.J. Cadbury, *The Style and Literary Method of Luke* (HTS 6; Cambridge, 1920 = New York, 1969), 106–07.

31. The explanation is therefore not that Luke would be using the singular *parabolē* even for several parables, as E. Schweizer thinks: *Das Evangelium nach Lukas* (NTD 3; 18th ed.; Göttingen, 1982) 82; ET: *The Good News according to Luke* (Philadelphia, 1987).

32. A. Plummer, *The Gospel according to St. Luke* (ICC; 5th ed.; Edinburgh, 1922) 478, is evasive: "A new introduction to mark a solemn utterance"; I do not understand why the words that follow should be considered more solemn than others.

33. Thus K.H. Rengstorf, *Il vangelo secondo Luca* (Brescia, 1980) 394; Marshall, *Luke* (note 19) 765.

34. Among others, Conzelmann, *The Theology of Luke* (note 4) 127.

35. J.M. Creed, *The Gospel according to St. Luke* (London, 1930) 255: "warnings . . . / . . . definitely prophetic passage."

36. The first group would suggest that here too the real beginning is in v. 10 (Dupont, *Distruzione* [note 10] 64, note 83; idem, *Le tre apocalissi* [note 10] 110). But then the question arises: Why not in v. 8?

37. Giblin, *Destruction* (note 28) 79.

38. Strictly speaking, it is the beginnings of the various events, not their endings, that are in chronological order; in other words, it is not being said that each event must end before the next begins. See E.E. Ellis, *The Gospel of Luke* (NCeB; London, 1966) 241. All of them end with the parousia.

39. R. Neyrey, *L'évangile selon Saint Luc. Analyse rhétorique* (Paris, 1988) I, 193.

40. Dupont, *Le tre apocalissi* (note 10) 110, 136.

41. *Ibid.* 139–40.

42. As in Geiger, *Endzeitreden* (note 7) 222: "V. 28 ends the whole complex with words of consolation"; *ibid.* 229–33; Ernst, *Lukas* (note 17) 567–68: the parable of the fig tree is not meant as an answer to the problem of signs, but is an independent image of the judgment.

43. See E. Lövestam, *Spiritual Wakefulness in the New Testament* (LUÅ, NF I/55/3; Lund, 1963) 122–32; V. Ott, *Gebet und Heil. Die Bedeutung des Gebetsparänese in der lukanischen Theologie* (STANT 12; Munich, 1965) 73–75. There is no reason for making vv. 28–33 part of the parenesis (as does Plummer, *Luke* [note 32] 476: "Exhortation to Vigilance Based on the Parable of the Fig Tree [vv. 29–30]"; Lambrecht, "Redactio" [note 9] 283–87; Keck, *Abschiedsrede* [note 7] 283). The imperatives in vv. 28–31 do not exhort the listener to act in a certain way but to observe and draw conclusions.

44. This is not to deny that the "before" may indicate importance as well as chronological sequence; see G. Braumann, "Das Mittel der Zeit.

Erwägungen zur Theologie des Lukas-Evangeliums," *ZNW* 54 (1963) 117–45, at 140–42; F. Schutz, *Der Leidende Christus. Die angefochtene Gemeinde und das Christuskerygma der lukanischen Schriften* (BWANT 89 = V/9; Stuttgart, 1979) 14.

45. This view is shared by various ancient and modern authors: see e.g., Godet, *Saint Luc* (note 25) 331; Lagrange, *Saint Luc* (note 25) 524; Plummer, *Luke* (note 32) 478–79; Rengstorf, *Luca* (note 33) 396; N. Walter, "Tempelzerstörung und synoptische Apokalypse," *ZNW* 57 (1966) 38–49, at 48–49; G. Bouwman, *Das dritte Evangelium. Einübung in die formgeschichtliche Methode* (Patmos Paperback; Dusseldorf, 1968) 49; S. Zedda, *L'escatologia biblica* I. *Antico Testamento e Vangeli Sinottici* (Brescia, 1972) 358–59; Marshall, *Luke* (note 19) 765–66; J.A. Fitzmyer, *The Gospel According to Luke* (AB 28; Garden City, 1981–85) 2:1334–35; V. Schmithals, *Das Evangelium nach Lukas* (ZBK III/1; Zurich, 1980) 201; H. Baarlink, *Die Eschatologie der synoptischen Evangelien* (BWANT 120; Stuttgart, 1986) 161; idem, "Ein gnädiges Jahr des Herrn – und Tage der Vergeltung," *ZNW* 73 (1982) 204–20, at 216–17.

46. J. Knabenbauer, *Evangelium secundum Lucam* (CSS I/3; Paris, 1896) 555; Loisy, *Les évangiles synoptiques* (note 27) II, 410–11; Grundmann, *Lukas* (note 26) 380, 384; E. Haenchen, *Der Weg Jesu. Eine Erklärung des Markus-Evangeliums und der kanonischen Parallelen* (STö II/6; 2nd ed.; Berlin, 1968) 455; A. George, "La venuta del Figlio dell'uomo (Lc 21, 25–28, 34–36)," in *Prima domenica di Avvento* (La Parola dell'assemblea festiva 2; Brescia, 1969) 121–32; Geiger, *Endzeitreden* (note 7) 169–72, 177–79; Keck, *Abschiedsrede* (note 7) 117–21, 192–94, 237–38; Schweizer, *Lukas* (note 31), 207–08; G. Schneider, *Das Evangelium nach Lukas* (Gekum. Taschenbuchkomm. zum NT 3; Gütersloh—Wurzburg, 1977) II, 417–19; Dupont, *Discours* (note 10) 53–57, 75–77; idem, *Distruzione* (note 10) 64–65, 155, 197–98; idem, *Le tre apocalissi* (note 10) 111, 115–18, 138–39; C. Ghidelli, *Luca* (Nuovissima versione della Bibbia dai testi originali 35; Rome, 1977) 389; F. Neirynck, "La matière marcienne dans l'évangile de Luc," in idem (ed.), *L'évangile de Luc. Problèmes littéraires et théologiques. Mémorial L. Cerfaux* (BEThL 32; Gembloux, 1973) 157–201, at 177–79 (reprinted in Neirynck, *Evangelica* [BETL 60; Louvain, 1982] 37–82, at 57–59); L. Sabourin, *Il Vangelo di Luca* (Rome, 1989) 322; J. Kremer, *Lukasevangelium* (Die neue Echter Bibel, NT 3; Würzburg, 1988) 202.

47. Volz, *Eschatologie* (note 21) 147–63.

48. Marshall, *Luke* (note 19), 761: ". . . even large-scale disorders are not a sign of the End."

49. For example: A.J. Mattill, *Luke and the Last Things. A Perspective for the Understanding of Lukan Thought* (Dillsboro, 1979) 130–33; C.H.

Talbert, *Reading Luke. A Literary and Theological Commentary on the Third Gospel* (New York, 1986) 199–205; Radl, *Lukas-Evangelium* (note 1) 130. Giblin, *Destruction* (note 28) 80–81, 86, holds that vv. 10–11a are developed in vv. 20–24, v. 11b in vv. 25–27.

50. See Flavius Josephus, *The Jewish War* 6:288–89; Tacitus, *Histories* I, 2–3: "Four emperors fell by the sword [Nero, Galba, Otho, Vitellius]; there were three civil wars, more foreign wars, and often both at the same time. . . . Besides the manifold misfortunes that befell mankind, there were prodigies in the sky and on the earth, warnings given by thunderbolts, and prophecies of the future" (trans. C.H. Moore [London, 1925]).

51. Wellhausen, *Evangelium Lucae* (note 23) 117.

52. As do Loisy, *Les évangiles synoptiques* (note 27) II, 414–15; and Haenchen, *Der Weg Jesu* (note 46).

53. Even more complicated is the hypothesis of Lambrecht (note 9), according to which the events of vv. 10–11 are identical with those of vv. 25–26, but precede both the parousia and the destruction of Jerusalem.

54. J. Schmid, *L'Evangelo secondo Luca* (Brescia, 1961) 390.

55. Among those who in various ways deny this: F.W. Danker, *Jesus and the New Age According to St. Luke. A Commentary on the Third Gospel* (St. Louis, 1972), 210–16; Schmid, *Luca* (note 54) 387; Geiger, *Endzeitreden* (note 7) 250–53; Ernst, *Lukas* (note 17) 554; Zmijewski, *Eschatologiereden* (note 7) 257–72.

56. See G. Nebe, *Prophetische Züge im Bilde Jesu bei Lukas* (BWANT VII/7 = 127; Stuttgart, 1989) 190–98.

57. Various authors, approaching the matter from a variety of viewpoints, are in agreement on this point: see H. Flender, *Heil und Geschichte in der Theologie des Lukas* (BEvT 41; Munich, 1968) 103–04; Maddox, *Purpose* (note 13) 120–21; Zmijewski, *Eschatologiereden* (note 7) 179–81, 203–04, 208, 240–41, 255; Lambrecht, "Redactio" (note 9) 285; idem, "Reading" (note 9) 602–06; H.-J. Michel, "Heilsgegenwart und Zukunft bei Lukas," in P. Fiedler and D. Zeller (eds.), *Gegenwart und kommendes Reich. Schülergabe A. Vögtle zum 65. Geburtstag* (Stuttgart, 1975) 101–15, at 107; Schweizer, *Lukas* (note 31) 211, 215–16; Marshall, *Luke* (note 19) 764; Ernst, *Lukas* (note 17) 555; Fitzmyer, *Luke* (note 45) 1329, 1337; A. Casalegno, *Gesu e il tempio. Studio redazionale su Luca-Atti* (Brescia, 1984) 120–23.

58. Conzelmann, *Theology* (note 4) 130.

59. Casalegno, *Gesu e il tempio* (note 57) 122; see E. Franklin, *Christ the Lord. A Study in the Purpose and Theology of Luke-Acts* (London, 1975) 13: "There is a hint of the future restoration, and this again suggests that even its fall is not to be divorced from Luke's eschatological beliefs."

60. Loisy, *Les évangiles synoptiques* (note 27) II, 435; Maddox, *Purpose* (note 13) 121–22.

61. Thus Conzelmann, *Theology* (note 4) 130; Grässer, *Das Problem* (note 26) 166; Geiger, *Endzeitreden* (note 7) 222; Dupont, *Discours* (note 10) 56–57; idem, *Distruzione* (note 10) 66–67, 196–202; idem, *Le tre apocalissi* (note 10) 136; G. Schneider, *Parusiegleichnisse im Lukas-Evangelium* (SBS 74; Stuttgart, 1975) 55–61; Ernst, *Lukas* (note 17) 552, 556, 568; Fitzmyer, *Luke* (note 45) 1349.—According to Keck, *Abschiedsrede* (note 7) 283–87, the sign is the judgment of the nations (vv. 25–26).

62. Vv. 10–11 are too distant to be meant by *tauta;* even if one regards vv. 10–11 as an anticipation of vv. 25–26 (see Section 5.1), *tauta* is more obviously to be connected directly with vv. 25–26.

63. Note that this hypothesis cannot be dismissed out of hand by saying that the sign then becomes that of the false prophets (Dupont, *Le tre apocalissi* [note 10] 116). In fact, the false prophets said the end was at hand as soon as they heard the first rumors of "wars and insurrections."

64. In effect, this is Conzelmann's thesis, *Theology* (note 4) 130, even though elsewhere he finds himself forced to admit that Luke does acknowledge signs, but after "a long period": "The Kingdom is announced for a long time—and then it comes like lightning" (129).

65. See E. Delebecque, *Evangile de Luc. Texte et traduction* (Coll. d'Etudes anciennes "Les belles lettres"; Paris, 1976) 132.

66. For this linking of persecution and liberation see G. Braumann, "Die lukanische Interpretation der Zerstörung Jerusalems," *NT* 6 (1963) 120–27; idem, "Das Mittel der Zeit" (note 44) 140–45.

67. Fusco, "Lc 21, 32" (note 14).

68. Plummer, *Luke* (note 32) 485; Caird, *Luke* (note 22) 233–34; Ghidelli, *Luca* (note 46) 395; A.L. Moore, *The Parousia in the New Testament* (NT.S 13; London, 1959) 132–35; Keck, *Abschiedsrede* (note 7) 288–90. See above, note 25.

69. With Wellhausen, *Ev. Lucae* (note 23) 118–19; see idem, *Das Evangelium Marci* (2nd ed.; Berlin, 1909) 107.

70. Keck, *Abschiedsrede* (note 7) 288–90.

71. Schneider, *Lukas* (note 46) 430–31; idem, *Parusiegleichnisse* (note 61) 59–60; earlier, but less clearly, Grässer, *Das Problem* (note 26) 166.

72. Conzelmann, *Theology* (note 4) 131.

73. Caird, *Luke* (note 22) 233–34, and D. Wenham, *The Rediscovery of Jesus' Eschatological Discourse* (Gospel Perspectives 4; Sheffield, 1984) 333–34, wrongly maintain that in v. 36 (and therefore, because of the parallelism, in v. 32 as well) *panta* does not include the parousia, since this cannot be escaped. In the context, "to escape all these things" does not mean to avoid the events, or to act as if they were not happening and

or did not involve oneself, but rather to face up to them in such a way as not to compromise one's salvation.

74. I do not share the view which admits a Lukan inconsistency regarding the parousia and then explains it by introducing theological and pastoral reasons of various kinds; thus S.G. Wilson, *The Gentiles and the Gentile Mission in Luke-Acts* (SNTSMS 28; Cambridge, 1973), 59–87 (= idem, "Lucan Eschatology, *NTS* 16 [1969–70] 330–47); J. Ernst, *Herr der Geschichte. Perspektiven der lukanische Eschatologie* (SBS 88; Stuttgart, 1978) 42–45. See Fusco, "Lc 21, 32" (note 14) 404, note 37.

"'REMEMBER' . . . THEN THEY REMEMBERED" (RIGATO)

1. I am thinking, for example, of the collective volume *Die Frau im Urchristentum* (Quaestiones Disputatae 95; Herder, 1983), or the series, *Teologia al femminile* (Palermo, 1985–90), edited by Cettina Militello and now numbering five volumes. Further: Salvatore Spera (ed.), *Uomini e donne nella Chiesa* (Atti della VII Primavera di Santa Chiara, 1987; Rome, 1988); various authors, *La donna nella Chiesa e nel mondo* (Naples, 1988).

2. These verses have not been made the subject of any special exegetical study. The same lack of attention can be seen in some of the more recent commentaries on the third gospel; for example: L. Sabourin, *Il Vangelo di Luca* (Casale Monferrato, 1989; French original, 1985) 367, where a brief reference is made to Lk 9:22; O. da Spinetoli, *Luca* (2nd ed.; Assisi, 1986) 727: "The 'men' recall the prophecy of the passion and resurrection to support their credibility"; J.A. Fitzmyer, *The Gospel According to Luke X-XXIV* (New York, 1986), 1531–48: no reference to "Remember"; C. Ghidelli, *Luca* (5th ed.; Roma, 1989) 461: "Here we are reminded that Jesus had predicted not only his death but also his resurrection."

3. See also M.-L. Rigato, "Donne testimoni della Risurrezione," in *Uomini e donne nella Chiesa* (note 1) 37–53.

4. See Nestle-Aland, *Novum Testamentum Graece* (26th ed.; 1981), *in loco*.

5. The particle *hōs* occurs with great frequency in Luke's work (Lk fifty times + one var.; Acts sixty-four times + two var.) and is used with a temporal, comparative, or quantitative meaning, as an adverb of manner, and, finally, to introduce a citation in the few cases (seven times) in which it is followed by *graphein, lalein,* or *legein*.

Lk 24:32d may be numbered among the instances (six in the gospel) in which *hōs* is a modal adverb; it should therefore be translated not as "while (he was opening)" (as it usually is in modern translations), but as "how (he was opening)." The Vulgate translates only the first *hōs* in v. 32 and makes it a temporal adverb on which both verbs then depend: "Et dixerunt ad invicem: Nonne cor nostrum ardens erat in nobis *dum* loqueretur in via *et* aperiret nobis scripturas."

6. The use of the verb *egeirein—egeiresthai,* "to rise" (from sleep, from a prone position, and therefore also from the sleep of death), for the resurrection of Jesus as prophecy and as event is not unambiguous: two meanings—"raise (bring back to life)" and "rise"—are established. It is clear that the transitive use—to bring someone back to life, to be brought back to life by someone—is demonstrated only if the verb is followed by an object raised or a raising agent. The gospels and Acts use the middle verb *egeiresthai* both transitively and intransitively; there are no sure examples of the middle-passive form being used transitively. I think it advisable here to translate what is definitely an aorist passive infinitive by "to be brought back to life," evidently by God, in contrast to having been "rejected by the elders (*apodokimasthēnai apo . . .*) . . . and . . . killed."— Some codices have the variant, *anastēnai.*

7. The verb *anistanai,* "raise oneself (from a sitting position, from rest and therefore also from death), arise," is always used intransitively in the gospel of Luke. See, in contrast, note 6 on *egeirein—egeiresthai.*

8. See E. Rasco, *La teología de Lucas: Origen, Desarrollo, Orientaciones* (AnGr 201; Rome, 1976) 119–20; here, in connection with the word *exodos,* "departure," Rasco cites I.A. Bengel, *Gnomen Novi Testamenti in quo ex nativa verborum vi simplicitas profunditas concinnitas salubritas sensuum coelestium indicatur* (2nd ed.; Tübingen, 1759) 259: "'A wonderful and very important word which refers inclusively to the passion, cross, death, resurrection, and ascension. Its opposite is *eisodos,* entrance: Acts 13:24.' Such appears to be the meaning of the 'exodus' of Jesus as understood by Luke: a journey that takes him beyond the city."

9. The literary contacts between Lk 9:30–31, 24:26–27, and 24:44–45 tell us a great deal.

10. Lk 2:50; 5:4, 21; 8:49; 9:11; 11:37; 22:47; 24:6, 32, 44.

11. The verb *astraptein,* "to flash, gleam, be dazzling," appears only in Lk 24:4 and again in 17:24, where it is accompanied by the noun *astrapē,* "lightning": "For as the lightning flashes and lights up the sky from one side to the other, so will the Son of Man be in his day." The intensive form, *exastraptein,* occurs only once, in the description of the garments of Jesus at the transfiguration: "His clothes became dazzling white" (9:29).

12. It is difficult not to see a harsh contrast between, on the one hand, these "two men . . . [who] appeared in glory (*andres duo . . . hoi ophthentes en doxē*)," their glory being a reflection of the glory of Jesus (the

apostles "saw his glory and the two men who stood with him [*eidon tēn doxan autou kai tous duo andras tous sunestōtas autō*])," and, on the other, the "two . . . criminals" crucified with Jesus, "one on his right and one on his left" (Lk 23:32–33).

13. On the famous section of Luke known as "the journey" see the masterly pages of E. Rasco, *La teología de Lucas* (note 8) 117–25. I agree with him in prolonging this "journey" to the ascension in Acts 1:10, 11, on the basis of a careful analysis of the verb *poreuesthai,* "to journey." See also note 8, above.

14. Ghidelli, *Luca* (note 2) 461: "It is not permissible to appeal to Lk 18:31–33, since when Jesus uttered this third prediction he was already in Judea."

15. A careful examination of the grammar shows that by the women "who provided for them out of their substance" are meant only Joanna, wife of Chuza, Susanna, and the many others, and not the women mentioned in v. 2, among whom is Mary Magdalene.

16. Some codices have a variant reading in Mt 14:21: "children (or servants: *paidōn*) and women." Mark, Luke, and John say only that there were five thousand men, *andres* (Mk 6:44; 8:9: "four thousand"; Lk 9:14; Jn 6:10).

17. It is significant that these two little words are lacking in cod D and a few others.

18. Matthew's notation (14:21): "besides women (*chōris gunaikōn*)," enables us to draw an analogous conclusion: the women may have been present even when he lists the narrowest circle of disciples, namely, the twelve. In fact, throughout his gospel Matthew does not refer to women "following" Jesus. Only at the death of Jesus does this evangelist mention that "*Many women* were also there, looking on from a distance; they had *followed* Jesus from Galilee and had provided for him (lit.: serving him, *diakonousai autō:* as though in a permanent position of service, *diakonia*)."

19. In addition to the most widely attested reading, "apostles," there are several variants in Lk 22:14: "the twelve," "the twelve apostles," "his disciples." Recall the passage: Jesus has told Peter and John to look for a suitable place "where I may eat the Passover with my disciples (*meta tōn mathētōn mou*)"; when the hour comes, he sits down to table with the apostles (*hoi apostoloi*) (Lk 22:11, 14). There is a comparable usage in Lk 17:1, 5. The twelve were certainly apostles (6:13: *hous kai apostolous ōnomasen*), but the "apostles" were not limited to the twelve. Finally, in biblical Greek the words "angel," "apostle," and "deacon" exist only in the masculine form.

20. The omission of a reference to the "first" christophany, the one to

Mary Magdalene at some distance from the tomb (Jn 20:14–17; Mk 16; Mt 28:9, with the addition of "the other Mary" in 28:1), appears in Luke at the redactional stage. Even though the appearance of the risen Lord to Peter is not described as chronologically "first," any more than it is in 1 Cor 15:5, Luke is anxious to bring out the primatial role of Peter in the beginnings of the church. For the same reason he omits the "command" to the women, even though he mentions the end result of the "command," namely, that "they told all this to the eleven and to all the rest. . . . [They] told this to the apostles," but were not believed (Lk 24:9–11). In Luke's work the proclamation of the event of the resurrection of Jesus is initially the task of the "official witnesses," and first of all the primary witness, Peter.

21. Recall how the law regarded women as radically incompetent to give sworn testimony (see Lv 5:1 with Dt 19:15, 17). See also Rigato, "Donne testimoni della Risurrezione" (note 3) 49.

LUKE 24:47: JERUSALEM AND THE BEGINNING OF THE PREACHING TO THE PAGANS IN THE ACTS OF THE APOSTLES (BETORI)

1. See E. Rasco, *La teología de Lucas, Origen, Desarrollo, Orientaciones* (AnGr 201; Rome, 1976) 114–25.

2. *Ibid.* 122.

3. H. Conzelmann, *Die Mitte der Zeit. Studien zur Theologie des Lukas* (BHT 17; 5th ed.; Tübingen, 1964) 8, note 1; ET: *The Theology of Luke,* trans. G. Buswell from the 2nd German edition (New York, 1960). [The note in the revised German version has changed much of what we read in the ET, 15, note 1—Trans.]

4. *Ibid.* 133.

5. *Ibid.* 210–12.

6. *Ibid.* 209.

7. G. Schneider, *Das Evangelium nach Lukas* (OkTKNT 3; Gütersloh-Würzburg, 1977) II, 501.

8. J.A. Fitzmyer, *The Gospel According to Luke* (AB 28; Garden City, 1985) II, 1581. See also W. Grundmann, *Das Evangelium nach Lukas* (ThHKNT 3; 4th ed.; Berlin, 1966) 453; J. Ernst, *Das Evangelium nach Lukas* (RNT; Regensburg, 1977) 668.

9. See e.g. I.H. Marshall, *The Gospel of Luke. A Commentary on the Greek Text* (NIGTC; Exeter, 1978) 906; C.F. Evans, *Saint Luke* (TPINT-Comm; London-Philadelphia, 1990) 924.

10. Marshall, *Luke,* 906. See also K.H. Rengstorf, *Das Evangelium nach Lukas* (NTD 3; 14th ed.; Göttingen, 1969) 286.

11. R. Meynet, *L'Evangile selon Saint Luc. Analyse rhétorique* (Paris, 1988) II. 239.

12. See P. Schubert, "The Structure and Significance of Luke 24," in W. Eltester (ed.), *Neutestamentliche Studien für R. Bultmann* (BZNW 21; Berlin, 1954) 165–86.

13. See A. George, "Les récits d'apparitions aux Onze à partir de Luc 24, 36–53," in P. de Surgy, P. Grelot, *et al., La résurrection du Christ et l'exégèse moderne* (LD 50; Paris, 1969) 75–104, especially 81.

14. J.-M. Guillaume, *Luc interprète des anciennes traditions sur la résurrection de Jésus* (EtB; Paris, 1979) 216; see too 181–83, 237–38. See also L. Dussaut, "Le triptique des apparitions en Luc 24 (Analyse structurelle)," *RB* 94 (1987) 161–213, especially 188.

15. See G. Gaide, "Les apparitions du Christ ressuscité d'après S. Luc. Lc 24, 13–48," *AssSeign,* 2nd series, no. 24 (Paris, 1970) 38–56, especially 53–54.

16. Deserving of special mention: J. Dupont, "Le salut des Gentils et la signification théologique du Livre des Actes," *NTS* 6 (1959–60) 132–55 = idem, *Etudes sur les Actes des Apôtres* (LD 45; Paris, 1957) 393–419, especially 401–04; F. Hahn, *Das Verständnis der Mission im Neuen Testament* (WMANT 13; Neukirchen-Vluyn, 1963) 111–19; E. Samain, "La notion de ARCHE dans l'oeuvre lucanienne," in F. Neirynck (ed.), *L'Evangile de Luc. Problèmes littéraires et théologiques. Mémorial Lucien Cerfaux* (BETL 32; Gembloux, 1973) 299–328, especially 303–03 and 324–27; S.G. Wilson, *The Gentiles and the Gentile Mission in Luke-Acts* (SNTSMS 23; Cambridge, 1973) esp. 47–58; J. Dupont, "La portée christologique de l'évangélisation des nations d'après Luc 24, 47," in J. Gnilka (ed.), *Neues Testament und Kirche. Für Rudolf Schnackenburg* (Freiburg-Basel-Vienna, 1974) 125–43 = idem, *Nouvelles études sur les Actes des Apôtres* (LD 118; Paris, 1984) 37–57; P. Zingg, *Das Wachsen der Kirche. Beiträge zur Frage der lukanischen Redaktion und Theologie* (OBO 3; Freiburg, Schw.-Göttingen, 1974) 136–53; R.J. Dillon, *From Eye-Witnesses to Ministers of the Word. Tradition and Composition in Luke 24* (AnBib 82; Rome, 1978) 203–20; M. Dömer, *Das Heil Gottes. Studien zur Theologie des lukanischen Doppelwerkes* (BBB 51; Cologne-Bonn, 1978) 95–128; R.J. Dillon, "Easter Revelation and Mission Program in Luke 24:46–48," in D. Durken (ed.), *Sin, Salvation and the Spirit. Commemorating the Fiftieth Year of the Liturgical Press* (Collegeville, 1979) 240–70; M. Bachmann, *Jerusalem und der Tempel. Die geographisch-theologischen Elemente in der lukanischen Sicht des jüdischen Kultzentrums* (BWANT 109; Stuttgart-Berlin-Cologne-Mainz, 1980) 86–92; J. Dupont, "La mission de Paul d'après Actes 26, 16–23 et la mission des apôtres d'après Luc 24, 44–49 et Actes 1, 8," in M.D. Hooker and

S.G. Wilson (eds.), *Paul and Paulinism. Essays in Honour of C.K. Barrett* (London, 1982) 290–99 = idem, *Nouvelles études* 446–56; J. Kremer, "Weltweites Zeugnis für Christus in der Kraft des Geistes. Zur lukanischen Sicht der Mission," in K. Kertelge (ed.), *Mission im Neuen Testament* (Freiburg, 1982) 145–63, esp. 147–52; M. Benéitez, "Un capítulo de narrativa bíblica. Los 'encargos' de Hch 1, 1–12," *MiscCom* 43 (1985) 329–82, esp. 362–71.

17. See Dupont, "Le salut des Gentils," 401–04; idem, "La portée christologique," 37–48; idem, "La mission de Paul," 452.

18. Hahn, *Das Verständnis der Mission,* 114.

19. C. Burchard, *Der dreizehnte Zeuge. Traditions- und kompositionsgeschichtliche Untersuchung zur Lukas' Darstellung der Frühzeit des Paulus* (FRLANT 103; Göttingen, 1970) 132, n. 297; confirmed by, among others, Dömer, *Das Heil Gottes,* 105, n. 29, and Bachmann, *Jerusalem und der Tempel,* 87, n. 57.

20. See Samain, "La notion de ARCHE," 303.

21. See Wilson, *The Gentiles,* 95 and 239–40.

22. See Samain, "La notion de ARCHE," 324–27.

23. See e.g. Wilson, *The Gentiles,* 95.

24. See Samain, "La notion de ARCHE," 301.

25. See Dömer, *Das Heil Gottes,* 160–64; Zingg, *Das Wachsen der Kirche,* 256, likewise maintains that the audience in the first five chapters is exclusively Jewish. For others, however, e.g. J.T. Sanders, *The Jews in Luke-Acts* (London, 1987), 29, the change comes after the persecution of Stephen.

26. See e.g. E. Haenchen, "Judentum und Christentum in der Apostelgeschichte," *ZNW* 54 (1963) 155–87, esp. 160–61.

27. U. Wilckens, *Die Missionsreden der Apostelgeschichte. Form- und traditionsgeschichtliche Untersuchungen* (WMANT 5; 3rd ed.; Neukirchen-Vluyn, 1974) 98 (italics added). Same view in Dupont, "La portée christologique," 46, n. 34, although he does not exclude here an appeal to the "acknowledged privilege of Israel" (with reference to the *prōton* of Acts 3:26 and 13:46).

28. See Wilson, *The Gentiles,* 229.

29. See G. Lohfink, *Die Sammlung Israels. Eine Untersuchung zur lukanischen Ekklesiologie* (SANT 39; Munich, 1975) 49 and 51.

30. See J. Jervell, "Das gespaltene Israel und die Heidenvölker. Zur Motivierung der Heidenmission in der Apostelgeschichte," *ST* 19 (1965) 68–96, esp. 83–84.

31. See Dillon, *From Eye-Witnesses,* 214–15; "Easter Revelation," 251. In Dillon's view, the theme of the prophet as doomed to death is the key to Luke's reading of the death of Jesus as messiah and, consequently,

the key to his reading of the role of Jerusalem—the city that kills the prophets—in the progress of preaching, because the missionaries share in the fate of the prophets. It is in this light that he explains the masculine plural *arxamenoi,* which emphasizes the part played by missionaries in the mission (see "Easter Revelation," 267, note 74). The same theme is taken up in Sanders, *The Jews in Luke-Acts,* 25–26.

32. See Benéitez, "Un capítulo de narrativa bíblica," 364–65 and 368–70.

33. I shall not undertake an analysis of the entire pericope, Lk 24:44–49, the Lukan character of which is acknowledged by all. For an overview of the problems relating to tradition and redaction see Guillaume, *Luc interprete,* 163–201, and Dillon, *From Eye-Witnesses,* 157–70, 184–200, and 227–66. With regard to Luke 24:47 in particular: since Hahn's study, *Das Verständnis der Mission,* 111–14, there is general agreement on seeing this verse as parallel to Mark 13:10, Luke having shifted from the apocalyptic perspective to the more dynamic perspective of "promise-fulfillment." To recall this here is to confirm the central place which the expression has in Lukan theology.

34. See F. Blass, A. Debrunner, and R.W. Funk, *A Greek Grammar of the New Testament* (8th ed.; Chicago, 1975) 137 (3), 419 (3).

35. D Δ^2 it[aur, b, (d), f, ff2, q] vg Diatessaron[f] have a genitive absolute, *arxamenōn (humōn* being understood). A masculine accusative absolute *arxamenon* (or a neuter singular, nominative or accusative, referring to all that has gone before in v. 47) is attested by π^{75} A C³ K W Δ^* η 063 f^1 f^{13} 28 700 892 1009 1010 1079 1195 1216 1241 1242 1344 1365 1546 1646 2148 2174 *Byz Lect* l^{185m} syr[2, p, h, pal] Diatessaron. Not lacking, of course, is the masculine nominative singular *arxamenos,* in keeping with the classical use of the pleonastic participle, as can be seen in θ ψ 565 1071 $l^{36, 47, 60}$. Finally in it[a, c, e, l, r1] geo[1] both *arxamenon* and *arxamenos* are found.

36. See B.M. Metzger, *A Textual Commentary on the Greek New Testament* (2nd ed.; London-New York, 1975) 188. This is the generally accepted view of scholars. Note that according to Metzger the nominative singular form may be due to an erroneous assimilation to *eipen* in v. 46.

37. The replacement of *kai aphesin* by *eph'aphesin* is of secondary importance in my opinion; both forms can occur in Lukan usage. The preference for the first is justified by Metzger, *A Textual Commentary,* 188, by reason both of the quality of the witnesses ($\aleph^{75}$ $\aleph$ B syr[p] cop[sa, bo] Diatessaron[a, (t), v]) and of the probable tendency of copyists to avoid *eis* because the same preposition occurs a little further on in *eis panta ta ethnē.*

38. This reading enjoyed a certain repute at the beginning of the century; see e.g. B. Weiss, *Die Evangelien des Markus und Lukas* (MeyerK I,

2; 2nd ed.; Göttingen, 1901) 690; Th. Zahn, *Das Evangelium des Lukas* (KNT 3; Leipzig, 1913) 713; even earlier as a marginal reading in B.F. Westcott and F.J. Hort, *The New Testament in the Original Greek* (London, 1881). It has been suggested once again recently, especially by Bachmann, *Jerusalem und der Tempel,* 86–87, note 49; J.T. Sanders, *The Jews in Luke-Acts,* 230–31. Meynet, *Luc* I, 237, and II, 238, has also adopted it.

39. Contrary to what Bachmann, *Jerusalem und der Tempel,* 87, claims, it is not true that the joining of v. 47b with v. 48 "does not cause any problems." In any case it is not at all "a sound exegetical principle . . . to prefer, when possible, a form of a text which can be said to be free of grammatical problems." We still ought to follow the principle that in textual criticism the more difficult reading is to be preferred.

40. See Dupont, "La portée christologique," 39, note 7, which refers to other literature.

41. See e.g. J. Dupont, "La conclusion des Actes et son rapport à l'ensemble de l'ouvrage de Luc," in J. Kremer (ed.), *Les Actes des Apôtres. Traditions, rédaction, théologie* (BETL 48; Gembloux-Louvain, 1979) 359–404 = idem, *Nouvelles études,* 457–511, esp. 490–501; idem, "La mission de Paul," 454–56.

42. See Benéitez, "Un capítulo de narrativa bíblica," 366–69.

43. *Ibid.* 363.

44. Among others, see in particular Dupont, "Le salut des Gentiles," 401–04; J. Kremer, *Pfingstbericht und Pfingstgeschehen. Eine exegetische Untersuchung zu Apg 2, 1–13* (SBS 63/64; Stuttgart, 1973) 179–90; Wilson, *The Gentiles,* 47–48 and 90–96; Dupont, "La portée christologique," 48–51; Dömer, *Das Heil Gottes,* 99–117; Dupont, "La mission de Paul," 451–53. My observations do not mean therefore that I agree with the questionable theory of D.R. Schwartz, "The End of the gē (Acts 1:8): Beginning or End of the Christian Vision?" *JBL* 105 (1986) 669–76, who uses the distinction between Luke 24:47 and Acts 13:47, on the one hand, and Acts 1:8, on the other, as the basis for interpreting the word *gē* in Acts 1:8 as the land of Israel, thus limiting the reference of this text to the first part of the book and the first stage of preaching, and therefore limiting the mission of the twelve to the Jews.

45. See e.g. Dupont, "La conclusion des Actes," 495. I have no interest here in going into the problem of whether we should distinguish a starting point (Jerusalem) and three stages, as most commentators do, or only two settings (Palestine and beyond), as Burchard does in his *Der dreizehnte Zeuge,* 134, note 309.

46. Some examples here from Acts might be the three accounts of the call of Paul (Acts 9:1–19; 22:5–16; 26:9–18) and the appearance first of Peter and John and then of all the twelve before the sanhedrin (Acts

4:1–22; 5:17–42). On Luke's methods of writing history, with reference especially to Acts, see G. Betori, "Gli Atti come opera storiografica. Osservazioni di metodo," in G.L. Prato, J.A. Soggin, *et al., La storiografia nella Bibbia. Atti della XVIII Settimana Biblica* (Bologna, 1986) 103–22.

47. Luke 3:23 also belongs in this group, since the verb is only apparently used in an absolute construction; it refers in fact to an implicit activity of Jesus.

48. See Samain, "La notion de *ARCHE,*" 301, note 8.

49. See Burchard, *Der dreizehnte Zeuge,* 132, note 297; he is followed by E. Nellessen, *Zeugnis für Jesus und das Wort. Exegetische Untersuchungen zum lukanischen Zeugnisbegriff* (BBB 43; Cologne-Bonn, 1976) 114; see also Dömer, *Das Heil Gottes,* 104. For a different view see, among others, Kremer, "Weltweites Zeugnis," 149, note 16.

50. Conzelmann, *The Theology of Luke,* 133.

51. See, among others, E. Lohse, "Siōn," *TDNT* 7:327–38; J. Navone, *Themes of St. Luke* (Rome, 1970) 64–70; J.C. O'Neill, *The Theology of Acts in Its Historical Setting* (2nd ed.; London, 1970) 59–76; Zingg, *Das Wachsen der Kirche,* 136–53; B. Corsani, "Gerusalemme nell'opera lucana," in M. Borrmans, S. Cipriani, *et al., Gerusalemme. Atti della XXVI Settimana Biblica in onore di Carlo Maria Martini* (Brescia, 1982) 13–26; Sanders. *The Jews in Luke-Acts,* 24–36.

52. These two faces of the city, which are always connected with its salvific function, emerge also in the most recent attempts at interpreting the alternating use of the Hebrew and Hellenistic forms of its name (*Ierousalēm–Hierosoluma*) in Luke-Acts. See especially: I. de la Potterie, "Les deux noms de Jérusalem dans l'évangile de Luc," *RSR* 69 (1981) 57–70 = L. Delorme and J. Duplacy (eds.), *La parole de grâce. Etudes lucaniennes à la mémoire d'Augustin George* (Paris, 1981) 57–70; I. de la Potterie, "Les deux noms de Jérusalem dans les Actes des Apôtres," *Bib* 63 (1982) 153–87; G. Morales Gómez, "Jerusalén-Jerosólima en el vocabulario y la geografía de Lucas," *RCatalT* 7 (1982) 131–86; D.D. Sylva, "Ierousalem and Hierosoluma in Luke-Acts," *ZNW* 74 (1983) 207–21.

53. See above, note 17.

54. The text is not clear, and the *hous* of v. 17 may refer only to *ethnōn* and not to *laou* as well; in this case the text would be comparable to Acts 22:21. See G. Schneider, *Die Apostelgeschichte* (HTKNT V/1-2; Freiburg-Basel-Vienna, 1980, 1982) II, 374.

55. The recovery of the historical dimension of Luke's works is one characteristic of present-day Lukan studies, in reaction against, or complementing, the emphasis on Luke as "theologian" that was typical of the early exponents of Redaktionsgeschichte, beginning with Conzelmann himself. See G. Betori, "La storiografia degli Atti. La recerca nel nostro

secolo: rassegna e valutazioni," *RivB* 33 (1985) 107–23. The following may be added to the literature studied there: D.L. Bar and J.L. Wentling, "The Conventions of Classical Biography and the Genre of Luke-Acts," in C.H. Talbert (ed.), *Luke-Acts. New Perspectives from the Society of Biblical Literature Seminar* (New York, 1984), 47–62; D.L. Balch, "Acts as Hellenistic Historiography," in K.H. Richards (ed.), *SBL Seminar Papers 1985* (Atlanta, 1985), 429–32; D. Schmidt, "The Historiography of Acts: Deuteronomistic or Hellenistic?" in *ibid.* 417–27; R.I. Pervo, *Profit With Delight. The Literary Genre of the Acts of the Apostles* (Philadelphia, 1987).

56. For the problem and the bibliography on the subject I refer the reader to V. Fusco, "Effusione dello Spirito e raduno dell'Israele disperso. Gerusalemme nell'episodio di Pentecoste (Atti 2, 1–13)," in Borrmans, Cipriani, *et al., Gerusalemme,* 201–18.

57. Kremer, *Pfingstbericht und Pfingstgeschehen,* 158.

58. See Lohfink, *Die Sammlung Israels,* 49. I do not understand how Lohfink (51) can take the messianic prophecy about the preaching of conversion to the pagan nations (Lk 24:47) as referring to this reunion of scattered Israel, which supposedly begins on Pentecost and comes to its conclusion in Acts 5. R. Maddox, *The Purpose of Luke-Acts* (FRLANT 126; Göttingen, 1982) 36, rightly reproaches Lohfink for not taking into account the centrality of the problem of the law for the identity of the people of Israel when, on the basis precisely of Lk 24:47, he tries to extend the concept of "Israel" to the nations once Christ has risen (see Lohfink, 79 and 95). The passage I am discussing says nothing about the problem of the law; this surfaces only in Acts 10.

59. Fusco, "Effusione dello Spirito," 217.

60. See Jervell, "Das gespaltene Israel." For a survey of this problem I refer the reader to G. Betori, "Chiesa e Israele nel libro degli Atti," *RivB* 36 (1988) 81–97.

61. See Fusco, "Effusione dello Spirito," 212–13 and 216–17.

62. Kremer, *Pfingstbericht und Pfingstgeschehen,* 131. See E. Lohse, "Die Bedeutung des Pfingstberichtes im Rahmen des lukanischen Geschichtswerkes," *EvT* 13 (1953) 422–36, esp. 432–34; J. Dupont, "La première Pentecôte chrétienne (Actes 2, 1–11)," *AssSeign,* 1st series, no. 51 (Bruges, 1963) 39–52 = idem, *Etudes,* 481–502, especially 498–502; idem, "La nouvelle Pentecôte (Acts 2, 1–11)," *AssSeign,* 2nd series, no. 30 (Paris, 1970) 30–34 = idem, *Nouvelles études,* 193–98, esp. 196; Dömer, *Das Heil Gottes,* 155–57.

63. Dupont, "La première Pentecōte," 501. See also Wilson, *The Gentiles,* 123–25, who emphasizes the proleptic and not purely symbolic character of the event in relation to the mission to the Gentiles; and Zingg,

Das Wachsen der Kirche, 145, who speaks of a missionary activity "with a universalist perspective."

64. Note: there is no context here of relations with persons of the pagan world such as elsewhere justifies taking the word in a "neutral" sense and allows the possibility that it may also refer to Israel (see above).

65. Reading *šᵉrīdīm* for *baššᵉrīdīm,* as proposed in the apparatus of the *BHS.*

66. I am obviously not excluding the reference to Is 49:6, but this verse applies only to the first part of Lk 24:47, namely, to the preaching of the message to all the nations. For the beginning in Jerusalem it is Jl 3:5b (LXX) that seems to be the most fitting reference, since it combines localization in Jerusalem with the idea of evangelization. The two Old Testament texts combined are thus the prophecy to which the *houtōs gegraptai* of Lk 24:46 refers the reader. I am not denying, however, that the mention of Jerusalem may contain an implicit reference to other passages of the Old Testament, among which I may mention Is 2:2 = Mic 4:2; Is 41:26–27; Zech 8:20–23; Ps 102:22–23; these would evidently correct any "centripetal" vision of the role of the city.

67. See Bachmann, *Jerusalem und der Tempel,* 90–91 and note 66.

68. On the identification of *patriai* with the "nations" see, among others, E. Haenchen, *Die Apostelgeschichte* (MeyerK III; 6th ed.; Göttingen, 1968) 169; ET: *The Acts of the Apostles,* trans. B. Noble *et al.* (Oxford: B.H. Blackwell, 1971); H. Conzelmann, *Die Apostelgeschichte* (HNT 7; 2nd ed.; Tübingen, 1972) 41; Dupont, "La conclusion des Actes," 500; Schneider, *Apostelgeschichte* I, 329.

69. Jl 3:5 seems therefore to be understood as a classical text on the universality of salvation; this is also shown by Paul's use of it in Rom 10:13.

70. The words *tois peitharchousin* refer first of all to the twelve, who thereby render their witness credible; but it cannot be restricted to them, precisely because in Luke's view the gift of the prophetic Spirit is not the privilege of a few but the mark of every believer.

71. This role of Jerusalem in relation to the preaching of salvation to the pagans has been especially brought out by e.g. Ph. H. Menoud, "Le plan des Actes des Apôtres," *NTS* 1 (1954–55) 44–51, esp. 46–47; J. Cambier, "Le voyage de S. Paul à Jérusalem en Act. IX, 26ss. et le schéma missionaire théologique de S. Luc," *NTS* 8 (1961–62) 249–57, esp. 252–53 and 256–57; Wilson, *The Gentiles,* 239–40.

72. It is this context that provides grounds for Dillon's hypothesis: he interprets "beginning from Jerusalem" in Lk 24:47 in light of the role of Jerusalem as persecutor of Stephen and his associates, a role which is in

continuity with its rejection of Jesus and, before him, of the prophets; all this in the framework of Jerusalem's role in the theology of the prophets as men doomed to death (see above, note 31). The future preaching to the pagan world has its roots in the persecution experienced in Jerusalem, but the life of the church in Jerusalem is not one solely of persecution, although persecution is a fundamental and often neglected element in Luke's picture of the church in the first chapters of Acts. If the proclamation to the pagans "begins from Jerusalem," this is not only because the witnesses to the resurrection are persecuted there, but also and above all because the testimony of these witnesses is already oriented, in its manner and content, toward the pagan world.

73. This is evidently the perspective of those passages of Acts which speak of Jews taking precedence over the pagans (Acts 1:8; 3:26; 13:46; 18:6; 28:28).

74. If there is to be any question of "non-repetition," it will have to do with the "apostolic" nature rather than the Jewish character of the Jerusalem community.

75. See G. Betori, *Perseguitati a causa del Nome. Struttura dei racconti de persecuzione in Atti 1, 12—8, 4* (AnBib 97; Rome, 1981) 26–40; J. Dupont, *Teologia della chiesa negli Atti degli apostoli* (Bologna, 1984) 16–18.

THE USE AND MEANING OF (HOI) IOUDAIOI IN ACTS (BARBI)

1. See E. Grässer, "Acta-Forschung seit 1960," *TRu* 42 (1977) 51–57; F. Bovon, *Luc le théologien. Vingt-cinq ans de recherches (1950–1975)* (Neuchâtel-Paris, 1978) 342–61; E. Plümacher, "Acta-Forschung 1974–1982," *TRu* 48 (1983) 46–51.

2. See J.T. Sanders, *The Jews in Luke-Acts* (London, 1987) 37–47; Sanders reduces the various positions to two main ones, with variations within each.

3. See W. Gutbrod, "Israēl," *TDNT* 3:379–80.

4. See H. Conzelmann, *The Theology of Luke,* trans. G. Buswell (New York, 1960) 145.

5. See A. George, "Israel," *Etudes sur l'oeuvre de Luc* (SB; Paris, 1978) 87–125.

6. *Ibid.* 109.

7. *Ibid.* 113.

8. *Ibid.* 120.

9. *Ibid.* 121.

10. See R.F. Zehnle, *Peter's Pentecost Discourse. Tradition and Lukan Reinterpretation in Peter's Speeches of Acts 2 and 3* (Nashville-New York, 1971) 65.

11. See G. Lohfink, *Die Sammlung Israels. Eine Untersuchung zur lukanischen Ekklesiologie* (SANT 39; Munich, 1975) 57–58.

12. See H.J. Hauser, *Strukturen der Abschlusserzählung der Apostelgeschichte (Apg 28, 16–21)* (AnBib 86; Rome, 1979) 246.

13. *Ibid.* 99.

14. See L. Gaston, "Anti-Judaism and the Passion Narrative in Luke-Acts," in P. Richardson and D. Granskou (eds.), *Judaism in Early Christianity* 1. *Paul and the Gospels* (Waterloo, 1986) 137–39.

15. See D. Slingerland, "The Jews in the Pauline Portion of Acts," *JAAR* 54 (1986) 314–19.

16. See Sanders, *Jews,* 71–72.

17. See the notes in F. Blass, A. Debrunner, and R.W. Funk, *A Greek Grammar of the New Testament* (8th ed.; Chicago, 1975) no. 262.

18. See Slingerland, "The Jews in the Pauline Portion of Acts," 315–16.

19. Thus, with variation among them: George, "Israel," 113; Sanders, *Jews,* 258–59; G. Schneider, *Die Apostelgeschichte* II (HTKNT V/2; Freiburg-Basel-Vienna, 1982) 103, note 14; E. Haenchen, *Die Apostelgeschichte* (MeyerK III; 6th ed.; Göttingen, 1968) 325; ET: *The Acts of the Apostles,* trans. B. Noble *et al.* (Oxford: B.H. Blackwell, 1971).

20. On the meaning of *laos* in Acts see Lohfink, *Sammlung,* 47–62; Sanders, *Jews,* 48–50; and, for Luke and Acts together, Zehnle, *Peter's Pentecost Discourse,* 63–66.

21. See J.B. Tyson, "The Jewish Public in Luke-Acts," *NTS* 30 (1984) 580.

22. Thus Hauser, *Strukturen,* 131.

23. Thus, correctly, Schneider, *Die Apostelgeschichte* II, 142, note 145, who compares the text with 14:3 and 20:32. Sanders, *Jews,* 261–62, gives a strange interpretation: the expression is an exhortation to "remain good Jews."

24. See O. Bauernfeind, *Kommentar und Studien zur Apostelgeschichte* (ed. V. Metelmann) (WUNT 22; Tübingen, 1980) 177.

25. See R. Pesch, *Die Apostelgeschichte* II (EKKNT V/2; Zurich-Einsiedeln-Cologne and Neukirchen-Vluyn, 1986) 41.

26. This is the interpretation of J. Roloff, *Die Apostelgeschichte* (NTD 5; Göttingen, 1981) 209, and Haenchen, *Apostelgeschichte,* 355.

27. J.T. Sanders, "The Salvation of the Jews in Luke-Acts," in *Luke-*

Acts. New Perspectives from the Society of Biblical Literature Seminar (New York, 1984) 108, has a different interpretation of this text and sees no reference in it to a coming to faith.

28. Conzelmann, *Theology of Luke,* had already referred to this (145).

29. See Schneider, *Apostelgeschichte,* II, 224, note 23; Pesch, *Apostelgeschichte,* II, 122.

30. See Haenchen, *Apostelgeschichte,* 545; Schneider, *Apostelgeschichte,* II, 313; Roloff, *Apostelgeschichte,* 317.

31. I agree with Sanders, "Salvation," 111–12, who takes the statement in Acts 21:20 as a summing up of the conversions among the Jews of Jerusalem which have already been mentioned at 6:7, and not as a reference to further conversions in Jerusalem after the Stephen episode.

32. Thus Schneider, *Apostelgeschichte,* 365.

PERSECUTION IN THE ACTS OF THE APOSTLES (KILGALLEN)

1. One goal of this essay is to evidence the persistent presence of persecution in Acts. This presence is particularly part of the fabric of chapters 13 and 14, which are a clear, lengthy unit characterized by the inclusion (E. Haenchen, *The Acts of the Apostles* [Oxford, 1971] 437 prefers "*eis to ergon* echoes 13,2"):

13,2:   *Aphorisate moi . . . EIS TO ERGON ho proskeklēmai autous*

14,26:   *. . . eis Antiocheian . . . hothen . . . paradedomenoi tē chariti tou theou EIS TO ERGON ho eplērosan*

The *ERGON* which typifies these chapters is not persecution, but witnessing; all the more striking, then, is Luke's willingness to allow persecution to play such a major role in this section.

2. The assumption of this essay is a conviction that the entire Acts narrative is an expression of that witness first mandated in 1:8. A. Wikenhauser, *Die Apostelgeschichte* (RTN; Regensburg 1956) 27, notes that the risen Jesus gives his apostles "den Auftrag der Predigt des Evangeliums, die er bezeichnenderweise ein Zeugnisgeben für ihn d.h. für seine Auferstehung, nennt. Dies wird die eigentliche Augabe der Apostel sein." But at 9:15–16 Wikenhauser speaks again of Auftrag: ". . . Er (Paul) soll die Botshaft von seinem Namen und Werk tragen" (110). Since Jesus announces not only that Paul will "bring my name before kings" *et al.,* but also that

Paul will "suffer for my name," it is easy to think of suffering as a further expression of witness to Jesus. So, too, in the case of other aspects and stories of Acts: forms of witness, of course for Theophilus' sake.

3. In chapter 11, only v. 19 speaks of persecution, and that as regards people whose persecution occurred some time prior to chapter 11. Yet, the desire to show a connection of cause and effect, persecution causing witnessing elsewhere, justifies to Luke the reference to earlier persecution he places at 11:19.

4. The material of chapters 1–3 of Acts is divided into introductory matter (chapter 1) and the beginning of a witnessing (chapters 2 and 3) of which we have two types: the explanation of Pentecost by Peter in christological terms (chapter 2) and the christological explanation of a miracle which should lead to repentance as well as acceptance of the rejected Jesus and of his way of life (chapter 3). With these matters in place, Luke proceeds, by connection particularly with the witnessing of chapter 3, to a further witnessing in the midst of opposition and persecution.

5. Probably *hoi hieroi* are principally some of the few chief priests who are always at the temple and who at this moment are available, with ordinary priests, to make an arrest; these latter priests are those who "had to be at the temple only one week out of every twenty-four apart from the three pilgrim festivals"; cf. J. Jeremias, *Jerusalem in the Time of Jesus* (London 1969) 160.

6. Cf. Jeremias, *Jerusalem,* 160–63.

7. "Dopo questo inizio lusinghiero incomincia il conflitto degli apostoli e i rappresentanti dei sadducei che hanno nel tempio il simbolo e zona del loro potere": R. Fabris, *Atti degli Apostoli* (Brescia,[2] 1982) 23.

8. Cf. Jeremias, *Jerusalem,* 229–30; later, 230: "We see then that the Saducean party was made up of chief priests and elders, the priestly and lay nobility."

9. This teaching recalls Paul's argumentation, many years earlier than Acts, to Corinthian Christians: "If Christ is preached as raised from the dead, how is it that some of you say *hoti anastasis nekrōn ouk estin?*" (1 Cor 15:12). Paul, however, saw a causal relationship between the resurrection of Jesus and the resurrection of the faithful, which was not within the argument of the Sadducees.

10. Though it is impossible to identify perfectly and absolutely the membership of sanhedrin of Acts 4–5 with that of the sanhedrin of Luke 22, there seems little reason to doubt that Luke intended such an identity. Cf. W. Lüthi, *Les Actes des Apôtres* (Geneva, 1958) 50: ". . . en face des mêmes personnage, exactement à la meme place ou il y a quelque mois leur Seigneur avait été condamné à mort."

11. J. Sanders, *The Jews in Luke-Acts* (London 1987) 17, suggests that

gerousia should be translated as the entire senate and seems to indicate that *gerousia* is a synonym for *presbutērion tou laou.* According to Jeremias, *Jerusalem,* 179, *gerousia* would be a specification of the chief priests who "formed an independent body competent to deal with affairs of the temple and the priesthood. . . ." But one wonders if *gerousia,* so similar in basic meaning to *presbutērion,* might not be distinguished as that body of elders of the people, who were of patrician families and who opposed Christian witnesses for the same reasons they opposed Jesus.

12. Acts 21:20–21 notes charges against Paul by Christian Jews in Jerusalem; these charges center on denial of the Mosaic laws, particularly of circumcision. Granted the particular attention reserved for the theology of the temple in the Stephen episode—cf. J. Kilgallen, "The Function of Stephen's Speech (Acts 7, 2–53)," *Bib* 70 [1989] 173–93), the main charges against Stephen coincide with those against Paul—and leads one to see a broad non-Palestinian Christian front which was very liberal as regards obedience to certain Jewish laws and traditions throughout the Mediterranean basin.

13. Luke has a specific reason for introducing the figure of the Son of Man at this point in Acts. It has to do with the fact that Stephen is judged and executed by the same body, the sanhedrin, as had judged and executed Jesus. Just as Jesus had revealed himself to the sanhedrin, so to the same sanhedrin does he reveal himself. Just as he had revealed himself to the sanhedrin as their future judge, so he renews this revelation now as the sanhedrin judges the Christian witness. The Son of Man is the appropriate judgmental figure to end Christ's life; so it is the proper figure with which to end the preaching of the risen one, of the one at God's right hand, in Jerusalem.

14. It is difficult to find any reasonableness in Sanders' argument (*Jews,* 18, 248–50) that the subjects of the verbs/participles *dieprionto, ebruchon, kraxantes, suneschon hōrmēsan, ekbalontes, elithoboloun* (7:54–58) refer to more Jews than those present at the trial of Stephen.

15. The reader often reads the term *Ioudaioi/hoi Ioudaioi* in Acts. Sometimes it seems valid to distinguish between the noun without the article and the noun with the article, as a way to understand clearly the meaning of *hoi Ioudaioi;* yet overall this articular distinction is not truly satisfactory. Perhaps the reality about this word is affected by two polar points. First, there is the reality of 28 A.D. when the forceful opponents of Jesus were those who disagreed with him over his claims to divine mission and obedience to a law of God in ways distinct from that practiced by authorities of his time. While this opposition could always be described by more individual terms (e.g. Sadducees, scribes, Pharisees, elders, priests, etc.—but even these classes hide the distinction between those who op-

posed Jesus and those who did not, and those who opposed Jesus without force and those who opposed him with force), the reality established was that of the difference between Jesus and all espousals of Yahwistic tradition; the easiest term for the opponents, then, was *hoi Ioudaioi,* meant to symbolize those who rejected the Jesus in favor of the tradition of the fathers. Secondly, there is the reality of the period of 35–85 A.D., in which the opposition between Jesus and his contemporaries continued on the same grounds and for the same reasons, now however between Jesus' followers and Jesus' contemporaries and those who held dear the perennial tradition of the fathers. This opposition is rooted, therefore, in the continuance or non-continuance of Yahwism; *hoi Ioudaioi* best expresses the root of this opposition. It is presumptuous to go beyond the framework of the disagreement to claim that Luke intends by the term *hoi Ioudaioi* to include all Jews, even those who knew nothing about Jesus, in his time, or about Christianity, in later times. His intent was to report the consistent disagreement that began with Jesus and continued with his followers over the intentions of Yahweh; not all *hoi Ioudaioi* proved unreceptive to Christian belief nor did they all turn to persecution, as is obvious from Acts. For a good bibliography on aspects of this subject and a provocative assessment of the data, cf. Sanders, *Jews.*

16. Acts 9:23 (messiah), together with 9:20 (Son of God), sums up the core affirmation of Paul in Damascus after his conversion. Since Acts uses two series of texts to argue the fact and meaning of the resurrection (a combination of Ps 132:11, 2 Sam 7:12–13 and Ps 16:8–11—cf. Acts 2:29–32), which deal with resurrection and messiahship, and Ps 2:7, Is 55:3 LXX and Ps 16:10—cf. Acts 13:33–37—which deal with resurrection and Sonship), one can assume that Paul's preaching of Jesus as Son of God and as messiah is centered on Jesus' resurrection.

17. Sanders, *Jews,* 21, suggests that in the long run ". . . it is irrelevant which Herod is active in the narrative at the time. In this sense, there is only one Herod in Luke's account." Such a reading appears forced, for it does not respect the reader's ability to be alert to historical realities.

18. One cannot forget either that very early the Marcan witness (3:6) says that Herodians opposed Jews. Luke's Agrippa may be finally catching up to this Marcan source.

19. The *de* of 13:50 suggests that the Jewish antagonism against Paul and Barnabas was in part owed to the fact narrated in the previous verse (13:49): *diephereto de ho logos tou kyriou di' holēs tēs Chōras.*

20. The theme, "the gifts of forgiveness and justification are yours today if you believe in Jesus," calls for belief that Jesus is messiah, and thus alive; cf. J. Kilgallen, "Acts 13,38–39: Culmination of Paul's Speech in Pisidia," *Bib* 69 (1988) 480–506.

21. *zēlōsantes* describes *hoi Ioudaioi* of Thessalonika, who became enemies both for love of their own religion and for distress at the loss of some Jews to Christianity.

22. Paul, some thirty years before Acts was written, criticizes those Corinthian Christians who divisively claim, "We belong to Apollos." In this criticism Paul never speaks against Apollos himself. One suspects that these Christians misunderstood the significance of Jesus as messiah (which Apollos, as Acts indicates, so ably proved Jesus to be), that they lost sight of the place of the crucifixion in the identity of Jesus (and thus those "who belong to Paul" are the most perceptive of the Corinthian Christians). All gospels, written later, continue to stress the significance of the cross in a life otherwise attractive for its messianic power, wisdom and holiness.

23. With chapter 21, the reader is about in the year 57 A.D., more than twenty-five years beyond the life and death of Jesus.

24. It is curious that the immediate impetus to preach to the Gentiles comes not from the experience of Paul on the road to Damascus, nor from Ananias, the interpreter of this experience, but from a later experience—and that in the temple, no less—of which we know nothing except what is told us in 22:17–21; one must be careful to reconcile this temple mandate with the Spirit-ordained work, which included witness to Gentiles, and which one finds given to Paul, not in the temple, but in Antioch (13:1–3).

25. Cf. Jeremias, *Jerusalem,* 230: "Since the Pharisees were on Paul's side, the plotters could only have been the Sadducee group in the Sanhedrin. . . ." While one sees no evidence of Pharisaic opposition in Acts because Luke favors those who support belief in the resurrection from the dead, Pharisees (Paul, for one) necessarily opposed Jesus for changing laws of Moses and the traditions and for thereby being called messiah of Israel.

26. So is the translation of *The New American Bible.* W. Arndt and F. Gingrich seem to support this interpretation; cf. *A Greek-English Lexicon of the New Testament* (Chicago 1957) 674 s. *plēthos* 2,b,g, "people, populace, population," as does F. Zorell, *Lexicon Graecum Novi Testamenti* (Paris,² 1931) 1072–3 s. *plēthos* "populus, vulgus." But one wonders if the sense might not better be kept to the strict meaning of the word, "the entire number of the Jews," thereby avoiding an unnecessary identification of all Jews with those who have turned enemy to Christianity and are represented by the sanhedrin members. E. Haenchen, *Acts,* 676–77, comments, ". . . despite 25,2 not only the Jewish leaders (so *Beg.* IV 313), but 'the crowd' "; Haenchen's translation is: "the entire Jewish people," 677. I. H. Marshall, *The Acts of the Apostles* (Leicester, 1980) 389–90, indicates that "the Sanhedrin is regarded as having spoken on behalf of the

whole Jewish nation." J. Roloff, *Die Apostelgeschichte* (NTD; Göttingen, 1981) 346: "die gesamte jüdische Bevölkerung." G. Schneider, *Die Apostelgeschichte* (Freiburg, 1982) II, 364: "alle Juden in Jerusalem und auch hier"; 366: "die gesamte Judenschaft."

27. Marshall, *Acts,* 390 calls *hapan to plēthos tōs Ioudaiōn* "a natural piece of rhetorical exaggeration." Recall that Marshall translates this phrase as "the whole Jewish nation" (390).

28. Why is there no article in the phrase *hypo tōn Ioudaiōn?* In the light of all that has been said before, Paul cannot mean with this phrase "by *some* Jews." Cf. Roloff, *Apostelgeschichte,* 347 at v. 7: "von den Juden"; Haenchen, *Acts,* 682, defers to Blass–Debrunner–Funk, *A Greek Grammar of the New Testament* (Cambridge, 1961) n. 262, 1, "The article is missing almost throughout with *Ioudaioi* in Paul's defences against the Jews: Acts 26, 2. 3. 4. 7. 21; 25, 10 (as with the name of the opponent in Attic court speeches) . . .)." Since, in 26, 2. 7, there is a question of charges brought and of disbelief in the resurrection, it is difficult to understand that *hypo tōn Ioudaiōn* includes all Jews or Israel taken as a whole.

29. The following bibliography concerning the general topic of Luke's making Acts conform to the gospel is noted by Sanders, *Jews,* 17 and note 8: R. Morgenthaler, *Die lukanische Geschichtsschreibung als Zeugnis* (Zurich, 1949) I–II; M. Goulder, *Type and History in Acts* (London, 1964); C. Talbert, *Literary Patterns, Theological Themes and the Genre of Luke-Acts* (Missoula, 1974); G. Muhlack, *Die Parallelen von Lukas-Evangelium und Apostelgeschichte* (Frankfurt, 1979); W. Radl, *Paulus und Jesus im lukanischen Doppelwerk* (Frankfurt, 1975). Sanders, 363, further cites Morgenthaler, *Geschichtsschreibung,* and E. Preuschen, *Die Apostelgeschichte* (Tübingen, 1913) in regard to relationships between Stephen and Paul in Acts. Another useful monograph on this entire subject is that of R. O'Toole, *The Unity of Luke's Theology* (Wilmington, 1984); finally, of good use is Sanders' own book, *The Jews in Luke-Acts.*

LUKE ON THE CLOSING OF THE EASTER APPEARANCES (O'COLLINS)

1. On the ascension see G. Schneider, *Die Apostelgeschichte,* I. Teil (Freiburg, 1980) 209–11, and J.A. Fitzmyer, *The Gospel according to Luke* (Garden City, 1985) 1586–89.

2. On the twelve apostles as witnesses see Fitzmyer, *Luke,* 253–55, 294, 613–16; J. Plevnik, "The Eyewitnesses of the Risen Jesus in Luke 24," *CBQ* 49 (1987) 90–103, esp. 100–03.

3. In the light of 1 Cor 15:5–7, Schneider lists among the prior ele-

ments used in the making of the ascension story in Acts "the concept of the closed nature of the Risen One's appearances"—*Apostelgeschichte,* 210.

4. Here we follow the general lines of H. Conzelmann's thesis about the three periods that make up Luke's historical-perspective: the period of Israel (from creation up to John the Baptist), the period of Jesus (from the start of his ministry to his ascension) and the period of the church (from the ascension to the parousia); see Conzelmann, *Theology of St. Luke* (New York, 1960) 16–17. "The description of the threefold division of Lukan salvation-history presented by Conzelmann is correct. Some modifications of it are necessary, but by and large it is still valid" (Fitzmyer, *Luke* 18; see ibid. 18–22, 181–87). At the same time, we must insist that Jesus is in no way confined to the second period (from his baptism to his ascension). Through his Spirit he is, for example, the moving force behind the whole story of Acts that ends with Paul in Rome "teaching about the Lord Jesus Christ" (Acts 28:31).

5. Schneider, *Apostelgeschichte,* 210.

6. Schneider comments (*ibid.* 211): "The apostles are ear-witnesses of Jesus' last promise [Acts 1,8] and eye-witnesses of his earthly activity right up to the ascension. It is precisely in the story of the ascension that they are portrayed as those who guarantee the continuity between Jesus and the time of the Church."

7. The twelve apostles are "witnesses not only because of their association with the earthly Jesus and not yet even through their post-Easter contact with the Risen One. To exercise their function as witnesses they need the power of the Spirit" (*ibid.* 224).

8. See V.P. Furnish, *II Corinthians* (Garden City, 1984) 528–31, 547–51.

9. This expression (featuring the Lord Jesus) is a variation on what we find in the LXX: "The Lord appeared to X and said" (e.g. Gen 12:7; 17:1; 26:2, 24; 35:9–10). This LXX usage does not justify interpreting the post-resurrection appearances (referred to in 1 Cor 9:1; 15:5–8 and narratives in the gospels) in terms of nonvisual bearing the word of revelation. However, the cases just discussed (Acts 9:10–19; 18:9–10; 22:17–21; 23:11) are different, and are clarified by the LXX and the Hebrew OT, where in many texts "vision" seems to refer principally or exclusively to a verbal message (e.g. Gen 15:1; Num 24:3–4; Is 1:1; 2:1; 13:1; Am 1:1; Ob 1:1; Mic 1:1; Neh 1:1; Hab 1:1; 2:2–3). On this OT usage see: A. Jepsen, *HZH* in G.J. Botterweck–H. Ringgren, *TWAT* 2 (1977) 822–35, especially 825–27; B. Kedar-Kopfstein, *Biblische Semantik. Eine Einführung* (Stuttgart, 1981) 154–55; B. Kedar-Kopfstein "Synästhesien im biblischen Alt-hebräisch in Übersetzung und Auslegung," *Zeitschrift für Alt-*

hebräistik, 1 (1988) 47–60, especially 50–53; H. Wildberger, *Jesaja 1–12*, BKAT X/1 (1972) 5; *Jesaja 28–39;* idem, BKAT X/3 (1982) 1590–91; H.W. Wolff, *Dodekapropheton, 3: Obadja und Jona*, BKAT XIV/3 (1977) 25–26.

10. The (varying) experiences of Paul's companions are meant to testify to the objective nature of Paul's encounter. He was not the victim of a merely subjective experience (see Schneider, *Apostelgeschichte*, 27–28).

11. E. Haenchen, *The Acts of the Apostles* (Oxford, 1971) 292, n. 4.

12. See Schneider, *Apostelgeschichte*, 496 and 503. To his bibliography (496) one should add: J. Dupont, "Les pèlerins d'Emmaüs (Luc xxiv, 13–35)," *Miscellanea Biblica, E. Ubach* (ed. R.M. Diaz) (Barcelona, 1953) 349–74; id, "The Meal at Emmaus," *The Eucharist in the New Testament*, ed. J. Delorme (Baltimore, 1965) 105–21; X. Léon-Dufour, *Resurrection and the Message of Easter* (New York, 1974) 160–63.

HISTORY AS A HERMENEUTICAL INTERPRETATION OF THE DIFFERENCES BETWEEN ACTS 3:1–10 AND 4:8–12 (MARCONI)

1. G. Betori, "La storiografia degli Atti. La ricerca del nostro secolo: rassegna e valutazioni," *RivB* 33 (1985) 107–33: over fifty titles ranging from the 1920s to the early 1900s. See idem, "Gli Atti come opera storiografica," in *Storiografia nella Bibbia. Atti della XXVIII Settimana Biblica, Rome, 10–14 settembre 1984* (Brescia, 1985) 103–22; E. Plümacher, "Acta-Forschung 1974–1982," *TRu* 49 (1984) 140–47.

2. H.-I. Marrou, *The Meaning of History*, trans. R.J. Olsen (Baltimore, 1966); P. Veyne, *Comment ont écrit l'histoire. Essai d'épistémologie* (Paris, 1971); J. Starobinski, "La letteratura: il testo e l'interprete," in J. Le Goff and P. Nora (eds.), *Fare storia. Temi e metodi della nuova storiografia* (Milan, 1981), 193–208; G. Duby, *Dialogues* (Paris, 1980); the great French medievalist speaks of "the inevitable subjectiveness of historical discourse" (45) and of the object of history as a "constructed object" (11). Historiography is preceded by epistemology—K.R. Popper, *The Logic of Scientific Discovery* (New York, 1959)—and followed by hermeneutics—H.-G. Gadamer, *Truth and Method*, trans. G. Barden and J. Cumming (New York, 1975); P. Ricoeur, *Temps et récit* I–III (Paris, 1983–85) has rejected the presumption of the historical objectivity of the data in favor of the primacy of interpretation; ET: *Time and Narrative* I–II, trans. K. McLaughlin and D. Pellauer (Chicago, 1984–85). The excellent synthesis of G. Betori, "Modelli interpretativi e pluralità di metodi in esegesi," *Bib* 63 (1982) 305–28, has provided me with ideas on theory.

3. P. Benoit, "Remarques sur les sommaires des Actes," in his *Exégèse et théologie* II (Paris, 1961) 181–92; H. Zimmermann, *Neutestamentliche Methodenlehre. Darstellung der historisch-kritischen Methode* (Stuttgart, 1967) 220–33.

4. P. Benoit, "L'ascension," in his *Exégèse et théologie* I (Paris, 1961) 363–411; H. Schlier, "L'ascensione di Cristo negli scritti di S. Luca," in his *Riflessioni sul Nuovo Testamento* (Brescia, 1969) 295–312; L. Panier, "Pour lire les Actes des Apôtres," *SemBib* 28 (1982) 7–16.

5. A. Casalegno, *Gesù e il tempio. Studio redazionale di Luca-Atti* (Brescia, 1984).

6. This is the thesis maintained, with variations, by many scholars. O. Bauernfeind, *Die Apostelgeschichte* (Leipzig, 1939) 59, sees a true and proper miracle story in the strict sense, as does G. Schneider, *Die Apostelgeschichte* I (Freiburg i. B., 1980) 413. R. Fabris, *Atti degli Apostoli* (Rome, 1977) 129, sees in the passage the classical pattern of miracle stories. According to J. Roloff, *Die Apostelgeschichte* (Göttingen, 1981) 103, the passage is a story of healing, but more schematic than those found in the synoptics. According to G. Theissen, *Urchristliche Wundergeschichten* (Gütersloh, 1974) 94–120, the account fits the typology of therapies; ET: *Miracle Stories of the Early Christian Tradition* (Edinburgh, 1983). D. Hamm, "Acts 3, 1–10: The Healing of the Temple Beggar as Lucan Theology," *Bib* 67 (1986) 305f., thinks of a "mimed story," symbolic of the eschatological restoration of Israel.

7. I think it useless to repeat what has already been set down by G. Betori, in his *Perseguitati a causa del Nome. Strutture dei racconti di persecuzione in Atti 1, 12—8, 4* (Rome, 1981) 42–44; to his list of verbal echoes I would add the one that connects 4:1–4 to the next section (4:3: *eis tēn aurion;* 4:5: *epi tēn aurion*).

8. In 3:1 some uncials (ψEP) prefix to *Petros de* the last three words of the preceding verse (2:47: *epi to auto*) in order better to justify the presence of initial *de*. The particle is justified, however, by the repeated mention of the temple and the day (2:46: *en tō hierō;* 3:2: *eis to hieron;* 2:47: *kath'hēmeran;* 3:2: *kath'hēmeran*).

9. Unlike the majority of exegetes, B. Reicke, *Glaube und Leben der Urgemeinde. Bemerkungen zu Apg 1–7* (Zurich, 1957), and some others do not regard 4:8–12 as a discourse.

10. C.H. Dodd, *The Apostolic Preaching and Its Developments* (4th ed.; London, 1970); M. Dibelius, *Studies in the Acts of the Apostles* (London, 1956); U. Wilckens, *Die Missionsreden der Apostelgeschichte. Form- und traditionsgeschichtliche Untersuchungen* (Neukirchen, 1961).

11. Wilckens, *Missionsreden,* 32–55.

12. J. Dupont, *Etudes sur les Actes des Apôtres* (Paris, 1967), 133–35.

13. Idem, "Les discours de Pierre," in F. Neirynck (ed.), *L'Evangile de Luc. Problèmes littéraires et théologiques. Mémorial L. Cerfaux* (Gembloux, 1973) 332–48.

14. For a very brief history of the interpretations of the discourses (Dibelius, Dodd, Wilckens, and Dupont), see J. Schmitt, "Les discours missionaires des Actes et l'histoire des traditions prépauliniennes," *RSR* 69 (1981) 166f. An excellent bibliography, which ends, however, with 1968, is to be found in the now unobtainable work of E. Rasco, *Actus Apostolorum, Introductio et exempla exegetica* II (Rome, 1968) 176–78. For a recent study of the composition of the discourse in light of the ancient rhetorical model see B. Standaert, "L'art de composer dans l'oeuvre de Luc," in *A cause de l'évangile. Mélanges J. Dupont* (Paris, 1985) 323–47, esp. 323–32. See R. Meynet, *Quelle est donc cette parole? Lecture "rhétorique" de l'évangile de Luc* I–II (Paris, 1979).

15. Wilckens thinks that v. 16 was part of the original story (*Missionreden,* 41f.), while others take it to be Lukan interpretation (E. Haenchen, *Die Apostelgeschichte* [7th ed.; Göttingen, 1977]) 205f; Schneider, *Apostelgeschichte,* 414).

16. The provenance of these three verses is much debated; one scholar even sees in them an allusion to Greek rhetoric (Haenchen, *Apostelgeschichte,* 209). For the structure see Schneider, *Apostelgeschichte,* 442.

17. After *hōs* D and p. add *hēmin te,* thus emphasizing the idea of the power belonging to the apostles.

18. V. 2: *hon;* v. 4: *eis auton;* v. 7: *auton, auton, autou;* v. 9: *auton;* v. 10: *auton, autō;* v. 11: *autou;* v. 12: *auton;* v. 16: *touton, hon, autō.*

19. H. Seesemann, "Pateō," *TDNT* 5:944–45.

20. The verb is used three times in vv. 8–9.

21. For a bibliographical survey (for 1961–1985) of the "intention of the reader" idea, see the first part of Umberto Eco's paper at the international congress on "Il discorso della critica letteraria" (Rome, March 1986): U. Eco, "Lo strano caso della intentio lectoris," *Alfabeta* 84 (1986) 15–16.

22. G. Bertram, "Stereos," *TDNT* 7:613, speaks of "a quasi-medical process."

23. In the Old Testament the word is found only as a variant of Is 1:6 in L and C.

24. In the New Testament *holos* is usually combined with a noun and adds the element of wholeness or integrity. See H. Seesemann, "Holos," *TDNT* 5:124–25.

25. See W. Foerster, "Holoklēria," *TDNT* 3:767; Schneider, *Apostelgeschichte,* 445, note 7.

26. See Mt 27:24: "Pilate . . . washed his hands before the crowd (*apenanti tou ochlou*)."

27. Lk 1:2; Acts 4:20; 10:41ff; 13:31. See J. Dupont, "L'Apôtre comme intermédiaire du salut dans les Actes des Apôtres," *RTP* 112 (1980) 342–58.

28. Classical exegesis raised the problem of who it is that has faith: the cripple (Foakes-Jackson, Bruce, Dupont, Haenchen, Conzelmann, Munck), the apostles (Preuschen), or both (Zahn, Wikenhauser, Stählin).

29. Before this indication of time, and at the very beginning of the sentence D and it[d] have the words *en de tais hēmerais tautais* ("in those days"), perhaps in order to connect the new passage with the preceding chapter (Haenchen). The CEI translation has "one day," which does not ensure continuity with what has gone before but provides an interesting parallel to Acts 4:5a; but it is not attested in the manuscripts.

30. After *aurion* D has *hēmeran.*

31. The article is repeated despite the fact that the nouns have the same gender and number; the repetition emphasizes the diversity in the membership of the sanhedrin; see F. Blass, A. Debrunner, and R.W. Funk, *A Greek Grammar of the New Testament* (8th ed.; Chicago, 1975), no. 328.

32. *Egeneto* + accusative + infinitive is a construction used chiefly by Luke: Acts 4:5; 9:3, 32, 37, 43; etc.; Lk 3:21f; 6:1, 6, 12; 16:22.

33. S 614 al read *eis Ierousalēm* as in 3:1 (*eis to hieron*) instead of the more accepted *en Ierousalēm.*

34. Given the problem of the historicity of the miracles in Acts (see Schneider, *Apostelgeschichte,* 423–30) and thanks to this parallelism, it seems to me legitimate to suppose a redactional intervention that fits the two passages into a pre-determined pattern.

35. *Anabainō eis to hieron:* Jn 7:14; Josephus, *The Antiquities of the Jews* 12:164, 362; 13:304; idem, *The Jewish War* 2:340, 405; 6:285. See J. Schneider, "Anabainō," *TDNT* 1:519–22.

36. For some exegetes (Roloff, *Apostelgeschichte,* 103), the presence of John is a later addition, since the purpose of the story is to give prominence to the important personalities of the early church.

37. R.E. Brown, K.P. Donfried, and J. Reumann (eds.), *Peter in the New Testament* (New York, 1973), 41.

38. G. Stählin, *Die Apostelgeschichte* (Göttingen, 1936) 135. For a full discussion of the sanhedrin see E. Schürer, *A History of the Jewish People in the Time of Jesus Christ,* trans. S. Taylor and P. Christie, Div. II, Vol. 1 (New York, n.d.), 163–95.

39. E. Lohse, *Umwelt des Neuen Testaments* (3rd ed.; Göttingen, 1977) 135; ET: *The New Testament Environment* (Nashville, 1975).

40. See P. Winter, *On the Trial of Jesus* (2d ed.; New York, 1974) 20–30; J. Blinzler, *The Trial of Jesus,* trans. Isabel and Florence McHugh (Westminster, 1959).

41. Some explain the presence of the name of Jerusalem by appealing to the Talmudic tradition which says that from 30 A.D. onward the place of meeting for the sanhedrin was changed from the temple portico to the portico of the traders; the appeal proves nothing because both venues were within the city (Stahlin, *Apostelgeschichte,* 135).

42. For the use of the imperfect of "ask" see Blass-Debrunner-Funk, no. 328.

43. A. Oepke, "Anēr," *TDNT* 1:360–63 lists five categories of meaning for this word in classical Greek, all of them applicable to the New Testament uses of it.

44. In the New Testament *anēr* is used much less than *anthrōpos;* the ratio is 2 to 5. Only in Acts and 1 Corinthians is the trend reversed:

	Mt	Mk	Lk	Jn	Acts	Rom	1 Cor	Rev	Total
anthrōpos	112	56	95	60	46	27	31	25	548
anēr	8	4	27	8	100	9	32	1	216

45. J. Jeremias, "Anthrōpos," *TDNT* 1:364.

46. G. Stählin, "Asthenēs," *TDNT* 1:491–92.

47. Acts 4:9–22 contains the heaviest concentration of the word *anthrōpos* (seven times) in the entire book of Acts, while *aner* does not occur at all in this passage; it occurs only once in chapter 4 (v. 4).

48. Translations generally have "in whose name?" but in strict logic *poios* can replace *tis* when the question does not refer to persons. See Blass-Debrunner-Funk, no. 298, 2.

49. L. Panier, "Pour lire les Actes des Apōtres," *SemBib* 29 (1983) 14.

50. *Euergesia,* 1 Tm 6:2; *euergeteō,* Acts 10:38; *euergetēs,* Lk 22:25.

51. For *peripatein* see Mk 2:9 par.; 5:42; Jn 5:8–12; etc. The verb *sōzein,* too, is used not only in the synoptic stories of healings by Jesus, in which it occurs sixteen times (*diasōzō* two times; *therapeuō* thirty-five times; *iaomai* fifteen times), but also, with the same meaning, in stories of healings worked within the first Christian community (Acts 14:9; Jas 5:15; etc.).

52. The verb *sōzō* in Acts 4:9, 12, is connected with *anthrōpos,* the universal scope of which has already been discussed.

53. According to R. Fabris, *Atti degli Apostoli,* 130, the cripple "is part of the choreography of the temple." His point is that the temple needs cripples in order to supply others with the opportunity for almsgiving;

consequently, to heal the man is to remove him from the temple and therefore to incur the wrath of the "guardians."

54. E. Schweizer, "Concerning the Speeches in Acts," in *Studies in Luke-Acts* (Nashville-New York, 1966) 214, maintains that the important change which affects the language of the discourse takes place not in the speaker but in the audience.

55. J. Schmitt, *Jésus ressuscité dans la prédication apostolique* (Paris, 1949); C.F.D. Moule, *The Speeches in the Acts of the Apostles* (London, 1945).

56. Haenchen, *Apostelgeschichte*, 73, 148–49, 172; Wilckens, *Missionsreden*, 99, 187–92; E. Käsemann, *Exegetische Versuche und Besinnungen* I (Göttingen, 1960) 214–23; H. Conzelmann, *Die Apostelgeschichte* (2nd ed.; Tübingen, 1972) 41. Between these two extreme positions—one seeing the discourses as giving the preaching of Peter, the other seeing in them only a reflection of the way the gospel was preached in Luke's time—can be placed Dodd and Dibelius, who find in the discourses the essential elements of the earliest apostolic preaching.

IDOLATRY COMPELLED TO SEARCH FOR ITS GODS (PRATO)

1. See the principal critical editions: C. Tischendorf, *Novum Testamentum Graece*. Editio octava critica maior (Leipzig, 1872) II, 61–62; E. Nestle and K. Aland (and others), *Novum Testamentum Graece* (26th ed.; Stuttgart, 1979) 340; A. Merk, *Novum Testamentum Graece et Latine* (8th ed.; Rome, 1957), 419.

2. J. Ziegler, *Duodecim Prophetae* (Septuaginta . . . XIII; 2nd ed.; Göttingen, 1967) 194–95; A. Rahlfs, *Septuaginta* (8th ed. [and later reprints]; Stuttgart, 1935) II, 507.

3. *En tē ēremō*, which some LXX witnesses place before and others place after *tessarakonta etē*, is little documented in the Greek text of Amos (Ziegler even omits it, unlike Rahlfs), but it is present in Acts 7:42 in almost all the manuscripts (for some omissions see the apparatus in Tischendorf).

4. According to some exegetes the purpose of the omission is to do away with the suspicion that the second of the two gods mentioned in Acts 7:43 is a god of Israel: T. Holtz, *Untersuchungen über die alttestamentlichen Zitate bei Lukas* (TU 104; Berlin, 1968) 14–19 at 14; E. Haenchen, "Schriftzitate und Textüberlieferung in der Apostelgeschichte," *ZTK* 51 (1954) 153–67 at 161; idem, *Die Apostelgeschichte* (KEKNT 3; 5th ed.; Göttingen, 1965) 235, note 3.

5. Tischendorf, *Novum Testamentum,* 61 app. cr.: "*Rephhan* or *Raiphan* could easily be substituted, as can be seen in most LXX witnesses."

6. According to Holtz (*Untersuchungen,* 17–18), these words might be regarded as influenced by Exodus 32:8 LXX, where God refers to the building of the golden calf (see Acts 7:40–41); he rejects the hypothesis, however, since he thinks that the citation of Amos in Acts 7:42–43 is due to Luke, who has reworked an earlier speech.

7. See the list of editions and translations in Nestle-Aland 443. In his commentary (*Atti degli Apostoli* [Casale Monferrato, 1978] 76–77), C. Ghidelli has a Greek text in which the whole of Am 5:25–26 is a question, but in his Italian translation the question extends only to v. 25.

8. See G. Stählin, *Gli Atti degli Apostoli* (Nuovo Testamento 5; Brescia, 1973) 201–02.

9. Many commentators call attention to the two different conceptions of punishment in Acts 7:42–43; see especially Stählin, *Atti* 201; Haenchen, *Apostelgeschichte,* 235; H. Conzelmann, *Die Apostelgeschichte* (HNT 7; 2nd ed.; Tübingen, 1972) 55; A. Weiser, *Die Apostelgeschichte, 1–12* (OTKNT 5/1; Gütersloh, 1981) 186–87 (the two punishments are located within the deuteronomistic conception of retribution); J. Kilgallen, *The Stephen Speech. A Literary and Redactional Study of Acts 7, 2–53* (AnBib 67; Rome, 1976) 86; Holtz, *Untersuchungen,* 7–8.

10. For so radical a reply see even back in the last century: J.A. Alexander, *The Acts of the Apostles* (2nd ed.; London, 1862) I, 291.

11. See W. Denton, *A Commentary on the Acts of the Apostles* (London, 1874) I, 237–38; C.J. Callan, *The Acts of the Apostles. With a Practical Critical Commentary for Priests and Students* (New York-London, 1919), 56; E. Jacquier, *Les Actes des Apôtres* (EtB; Paris, 1926) 227–28.

12. For this as a hypothesis see Jacquier, *Actes,* but see especially R. Fabris, *Atti degli Apostoli* (Commentari Biblici; Rome, 1977) 225, note 10.

13. Haenchen, *Apostelgeschichte,* 234.

14. M. Simon, "Saint Stephen and the Jerusalem Temple," *JEH* 2 (1951) 127–42; the same author has summarized the arguments in his *St. Stephen and the Hellenists in the Primitive Church* (London-New York-Toronto, 1956), 39–58 (= Chapter III); Conzelmann, *Apostelgeschichte,* 55–56. Against the view that the theme of the temple is the central core of Stephen's speech see A.F.J. Klein, "Stephen's Speech—Acts VII. 2–53," *NTS* 4 (1957–58) 25–31.

15. Haenchen, *Apostelgeschichte,* 238–41, especially 240.

16. Holtz, *Untersuchungen,* 87–80 (in like manner Holtz thinks that the citation of Isaiah 66:1–2 in Acts 7:49–50 is due to Luke).

17. Weiser, *Apostelgeschichte,* 180–82.

18. R. Pesch, *Die Apostelgeschichte* 1. *Apg 1–12* (EKKNT; Zurich and Neukirchen-Vluyn, 1986), 255. An intermediate stage between the LXX text of Amos 5:25–27 and its introduction into Acts 7:42b–43 is also supposed by G.D. Kilpatrick, but only because of the variant *proskunein autois* (LXX: *heautois*) and without facing the question of the different theological perspectives: see "Some Quotations in Acts," in J. Kremer (ed.), *Les Actes des Apôtres. Tradition, rédaction, théologie* (BETL 48; Gembloux-Leuven/Louvain, 1979) 83. For a defense of the redactional unity of the entire speech (still in the supposition of a group of Judeo-Christian Hellenists who are opposed to the temple), see P. Dschulnigg, "Die Rede des Stephanus im Rahmen des Berichts über sein Martyrium (Apg 6, 8–8, 3)," *Judaica* 44 (1988) 195–213.

19. Here, in chronological order, are some commentaries that dwell, more or less extensively, on the problem of the identification of the two divinities: Alexander, *Acts*, 292; Denton, *Commentary*, 239–40; Callan, *Acts*, 57; Jacquier, *Actes*, 228; A. Wikenhauser, *Die Apostelgeschichte* (RNT 5; Regensburg, 1956) 89–90; L. Cerfaux, *Les Actes des Apôtres* (La Sainte Bible . . . de Jérusalem; 2nd. ed.; Paris, 1958), 81; Fabris, *Atti*, 225, note 10; G. Schneider, *Die Apostelgeschichte* I. *Einleitung. Kommentar zu Kap 1, 1–8, 40* (HTKNT 5/1; Freiburg-Basel-Vienna, 1980), 445–46; G. Schille, *Die Apostelgeschichte* (THNT 5; Berlin, 1983), 183–84.

20. See e.g. W. Bauer, W.F. Arndt, and F.W. Gingrich, *A Greek-English Lexicon of the New Testament and Other Early Christian Literature* (2nd ed.; Chicago, 1979) 526 (*Moloch*) and 737 (*Rompha*); B. Reicke and L. Rost (eds.), *Biblisch-historisches Handwörterbuch* (Göttingen, 1966) 3:1622 (the entry on *Rompha* is by K.-H. Bernhardt) and 1589 (the entry on *Remphan* refers the reader to *Rompha*).

21. Text according to Sperber's edition, *The Bible in Aramaic* III. *The Latter Prophets* (Leiden, 1962) 424; his text is substantially identical with that of P. de Lagarde, *Prophetae chaldaice* (Leipzig, 1872), except for the graphic variant *ṭ'wwtkwn* found in the latter. In B. Walton's polyglot (*Biblia Sacra Polyglotta* [London, 1657], III, 48), the first part of the verse has the variant *skwt ptkwmrkwn* (the second word is also attested in ms. p. 116 of the Montefiore Library in London, in the form *ptkmrykwn;* see the critical apparatus in Sperber), while the second has a text that inverts the order of two words: *wyt kywn ṣlmykwn kwkb ṭ'wtkwn dy 'bdtwn lkwn* (attested not only in the various printed editions but also in the Codex Reuchlinianus, where, however, as I noted above, the writing of one of the two inverted terms is *ṭ'wwtkwn;* de Lagarde does not follow the Codex Reuchlinianus in this instance).

22. Text according to the Leiden edition: *The Old Testament in Syriac according to the Peshiṭta Version* (Leiden, 1980), III/4, 31. Walton's

polyglot has only the variant *wk'wn for wkwn.* One British Library ms. (= Add. Ms 18.715) has *mlkwm* alone in place of *mšknh dmlkwm* (see the critical apparatus in the Leiden edition).

23. The situation is not improved by the variant *ṣlmykwn kwkb ṭ'wtkwn/ṭ'wwtkwn,* "your images [*sic!* not the singular *imaginem vestram,* which appears in Walton's Latin translation], star of your idol" (see note 21).

24. For Aquila, Symmachus, and Theodotion see F. Field, *Origenis Hexaplorum quae supersunt* (Oxford, 1875) II, 975. For TJ see above, note 21; the word *ptkwmryn* of the variant is understood here as a synecdoche, since by itself it means the veil on statues of idols (thus in M. Jastrow, *A Dictionary of the Targumim . . .* [New York, 1950] 1254).

25. See S. Schechter, *Documents of Jewish Sectaries* (Cambridge, 1910 = 1970) I, 112 (Hebrew text) and 72 (translation and critical notes); Ch. Rabin, *The Zadokite Documents. I. The Admonitions; II, The Laws* (Oxford, 1954) 28–31 (Hebrew text and translation); E. Lohse, *Die Texte aus Qumran* (Munich, 1964) 80–81 (vocalized Hebrew text and translation).

26. For a different view, Schechter (*Documents,* 72, note 12) and Rabin (*Zadokite,* 28 and 29), who want to introduce into CD parts missing from the passage in Amos. For a fuller discussion see P. von der Osten Sacken, "Die Bücher der Tora als Hütte der Gemeinde. Amos 5, 26f. in der Damaskusschrift," *ZAW* 91 (1979) 423–35, especially 427–30; J. de Waard, *A Comparative Study of the Old Testament Text in the Dead Sea Scrolls and in the New Testament* (Studies in the Texts of the Desert of Judah 4; Leiden, 1966) 41–47 (given the nature of the citation, de Waard's procedure does not seem justified, that is, to purge and shorten the text of Amos on the basis of CD and the suggestions of other authors: *ibid.* 42).

27. Since these verses are so important for the literary problems and the problems of religious history that are connected with them, it is inevitable that they should be the subject of extensive discussion. For an initial guide to the research and its development it will be enough to consult W.R. Harper, *A Critical and Exegetical Commentary on Amos and Hosea* (ICC; Edinburgh, 1905) 129–41; E. Sellin, *Das Zwölfprophetenbuch,* Erste Hälfte: *Hosea-Micha* (KAT [ed. E. Sellin], 12; 2nd–3rd ed.; Leipzig, 1929) 233–40; M. Bič, *Das Buch Amos* (Berlin, 1969) 122–26; H.W. Wolff, *Dodekapropheton 2. Joel und Amos* (BK 13/2; Neukirchen-Vluyn, 1969) 303–13; W. Rudolph, *Joel-Amos-Obadja-Jona* (KAT [ed. W. Rudolph, K. Elliger, F. Hesse, O. Kaiser], 13/2; Gütersloh, 1971) 205–13. In particular, see the summary presentation in K. Koch, and others, *Amos.*

Untersucht mit den Methoden einer strukturalen Formgeschichte (AOAT 30/1–3; Neukirchen-Vluyn, 1976) I, 178–83; II, 40–41.

28. A full description of the literary genre is to be found especially in Wolff, *Dodekapropheton,* 304–06; somewhat less clearly in Rudolph, *Amos,* 207–13. See also J.A. Soggin, *Il profeta Amos* (Studi Biblici 61; Brescia, 1982) 130–36.

29. See, e.g., I. Willi-Plein, *Vorformen der Schriftexegese innerhalb des Alten Testaments. Untersuchungen zum literarischen Werden der auf Hosea, Amos und Micha zurückgehenden Bücher im hebräischen Prophetenbuch* (BZAW 123; Berlin-New York, 1971) 39.

30. O. Loretz, "Die babylonischen Gottesnamen Sakkut und Kajamānu in Amos 5, 26. Ein Beitrag zur jüdischen Astrologie," *ZAW* 101 (1989) 286–89.

31. Wolff, *Dodekapropheton,* 309–11; Soggin, *Il profeta Amos,* 132–33, 135–36; J.L. Mays, *Amos. A Commentary* (OTL; London, 1969) 110–13; C. Van Leeuwen, *Amos* (De prediking van het oude testament; Nijkerk, 1985) 228–33; A.S. van der Woude, "Bemerkungen zu einigen umstrittenen Stellen im Zwölfprophetenbuch," in A. Caquot and M. Delcor (eds.), *Mélanges bibliques et orientaux en l'honneur de M. Henri Cazelles* (AOAT 212; Kevelaer and Neukirchen-Vluyn, 1981) 483–99, at 485–90; R. E. Clements, "*kôkâb,*" *TWAT* 4:79–91, at 90. Against a deuteronomist redactional framework: F.I. Andersen and D.N. Freedman, *Amos* (AB 24A; Garden City, N.Y., 1989) 536–37.

32. See J. McKay, *Religion in Judah under the Assyrians* (SBT 2/26; London, 1973) 31, 67–73; P.D. Miller, Jr., P.D. Hanson, and S.D. McBride (eds.), *Ancient Israelite Religion. Essays in Honor of Frank Moore Cross* (Philadelphia, 1987). Prescinding from the Assyrian invasion and conquest of Samaria, Andersen and Freedman suggest (534, 544), without any real foundation, that Jeroboam II wanted to enter into an alliance with the Assyrians, even before the latter became a greater threat under Tiglath-Pileser III; this unlikely historical reconstruction is based on an equally hypothetical exegesis of the expression "your king" in Amos 5:26, which, according to them, refers not to a divinity but to a king who is responsible for Israel's idolatry (533).

33. See S. Amsler, *Amos* (CAT 11a; Neuchâtel, 1965) 214–16; Sellin, *Zwölfprophetenbuch,* 233–39; Wolff, *Dodekapropheton,* 303, 309–11; van Leeuwen, *Amos,* 228; van der Woude, "Bemerkungen," 485; V. Maag, *Text, Wortschatz und Begriffswelt des Buches Amos* (Leiden, 1951) 34–36.

34. The answer is at times made to depend on the value assigned to *w-* in *ûn⁽e⁾śā'tem:* copulative or conjunctive-adversative? See S. Erlandsson,

"Amos 5:25–27, ett crux interpretum," *SEÅ* 33 (1968) 76–82; Sellin, *Zwölfprophetenbuch,* 233–39 (both verses are in the past tense); Wolff, *Dodekapropheton,* 303, 309–11 (same); Maag, *Text,* 34–36 (same); E. Hammershaimb, *The Book of Amos. A Commentary* (Oxford, 1970) 91–94 (summary of the various possibilities).

35. For v. 26 as referring to the present: Harper, *Amos,* 137–38; as referring to the future: Mays, *Amos,* 110–13; Rudolph, *Amos,* 206–08; A. Weiser, *Die Propheten Hosea, Joel, Amos, Obadja, Jona, Micha* (ATD 24; seventh ed.; Göttingen, 1979) 172, 174 (Weiser also proposes the passive voice: *niśśā'tem,* "you will be taken together to . . .": a correction that has even found a place in the critical apparatus of the *BHS*); N. Snaith, *The Book of Amos.* Part Two (London, 1958 = 1946), 106. Willi-Plein, *Vorformen,* 39, also supposes that the verse already refers to v. 27, but she keeps it in the past tense. Andersen-Freedman (*Amos,* 529, 532–33, 543–44) translate v. 26 in the future and v. 27 in the present, claiming even that the two verses form a period in which the principal statement (v. 27) refers to an exile, while the secondary statement (v. 26) is not only subordinate to it but expresses an action which is later in time.

36. The wilderness as an ideal is one of the cornerstones of the religious vision of J. Wellhausen; it is therefore not surprising to find it in his commentary on Amos (*Die kleinen Propheten* [3rd ed.; Berlin, 1898] 83–84. The same idea is found in other works published at the beginning of the twentieth century: W. Nowack, *Die kleinen Propheten* (HAT 3/4; 2nd ed.; Göttingen, 1903), 153–54 (Amos 5:25 shows no knowledge of P); K. Marti, *Das Dodekapropheton* (Kurzer Handkommentar zum Alten Testament 13; Tübingen, 1904) 196–97 (Amos 5:25 shows as yet no knowledge of P). According to Sellin (*Zwölfprophetenbuch,* 236), there is disagreement with E; according to Mays (*Amos,* 111), with the Pentateuch. On the impossibility of Amos speaking of sacrifices in the wilderness: R. Dobbie, "Amos 5, 25," *TGUOS* 17 (1957–58) 62–64.

37. In addition to Wellhausen, Nowack, and Marti (see note 36), see E. Würthwein, "Amos 5, 21–27," *TLZ* 72 (1947) 143–52; R.S. Cripps, *A Critical and Exegetical Commentary on the Book of Amos* (London, 1929) 199–201.

38. The hypothesis of such a connection had already been proposed at the beginning of the century, but with the supposition that v. 25 is a question calling for a positive answer and that it refers to legitimate sacrifices in the wilderness: see A. van Hoonacker, *Les douze petits prophètes traduits et commentés* (EtB; Paris, 1908) 250–52. The question was taken up again more recently in terms of the history of religions: it is not possible to believe that Israel did not have sacrifices while it was in the wilderness, since sacrifice was an essential element in the semitic religions; the

need is rather to determine how these were judged at a later time; thus considered, Amos does not utter a sweeping condemnation of every kind of sacrificial cult. See Würthwein, *Amos,* 143–52; Rudolph, *Amos,* 212; Soggin, *Il profeta Amos,* 135–36.

39. Amos 5:26 "along with 4:3 is the most discussed verse in the entire book" (Sellin, *Zwölfprophetenbuch,* 236); see also H.M. Barstad, *The Religious Polemics of Amos. Studies in the Preaching of Am 2, 7B–8; 4, 1–13; 5, 1–27; 6, 4–7; 8, 14* (VTS 34; Leiden, 1984) 118–26 ("Am 5, 26—the most difficult passage in the whole Book of Amos," 119). As for v. 25, it presents no difficulties for Barstad, but Snaith (*Amos,* 100) finds it to be "one of the most difficult verses in the Old Testament"!

40. Among the commentaries already cited in the preceding notes see those of Wellhausen, Nowack, Marti, Snaith, Cripps, van Hoonacker, Mays (uncertain), Hammershaimb, Rudolph, Wolff, Soggin, van Leeuwen, and add: T.H. Robinson, *Die zwölf kleinen Propheten. Hosea bis Micha* (HAT 1/14; 3rd ed.; Tubingen, 1964) 92–93; L. Alonso Schökel and J.M. Valverde, *Doce profetas menores* (Madrid, 1966) 75; L. Alonso Schökel and J.L. Sicre Diaz, *I Profeti* (Commenti biblici; Rome, 1984) 1112–13. Sikkut/Sakkut and Chiun/Kaiwan have therefore also found a place as divine names in the biblical dictionaries: see K.-H. Bernhardt in B. Reicke and L. Rost (eds.), *Biblisch-historisches Handwörterbuch,* 1:300; 3:1792–93; K. Koch, "*kûn,*" *TWAT* 4:95–111. at 98; more cautious is J. Gray in *IDB* 4:165.

41. The expression *sikkut malkᵉkem* leads some commentators to think of a divinity named Adar-Melek, Adrammelek, Anammelek, who would be a further equivalent of Saturn; see Nowack, Cripps, Rudolph. It is odd to assimilate the two possible names for Saturn in 5:26 to those of El and Baal of the Cananite religion, as proposed by Andersen and Freedman (*Amos,* 534), who in addition revive an ancient connection made between Saturn and the Jewish sabbath among the Kenites, but make no reference to more recent discussions of the subject (*ibid.* 533).

42. *AHW* 1:420; *CAD* 8:36–38. The steadiness of Saturn is connected with his function as guarantor of order and justice.

43. See K. Schrader, *Die Keilschriften und das Alte Testament* (2nd ed.; Giessen, 1883) 442–43; in the first edition of this work (1872), there was nothing about this identification, whereas it is repeated in the third edition (1902), which is the one mostly cited in commentaries on Amos. In this work Schrader made more accessible to exegetes what he had already proposed in an essay entitled "Assyrisch-Biblisches" (included in *Theologische Studien und Kritiken,* 1874, 324–33) and what was said in a summary in *JA* 18 (1871) 443–49, at 445, about M. Oppert's correct reading of an Akkadian text (the planet which others identified with Ju-

piter should in fact be understood as Saturn). On the other hand, the equating of Ninib/Ninurta with *ᵈSAG.KUD* was commonly accepted at that time: see, e.g., W. Muss-Arnoldt, *Assyrisch-englisch-deutsches Handwörterbuch* (Berlin, 1905) 2:693–95, especially 694.

44. H. Zimmern, *Beiträge zur Kenntnis der babylonischen Religion, Die Beschwörungstafeln Šurpu, Ritualtexten für den Wahrsager, Beschwörer und* Sänger (Leipzig, 1901) 12–13; among the texts published here the god *Sag-kud* is also attested in one of the "Ritualtafeln für den Sänger" (187, no. 70, line 10: *i-na pa-an* ⁱⁱ*Sag-kud;* see also line 8: ⁱⁱ*Sag-kud-da*).

45. E. Reiner, *Šurpu. A Collection of Sumerian and Akkadian Incantations* (*AfO* Beiheft 11; Graz, 1958) 18 (here the line with the names of the two gods corresponds to II, 180).

46. R. Borger, "Amos 5, 26, Apostelgeschichte 7, 43 und Šurpu II, 180," *ZAW* 100 (1988) 70–81, especially 74–77.

47. According to Borger, any future translator rendering this term as "Sakkut" should follow it with a question mark ("Amos 5, 26," 77). Loretz (*Die babylonischen Gottesnamen*) perhaps has this warning in mind when he introduces a new form of the divine name: "Sukkut," for which, however, he offers no justification.

48. See K. Tallqvist, *Akkadische Götterepitheta* (StudOr 7; Helsinki, 1938), 424, 440; F. Gössmann, *Planetarium Babylonicum oder die sumerisch-babylonischen Stern-Namen* (Šumerisches Lexikon IV/1; Rome, 1950) 20–21 (no. 69), 49–50 (no. 133), 57–58 (no. 141), 129 (no. 336). D.O. Edzard, "Ninurta," in W. Haussig (ed.), *Wörterbuch der Mythologie* (Stuttgart, 1965) 1:114–15, makes no reference at all to the astral character of the god Ninurta.

49. M. Cogan and H. Tadmor, *II Kings* (AB; New York, 1988) 211. The LXX at this point is satisfied to transcribe the name as *Sokchōthbainith* (and variants), the second part of which may contain the Akkadian epithet *Banītu* (the "creatress"), which was assigned to Ishtar (Cogan and Tadmor say the same but without reference to the Greek).

50. The failure of this argument should lead to a different evaluation of the term *ṣelem* in Amos 5:26, which is sometimes taken as the name of a constellation with a human form or as the name of an astral divinity of the same kind as Saturn (*Ṣalmu*), supposedly attested in some inscriptions from Tema: see E.A. Speiser, "Note on Amos 5:26," *BASOR* 108 (1947) 5–6; among the commentaries, Cripps, *Amos,* 200; Hammershaimb, *Amos,* 95 (but he rejects this identification); van Leeuwen, *Amos,* 230–31 (where the mention of Assyrian divinities in Amos 5:26 is taken for granted!). The certainty with which Speiser sticks to his reading of Amos

5:26 is therefore not justified ("As the verse stands, however, its astral import is unmistakable and any attempt to purge it of that content would seem to create more problems than it can solve," 5).

51. Sellin, *Zwölfprophetenbuch,* 233, 238–39; so also Amsler, *Amos,* 214–16.

52. Bič, *Amos,* 123–26.

53. Maag, *Text,* 35–36 and also in his "Vokabular," nos. 424–25 (pp. 88–90) and 280–81 (pp. 81–82); but Maag regards the *melek* of Amos 5:26a as a divine name (see no. 340, p. 85).

54. Weiser, *Amos,* 172, 174; this emendation, too, has found a place in the critical apparatus of *BHS.* Weiser's solution has been accepted by Willi-Plein, *Vorformen,* 37–39, who thus eliminates any reference to the Babylonian *Sag/Sakkud,* but who still holds on to Kêwan, appealing to the cuneiform witness, that is, to what was subsequently challenged by Borger.

55. S. Gevirtz, "A New Look at an Old Crux: Amos 5, 26," *JBL* 87 (1968) 267–76; Gevirtz, like Maag before him (see note 53), regards *melek* as a divine designation.

56. H.H. Hirschberg, "Some Additional Arabic Etymologies in Old Testament Lexicography," *VT* 11 (1961) 373–85 at 375–77.

57. É. Lipiński, "*SKN* et *SGN* dans le sémitique occidental du Nord," *UF* 5 (1973) 191–207, especially 202–04.

58. Koch, *Amos* 2:41.

59. See Barstad (*Religious Polemics*), who explicitly acknowledges his indecision. On the other hand, see S. Schroer, *In Israel gab es Bilder. Nachrichten von dorstellender Kunst im Alten Testament* (OBO 74; Freiburg, Switz.-Göttingen, 1987) 267–72; in her effort to provide iconographic representations to illustrate what is said in the text, the author tends to see in Amos 5:26 images or banners of divinities, these being pictured, however, with their astral characteristics.

60. The dictionaries behave strangely when they come to *kywn.* According to W. Gesenius, *Hebräisches und aramäisches Handwörterbuch über das Alte Testament* (17th ed.; Leipzig, 1921) 343b, it was the Masoretes who made the word a common noun ("statue"), but the text "undoubtedly contains the Babylonian name of a planet, *kaimânu/ kaiwânu.*" In *HALAT* 2:450A, "stand" (*Gestell*) is given as the first meaning, but it is pointed out that the word is usually understood as a divine name, "Saturn," from the Akkadian *kayyamānu/kayyawānu; sikkût* is said (3:771b, 712a) to be first of all an Assyrian divine name, along with *kiyyûn* (and an epithet of the god Ninib-Ninurta), but room is also made for the reading *sukkat,* alongside the common noun *kiyyûn* or

kēn, "pedestal." With regard to the formation of the noun, there are no sound reasons for denying that *kywn* resembles *kiyyôr* ("vessel," "basin"), nor is there any need to have recourse to the root *kwn;* Borger ("Amos 5, 26," 78–79) is too rigid in arguing for the contrary, and he finds himself forced later on to end with a more nuanced statement: "The formation of nouns in Hebrew is far too thorny a subject when it comes to foreign words" (but it remains to be shown that we are dealing here with a "foreign word"!).

61. In the context of Amos 5:21–27 a translation using the past tense seems more probable. But this point is not directly related to my subject. For the translation of the last part of the verse as an independent noun sentence see also Schroer, *In Israel,* 210. By vocalizing *kwkb* in the construct state (*kôkab*), the Masoretes eliminated this possible reading.

62. Rudolph, *Amos,* 208, holds that the words cannot be from Amos, simply because he could not have reproached the Israelites for making for themselves gods originating with the Assyrians. Once the words are taken as common nouns this objection no longer holds.

63. It is difficult to maintain that the LXX presupposes a Hebrew text which already has this form, and therefore it is not possible to use the Greek in order to reconstruct an original which it would have as its model. For a different view see Ch.D. Isbell, "Another Look at Amos 5:26," *JBL* 97 (1978) 97–99. The Hebrew *ṣelem* is translated, then, as *tupos.* De Waard, *A Comparative Study,* 43–44, maintains that this translation signals an affinity between the text in the LXX and the text in CD VII, 14–15, especially since this is the only instance in which *tupos* is used to translate the Hebrew *ṣelem;* but de Waard does not take into account that *tupos* appears only four times in the Greek of the LXX; if we leave aside 3 Maccabees 3:20 and 4 Maccabees 6:19, only Exodus 25:40 is left for comparison (but there *tupos* corresponds to *tabnît*). On the other hand, when Theodotion translates *ṣelem* with *eidōlōn,* he does the same as the LXX in Numbers 33:52 and 2 Chronicles 23:17, while when Aquila and Symmachus use *eikonas* for the Hebrew word they imitate the LXX in 2 Kings 11:18 and Ezekiel 7:20 (see de Waard, *ibid.* 44, note 3).

64. *k'wn* is the variant in Walton's polyglot (see above, note 22).

65. See C. Brockelmann, *Lexikon syriacum* (Halle, 1928) 332b; R.P. Smith, *Thesaurus syriacus* (Oxford, 1879) 1:1659–60 + *Supplement* (Oxford, 1927) 158; E.S. Drower and R. Machuch, *A Mandaic Dictionary* (Oxford, 1963) 212a; *Vocabolario arabo-italiano* (Rome, 1973) 3:1305b. The connection between the Syriac and Mandaic words and the Akkadian *kayyamānu/kayyawānu,* which Brockelmann and Drower-Machuch

point out, is quite uncertain (Brockelmann in fact appeals only to Oppert; see above, note 43); Kêwan is regarded as being rather of Persian origin.

66. So in the editions of Sperber and de Lagarde; for the variant see above, note 21.

67. See Ziegler, *Duodecim Prophetae,* 195 in the critical apparatus. Rudolph, *Amos,* 207, claims that Theodotion was trying to "etymologize" when he saw in *kywn* the Hebrew verb *khh,* "to be dark/overcast."

68. For a survey of the state of research on this point see especially O. Eissfeldt, *Molk als Opferbegriff im Punischen und Hebräischen und das Ende des Gottes Moloch* (Beiträge zur Religionsgeschichte des Altertums 3; Halle, 1935); R. de Vaux, *Ancient Israel: Its Life and Institutions,* trans. J. McHugh (New York, 1961) 441–46; M. Weinfeld, "The Worship of Molech and the Queen of Heaven and Its Background," *UF* 4 (1972) 133–54; P.G. Mosca, *Child Sacrifice in Canaanite and Israelite Religion. A Study in Mulk and mlk* (unpublished dissertation; Harvard University, 1975); G.C. Heider, *The Cult of Molek. A Reassessment* (JSOT Supp. 43; Sheffield, 1985); A.R.W. Green, *The Role of Human Sacrifice in the Ancient Near East* (ASOR DS 1; Missoula, Montana, 1975).

69. A brief presentation of this hypothesis can be found in J. Trebolle Barrera, "La transcripción *mlk* = *moloch.* Historia del texto e historia de la lengua," *Aula Orientalis* 5 (1987) 125–28. J. Lust reaches the same conclusion by a different route in his review of Heider's book (see note 68): "The Cult of Molek/Milchom. Some Remarks on G.H. Heider's Monograph," *ETL* 63 (1987) 361–66. Such a hypothesis also leads to the denial that in the earliest Hebrew the word *mlk,* understood as meaning "king," could have referred to a particular divinity (Melek = king); at most it could have been used as a title (see Trebolle Barrera, *ibid.* 128).

70. The Syriac text of Acts 7:43 also has Milcom in place of the Moloch of the LXX; see R.P. Smith, *Thesaurus* 2:2146b.

71. It seems obvious that *horasis* should be understood as "vision" (see also *visio* in the translation of Jerome cited by Field, *Origenis Hexaplorum,* 2:975, and in Ziegler, *Duodecim Prophetae,* 195, critical apparatus). I do not understand how von der Osten Sacken, *Die Bücher der Tora,* 425, can try to make it mean "abomination." Rudolph, *Amos,* 207, hypothesizes that here again we have an etymological interpretation based on *skh/śkh,* "to see" (but this had already been proposed by Field, *ibid.*).

72. See notes 21 and 24 for the variants.

73. Only in some Punic witnesses is the Latinized word *molchomor* (which however is a sacrificial term) linked iconographically with Saturn, venerated under the name of Baal-Hammon; see W. Röllig, "Moloch," in

Wörterbuch der Mythologie 1:299–300; idem, "Baal-Hammon," in *ibid.* 271–72. On the other hand, Saturn has numerous "faces" at this period; at Palmyra he even takes on the characteristics of a vegetation god and is assimilated to a solar deity (diurnal and nocturnal); see M. Hoffner, "Malakbēl," in *ibid.* 452.

74. As I noted earlier, the citation of the text takes two forms: *kynyy hṣlmym* and *kywn hṣlmym.* The second repeats the noun in the Hebrew text cited earlier, while the first, usually regarded as erroneous (but for a contrary view see Rabin, *Zadokite Documents,* 30), would be even more suited to an understanding of the second object in Amos' text as a common noun ("pedestals"), although the difficulty of its vocalization would remain: if at the base of the word is the *kēn* of biblical Hebrew (see Ex 30:18, 28), the construct plural should be *kannē,* while the spelling *kynyy* should be read as *kînê(y),* that is, a later and rabbinical word (thus von der Osten Sacken, *Die Bücher der Tora,* 429–30, who nonetheless acknowledges that this question is not pertinent to the exegesis of Amos in CD; later Hebrew, however, like biblical Hebrew, has both *kēn* and *kannê:* if the latter is not found in CD VII, 15, in this form, this may be a further, even if not decisive, argument for regarding *kynyy* to be erroneous).

75. The passage with the citation of Amos 5:26–27 and the commentary on it is found in ms. A of CD but not in ms. B (see the synoptic presentation of the translations of the two mss in Schechter, *Documents,* 72). According to G.J. Brooke, "The Amos-Numbers Midrash (CD 7, 13b–81a) and Messianic Expectation," *ZAW* 92 (1980) 397–404, the idea of two messiahs is due to a later recension (to which he gives the abbreviation A_1), which replaced an older recension (= A_2, B) that spoke of a single messiah, eliminating some of its material and introducing the citation of Amos 5:26–27 and Numbers 24:17; the result was a greater consistency with other Qumran documents (1QS, 1QSb, 4QTestim, 4QFlor). The biblical texts (says Brooke) are cited in accordance with specific techniques; to be precise, Amos 5:26–27 is not cited here but rather 5:27, with 5:26aA2-b being inserted into it (*ibid.,* 400).

76. Schechter (*Documents* 72), Rabin (*Zadokite Documents,* 28, 30), and Lohse (*Die Texte aus Qumran,* 80–81, with vocalization of the Hebrew-text) hold to the masoretic pronunciation. L. Moraldi's translation, *I manoscritti di Qumrān* (Turin, 1971) 244–45, even cites, in Italian transcription, the words of the masoretic Hebrew text. But the German translation of J. Maier, *Die Texte vom Toten Meer* (Munich-Basel, 1960), 1:56, reads thus: "I lead away Sakkut, your king, and Kewan, your images (Ich führe den Sakkut, euren Konig, and Kewan, eure Bilder, fort . . .)." It is odd that Wolff, *Amos* 311–12, should cite the text of CD VII, 13–19,

perhaps with Lohse in mind (though the latter has "Sikkut" and "Kij-jun"), but introducing on his own "Sakkut" and "Kewan"; von der Osten Sacken (*Die Bücher der Tora,* 423–25), rightly criticizes him for this.

PAUL'S VISION AT TROAS (FARAHIAN)

1. On the division between Asia and Europe see G. Betori, "Lo Spirito e l'annuncio," *RivB* 35 (1987) 399–441, especially 430, note 61.

2. Just a short time ago, on occasion of the pope's visit to South Korea, Indonesia, etc., we were reminded that of the approximately three billion people in Asia only sixty-five million are baptized. See *Le Monde,* Tuesday, October 19, 1989, p. 1.

3. I am glad to offer this essay as homage to Rev. Father and Professor Emilio Rasco, who was my teacher and guide, especially in the study of Luke's works. I wish here to mention especially his article, "Spirito e Istituzione nell'opera lucana," *RivB* 30 (1982) 301–22.

4. See F. Bovon, *Luc le théologien* (2nd ed.; Geneva, 1988) 318–19 and 375. There are only two articles devoted to the study of the passage I am examining. One of these I have unfortunately been unable to consult: B. Schwank, " 'Setze über nach Mazedonien und hilf uns!' Reisenotizen zu Apg 16, 9—17, 15," *ErbAuf* 39 (1963) 399–416.

5. The bibliography is very meager. See J. Dupont, *Etudes sur les Actes des Apôtres* (Paris, 1967); idem, *Nouvelles études sur les Actes des Apôtres* (Paris, 1984); Bovon, *Luc.* For a more detailed bibliography see G. Schneider, *Gli Atti degli Apostoli* (2 vols.; Brescia, 1986) II, 267.

6. C.M. Martini, *Atti degli Apostoli* (4th ed.; Rome, 1977) 230.

7. See F. Bovon, "L'importance des médiations dans le projet théologique de Luc," *NTS* 21 (1975) 23–39. Referring to S. Schulz and E. Haenchen, Bovon remarks on the failure to consider the role of human freedom in the Lukan narrative.

8. See F.F. Bruce, *The Acts of the Apostles* (2nd ed.; Leicester, 1952) 309–12; O. Glombitza, "Der Schritt nach Europa. Erwägungen zu Act 16, 9–15," *ZNW* 53 (1962) 77–82. I may mention that in his article Glombitza studies the use of the accusative after the verb *euaggelisasthai,* "to evangelize."

9. See E. Jacquier, *Les Actes des Apôtres* (Paris, 1925) 478–84; I. Howard Marshall, *The Acts of the Apostles* (Grand Rapids, 1980) 261–64; J. Munck, *The Acts of the Apostles* (New York, 1981) 157–58.

10. See Schneider, *Atti,* II, 271; J. Cantinat, *Les Actes des Apôtres* (Paris, 1966) 118; H. Binder, "Die angebliche Krankheit des Paulus," *TZ* 32 (1976) 1–13; R. Pesch, *Die Apostelgeschichte* II (Zurich, 1986) 99–103.

11. See E. Haenchen, *The Acts of the Apostles* (Oxford, 1971) 489–90.

12. See W.M. Ramsay, *Saint Paul: The Traveller and the Roman Citizen* (London, 1920) 200–05.

13. See G. Stählin, *Gli Atti degli Apostoli* (Brescia, 1973) 374–80, especially 380; but there is nothing here comparable to what we find in Revelation 2—3.

14. See Munck, *Acts,* 158: "He was in a state of great uncertainty." In light of this approach to the vision of the Macedonian see the following explanations of a psychological kind: A. Loisy, *Les Actes des Apôtres* (Paris, 1920, 1973) 628; Jacquier, *Actes,* 482; C.S.C. Williams, *A Commentary on the Acts of the Apostles* (2nd ed.; London, 1964) 193. Marshall, *Acts,* 263, mentions a variant of this explanation: the vision was occasioned by an actual visit which Paul received at Troas (during the day) from a group of Macedonians, perhaps with Luke among them. All four authors cite opinions of this kind without agreeing with them.

15. This would then be a reason for placing Luke's work in a Macedonian setting.

16. See H. Conzelmann, *Acts of the Apostles* (Philadelphia, 1987) 126–27.

17. See E. Trocmé, *Le "livre des Actes" et l'histoire* (Paris, 1957) 138–47; Haenchen *Acts,* 490–91.

18. See Loisy, *Actes,* 630.

19. On the other hand, if one thinks that the author is not a disciple closely linked to Paul but is of another generation (see Bovon, *Luc le théologien,* 29, who agrees with G. Klein—rightly in my opinion—that Luke belongs to the third Christian generation), this would be a further reason for locating Luke's work in Macedonia.

20. See, long ago, Loisy, *Actes,* 628–31. For the opposite view: S. Dockx, "Luc a-t-il été le compagnon d'apostolat de Paul?" *NRT* 103 (1981) 385–400, especially 387–88.

21. See P. Vielhauer, "Zum Paulinismus der Apostelgeschichte," *EvTh* 10 (1950–51) 1–15; G. Bornkamm, *Paulus* (Stuttgart, 1969); E. Farahian, *Le 'je' paulinien* (Rome, 1988) 266.

22. Except, in my opinion, in his last trial (as told in Galatians 2:19–21). See Farahian, *Le 'je' paulinien,* 266.

23. See Loisy, *Actes,* 627, who cites the case of Apollonius as reported by Philostratus: Apollonius learns in a dream that he should leave Crete (*Vita Apollonii* IV, 34); A. Wikenhauser, "Religionsgeschichtliche Parallelen zu Apg 16, 9," *BZ* 23 (1935) 180–86.

24. See R. Fabris, *Atti degli Apostoli* (Rome, 1977) 493–97, especially 497, note 6, where he cites Josephus, Herodotus, and others.

25. See R. Penna, "Lo 'Spirito di Gesu' in Atti 16, 7. Analisi letteraria e teologica," *RivB* 20 (1972) 241–61; A. George, "L'Esprit Saint dans l'oeuvre de Luc," *RB* 85 (1978) 500–42; G. Bettori, "Lo Spirito e l'annuncio della Parola negli Atti degli Apostoli," *RivB* 35 (1987) 399–441.

26. See J. Kürsinger, *The Acts of the Apostles* (London, 1969) 264–68.

27. E. Haulotte, *Actes des Apôtres* (Supplément Vie Chrétienne no. 212; Paris, 1977). Italics added.

28. M. Dibelius, *Aufsätze zur Apostelgeschichte* (3rd ed.; Göttingen, 1957) 170.

29. The majority of authors think that a second main part of the book begins in 13:1 or 15:36.

30. Note how the "marvelous" is described in the literature, in, e.g., P. Malandain, *Madame de la Fayette. La Princesse de Clèves* (Paris, 1989) 33: "supernatural interventions, miraculous meetings, ghosts and visions."

31. See C. Perrot, "Les Actes des Apôtres," in A. George and P. Grelot (eds.), *Introduction critique au Nouveau Testament* 2 (Paris, 1976) 253.

32. Penna, "Lo 'Spirito di Gesu,' " 243–44. Penna's analysis offers further proof of the limits of the pericope I am discussing.

33. See E. Delebecque, *Les deux Actes des Apôtres* (Paris, 1986) 18–19, 373–96.

34. See *ibid.* 100–01.

35. See Schneider, *Atti,* II, 268–69.

36. See P. Gibert, *La Bible à la naissance de l'histoire* (Paris, 1979), 431: "Heroes [David, Solomon, etc.] do not succeed simply for our pleasure; they succeed because in the final analysis God is with them and because their fortunes are no longer theirs alone but the fortunes of Israel itself."

37. See H. Bachmann and W.A. Slaby, *Computer-Konkordanz zum Novum Testamentum Graece* (Berlin-New York, 1985) 1361.

38. It is worth noting that the only other New Testament writer to use a word like *horama,* namely, *onar,* "dream," with some frequency is Matthew, who uses it six times (Bachman-Slaby 1347). Among words of related meaning I may mention *horasis,* which occurs four times in the New Testament: once in Acts, three times in Revelation (*ibid.* 1361). Finally, *enupnion* appears only once, in Acts (*ibid.* 628).

39. See *ibid.* 1361.

40. The LXX has *horama,* the TM *ha-mar'eh,* which can be vaguer.

41. See Dupont, *Nouvelles études,* 329–42, especially 335–42.

42. See *ibid.* 63, note 8. In this lengthy note the author says: "The promise, 'whoever calls upon the name of the Lord shall be saved,' applies

also to 'those who are far off' (2:39): in Luke's perspective the expression alludes to the Gentiles." See also Dupont, *Etudes,* 408–09, where he brings out this same extension.

43. See Bovon, *Luc le théologien,* 273, note 1, apropos of G. Voss; C.L'Eplattenier, *Les Actes des Apôtres* (Geneva, 1987) 35.

44. Some of these words are found together in some passages:

7:31: *horama;* 7:30: *aggelos;* 7:31: *phōnē;* 7:45: *Iēsous;* 7:35: *cheir.*

9:10, 12: *horama;* 9:4, 7: *phōnē;* 9:17: *pneuma;* 9:5, 17: *Iēsous;* 9:12, 17: *cheir.*

10:3, 17, 19: *horama;* 10:3, 7, 22: *aggelos;* 10:13, 15: *phōnē;* 10:19: *pneuma;* 10:36, 38, 48: *Iēsous.*

11:5: *horama;* 11:13: *aggelos;* 11:7, 9: *phōnē;* 11:12, 15, 16: *pneuma;* 11:17: *Iēsous;* 11:21: *cheir.*

12:9: *horama;* 12:7, 8, 9, 10, 11, 15: *aggelos;* 12:14: *phōnē;* 12:7: *cheir.*

16:9, 10: *horama;* 16:6, 7: *pneuma;* 16:7: *Iēsous.*

18:9: *horama;* 18:5: *Iēsous.*

45. See note 44.

46. See Haulotte, *Actes des Apôtres,* 132.

Index of Biblical References

Index of Names